INTO
THE HEART
OF
DARKNESS

The trouble with Eichmann was precisely that so many were like him, and the many were neither perverted nor sadistic, but they were, and still are, terribly and terrifyingly normal ... this normality was much more terrifying than all the atrocities put together.

Hannah Arendt
Eichmann in Jerusalem
A report on the banality of evil

INTO THE HEART OF DARKNESS

Confessions of Apartheid's Assassins

Jacques Pauw

Jonathan Ball Publishers
Johannesburg & Cape Town

© Text Jacques Pauw 2017
© Published edition 2017 Jonathan Ball Publishers

Originally published in South Africa in 1997 by
JONATHAN BALL PUBLISHERS
A division of Media24 (Pty) Ltd
PO Box 33977
Jeppestown
2043

ISBN 978-1-86842-892-2
ebook ISBN 978-1-86842-893-9

*Every effort has been made to trace the copyright holders and to obtain their permission
for the use of copyright material. The publishers apologise for any errors or omissions and
would be grateful to be notified of any corrections that should be incorporated in future
editions of this book.*

Twitter: www.twitter.com/JonathanBallPub
Facebook: www.facebook.com/JonathanBallPublishers
Blog: http://jonathanball.bookslive.co.za/

Design by Michael Barnett, Johannesburg
Typesetting by Wouter Reinders
Reproduction of cover and picture section by RT Sparhams, Johannesburg
Index by Naomi Musiker

Printed by **novus print**, a Novus Holdings company

Contents

Acknowledgements

This book is the culmination of an investigation spanning several years into state-sponsored apartheid death squads that led to the publication of a series of articles in *Vrye Weekblad, Sunday Star* and *The Star* and television documentaries broadcast in South Africa and abroad.

This book is not a complete work. It is published at a time when the Truth and Reconciliation Commission is trying to unearth part of the truth of three decades of National Party tyranny and political violence that engulfed this country. A host of perpetrators have thrown themselves at the mercy of the Amnesty Committee, gushing forth an endless tale of murder, torture and disappearances, while more bones and skulls are emerging from the bowels of the South African earth.

It is a story far too great for a single author to attempt to tell. That is why this book is not a definitive history of the brutality or extent of death squads, but merely a collection of stories and sketches of the secrets and turmoil which lie at the heart of some of the operatives who perpetrated so much evil and brought about so much misery.

This book would not have been possible without the help of many people – friends and foes; lawyers and investigators; policemen and soldiers; killers and torturers; victims and their families; and just ordinary people – who have over many years provided me with information, introductions, leads, documentation, suggestions, advice, inspiration and guidance. There are simply too many to name.

I however wish to pay special tribute to my colleagues in the media who contributed to unearthing the truth, amongst them Eddie Koch, Peta Thornycroft, Phillip van Niekerk, Max du Preez, John Carlin and the late Kitt Katzin.

Many thanks also go to:
- The SABC's Truth Commission Special Report for opening their files to me and providing me with transcripts and records of Truth and Reconciliation Commission hearings;
- State advocates Torie Pretorius and Anton Ackermann for providing me with the court records of the Eugene de Kock case. They are both criminal prosecutors that I have come to respect and admire for their contribution in bringing justice to my country; and

- The SABC's Joe Thloloe and Sarah Crowe for giving me the time to write this book.

My deepest thanks to Elize and Louis for their unfaltering encouragement, support and devotion.

My publisher Jonathan Ball undertook the task of publishing a painful and controversial book. My sincere thanks to him and Francine Blum, his production manager, for understanding the project and being so supportive.

Over the past years I have been witness to a story of tragedy and waste and brutality, but also of incredible hope and humanity and courage. That is why this book is intended as a tribute to all South Africans emerging from and making peace with a dark and secret past.

Abbreviations

ANC   African National Congress
CCB   Civil Co-operation Bureau
DCC   Directorate of Covert Collection
PAC   Pan-Africanist Congress
SADF   South African Defence Force
SAP   South African Police
SSC   State Security Council
Swapo South West African People's Organisation
TRC   Truth and Reconciliation Commission

Preface

A confession

His head was bouncing and hopping like a rubber ball on his broad shoulders, while clutched between his thumb and forefinger was a thin glass syringe, stuffed with a mixture of tobacco and small cocaine crystals. He had lit the pipe a minute before, and a whiff of cigarette tobacco and chemical substance was filling the car.

'It's true, I killed him,' he suddenly said; kept quiet for a second or two, and let rip again: 'It's true, I shot him.'

'Who?' I asked him.

'David Webster.'

Sitting next to me sucking on his crack pipe was Ferdi Barnard, one of apartheid's most infamous hoodlums, a Rambo-esque killer who moved between the criminal underworld of drug dealing, prostitution and diamond smuggling, and South Africa's official business in the government's dirty tricks units and death squads.

The tiny orange coal in his crack pipe glowed brightly in the afternoon light as it slowly burned down the syringe, consuming the crystals and tobacco. He blew a streak of white smoke against the front window of the car where it exploded into a million molecules.

'He flew through the air and landed on the pavement. I saw it, because I shot him. I did it.'

Before he continued, he put the pipe in his mouth again and inhaled the mixture into his lungs.

'It was all that tea parties and shit. That's why we killed him. I pulled the trigger, I shot him.'

We looked at one another. I didn't say anything, too scared to interrupt him and stop a confession.

'I was paid a R40 000 production bonus after the killing. For a job well done. It was an approved operation and Joe Verster knew about everything.'

Silence again. The coal had nearly burned its way to the bottom of the pipe.

'Who were the other two people in the car with you?'

'There was only one other person.'

'Was it Eugene Riley?'

'No.'

'Chappies Maree?'

'No.'

'Calla Botha?'

He laughed. I'm not going to say anything. Maybe he was, maybe he wasn't. Make your own deduction.'

'Why don't you confess and ask for amnesty?'

'I won't, I won't. I will never ask for amnesty.'

'And what about Anton Lubowksi?'

'No, I didn't kill him.'

'You told me three years ago you tried to shoot him at one stage.'

'Yes, that's true. Everything I told you was true. But I didn't pull the trigger.'

His pipe was finished.

'Come on,' he said, 'let's go back. People are going to think that we are two *moffie-tjies* (little gays) sitting here in the car.'

He laughed.

The last shred of normality in the lives of David Webster and his lover Maggie Friedman was a Saturday morning frolic with their dogs.

On May 1, 1989, Dr David Webster, a university lecturer and a tireless anti-apartheid campaigner, was opening the back door of his van, parked in front of his house in Troyeville, Johannesburg, to let his dogs out. A car pulled up along-side him. A shotgun was fired at close range. Sixteen coarse-grain pellets entered his body, and as he was dying, the assassin sped away.

The last words he spoke were: 'I've been shot with a shotgun … call an ambulance.' Less than 30 minutes later, he died.

David Webster was never a prominent figure in the struggle, but a passionate campaigner against detention without trial. Webster became famous among former detainees and detainees' parents for intervening on their behalf and arranging gatherings at which people could sing, pray and be comforted. They became known as Webster's 'tea parties' and made him the subject of attention by the security forces.

In the days, weeks and months that followed, the murder of David Webster became one of the most highly publicised assassinations in the history of this country. Few murders in South Africa's violent history have been the subject of so much publicity, investigation, suspicion, false leads and accusations.

Six months after the murder of Webster, a former narcotics bureau detective and convicted murderer by the name of Ferdi Barnard was detained under Section 29 of the Internal Security Act for the murder. Shortly afterwards, a former murder and robbery detective and provincial rugby player, Calla Botha, was also taken in.

Although they were released a few months later for lack of evidence, their detention led to the exposure of a sinister and secret death squad within the

South African Defence Force (SADF) that was ominously known as the Civil Co-operation Bureau (CCB), a network of criminals, former reconnaissance soldiers and murder and robbery unit policemen who operated all over southern Africa. Their actions ranged from shootings, bombings and poisoning to intimidation, breaking windows, stealing heart pills and hanging a monkey foetus in a tree at the residence of a Nobel Peace Prize laureate.

None of the long list of unsavoury CCB agents who were exposed was more menacing than Ferdi Barnard, an underworld gangster with a reputation as a man of violence. Those who dared to speak about his nefarious secrets were threatened and withdrew their statements. Several people once close to him are now dead or fear for their lives.

That is probably why he was on the loose for so long.

October 23, 1996, and in the car sitting next to me, Ferdi Barnard was hiding his crack pipe under the carpet. He had called me earlier that morning to obtain a tape recording of a documentary I had produced on the life and times of his friend and former police death squad commander, Colonel Eugene de Kock. The documentary had been screened the previous night and Barnard was one of the characters I had interviewed.

Barnard loved seeing himself on television. When he walked into the fish restaurant in Seventh Street in Melville, Johannesburg, he said: 'It was good for business.' He was referring to the brothel he managed in the northern suburbs of Johannesburg. The killer had very much become one of the 'kings of smut' of Johannesburg's booming sex industry. I had interviewed him ten months earlier in another upper-class brothel, aptly named The Palace, in a double storey house in the affluent northern suburbs.

For several days, we had waited for Barnard at the brothel as young, 'R300-a-time' hookers were whisked away in taxis to clients in plush hotel rooms, while others, showing off their wares in miniskirts and black stockings, lined the fake marble foyer of the brothel. From time to time, a stolid-looking guard, an economy-size version of Barnard and armed with a sub-machine gun, scrutinised us. A night or two later, the same man grabbed one of the girls in the brothel's strip club, pinned her to the ground and simulated sex with her.

One of the managers of the club, a former Military Intelligence operative, told me then that he was worried that Barnard was taking too much cocaine. The manager, a self-confessed drug smuggler and hit-man, said that he personally supplied Barnard with several grams of cocaine every day.

Barnard finally walked into the plastic foyer of The Palace, followed by a blonde girl who obviously adored him, sat down on the couch in the casino and spoke about Eugene de Kock. His head was veering around, probably from too much cocaine.

I had met Ferdi Barnard for the first time at the end of 1992 after he had testified in the judicial inquest into the murder of David Webster. Barnard attended the court proceedings virtually every day as the lawyers representing the Webster family tried to pin the murder on him and the CCB.

On days when Barnard thought he might be called to testify, his big frame was tightly packed into a pink-brown double-breasted suit. On other days, he looked more comfortable in jeans, ankle-high white sneakers and a multi-coloured shortsleeved shirt. When he finally took the witness stand, he denied any complicity in the murder.

In a crucial testimony, a Springbok sprinter and former employer of Barnard told the court that the CCB man had described how Webster's body 'flew through the air' after he had pulled the trigger. But soon afterwards, he astounded the court when he said that his testimony was false and that he no longer wished to testify. Years later, I was told that a close friend of Barnard had threatened the witness during the tea break: 'You will be pissing in your pants when I'm finished with you.' The friend, a criminal and former Military Intelligence operative, mysteriously died in January 1994.

The inquest judge found that although Barnard was a prime suspect, no proof beyond a reasonable doubt could be established that Barnard had been responsible for the murder of David Webster.

Soon after the inquest, I met Barnard several times. On these occasions he volunteered information about the illegal weapons dealings of his close friend Colonel Eugene de Kock, with whom he had fallen out at the time.

One day, Barnard visited me at my home and told me how he had had to shoot Swapo leader Anton Lubowski in 1989 on the eve of the Namibian elections. He said he twice waited with an AK-47 assault rifle to kill Lubowski, but couldn't get a clear aim and had to abandon the project. His CCB colleagues then flew to Namibia to finish Lubowski off, four months after the killing of Webster. When he left later that afternoon, he said I was never to speak about Lubowski. 'Ask Webster what happened to him,' he said and laughed.

When Ferdi Barnard arrived at the Melville restaurant, he was accompanied by a man by the name of 'Rassie', who didn't speak much and was clearly there to look after Barnard, who would from time to time excuse himself and go to the toilet, probably to take another fix of coke.

I later discovered that 'Rassie' was none other than Lieutenant Erasmus of the South African Police Organised Crime Unit, and that instead of investigating Barnard for a series of crimes ranging from murder to diamond smuggling, was acting, it seems, as his guardian.

At about four o'clock that afternoon, Barnard must have run out of drugs and ordered me to go with him to his car.

As he was fiddling around looking for his crack and pipe, a hundred dollar note fell out of a compartment between the two front seats. He picked it up and said: 'This is for you. Take it.' I knew it had to be a counterfeit note as I had been told that Barnard and his criminal network were involved in the smuggling of bogus dollars. I afterwards took the note to a foreign currency dealer, who told me that it was a 'near-perfect' forgery.

The same day that Barnard confided in me about Webster, I told two friends and colleagues about the confession. A few months later, I made an affidavit about what Barnard had told me, and I decided then that if ever I was subpoenaed to testify against him, I would have to do so.

I had lunch again with Barnard in the same restaurant in December 1996, but when he sat down on that occasion, he said: I'm clean. I'm not taking drugs any more.' He was indeed sober, the name of David Webster wasn't mentioned and no further confessions were forthcoming.

Barnard clearly has a tendency to talk, especially when he is high on drugs. When he told me about Webster, he was certainly stoned and intoxicated by all the drugs he had consumed, but his speech was composed and sensible.

I have often wondered why he told me about the killing, as he knows that I am a journalist and have been working on and exposing death squads for several years. He trusts me, and the fact that I had never spoken about his attempted killing of Anton Lubowski probably reinforced that perception. Maybe he thinks that I am afraid of him, since he rules by fear and nobody dares to stand up to him.

Since his confession, I have been torn between some loyalty to Barnard, journalistic ethics and my simple citizen's duty to report and speak of a murder that was committed. The murder of David Webster has caused incredible pain, not only to those who were close to him, but has also contributed to tearing this country apart at a time when we were fighting for human dignity and civil rights. I do not believe that Ferdi Barnard should go unpunished and continue his mafiosi schemes, planned and executed from his dives in Johannesburg's northern suburbs.

Towards the end of 1996, new evidence against Ferdi Barnard emerged when his former live-in lover provided details of the murder of David Webster and a host of other crimes. The previously bungled and half-hearted investigation was reopened, but this time it was handled by an invigorated and dedicated special team of policemen. On September 2, 1997 Barnard was arrested and charged with the murders of David Webster and a Johannesburg drug dealer, as well as 22 additional crimes ranging from attempted murder to the illegal possession of firearms. Barnard's reign of supremacy over Johannesburg's gangland may at last have come to an end.

Over the past seven years, I have listened to many confessions by apartheid's killers, some so cruel and savage they were beyond comprehension. Of how police killers had a barbecue and a drinking orgy next to the burning body of an African National Congress (ANC) member they had just murdered; of three civic leaders who had iron pipes smashed into their heads; and an SADF assassin who boasted about the 'mincemeat' he made out of an arm of an ANC lawyer he blew up with a car bomb.

But none was more uncanny than the confession about the activist who 'flew through the air'.

Chapter One

A very bloody business

Eliminate (v.) to remove somebody/something, especially somebody/something that is not wanted or needed; to get rid of; to kill somebody, especially a potential opponent (*Oxford Dictionary*)

Once upon a time, there were three boys: two white and one black. The two white boys were born in the 1940s, the black child a decade later. The white boys grew up in typical Afrikaner homes where their fathers told them of the *Groot Trek* (Great Migration) more than a hundred years earlier, and the concentration camps where Afrikaner women and children were incarcerated by the English during the Second Boer War at the turn of the century. One boy's father was a magistrate, the other's a postmaster.

And then there was the black boy, who grew up as the son of a labourer in a township. When the white boys reached adulthood, they prepared themselves for a career in the South African Police (SAP), while the black boy became embroiled in student politics and the rising tide of resistance against apartheid.

On the face of it, there was nothing unusual about these boys. They could have been me or you in apartheid South Africa a few years or a few decades ago. But one morning in December 1993, extraordinary circumstances brought them together in a shopping centre in Pretoria where they broke garlic bread and had coffee.

They were now grown men, and it was the first time that the two whites had set eyes on one another. The black man had worked for both and brokered the meeting between his former employees. They looked no different from the people around them and spoke about the political situation and the dawn of democracy in their fatherland – something most South Africans discussed at the time.

But they were not everyday South Africans. Their business was a very bloody one. The three men had between them murdered more than 100 people. Their victims were black and thought to be opponents of apartheid. The black man, once a soldier against apartheid, had killed 40 people in upholding and defending the very system he had once opposed.

United in blood they were no more. Four years before the meeting, one had left South Africa to tell the world about the murders the other two had committed, resulting in one sending the other first a parcel bomb and then an assassin to track him down. This meeting took place five months before one was arrested, charged and eventually convicted of 121 apartheid crimes. The other two testified against him, but months later, one of them was also charged with murder. Today, one is in prison for life, the second is a convicted murderer and the third is in hiding somewhere in fear for his life.

A bizarre story? Not so – it is all too true. These three were the foot soldiers of apartheid's secret wars. They were the men who went out to kill, and kill again. One would be remembered for burning the bodies of his victims to ashes while gorging himself on meat and brandy, one for packing explosives around bodies and blowing them to nothingness, and the third for luring 15-year-olds into deadly ambushes. They were the people who watched life's blood spilling out as they got up close to their victims, twisting knives into guts and firing bullets into brains.

Dirk Coetzee, Eugene de Kock and Joe Mamasela – three of apartheid's assassins whom you are going to meet in this book.

Killing was their business. And business was good.

These men represent the banality of the evil which was South Africa's culture, as much as it had been the country's system of government since the National Party took power in 1948 and legalised apartheid.

They were apartheid's ultimate and most secret weapon. When all else had failed – detention without trial, harassment and dirty tricks, state of emergency regulations and criminal prosecution – the death squads were sent out to finally 'solve the problem'. They acquired the power to decide over life and death. In the process, they not only abandoned their police or SADF oaths to serve and uphold law and order, but were also forced to abandon their own morality.

The system they served rewarded them richly. The police counter-insurgency unit based at Vlakplaas, a farm outside Pretoria, stole hundreds of thousands of rands from the police secret fund – with the connivance of the generals. Members of SADF death squads paid themselves 'production bonuses' for successful operations. The more they killed, the more they were honoured. This system made a killer like Eugene de Kock one of apartheid's most decorated policemen.

This book will take you on a journey to uncover the innermost secrets of the men based at Vlakplaas, killer policemen of the Northern Transvaal Security Branch, operatives of an SADF death squad called the CCB and several military intelligence and security police agents.

What caused these souls to become so dark and led them to so much wickedness?

These are people I have dealt with over a period of many years. Some I have come to know very well, like Dirk Coetzee, whom I met more than 12 years ago and eventually persuaded to leave the country in November 1989 to write his story. I have spent time with him not only in this country, but also in Mauritius, Zimbabwe, Zambia and England.

Tracking down the cut-throats of apartheid has taken me from the drinking taverns of Pretoria to pubs in London, from Pretoria Central Prison to Her Majesty's Prison in Dorchester in England, from the Weskoppies Psychiatric Institution in Pretoria to brothels in Johannesburg's northern suburbs, and from the smelly city of Beira in Mozambique to the opulence of the Hotel National in Lucerne in Switzerland.

In the process, I had to consume enormous quantities of liquor and listen to bloody bravado and gleeful torture talk. There was a time, especially in the early 1990s, when I had to listen to a flood of confessions by these outcasts of society. In many cases, I couldn't write their stories, either because they wouldn't allow me to or because I didn't know whether or not they were true.

A security police agent once dumped an arsenal of weapons on me: an R-1 assault rifle with a bag of bullets and extra magazines, an assassination pistol with a telescope and a throwing knife. I drove around for weeks with the weapons in the boot of my car before dumping them on a friend who, before passing them on to somebody else, hid them in the home of the former leader of the Progressive Federal Party, Dr Frederik Van Zyl Slabbert. The friend was at the time living in Slabbert's home while his host was on a study tour abroad.

Why did they speak to me when I was at the time perceived to be anything from a Communist to a traitor to a National Intelligence Service agent? Certainly not out of remorse, nor to get rid of a heavy burden in their hearts. When the politicians and the generals abandoned their foot soldiers in the early 1990s and left them to fend for themselves, they opened the floodgates of confession.

'I only followed orders ... the generals knew everything ... I was just a soldier,' most would say as they pointed fingers at their superiors. Others spoke out of fear of prosecution or tried to justify their deeds. 'It was a war ... they were killing us and we were killing them.'

Many of the confessions were published in the anti-apartheid Afrikaans newspaper *Vrye Weekblad*, which I helped to found at the end of 1988. Although they hated what we stood for, they knew that we were not afraid to publish. What is more, I was also born an Afrikaner; we spoke in our mother tongue and I understood what they meant by the religious doctrine of the Afrikaans churches and that their crusade was a '*stryd vir Volk en Vaderland*' (a battle for people and fatherland).

Who are these people, I am often asked. What are they like, and why did they do it? Most of them, I am afraid to say, seem to be as normal as you or I and could be our next-door neighbours. They don't walk around with the mark of Cain on their foreheads, and it is only when you start scratching at the surface of their ordinariness that their true colours emerge.

These were men who had their own rules, their own language, their own culture. Informal rules required that only two people should ever be present when orders were given, turning the only witnesses into co-conspirators.

The conspiracy needed its own language – one that didn't leave any suggestion of blood, pain, loss or suffering. Never, but never, did they use words like 'kill' or 'murder' or 'assassinate'. '*Maak 'n plan met*' (make a plan with), '*vat hom uit*' (take him out), '*raak ontslae van hom*' (get rid of him), '*los die probleem op*' (solve the problem) and the favourite: '*elimineer*' (eliminate). This allowed the killers to pray and attend church, get married and raise families, hold funerals and cry when their pets passed away.

In their eyes, 15-year-old township activists armed with stones and sticks were '*gewapende terroriste*' (armed terrorists) and civic leaders who led disobedience campaigns in the townships were '*opgeleide revolusionêres*' (trained revolutionaries). Any black person opposed to apartheid was easily branded as a '*Marxsis*' (Marxist) or '*Kommunis*' (Communist). And once labelled as an '*opstoker*' (agitator), you could have been listed for '*eliminasie*' (elimination). When a detainee was tortured by attaching electrodes to his testicles, toes or fingers and an electrical current sent through his body by turning an old manual telephone, he was simply '*gebel*' (phoned); and when the inner tube of a car tyre was pulled over his face to suffocate him, he was '*getjoep*' (tubed).

The linguistic circumnavigation of deeds of evil was not restricted to the death squad operatives. When the State Security Council (SSC), a secret cabinet committee that co-ordinated the government's security police, met on June 28, 1983 under the chairmanship of State President PW Botha to discuss the destabilisation of southern Africa, it decided '*dat die pot van interne konflik in Zimbabwe subtiel aan die kook gehou word*' (that the pot of internal conflict in Zimbabwe should subtly be kept boiling). At the time, the S ADF was stirring up a civil war in Matabeleland in which thousands of people died.[1]

This control of language enabled FW de Klerk, who was present at the SSC meeting, to say to the Truth and Reconciliation Commission (TRC) 14 years later: 'I am not aware of any initiative to support any other movements or organisations in other countries that sought to overthrow or influence the policies of those countries.'[2]

We may never know to what extent the apartheid government conspired with the death squads to annihilate their political opponents, but there can be little doubt that statements by National Party politicians ignited the fire in the bellies of killer policemen and soldiers.

For example, former Minister of Defence Magnus Malan said in September 1981 in Parliament: 'As point of departure we have to accept that the onslaught here in southern Africa is Communist-inspired, Communist-planned and Communist-supported ... They want to establish a dictatorial state for elite black Marxists in the Republic of South Africa ... The security of the Republic of South Africa must be maintained by every possible means at our disposal.'[3]

Days after Malan's speech, Dirk Coetzee burnt one of his victims to ashes on a pyre of tyre and wood. 'It was just another job to be done. We would have our own little braai (next to the burning body) and just keep on drinking ... Hell, we didn't care. It wasn't as if we had killed human beings.' On Coetzee's pyre was a Communist, a Marxist, a revolutionary. Not an innocent law student who had been detained and interrogated, and had fallen through a window and been so seriously injured that Coetzee had been called in 'to get rid of the problem'.

Because activists became terrorists, Communists and revolutionaries, it became easy to 'eliminate', 'tube' or 'solve a problem'. In the process, not only were black people dehumanised, but so were apartheid's assassins.

That is why, I believe, they seem to be unable to open their hearts and souls to the pain of the victims and their own pain at having caused it. They show little remorse and their only regret seems to be the fact that they have been forced to the TRC's confession table. They may say how sorry they are, but with few exceptions the only emotion they show is their feeling of desperation about their situation, which compels them to face their victims.

Eugene de Kock said in testimony during his trial: 'I can't tell you how dirty I feel. I sympathise with my victims as if they were my own children.' Yet, De Kock and his death squad never showed mercy for any of their victims. They killed recklessly and never questioned their orders. In the words of Vlakplaas killer Leon Flores: 'We were just a great bunch of guys who had a great time with the work we did.'

That's why many people don't accept that De Kock felt shame and sorrow. He uttered these words after being convicted of six murders and when he faced a life behind bars. At the time, though, he had already been incarcerated for more than two years, and maybe the loneliness of being locked away in a solitary cell has compelled him to come to terms with his evil deeds and the futility of his dirty war.

Dirk Coetzee said the many months he had spent alone in exile in Zambia and England forced him to confront his past and think about his victims. 'Their faces came back to me. I could see the body jerking when the bullet hit it … I had to make peace with what I had done.'

Paul van Vuuren, a death squad policeman who applied for amnesty for a spate of murders, bombings and torture during the 1980s, is at least honest when he says that at the time he enjoyed what he did because he thought he was busy with a big and important mission: fighting Communism.[4]

The death squads were not a place for '*sissies*', but for men who would unflinchingly carry out orders without even knowing why they were pulling the trigger or planting the bomb.

'You ask no questions, you hear no lies,' was the explanation of Captain Rolf Gevers when he explained why he obeyed an order from Eugene de Kock to execute an activist at point-blank range and blow his body up with explosives.[5]

The death squad's culture, its techniques, skills and methods had much in common with those of a gang of ordinary thugs. What distinguished the squad's members from common criminals was that they believed themselves to be fighting a secret twilight war against an evil enemy. Any method that could lead to the destruction and disruption of the enemy was permitted and tacitly condoned. In committing these atrocities, there was one golden rule: never get caught. They referred to it as the 'eleventh commandment'.

They were once closer than brothers; bound by blood. Like the Sicilian Mafia, treason was punishable by death. But when the brotherhood broke apart and the truth started to emerge, brother ate brother, love turned into hate and respect became revulsion.

Many executions were performed with a Makarov or Tokarev pistol in one hand and a glass of '*polisie-koffie*' (police coffee – a glass of rum or brandy topped up with a little Coca-Cola) in the other. Some killings were preceded by heavy boozing, many operations followed by a drinking orgy. This enabled the killers to numb their senses, to comfort one another and to pat each other on the shoulder. If a killer should get sick in the aftermath of killing, one could always put it down to too much rum or brandy.

Because in the end, they also were human beings. And sometimes, in a private moment that they perceive as momentary weakness, they show emotion. I was sitting late one night in a Pretoria pub with Captain Wouter Mentz when he burst into tears because he was truly haunted by the killings he had participated in, amongst his victims a security policemen and two deaf children.

One morning, former paratrooper Rich Verster, tears rolling down his cheeks, started telling me of the day he performed mercy killings in Angola: shooting a young boy clutching a wooden rifle and taking a baby from a dying mother before firing a bullet into her. 'Do you know what it feels like?'[6]

Late last year, three months before his death, I sat with security police agent Peter Casselton in the Mozambican city of Beira. It was stinking hot and as sweat rolled down his overweight body, he told me that he was finished, that he had nothing more to live for and that his life had been wasted. 'I achieved nothing in working for them,' he said. He was ready to die.[7]

In fact, all the killers I have spoken with echo the same sentiment: we have achieved nothing. All the killing was a waste of time and human life. They all say so: Eugene de Kock in Pretoria Central Prison, Paul van Vuuren on his farm near Warmbaths, Ferdi Barnard in his brothel in Johannesburg, Rich Verster in prison in the south of England.

That is why so many of them suffer from post-traumatic stress disorder (PTSD), commonly known as the Vietnam Syndrome. The most prominent symptom of PTSD involves distressing recollections of one or more traumatic events from the past, such as war trauma and extreme violence. The person suffering from this disorder usually has nightmares and struggles to sleep at night. He may be highly irritable and startle at the slightest sound. Interest in everyday activities is reduced. Finally, feelings of anxiety or depression are common.

In March 1992, a group of Vlakplaas and murder and robbery squad policemen executed four suspected bank robbers in a minibus near Nelspruit before setting them alight. The fifth suspect was executed and blown up with explosives. Most of the policemen who participated in that operation suffer from PTSD. Eugene de Kock said that several of his men had to go for psychiatric treatment. 'Two or three landed up in Weskoppies [Psychiatric Hospital] for two or three weeks. But I didn't ask them about their symptoms. It was very sensitive and people didn't want to speak about it.'[8]

Sergeant Dougie Holtzhausen, the security policeman who supplied the information that led to the ambush, testified against De Kock one day after waking up from yet another session of sleep therapy. 'Our lives have been destroyed,' he said.[9]

South Africa's secret wars have created a new 'lost generation' – the men of the death squads who have been left to fend for themselves. Many are jobless and have difficulty in adapting to our new society. Three of the death squad operatives I describe in this book are dead, one is in prison in South Africa, another in England, one is awaiting trial for murder and five more are incarcerated in Zimbabwe.

Underneath the bravado and swagger are deeply damaged men. Their demeanour is uncompromising and macho, but when you meet them individually face to face, they don't measure up to their bloodcurdling reputations. They usually hunted in packs and killed as a group.

Most of them nurture extreme resentment of FW de Klerk, the politicians and the generals, who they believe have abandoned them and left them to bite the bullet.

Paul van Vuuren: 'I will chase FW de Klerk off my farm like a dog.'[10]

Eugene de Kock: 'De Klerk was a petrified puppy who lay on his back and wet himself. He just gave over.'[11]

Peter Casselton: 'The generals have no moral fibre. I don't think even the Italians were so yellow.'[12]

Guy Bawden: 'They've got rubber necks. The generals have taken their money and run. The fat cats.'[13]

I have often grappled with the question: did apartheid create these monsters? Or are they simply evil? What drives one to push the barrel of a gun against somebody's head and blow his brains away? Or pull a car tube over somebody's face and suffocate him while he moans and pleads: '*Asseblief, my baas, asseblief* (please, boss, please). Or push an iron rod into somebody's anus or electrocute him with a power generator?

Most of the apartheid assassins grew up in good, conservative homes and entered the armed forces as ordinary Afrikaners at a time when the ruling National Party was creating a united white front to prevent black majority rule and counter an external 'Communist' threat. On every level – in the homes, churches, schools and civil society in general – they were indoctrinated to embrace the National Party dogma of 'a Christian lifestyle based on Western civilisation and values'. Most became policemen or soldiers because of a quest for adventure and a healthy sense of patriotism.

For years, white minds were bombarded with this message: there is a revolutionary 'total onslaught' against the white man, orchestrated and dictated by the red bear in Moscow. 'Revolutionary organisations' like the ANC, the South African Communist Party and the United Democratic Front were portrayed as tools of an international Communist conspiracy.

Said former State President PW Botha: 'It is a struggle between the powers of chaos, Marxism and destruction on the one hand and the powers of order, Christian civilisation and the upliftment of people on the other ... we will not surrender.'[14]

Magnus Malan: 'South Africa has for a long time been subjected to a total and protracted revolutionary onslaught ... The onslaught is not just military: it is political, diplomatic, religious, psychological, economic and social.'[15]

Former Minister of Law and Order Adriaan Vlok: 'The ANC is a barbaric organisation of killers that doesn't care about the destruction of human life ... the [police] force has always maintained Christian norms and civilised standards. The force has ensured the acknowledgement and maintenance of individual freedom of faith and worship and has ensured the inviolability of freedom in our country.'[16]

In order to counter the revolution and the onslaught, a 'total strategy' was devised which came to a peak with the declaration of a state of emergency in the mid-1980s. The security forces were given extraordinary powers to counter the tide of black resistance. As a result, a new culture took hold in the security forces: one of no accountability and no rules. This soon bred an evil offspring: death squads. These units were never officially formed or sanctioned by the political leaders, but the fruits of the 'total strategy' were soon evident. Anti-apartheid activists disappeared and were mysteriously killed.

Major Craig Williamson, former commander of the Security Branch's foreign section and National Party member of the President's Council in the latter half of the 1980s, says: 'The myth that was put forward was that there were factions inside the ANC and the Communist Party who were busy killing each other. I expect some naive people on the Parkhurst bus maybe believe that story, but people who were in the management systems of the state didn't believe that story. They knew who was killing the ANC.[17]

'We were dealing with a system of the most incredible hypocrisy. On the one hand we had to pretend that we were God-fearing Christians who walked around with Bibles under our arms, and then on the other hand we were supposed to go around making sure that the white National Party government wasn't overthrown. And that was done very effectively.'

That is why theologian Dr Beyers Naude, probably the prime example of an Afrikaner who abandoned his tribe and joined the struggle for justice, believes that the moral responsibility for the actions of the hit men lie not only with them, but also with the National Party government which created special units like Vlakplaas and the CCB, structured them, allowed them, approved of them, financed them, blessed them and exploited them for their own ends.[18]

'Such a government should come forward and say: even if we do not know everything that was done, we have to stand before the whole nation and say: "Forgive us, including the way we used these people to do what they did."'

A notion close to the hearts of the assassins is that of a biblical justification not only for apartheid, but also for fighting the revolutionary onslaught. The policies of the powerful Dutch Reformed Church (DRC) on racial and political matters had until the 1980s read like a blueprint of the policies of the National Party. In the 1970s 63% of all Afrikaners were members of the strongest branch of the DRC. Where were the Afrikaans churches when people died in detention or complained of torture and when innocent people disappeared or were assassinated? In the hearts and minds of those very people who committed the atrocities, the silence of the church – added to the silent approval of the government – justified their deeds.

The assassins all say that they believed deeply in what they did, on the one hand because their political leaders told them that they were fighting Communism, and on the other because the Afrikaans churches were marching shoulder to shoulder with them into war. At the same time, the generals decorated and promoted the killers, who were regarded as heroes in the security forces.

But then: I am also an Afrikaner who grew up in a conservative home, was baptised in the DRC and indoctrinated by the total onslaught ideology. Yet, I did not kill. Neither did every security policemen torture or kill.

For the assassins, it was a question of: all's fair in love and war. There were numerous occasions on which they murdered and when it wasn't necessary to kill.

When Eugene de Kock and his men executed five people in Nelspruit, they did it to 'show results' in order to ensure the continued existence of their unit and to enable them to claim money for weapons they said they found afterwards (they lied – the people were unarmed). That was plain and simply evil.

In June 1986, ten Pretoria township activists, the youngest only 15, were lured by Joe Mamasela, acting as an ANC member, into a minibus and driven towards the Botswana border to join the ANC. On their way, they were intercepted by security policemen and Special Forces soldiers who killed them by injecting them with poison. That was plain and simply evil.

It is not difficult to condemn the assassins outright as evil. They not only fought an unjust war, but they did so in an immoral way. On the one hand, the answer is as simple as: you are human beings like me, and as such you were free to commit a crime, to become guilty – which you did.

Beyers Naude said that in the final analysis, the assassins must bear the responsibility for their actions. 'The decision to do what I do, must rest with me as an individual and I cannot blame either the government or the church or the system, because I, and I alone, must ultimately stand before my God and my conscience.'[19]

Psychiatrist Dr Viktor Frankl, who endured years of unspeakable horror in Nazi death camps, believed that human kindness could be found in all groups, even in those which it would be easy to condemn. Writing about his experiences in Auschwitz, he said: 'From all this we may learn that there are two races of men in this world ... the race of the decent man and the race of the indecent man. Both are found everywhere; they penetrate into all groups of society. No group consists entirely of decent or indecent people. In this sense, no group is of 'pure race' – and therefore one occasionally found a decent fellow among the camp guards.[20]

'Life in a concentration camp tore open the human soul and exposed its depths. Is it surprising that in those depths we again found only human qualities which by their very nature were a mixture of good and evil? The rift dividing good from evil, which goes through all human beings, reaches into the lowest depths and becomes apparent even on the bottom of the abyss which is laid open by the concentration camps.'

In Hannah Arendt's famous report on the Adolf Eichmann trial after the Second World War, she says that evil becomes widespread not so much because its proponents are profoundly diabolical, but because their work has become so routine, so banal, that they can do it without even thinking of morality.[21]

While I was writing this book, the TRC was hearing the stories of our shameful – and proud – past. The Great Telling started on April 15, 1996 in the East London town hall when ordinary South Africans spoke about massacres and wars, about the death of a child and about the killing of whole families, about loved ones who had disappeared without a trace or returned as corpses. Twice in the first two days, commission chairman Desmond Tutu wept openly.

Over the following months, the commission sat in noisy cities and quiet *dorpies* (small towns). They sat in big imposing town halls and dingy schools and churches – from Messina in the north to Cape Town in the south. It was time for our 'small people', 2 000 of them, previously unheard and not believed, to tell of their pain and suffering.

But the common thread was that the extent of the horror was more than anyone had ever suspected. Even the smallest town had its casualties: like the two boys from Hanover in the Karoo who told the story of how their torture at the hands of the police had caused them to lose their minds.

When I sat down in 1991 to write the book *In the Heart of the Whore*, I tried to compile a list of anti-apartheid activists who had been killed and murdered by the apartheid forces. I studied the files of human rights lawyers and human rights organisations and came up with a list of 87 people who had been killed inside South Africa and 138 outside the country. I listed nine people who had completely disappeared.

Today we know that many hundreds of people who were opposed to apartheid were killed by the security forces or made to disappear. Many more were tortured. When I wrote *In the Heart of the Whore*, the police death squad at Vlakplaas stood out as the main instrument in the security police killing arsenal. Today we know that every security branch unit in the country killed and tortured.

There is a mountain of evidence before the TRC to suggest that murder, torture and sabotage were commonplace and reached into the highest echelons of the security forces and the government. Former Minister of Law and Order Adriaan Vlok said in his amnesty application that PW Botha had instructed him to blow up a building, while a former commissioner of police admitted his complicity in the killing of eight student activists on the East Rand. A police brigadier and his death squad appeared twice before the commission to support their amnesty application for the deaths of more than 40 activists while a host of senior police-men, amongst them generals, are due to testify in the coming months.

And yet, FW de Klerk maintained in his submission to the commission: 'It has never been the policy of the government, the National Party, that people should be murdered, that they should be assassinated ... Totally unacceptable things for which we are so sorry and which we abhor, all of us so much, have taken place without the knowledge of superiors.'[22]

I am sure that if you read this book, you will come to the same conclusion as me: that FW de Klerk and the National Party government must have known what was going on. I have found no evidence that De Klerk authorised the killing of any person, but he miserably failed in his duty as State President to clean up the security forces and bring the perpetrators of death squad activities to justice.

All over the country, Commission investigators have dug up the skeletons of police victims who were killed and buried in secret graves. Every security police unit devised its own methods of getting rid of bodies. Vlakplaas operatives packed explosives around the bodies of their victims, the Northern Transvaal Security Branch blew them up with landmines, the Eastern Cape Security Branch burnt them and threw their ashes into the Fish River, while evidence suggests that the Natal Security Branch buried them in secret graves and the Johannesburg Security Branch threw some of its victims down mineshafts.

Listening to so many confessions of murder over a protracted period of time threatened to diminish my own sense of the value of life. After spending so much time with apartheid's assassins, death tends to make less sense and the victims of the atrocities become mere statistics. Fortunately, there have always been those victims who have bolstered me with their hope and humanity and reminded me that there was a purpose behind what I had been doing. Although this book is about the killers and their stories, I will also introduce you to some of their targets.

None was more haunting than the agony of Sipho and Joyce Mtimkulu, the parents of Eastern Cape student leader Sipiwo Mtimkulu – detained, tortured, poisoned, kidnapped, murdered and cremated by a group of security policemen.

When Mtimkulu was arested on May 31, 1981, he was in perfect health. When he was released from security police detention five months later, he was a shadow of his former self. He told his parents: 'They have finished me. Even my memory is not like before. I will never be that old Sipiwo again.'[23]

A day after his release, his father found him crawling from the bedroom to the kitchen. His feet were swollen and cold and he was suffering from severe stomach cramps. He was admitted to hospital where thallium poisoning was diagnosed. As the poison seeped into his veins, Sipiwo Mtimkulu was confined to a wheelchair and his hair started falling out.

He kept a diary of his detention – a chronicle of abuse at the hands of his interrogators. 'I still had on only my underpants. Nieuwoudt left the office with the towel. He returned. The towel was wet and dripping with water. He tied it over my nose and mouth. Breathing was difficult. I lost consciousness and fell. The towel was removed. It was done until I lost consciousness several times. Each time I fell on my back. At times he would hit me. The others would kick me …'

For several years before his detention, Mtimkulu was mercilessly hunted by Colonel Gideon Nieuwoudt, the Eastern Cape's most notorious security policeman, a thin-lipped savage with a swagger in his walk and hawklike eyes.

His pursuit of Mtimkulu knew no limits. One day, a 'priest' arrived at the Mtimkulu household. Says Sipho Mtimkulu: 'The man had a white collar and a Bible. He spoke about God and asked questions about Sipiwo. But I saw a gun at his side and wondered: why is a priest carrying a gun?' Later, Sipiwo Mtimkulu warned his parents that the 'man of God' was none other than Gideon Nieuwoudt. But true to his reputation, Nieuwoudt eventually got his man.

Ten months after Mtimkulu was hospitalised, he had regained some strength, although he couldn't wear shoes and had to use a walking stick. He instituted two civil claims against the Police for being tortured in detention, and for being poisoned in prison. By doing that, Sipiwo Mtimkulu signed his own death warrant. Two weeks later, Mtimkulu was given a lift to Livingstone Hospital by a friend, Topsy Madaka. They disappeared and were never seen again. The Mtimkulus searched for their son for nine years, until in 1989 Dirk Coetzee said that the security police had kidnapped him, killed him and disposed of his body. One morning in May 1996, Joyce Mtimkulu left her green-painted matchbox home in the township of New Brighton near Port Elizabeth to testify before the TRC about the disappearance of her son. Clutched under her arm was Sipiwo's diary, hidden by Joyce for many years, waiting for the day she could reveal it to the world and expose his torturers and probable killers.

'Although he is dead, he can still talk. And he is talking now,' Joyce said the night before as she prepared for one of the most important days of her life. She was not only taking his diary to the commission; in a plastic shopping bag was his hair which she had collected as it started falling out.

Joyce Mtimkulu would have been the latest in a long line of anti-apartheid activists that recalled events of incredible depravity committed by Gideon Nieuwoudt.

Sicelo Apleni: 'He took my genitals. They opened a drawer. He took my genitals and shut the drawer. All my genitals were in this drawer and it was shut closed. He squeezed and squeezed …'

Mkhuseli Jack: 'Seventy per cent of my testimony concerns this man. He was very busy torturing people. The first time I was tortured, it was by Nieuwoudt, and the last time I was tortured, it was by Nieuwoudt.'

The residents of New Brighton formed a line of honour for the Mtimkulus as they entered the brand new community hall officially opened by Her Majesty the Queen of England during a visit to Port Elizabeth the previous year.

Then Commissioner Bongani Finca broke the news: Eastern Cape security policemen had obtained a Supreme Court interdict to prevent Joyce Mtimkulu from testifying. When she heard the news, she collapsed and wept. Sipho Mtimkulu buried his face in a white handkerchief.

That night, the community of New Brighton assembled in their home and sang and prayed. 'Oh Lord, we are praying to preserve the dignity of Sipiwo and his parents. Help us to remove the hatred around the name of Sipiwo.'

A few weeks later, Joyce Mtimkulu, flanked and supported by her husband and family members, took the stand at the TRC. She swore an oath, and told the tale of her son who had been broken by those who professed to maintain law and order and uphold Christian values. She read passages from his diary, took the contents from the plastic shopping bag and pointed to the pieces of flesh still attached to his hair. When she was finished, she cried again, but this time out of sheer relief. A nation listened and embraced her with understanding and empathy.

That same week, Gideon Nieuwoudt was sentenced to 20 years' imprisonment in the Port Elizabeth Supreme Court after having been found guilty of blowing up four people with a car bomb in 1988. In mitigation he was presented to the judge as a God-fearing Christian who occupied the front pew in church every Sunday. Nieuwoudt, released on bail, has applied for amnesty for not only the car bomb killings, but also for being a member of a group of Eastern Cape security policemen who have admitted their complicity in a spate of murders, torture and disappearances. Amongst their victims: Sipiwo Mtimkulu. His body was burnt on the banks of the Fish River and his ashes thrown into the river.

On a crisp and sunny Karoo morning in January 1997, the families of Sipiwo Mtimkulu, Topsy Madaka and several other murdered Eastern Cape activists arrived at the Fish River to enact a special ritual. They came not to mourn the deaths, but to remember and pay homage to lives devoted to struggle and freedom. White petals and bouquets of flowers were cast onto the water as the families bowed their heads in prayer.[24]

'In the midst of big things, in the midst of strong winds, the father of my king Jesus Christ, you looked after us. Today at the start of 1997, our God who is extremely good said we must come and stand over this river. We heard, after these long years when we were in the dark that the bones, the remains of our husbands and children got thrown here in plastic bags, by the Boers, the people who were ruling at the time. But they got caught out, because you said a human being's bones can't just disappear.'

Chapter Two

The making of a man called Prime Evil

The hollow sound of our footsteps echoed through the long, badly lit passage that led to the visitor's section of the Pretoria Central Prison. Streaks of sunlight gleamed through the barricaded windows and the smell of floor polish filled the air. The faint sound of sombre religious music came from somewhere deep in the bowels of the stark, yellow-brick complex.[1]

It was Sunday morning, visitors' day, and walking next to me was a big, bulky black man with a square face and a deep voice. In one hand, he clutched a Bible inscribed with the words: 'The Lord will decide what is right and what is not.' His other hand was holding that of his 12-year-old son.

'This is going to be very difficult for me. It's the first time I've come here,' he said to me in Afrikaans.

We arrived at the row of visitors' cubicles at the end of the passage and stopped at the very first one. Sitting behind the thick, bullet-proof glass was a man with equally thick black-framed spectacles. His dark hair was combed sleekly across his forehead.

He looked up at his visitor whose bulk filled nearly all the space in the cubicle. His usually expressionless face lit up, he smiled and said: 'My God, it's you! How wonderful to see you.'

'Good morning, Colonel. And how's the Colonel?'

It was only the glass that prevented the two men from embracing one another.

'I have come to show you my son, Colonel. He's now 12 years old and it's time that he meets his namesake. He's been nagging me to see you.'

The young boy stood closer to the window. The man put his hand on his son's shoulder, and said: 'Colonel, this is my son, Eugene de Kock. And Eugene, this is the Colonel.'

I was standing a few paces back, witnessing one of the most peculiar events of my journalistic career. The man behind the window was a political serial killer, on trial for 121 crimes ranging from murder through kidnapping to fraud. His visitor was Lukas Kalino, a black Angolan comrade-in-arms who had fought with him in the security police counter-insurgency force called Koevoet (Afrikaans for 'crowbar') during the Namibian bush war. Together, the two men were involved in 350 shoot-outs with Swapo guerrillas.

Kalino respected and admired his commander so much that he had given his son, born around the time when De Kock was transferred from Koevoet to Vlak-plaas, the names 'Eugene de Kock'.

'I love that man,' Kalino had said to me when he had arrived at the prison ear-lier that Sunday morning in January 1996.

The young Eugene just stared at his namesake, not saying a word and proba-bly not quite understanding what was going on.

'You have probably heard many bad things about me. You mustn't believe all you hear. You must carry your name with pride. Don't be ashamed of it. I'm not a bad man,' De Kock said to the young boy.

When visiting time was over, Kalino left the Bible for De Kock.

He would afterwards tell me that he owed his life to the man behind bars. They fought and killed side by side, were ambushed and were in several land-mine explosions. They slept alongside each other in the bush and ate from the same bully beef tins. Lukas Kalino had cried the day when Eugene de Kock left Koevoet. 'He is my best friend, that man. I love him.'

I don't know whether the Angolan understands the implications of sending a township boy into the world with the names 'Eugene de Kock', but he said it was at the time the greatest honour he could bestow on his former commander.

'My son had to see his namesake. When I saw the Colonel, my heart had a big shock. I feel very, very sorry for him.'

He didn't only pray for him every day, but would later travel to northern Mozambique to search earnestly for a magical beetle that he believed would have granted De Kock the power to get out of prison.

I decided on that Sunday at Pretoria Central Prison that there are certain things I may never understand. The one is the bond between men who have done battle together, stared death in the face and killed.

At the time of our visit, Lukas Kalino was one of a few men who had not aban-doned Eugene de Kock and turned against him. Many of the Vlakplaas operatives, who had killed and tortured with him, were lining the Pretoria Supreme Court to testify against their former commander in return for indemnity from prosecution. Eugene de Kock was a lonely and deserted man, facing a life in prison after two decades at the forefront of southern Africa's secret and dirty wars.

For a long, long time to come, Eugene Alexander de Kock will remain a symbol of apartheid's most evil face: that of murdering and torturing the opponents of its racial policies.

September 19, 1996. In Court GD of the Pretoria Supreme Court, Colonel Eugene de Kock was unravelling the web of debauchery committed by a blood-soaked band of brothers at the police counter-insurgency unit based at a farm called Vlakplaas. It was a world in which murder was commonplace, where mercy and compassion counted for little.

The man they called Prime Evil was sitting in the witness box, gushing forth a tale of banality and depravity. Senior state advocate Anton Ackermann asked him: 'How would your enemies describe you?'

De Kock: Cold-blooded.

Ackermann: Other words you want to use?

De Kock: Determined and persevering.

Ackermann: How do your enemies see you?

De Kock: As merciless.

Ackermann: What else?

De Kock: I haven't met that many, because most are dead.

Ackermann: Mr de Kock, have you ever tried to establish how many lives you've taken?

De Kock: No, one doesn't do it. It's a terrible thing to think about.

For eighteen months, the former Vlakplaas commander had sat expressionless and impassive in the dock, making notes or staring straight in front of him. Those who saw him for the first time were surprised by his meek look and mild manner. Day after day, state witnesses had painted a picture of a man who ruled Vlak-plaas like a despot, who ordered his men to murder simply by using security police euphemisms like *'elimineer'* or *'maak 'n plan'*. The Vlakplaas operatives were expected to ask no questions, unflinchingly carry out his orders and be at his beck and call at all times. Those who obeyed him were well rewarded; the security police secret fund provided an endless flow of cash that found its way into their pockets. When investigations into their murderous activities were launched from time to time, the Vlakplaas death squad banded together, lying under oath, destroying evidence and creating alibis. If need be, they killed colleagues to protect their nefarious secrets.

Many of the state witnesses were once De Kock's confidants, co-conspirators and even close friends. The main state witness was the godfather of one of his children. The two had once been closer than brothers, but when Warrant Officer Willie Nortje realised that his former commander was doomed by the mass of evidence against him and that Nortje's own freedom might be on the line, he turned state witness.

At the start of the case, Anton Ackermann assured Mr Justice Willem van der Merwe that the trial would be neither a witchhunt nor a Nuremberg hearing. It would expose crimes 'universally recognised for centuries', committed for personal gain or to conceal covert operations carried out in the name of state security.

In August 1996, Eugene de Kock was convicted of six murders, conspiracy to commit murder, attempted murder, kidnapping, assault, manslaughter, defeating the ends of justice, the illegal possession of arms and ammunition, and fraud.

This was, however, only a fraction of the crimes and atrocities committed by the death squad commander. He was in command of Vlakplaas for eight years, during which time he was involved in the killing of about 65 people. During his four-and-a-half year stint with Koevoet in Namibia, he commanded a unit which killed hundreds of South West African People's Organisation (Swapo) infiltrators and supporters. And during the early 1990s De Kock and his men became a 'third force' when they flooded the townships around Johannesburg with weapons to enable Inkatha to wage civil war against the ANC. Thousands of people died during this conflict.

But on that day in September 1996, one of the South African security forces' most effective assassins was driven to confession and to breaking his silence for the first time when he testified in mitigation of sentence. He pointed fingers at those who had given the orders and instructed him to kill.

In a moment of emotion, he said: 'There are times when I wish I wasn't born. I can't tell you how dirty I feel. I shouldn't have joined the South African Police. We achieved nothing. We just left hatred behind us. There are children who will never know their parents and I will have to carry this burden for ever. I'm a very private person and I don't like to show emotion, but I sympathise with my victims as if they were my own children. This is all I can say.'

But remorse came too late for the 47-year-old killer. His crimes were just too barbarous and brutal to justify any leniency in sentencing. Six weeks later, Willem van der Merwe sentenced him to two life sentences and 212 years' imprisonment. If the death penalty had not been abolished, De Kock could have been on his way to the gallows.

As black people danced and celebrated outside the court building, their fists clenched in the air, Eugene de Kock was driven away to start his sentence in the maximum security section of the Pretoria Central Prison. For the first time, justice was seen to be done to an apartheid killer.

For many years Eugene de Kock had been an elusive and secretive man. His name first appeared in the headlines when convicted killer and former Vlakplaas operative Almond Nofemela and former Vlakplaas commander Captain Dirk Coetzee spoke out towards the end of 1989. Nofemela identified him as his former commander and implicated him in several killings while Coetzee named him as his death squad successor at Vlakplaas.

Little was known about the man with the thick spectacles. His name had appeared two or three times in newspapers after he had testified in judicial inquests into the deaths of activists ambushed or killed by his unit. But the words Vlakplaas, askari, death squad and counter-insurgency unit were never mentioned. De Kock didn't grant interviews, never appeared in public and the courts and judicial commissions of inquiry prohibited the taking of photographs of him.

Looking back at his reign of terror during the 1980s, judges and magistrates must carry a great deal of blame for exonerating him and his unit and thereby allowing them to continue their dirty work. Time after time, magistrates found that Eugene de Kock and his men had fired in 'reasonable defence' – while such incidents were in fact nothing but murder.

The most blatant disregard of justice happened in June 1988 when De Kock and a group of security policemen ambushed nine people in two separate incidents near Piet Retief in the Eastern Transvaal. The police claimed that the infiltrators had been armed and had opened fire at them first. In the two years preceding the Piet Retief incidents, eight other people – four in the Eastern Transvaal and four near Durban – had died in similar mysterious circumstances. In each case, the death squads of Vlakplaas were involved in the operations, and there were never survivors to tell their stories.

Eugene de Kock testified at the Piet Retief inquest that he had prayed that the people into whom he was emptying his Uzi sub-machine gun would not die. De Kock assured the magistrate that it was never his intention to kill anybody and that he had planned the entire operation to avoid deaths and injuries at all costs.[2]

De Kock said he had received information from an ANC informant in Swaziland about the infiltration the day before the shoot-out. De Kock sent an askari to meet the infiltrators at a certain spot and lead them into his ambush. (The word 'askari' is Swahili and means 'black soldier'.)

De Kock said in his evidence that he had set up a police road-block to stop the infiltrators and arrest them. 'The next moment, the back window of the car was opened and one of the infiltrators started firing at me. I only had my weapon. One would not use it injudiciously and kill people on purpose. It was a tragedy that the people were killed. If I had wounded them, I would have applied first aid and taken them to hospital.'

The magistrate not only accepted De Kock's version of events, but ignored a number of highly irregular acts committed by the police in an attempt to cover up their actions. Incredible as it may seem, a security policeman who participated in the killings appointed himself as investigating officer. The motor car in which the infiltrators had travelled was removed before any ballistic examination was done. No photographs of the inside of the car were taken and the Makarov pistol which police said was found next to one of the bodies was not sent for fingerprint analysis.

There were at least 62 entry wounds in the four bodies – many more than the number of shots the police claimed they had fired. The bloodied clothes of the deceased were burnt without any investigation having been conducted. The investigating officer explained that he was afraid that they might have had AIDS.

During the inquest, a former police constable by the name of Marthinus Grobler came to me and told me that he was in the charge office of the Piet Retief police station on the night of one of the incidents.

When the policemen returned later that night, he had to help to carry the dead bodies into the mortuary and was told by one of the security policemen how they had been executed in cold blood. No weapons were found on the dead, he said.[3]

Grobler told of a macabre ritual in the mortuary: four security policemen walking around the bloodied corpses and gloating, passing a bottle of Old Brown sherry around as they congratulated each other on the magnificent blow they had dealt the enemy.

Days after we had published the story in *Vrye Weekblad,* Grobler left the country in fear for his life. There was, however, no attempt by the court to trace him to give evidence at the inquest. The magistrate eventually found that there was not enough evidence to show malice on the part of the security policemen.

More than six years after De Kock had testified in the Piet Retief magistrate's court, Anton Ackermann asked him: 'Were you telling the truth in the Piet Retief inquest?'

'No.'

'Chesterville?'

'No.'

'Maponya?'

'No.'

'Harms Commission?'

'No.'

'Goldstone Commission?'

'No.'

'Mr de Kock, I read your evidence in the different cases and I must say you have improved with time.'

'Maybe one graduates after every case.'

De Kock admitted in the Pretoria Supreme Court that the people at Piet Retief were unarmed, never fired on the police and that the Makarov pistol and hand grenade were planted on the dead bodies afterwards. They were simply executed.

Ackermann: Why did you lie at the judicial inquest?

De Kock: It was in the interests of the police, it was in the interests of the government. We had to protect the police and army so that the revolution-ary forces couldn't flood into the country and cause the same bloodbaths as in Angola, Mozambique or the former Congo.

Ackermann: So you committed perjury for *Volk and Vaderland* (for country and people)?

De Kock: Yes, that is correct.

But no judicial officer was more naive than the blundering Mr Justice Louis Harms, appointed in February 1990 by the State President, FW de Klerk, to inves-tigate the existence of police death squads. Harms was the dupe of a massive police cover-up when he found that there was no police death squad at Vlakplaas. Ironically, Harms chose to introduce his report with a Latin expression: *Felix qui potuit verum cognoscere caucas* (Blessed is he who can recognise the truth).[4]

Eugene de Kock was involved in killing about 70 people in the ten years be-tween 1983, when he arrived at Vlakplaas, and 1993, when he left the police force. That's how long it took the state to stop him. The country and the majority of its people had to wait for the coming of democracy before Eugene de Kock could be charged, prosecuted and convicted. He was arrested one week after South Africa's first democratic election on April 27, 1994. He pleaded not guilty to all the charges against him.

In the end, it took nearly two years and more than 80 state witnesses, a special investigations team, a judge and state prosecutors with integrity, an elaborate witness protection programme that could fly co-conspirators to safety around the world, and millions of rands to bring the killer to justice.

Eugene de Kock was born in January 1949 into a typical Afrikaner home. His father, Lourens de Kock, was a magistrate who in later years became president of the regional court in Johannesburg. 'There wasn't time for play. If you weren't doing homework, you had to work. My father grew up during the years of the Great Depression and suffered a great deal. We had to go and work on farms during the school holidays. He said if we didn't learn hard at school, we would become railway workers. He was very aggressive, and would hit us till the stick broke. If we cried, he would hit us again.'

Eugene's younger brother, Vossie, describes him as a quiet, lonely child. 'He loved his music. He mostly listened to classical music. He was a soft child who was never violent, not aggressive at all.'[5]

According to evidence in court, his father drank excessively, was aggressive and fought with his mother. When Vossie was five and Eugene six years old, his mother got into the car and drove away. 'My younger brother and I stood in the study and looked through the window at what was happening outside. Vossie started crying and was afraid, and although I didn't cry, I was afraid we were going to be alone. It was an unknown fear, one that I never felt again during unrest, skirmishes or any other situation.'

University of South Africa criminologist Professor Anna van der Hoven examined and analysed De Kock. She explains that because of his childhood experiences De Kock learned to suppress emotions such as sadness and empathy and that he is, therefore, emotionally cold. It helped him in later years mercilessly to hunt down his enemies. De Kock learnt his aggressiveness from his father.

Both brothers remember their father as a strong supporter of the National Party who told them stories about the Great Trek and the Second Boer War and reminded them that thousands of women and children had died in the British concentration camps. His opinion was that *hensoppers* and *hanskakies* (Boer traitors) deserved the firing squad. During their father's youth, he was a member of the Ossewa-Brandwag, an Afrikaner nationalist organisation which had strong links with the Nazis in Germany. The brothers later discovered that he was a senior member of the Afrikaner Broederbond (a secret Nationalist organisation of more than 12 000 'super Afrikaners') and a friend of former Prime Minister John Vorster.[6]

De Kock said: 'I was a member of the Voortrekkers (a conservative Afrikaner youth movement) for 12 years. I wouldn't say it was quite the same as the Hitler youth, because there wasn't a war at that stage, but we wouldn't have dared to miss any such activity. Every grain in my body was Afrikaner.'

Their mother was English-speaking and, according to his own evidence, 'a very soft woman'. When she was dying of cancer in later years, De Kock could not be with his father to comfort him because he had to go on a Vlakplaas operation. He had to ask a friend to stay with his father.

Vossie never testified in court, but according to friends, the two brothers were never close. Vossie hardly ever visited De Kock in prison and seldom attended the trial. He was, however, in court when his brother was sentenced, and shook his hand before he was led away to the cells downstairs.

Vossie, also a policeman, said his brother had wanted to join the army after school, but was rejected because he stuttered. De Kock himself said he wouldn't join the permanent force because the instructors used foul language, to which he wasn't accustomed.

De Kock said he was 17 years old and untouched by the cruelty and harsh realities of the world when the army showed the film *Africa Adieu* – the story of the rebel uprising in the former Belgian Congo – to the young recruits.

'We saw things like pregnant women with their stomachs ripped open, nuns that were raped and killed and dead people with their hands chopped off. Churches were burnt down and people massacred. I never thought that things like that could happen. It brought about a belief that what had happened in the Congo would happen here if we allowed Communists to take over.'

De Kock decided to join the police and went to Police College on January 3, 1968, at the age of 19. Former security policeman Warrant Officer Paul Erasmus was at college at the same time as De Kock. 'We were literally taught to hate. If you look at the security course I went on, for five weeks we were subjected to, and we swallowed all of this, the ranting and raving of a person that I'll describe as a cross between Adolf Hitler and Eugene TerreBlanche. About the satanic, godless Communists and their black surrogates that were going to swamp us. Officially we were taught to hate. It was a culture of hatred.'[7]

This is a passage from a Criminology and Ethnology textbook: 'The Bantu are less civilised. The more primitive a people is, the less they are able to control their emotions. At the slightest provocation they resort to violence. They cannot distinguish between serious and less serious matters. They are less self-controlled and more impulsive.'

Dirk Coetzee still remembers the spellbinding lectures he received at police college from the legendary Sagmoedige Neelsie (Gentle Neelsie), Brigadier Neels du Plooy of security police headquarters. Du Plooy was a soft-spoken and humble Christian who opened and closed his lectures with a scripture reading and prayer. When Neelsie spoke, you could hear a pin drop. His lectures consisted of cycles of emotion. He would start in a calm and collected manner and gradually work himself up into a frenzy that left the policemen in a trance. He supported his claims with a display of subversive and banned literature that ordinary citizens could never see. The ANC were the heathens – callous, heartless and cruel killers of innocent people like nuns and children.[8]

After his basic training, De Kock applied to join the elite police Special Task Force, but was again rejected, this time because of his poor eyesight. Shortly after, he did his first tour of duty in the former Rhodesia, where the white-dominated forces of Ian Smith were doing battle with the liberation armies of Joshua Nkomo and Robert Mugabe. De Kock did altogether nine tours of duty, of between three and four months each, in Rhodesia.

'During my third tour in Rhodesia, policemen were swimming in the Zambezi River at Fish Camp number one when they were captured and abducted by terrorists. One was tortured to death. The other three were executed. At one stage, there was a formal cease-fire between the warring factions. Seven members of the police were driving to Bindura when they were stopped by a group of terrorists. They didn't even have their R-1 rifles with them. They were also executed. Two policemen got away by diving into a river. These incidents made me realise: if you shoot second, you are dead. You can never expect any mercy.'

Vossie de Kock was also in Rhodesia. 'We were divided into small units, what we used to call sticks, up to six people. After you left camp with gun, ammunition, little bit of water, little bit of food, you were out in the bush, hunting down the terrs. If I say hunting, I mean hunting. There's no mercy. If you get the terrs, you kill them, there's no two ways about it.'

Former colleague Riaan Stander did several tours of duty in Rhodesia. He said already then the young De Kock showed that he was extremely brave. 'Eugene was never a policeman. I think we must understand it right from the start that Eugene was a warrior. I would say he must have had some roots in the Old Vikings because he was really an excellent soldier. He was a warrior by heart and he was very loyal to the cause. He was a good leader. He could lead men. Men believed in Eugene de Kock like they believed in their Bible, even more.'[9]

Vossie de Kock said he never discussed Rhodesia with his brother. 'Why must we? It was a job to be done and we did it.'

The Rhodesian experience left a deep impression on Riaan Stander. He remembers a specific incident where a guerrilla leader by the name of Lebandi was interrogated by the Rhodesian forces.

'He was hung upside down and hit from one side to the other. There were two parties and you'll hit him from one side and he would swing over to the other side, and another one would hit him from that corner. They also forced a burning stick up in the anus area as far as possible and then he would start talking.'

De Kock testified in court that the Rhodesians taught him a very important lesson: 'Shoot first, and then ask questions.' It became a philosophy he would apply throughout his life.

Dirk Coetzee was sent to Rhodesia as a dog handler and stationed at a police base near Mount Darwin. Although he was not directly involved in military operations, this was where he had his first lesson in how to dispose of an unwanted body. The Rhodesian Special Branch would put as many as seven bodies in a shallow grave and cover them with branches, douse them with petrol and set them alight. As soon as the bodies were burnt beyond recognition, the graves were covered with soil. Later on, he witnessed the mutilated bodies of landmine victims and massacred villagers. These killings made a deep impression on him and he took photographs of the bodies to show the people back home what was really going on in the Rhodesian bush.

Riaan Stander said the war changed his whole view of life. 'It changes the value of life, to the point where a life means nothing. We were trained in the college to protect and serve. At the same time though, you became part of a totally different discipline, and that is to kill and destroy. It changes a person completely.'

In 1977, De Kock was posted to Ruacana in Ovamboland, Namibia. 'I was then an officer with the rank of lieutenant. I requested this transfer because I wanted to be in a position where I could fight terrorism.'

Two years later, he was transferred to a new security police counter-insurgency unit with the codename 'Koevoet', which became the most successful fighting unit in Namibia, making use of a handful of white security policemen who were in command of 'turned terrorists', Ovambo trackers and former Angolan soldiers who had come to Namibia after Angola became independent in 1975.

Eugene de Kock was in command of one of the two first fighting units that were formed. 'The first operation we went on was to look for Swapo terrorists who had attacked a farmhouse and killed three people. An old woman had been bayoneted, and two young children of six or seven had been picked up by their legs and their heads were smashed against the wheel of a tractor. Myself and seven Koevoet men were dropped by helicopter not far from the Angolan border to wait for the murderers. Within two hours, we were ambushed. The area we were in was a socalled liberated area controlled by Swapo. Over the next four or five days, we were in "contacts" every day until our ammunition was finished. While we were tracking one group of terrorists, another group was hot on our heels, hunting us down. One night, they had to drop parabats to bring us more ammunition.'

It was in Ovamboland that Eugene de Kock teamed up with Lukas Kalino in what was the beginning of a very close camaraderie. Kalino had been a soldier for most of his life. He was 15 when he joined the FNLA in Angola and took up arms against Portuguese occupation of the country. But the independence of his fatherland in 1975 promised little freedom as the MPLA seized power and civil war broke out. Kalino fled to Namibia where he joined 32 Battalion before being recruited to Koevoet.

The two men forged a formidable fighting unit. 'When we went into a contact, my heart thought for him, and he thought for me. When we went forward, I first looked to see where he was, and he looked to see where I was. If he shouted, I shouted. Then I could see he was still alive. That gave us the strength to go forward.'

De Kock said they were in 'contacts' with fighting members of the South West African People's Organisation (Swapo), fighting for the liberation of Namibia, approximately every second day. 'We were quite often outnumbered three to one. Swapo was dedicated and prepared to fight till the bitter end. Sometimes you felt as though you wanted to hide away until it was all over. In one instance, we were in a fight with 120 terrorists – and it was the second fight within half an hour.'

As always, Lukas Kalino was next to him. 'They shot the trees out of the ground and we didn't know whether we would ever get out alive. But we went forward and fought until they ran away.'

'How many Swapo guerrillas did you kill that day?' I asked him. 'It was 27.'

Kalino was next to De Kock the day he lost his spectacles in battle. 'We were in an ambush. The Colonel was the only white man amongst us and all the Swapo guns were aimed at him. A bullet ripped his spectacles from his face. The shot burnt his hair. I thought he was dead and crawled towards him, but when I got there, he lifted his head and said he was okay, but couldn't see anything. He was looking for his spectacles, but I told him they were smashed. He said it didn't matter, we must go forward.'

'How many Swapo soldiers did you kill that day?'

'I think it was six.'

'In how many battles were you and De Kock?'

'350.'

'And how many people did you kill?'

'I don't know, it was too many.'

De Kock said he was in two landmine explosions. One hurt his back and damaged his hearing. During one of the landmine explosions, he was strapped to a seat inside a Casspir (a police armoured vehicle). The Casspir was thrown 43 metres down the dirt road. His men had to prise him out of the vehicle.

He said when he arrived at Koevoet, there were different food rations for white and black members. 'I saw the same thing in Rhodesia: the blacks would get mealie meal and maybe one tin of meat, while the white men had virtually a menu to eat from. The black Koevoet members never complained, but I could see that it had an effect on their performance. Yet, they did the same work, carried the same load and fought as hard as we did. I asked for the same rations for black and white, but my request was rejected. I said fine, but in future the white members would only eat black rations, and it was only then that my black members could get white man's food. The same happened whenever I required air assistance to transport a wounded soldier to hospital. I would be asked if the soldier was white or black. If you were white, you would get a helicopter, if you were black, you might be left in the bush to die.

'One day we were on the heels of Swapo terrorists. They were already discarding some of their equipment to make their load lighter. I requested helicopters to assist us, but I was told that General Hans Dreyer [commander of Koevoet] and the rest of the unit were having a braaivleis somewhere and couldn't assist us. This gave the terrorists the chance to lay anti-personnel mines for my troops. Three of my men were killed and 13 wounded before the helicopters arrived.'

De Kock was one of the architects of the Koevoet fighting formation which became both famous and notorious. The men initially operated on foot until they were introduced to Casspirs.

The men became a feared sight in northern Namibia, the white policemen riding on top of the Casspirs behind their heavy machine guns, while Ovambo trackers would run on the spoor of Swapo insurgents.

In 1981, Koevoet killed 510 Swapo insurgents. The men were paid bounty money of R2 000 for every dead or captured Swapo infiltrator. This meant that sections kept scoreboards and competed for the most kills. De Kock was the commander of Section Zulu Delta, one of the Koevoet units boasting the highest kill rate.

'Every time you climbed into your Casspir, you knew that within an hour you could be a corpse, a paraplegic or brain dead. We usually brought the dead terrorists back to the base with us. I tied them to other Casspirs because I had an aversion to corpses.

'I never had any problems with dead Swapo terrorists, but was greatly disturbed by my own wounded or dead. Sometimes, you could just not avoid that incoming bullet. Many nights, I could hear my Ovambo soldiers cry, especially when one of them had been wounded in a heavy fight. I sometimes gave them injections to make them sleep.'

Koevoet was notorious for driving through villages and houses, killing innocent civilians and torturing detainees. The bodies of dead Swapo soldiers were often strapped across the spare wheel of the Casspir to scare and intimidate the local people.

It was a war without rules, conventions or decrees. Anything was permitted in fighting and defeating the enemy. During the final days of the Rhodesian bush war, tinned food poisoned with thallium was obtained from friends in Ian Smith's defeated forces and passed on to Koevoet which would distribute the supplies in regions controlled by Swapo.[11]

De Kock told the court: 'Terrorists who were captured and interrogated and refused to co-operate were executed and buried. They were the enemy, they showed no mercy and we showed no mercy. They cut people's throats with bayonets. You used this to justify killing them, but we knew what we were doing was not right.' When De Kock and his unit combed an area after a skirmish, they would sometimes just drive over the wounded with the nine-tonne Casspir.

Two white Koevoet policemen murdered a Swapo detainee and buried him in the Etosha game reserve in northern Namibia. Unfortunately for them, game wardens came across the grave and dug up the body. Next to the grave was an empty Red Heart rum bottle and six tins of Coca-Cola. Fingerprints were found on the bottle, and General Hans Dreyer told De Kock to be ready to go to Windhoek to steal the evidence. Fortunately for them, somebody else 'solved' the problem first.

De Kock said there was a white Koevoet member who was completely deranged and was known for killing innocent women and children. He would throw hand grenades into huts and burn people to death. His hobby was catching and playing with snakes. He had a female dog and every time the bitch went on heat, he would open the gates of his yard to attract other dogs, but as soon as they entered his property, he would club them to death.

Eugene de Kock became entangled in the madness of Ovamboland. Photographs taken by one of his men show him bearded and unkempt amongst the bullet-riddled bodies of dead Swapo soldiers, standing next to the twisted wreck of a landrnined Casspir and assaulting a Swapo detainee.

'When we returned to base after a week in the bush, the first two days were marked by rather wild parties. In the bar, bottles would be shot from the shelves and the boys would get involved in brawls with members of other units.'

Eugene de Kock was transferred from Koevoet after a fall-out with General Hans Dreyer. One night, a Koevoet unit was drinking in the bar and the celebration got out of hand. Members of the unit shot liquor bottles from the shelves, and used their guns to shoot at targets on the walls. They activated fire extinguishers and everything was covered with a layer of white powder. De Kock said when he arrived there, one of the members was shoving his pistol in the barman's ear. De Kock had to calm them down, but by that time, they had already bought the whole supply of liquor, and the drinking and rampaging continued through the night.

'A few days later, while my unit was out in the bush, Dreyer instructed me to return to base. I had a feeling that trouble was brewing, and told my unit that if they heard any shooting coming from the base, they must attack and flatten it. They waited outside the base while I went to see Dreyer, armed to the teeth. When I walked into his office, he accused me of being responsible for the mess in the bar. He threatened to assault me with his walking stick, but I told him I would break it and hurt him.'

In May 1983, Dreyer sent a telex to police headquarters in Pretoria: 'This officer was involved in many contacts with Swapo terrorists. It is in his own interest that he returns to normal service and I, therefore, request his urgent transfer.' Dreyer might well have realised that Eugene de Kock was becoming unstable.

De Kock said: 'I also wanted to go. I had reached the point where I was losing myself and could become a danger to my men. You know, I wouldn't have thought twice about flattening a house with my Casspir.'

Lukas Kalino said he was never as sad as the day his commander left Koevoet.

'Six hundred men asked him to stay. The blacks cried when he left and said that they were breaking Koevoet down. The only difference between us was that he had a white skin and I had a black skin. In every other way we were brothers.'

Vossie de Kock said when his brother returned from Koevoet he 'was going out of his mind' and was a completely changed person. 'I think his nature rebelled against all the fighting and killings. I think at a later stage they were pushed a little too far and had to commit too many atrocities.'

De Kock said he suffered from anxiety attacks, nightmares and flashbacks of his experiences. 'I would wake up at night and could smell the Mopani bush and taste the gunpowder on my tongue. I couldn't breathe and had to get up and was too scared to go and sleep again. I was sometimes so afraid that I couldn't move. My doctor said I was suffering from anxiety and stress and gave me pills. I once went to see a psychologist, but when he heard I came from Koevoet, he couldn't get rid of me quickly enough.'

De Kock was suffering from symptoms of post-traumatic stress disorder. This is how Vossie described his behaviour: 'If you talk to him, don't make a sudden movement or taunt him, because he'll jump over the table and grab you by the throat. Don't come up from behind and touch him, because when he turns around he is not going to wait to see who you are. He's going to hit you.'

The Koevoet soldiers, exposed to extreme battle fatigue and war stress, never received any psychological treatment. De Kock said: 'The closest you would get to that would be police chaplains that would pray to the Lord to deliver the enemy into your hands. One day, we captured a Swapo terrorist. In his pocket was a Bible, and I then wondered whether he hadn't also sat that morning under a tree and asked the Lord to give us into his hand. It confused me, and I wonder about it till this day.'

Former security policeman Paul Erasmus was also sent to Ovamboland, and before long, he had an opportunity to take aim at the enemy. 'An elderly black man, a Swapo medic, was arrested. Two of my colleagues and I took the guy out early in the morning after we had interrogated him. He took us out into the veld about ten kilometres outside Oshakati. We were drinking as was usual and this was eight o'clock in the morning when he made a break and ran off into the bushes and we all started shooting at him. I eventually shot him twice in the back. It was the first person that I killed, that I knew I had actually killed. He was still alive when I posed with my rifle in my hand and my boot on his back like a big game hunter and somebody took a photo of it.'

'How did you feel afterwards?'

'It only hit me late that night after a lot of celebrating when I was initiated as one of the "old salts" of Ovamboland. After a heavy drinking session I got into bed and I started crying, which I put down more to the amount of alcohol I had consumed. But when it really came home to me was the following day when we went to the kraal where we had shot him. He was a grandfather, and there were his children, looking at me. And I have never forgotten, and it haunts me every day and every moment that I sleep: I'll never forget their eyes.'

Nobody, it seems, emerged unscathed from the Namibian experience. When Shaun Callaghan was conscripted into the SADF in 1982, he applied to become a medical orderly, because he said: 'I would rather help people than kill them.' After his training, he was sent to the operational area in northern Namibia. [12]

In February 1983, he was told to exchange his army 'browns' for a camouflaged Koevoet uniform and joined Section Zulu India as their operational medical orderly, where he remained for seven months.

The young man emerged traumatised and mentally broken from his Koevoet experience, and for years would have nightmares of swimming pools filled with blood and patients without legs or arms dying in his room. For more than ten years, he fought post-traumatic stress disorder, and finally came to the TRC in June 1997 to tell why he had broken down.

He told the Commission of Swapo detainees who were tortured with boiling water and electrical shocks, and had to dig their own graves before being executed, mutilated bodies strapped to the spare wheels of Casspirs for days, and mates and comrades who had their limbs blown off by landmines.

And then there was a Section Zulu Yankee commander by the name of John Deegan. Callaghan recounted an incident in Ovamboland in 1983 when Section Zulu India chased a political commissar for two days.

'There were 50 of us chasing one person with an AK-47. We caught him two days later where he was hiding in a kraal. John Deegan chased everybody out of the kraal, but the commissar stayed in the hut. We drove over the hut with a Casspir, and everybody fired into the hut afterwards. They pulled out the wounded political commissar who was handed to me to treat. I started applying bandages and put up a drip. At the same time, John interrogated him. I was still applying the drip when John got so frustrated that he shot the patient through the head. The commissar was also tied to the bumper of a Casspir.'

In early 1997, nearly 15 years after they had shared death in Koevoet, Callaghan met up with John Deegan in Johannesburg.

'He still wears camouflage uniforms and the room where he was living was covered with camouflage netting. He has dropped out of society, he is on drugs, he's an alcoholic, and he told me it is all because of that day when he had completely lost it.'

John Deegan is indeed a man surrounded by memorabilia of war and memories of killing. Jobless, floating around, haunted and mentally scarred, he says: 'My life since [Ovamboland] has been very, very difficult. There's a big element of selfdestruction. I went through two marriages. I have a daughter. But really I've just destroyed the people around me. My friends. My family. And, I think that's enough now.' [13]

He tells of the political commissar: 'He wouldn't respond. And I just remember feeling the most incredible rage and anger. I took out my pistol and put a bullet between his eyes. Shot him. I executed him. It was as if I was looking at the scene from above and I could see myself standing there with this gun in my hand. The family from the kraal; they were very shocked. And the kids were very shocked. And I walked away …

'We would just kill and that's how we got our kicks. We were adrenaline junkies, basically. The killings … obviously I have deep remorse now. But at the time, that's what we had to do. And we did it well. We were the best. And that's what Koevoet was all about.'

Major Craig Williamson, who was at the time of the Namibian war a good friend of De Kock, said he was one of the bravest and toughest men he had ever met. 'If he had gone to Vietnam, he would have been sent for one tour of six months, and perhaps a second tour of six months, and if he had completed a third tour of six months he would have been regarded as some type of a hero. There are people who couldn't complete one tour of six months and ended up suffering from post-traumatic stress disorder. Here is a man who was in the frontline for 20 years, and a man who was burnt by that 20 years of war.'[14]

A day after De Kock returned to South Africa, an ANC car bomb exploded in front of Air Force headquarters in Church Street in Pretoria, killing 19 people and injuring more than 200. 'I visited the site, and it had a formidable effect on me. I thought that this was nothing but terror against the public. It gave me the impression that we are sitting here with an enemy that would do anything.'

Williamson said the Pretoria bomb also had a profound effect on him. 'I don't know whether I was taught to hate, but the day I stood in Church Street among all the bodies, I hated.'

'What effect did it have on you?' I asked him.

'Made me want to kill ANC members.'

Without ever being debriefed or treated for war trauma, Eugene de Kock was transferred from one fighting unit to another when he was sent to Vlakplaas. He said in his testimony in court: 'I walked from one war to the next. There was a difference in tactics, but the enemy remained the same. The war never stopped.'

Craig Williamson said De Kock was certainly groomed for his job at Vlakplaas. 'He was part of an élite in the security police. He believed absolutely that he had a mission. The Rhodesian and Koevoet episodes primed him for what he became and for the job he did at Vlakplaas. And let nobody deny that Eugene de Kock's superiors knew who Eugene de Kock was and knew what Eugene de Kock was good at.'

It was in fact Williamson who helped to prepare De Kock for the reputation he would achieve at Vlakplaas and bring him to the attention of the generals at Security Branch Headquarters and the Minister of Police, Louis le Grange.

Towards the end of 1981, Craig Williamson and his men planned a highly secret operation in Europe: to bomb the ANC headquarters in London. Explosives were sent via the diplomatic bag to the South African Embassy in the British capital where they were collected by one of Williamson's agents, Peter Casselton.

De Kock testified that he met Craig Williamson during one of his visits to Koevoet. The two men struck up a friendship when De Kock took Williamson on a tour of the operational area in northern Namibia.

A week after Williamson had left, De Kock received a message to report to Security Branch headquarters in Pretoria. When he got there, he was told that he had been selected as a member of the London bombing team. De Kock said he was told that the bomb was not only intended to damage the building, but was aimed at killing the ANC leadership during a meeting that was going to take place at the same time. De Kock was included in the team because he was a trained explosives expert and could do reconnaissance of the building. He was instructed that should there be any guards, he had to 'neutralise' them. False passports were issued and the men had instructions that they should under no circumstances contact the South African Embassy in London.

The men flew to London in two teams. When De Kock arrived at Heathrow, he was questioned for four hours by customs officials, but said he got the impression that they suspected him of drug trafficking. They released him and the planning for the bombing could continue.

Most of the men left London a few hours before the bomb exploded. De Kock and another security policeman, Colonel Vic McPherson, flew back to South Africa via Frankfurt.

McPherson, a long-time friend of De Kock, said that while they were waiting in the international departures hall at Frankfurt airport in Germany for their connecting flight to South Africa, they heard an announcement: 'Attention: telephone for Herr Joe Slovo. Herr Slovo, telephone, please.'[15]

McPherson said they couldn't believe their eyes when the leader of the South African Communist Party walked past them towards a telephone booth to take the call. De Kock decided there and then that he was going to kill Slovo. He simply couldn't let the opportunity go. The only weapon he could find was a ball-point pen. He said to McPherson that he was going to stab it into Slovo's heart. McPherson had to hold him back and calm him down.

The London operation was seen as a huge success and Louis le Grange decorated all the bombers with the Police Star for Outstanding Service at a private and secret ceremony in his office.

Vic McPherson has against all odds survived the clean-up in the police after the ANC won the elections in 1994 and became a senior officer at John Vorster Square in Johannesburg. He remains one of De Kock's biggest supporters.

'I would say he was brilliant in what he achieved for the South African Police. He should be regarded as a hero. What he did, he did very, very well.' He says Eugene de Kock is nothing but a modern-day Christiaan de Wet, an equivalent of the legendary Boer general who fought and nearly defeated the English during the Second Boer War.

He quotes from *The Boer War,* in which Thomas Packenham recounts how De Wet and 1 500 Boer soldiers outfought an English force of more than 10 000 men near the Modder Spruit in the Orange Free State. McPherson reckons that De Kock showed the same strategic qualities as De Wet when he and his men did battle in Namibia against the Swapo enemy, who were also superior in numbers.

McPherson says he has many delightful memories of visiting De Kock at Koevoet. 'I once visited the boys at Oshakati with the former head of the intelligence service of Mozambique, who had just defected to South Africa. While we were having a fish braai, Eugene grabbed one of the fish, which was still half frozen, and started hammering people with this fish. He hit one of the chaps on the side of the head and the man fell down, out, cold! Then they started performing a mock funeral. Ovamboland has this loose sand, and everybody lent a hand. While this man was lying out cold on his back, they made a grave over him with just his face sticking out. And I find it quite funny.'

McPherson said he introduced De Kock to his future wife, Audrey, during one of his friend's visits to South Africa. McPherson was a commander of a security police dirty tricks unit called Stratkom (Strategic Communications) and Audrey worked for him. De Kock married Audrey when he was 37 and she was 22 or 23 years old.

A Koevoet operative told me that De Kock once called his men together and said to them that his father was worried that his son was getting old and that it was time to get married. They had to be on the look-out for the right woman for him, but he warned them that she had to be a virgin.

Eugene de Kock arrived at the police counter-insurgency unit at Vlakplaas towards the middle of 1983. He served for two years under the command of Brigadier Jack Cronje before he became commander of what was known as Section Cl.

Cronje, who later became the head of the Northern Transvaal Security Branch, applied for amnesty for his involvement in the killing of more than 40 activists. Most were killed between the years 1985 and 1988, when he commanded a death squad operating in and around Pretoria.

Cronje said he never wanted De Kock, who was then a captain, in his unit. He knew that the man had a reputation for being a 'trouble-maker'. At the time, he said, Vlakplaas was a disciplined and organised unit. He hadn't allowed the excessive drinking that in later years would become such a trademark of the Vlakplaas death squad.[16]

When De Kock arrived at Vlakplaas, it wasn't much more than a unit accommodating 'turned' ANC and Pan-Africanist Congress (PAC) activists or askaris. Little happened at Vlakplaas after Dirk Coetzee left at the end of 1981, except for the unit's involvement in one incident in Swaziland in June 1982 when two

ANC activists were blown up by a car bomb. The askaris Joe Mamasela and Almond Nofemela carried out the reconnaissance for the operation.

Eugene de Kock was a trained and battle-hardened counter-insurgency operative and with his arrival Vlakplaas entered a new phase. When he took command on July 1, 1985, a new wave of civil rebellion had spread through the townships as the ANC embarked on a 'people's war' against apartheid.

This is how Joe Mamasela describes his first impression of De Kock: 'On the surface he appeared to be a relatively nice chap, but behind that mask lurked a terrible mamba. He was a brutal man, he was an aggressive man. He never laughed with us and he changed a lot of things.'[17]

There was never any love lost between Eugene de Kock and Joe Mamasela. The askari was probably just too arrogant for the likes of Eugene de Kock who, he said, threatened to kill him and throw his body into the sea. He left Vlakplaas about six months after De Kock became commander and joined Jack Cronje's death squad at the Northern Transvaal Security Branch.

When Eugene de Kock arrived at Vlakplaas, there were already a variety of weapons in the unit's storeroom that were used for assassinations and raids into neighbouring states. De Kock got an additional six P38 pistols, eight Scorpion and twelve Uzi machine pistols, and 21 AK-47 assault rifles, all fitted with silencers. De Kock said he was told that there was a 'commissioner's fund' at Vlakplaas that was supplemented with money illegally obtained from submitting false claims. The fund was used, for instance, to pay for a hunting expedition in the Western Transvaal that went wrong when one of the men mistook a stud bull for a kudu. They had to replace the bull with money from the 'commissioner's fund'.

Five months after joining Vlakplaas, De Kock went on his first operation when operatives raided a house in Swaziland. The target was Zweli Nyanda, commander of Umkhonto we Sizwe in Swaziland, who De Kock said was giving the security police a headache. Cronje was in command of Vlakplaas raiders who hurled a hand grenade through a window before bursting into the house. De Kock said he shot and killed Nyanda as he was trying to escape through a window. A Swazi national, Keith McFadden, was shot dead in his bed as the raiders sprayed the house with bullets fired from their silenced machine guns. A third man managed to escape through a window.

Three months after the operation, De Kock and some of the other operatives were decorated with the Police Star for Outstanding Service for killing Nyanda. It was De Kock's second medal for a clandestine operation.

Among the thousands of killings which marked the township rebellion of the middle 1980s, few were as tragic as that of a young woman by the name of Maki Skosana, a 24-year-old unmarried mother of a five-year-old boy. She was murdered when a mob of mourners attending a funeral in the township of Duduza on the East Rand turned on her. They chased her across the veld, beat her with sticks and stoned her to death, tore her clothes off, set her on fire and rammed a broken bottle into her vagina. All the while, the television cameras were rolling. That night, her death was shown at length on public television and broadcast around the world.[18]

The killing of Maki became an important propaganda tool in the hands of the government as it illustrated the brutality of the young comrades in the townships and legitimised the imposition of a state of emergency. Ordinary South Africans were justifiably appalled by the scene of the burning woman and the message to white people was clear: we cannot negotiate with these people and extraordinary measures are needed to deal with an extraordinary situation.

The story behind Maki's death started in June 1985 when a man made his appearance in the townships of Duduza, Tsakane and KwaThema and introduced himself as a member of Umkhonto we Sizwe. He made contact with the leadership of the Congress of South African Students and told them he had a supply of weapons for them. The students agreed to work with him.

On June 24, a group of students were collected by the ANC man and driven to an old mine dump. He produced two hand grenades and gave them a crash course in how they should pull out the pins, count to three and then throw them. The students threw the two hand grenades and they exploded exactly as the man had explained. They returned to the township and agreed to meet him again the next night. Hand grenades were to be thrown at the homes of two policemen, while a limpet mine was to be used to blow up a power sub-station at KwaThema. At their collection points, the man gave them the hand grenades and told them to co-ordinate their attacks to take place at midnight.

In KwaThema, three of the students headed for the policeman's home. When the first student pulled the pin, the hand grenade exploded immediately, blowing him apart. In Tsakane, two students died a similar death. In Duduza, more students blew themselves up. At the power station, another student was blown to pieces.

In Duduza, the bodies were left lying in the street. A local journalist, Rich Mkhondo, described the scene in *The Star:* 'We joined about 2 000 residents who had gathered around the bodies of the youths who had died at about midnight. The most horrifying moment of my life was when I was shown the bodies of the youths. I had never before seen the body of a man without a head. Nor had I seen pieces of human flesh scattered around and people trying to put them together again.'[19]

Shortly after the death of the eight students, rumours began to circulate in Duduza that the ANC man had been seen with a woman called Maki and that she had introduced him to the students. Maki Skosana said it wasn't her and that there was another Maki in the township. Stubbornly and against the advice of her family, she insisted on going to the funeral of the students.

The memory of Maki's death was re-awakened by Joe Mamasela when he testified against De Kock and admitted that he was the mysterious ANC man who had infiltrated the students and given them booby-trapped grenades and the limpet mine. The operation was known as 'Zero Zero Hour'.

Mamasela later told me that he had waited in the car when one of the students tried to plant the SPM mine at the power sub-station. 'Once he started pulling out the safety pin, the mine went off. There was this black smoke billowing in the air with a tongue of red smoke. It was like a red flashlight, and one could see it was blood. It was terrible, and my car shook vigorously.'

Mamasela was promoted to the rank of sergeant after the operation, while the other two askaris who were involved were each paid R2 000.

In his evidence, De Kock admitted his involvement and said he acted upon instructions from Jack Cronje. In turn, Cronje applied for amnesty for the incident and said that the former Commissioner of Police, General Johan van der Merwe, had authorised the operation.

Van der Merwe, in a submission to the TRC in 1996, said the operation was necessary in order to 'protect and save the lives of black members of the South African Police'. He said he had made a recommendation to the Commissioner of Police, General Johan Coetzee, to provide the activists with hand grenades 'which had been suitably modified'. Coetzee presented the proposal to the Minister of Police, Louis le Grange, who approved the operation.[20]

'Whoever authorised that was guilty of a very gruesome and totally unaccept-able decision. It was wrong, it wasn't part of the policy and whoever authorised it was acting against the interests of South Africa,' FW de Klerk said in his evidence before the Commission in May 1997.

A few days after the killing of Maki Skosana, Eugene de Kock took command of Vlakplaas. Shortly afterwards, he and his death squad abducted, tortured and killed an innocent man whose only crime was that his brother was an ANC member. It was a crime so cruel and inhuman, that 11 years later, Mr Justice Willem van der Merwe decided that it justified life imprisonment.

Chapter Three

A shallow grave

'What's a little murder between friends?' – from the film *Shallow Grave*

Japie Maponya was, in the words of his fiancee, 'a sweet somebody. He was a Christian.'

The young man must have been in a buoyant mood as he made his way from his home in Kagiso to a bank in Krugersdorp where he worked as a security guard. In four days, he was to marry his childhood sweetheart and the mother of his child.

Later that day, a man approached him and engaged in conversation. He wanted to know where he could find Odirile Maponya, Japie's older brother who had fled South Africa in 1977 to join the ANC and who was wanted for the murder of a policeman. The man said to Japie that he was an ANC cadre and was looking for his friend, Mainstay, which was Odirile's MK name. He showed Maponya a Makarov pistol to confirm his status as a trained guerrilla. Maponya ignored the man and turned away.[1]

By doing that, he unwittingly signed his own death warrant.

What Maponya didn't know was that the strange man who had approached him was no longer an MK member, but an askari at Vlakplaas. His name was Chris Mosiane, once an ANC operative who had been trained in the former Soviet Union and Angola. He knew Odirile from the military camps in Angola. In 1984, he was kidnapped and abducted from Swaziland, and interrogated and tortured until he agreed to co-operate with the Security Branch.

'Japie Maponya was not an easy man. It was difficult to get through to him. He had built a wall around him which I couldn't penetrate. He wouldn't listen to me,' Mosiane reported back to his Vlakplaas superiors.

Another plan had to be made with Japie Maponya. Later that day, Eugene de Kock and his confidant, Warrant Officer Willie Nortje, went to General Johan le Roux, then a colonel in charge of the Security Branch on the West Rand.

Nortje: We said to him we will kidnap him, but if he doesn't want to talk, we will have to take him away.

Ackermann: What did you mean by that?

Nortje: Eliminate.

De Kock said in his evidence that he asked Le Roux what they should do with Japie Maponya. 'He said to me he never wanted to see the man again. The man was a supporter of the ANC. He made it very, very clear to me that he never wanted to see him again.'

In police language, it simply meant that he had to be killed.

By five o'clock that same afternoon, the askaris had snatched Maponya from a sidewalk and had forced him to lie on the floor of a Volkswagen Jetta.

'He tried to resist, but our actions were so fast that whatever resistance he tried to offer was in vain, because we got him into the car. We immediately covered him with the blanket,' testified Moses Nzimande, one of the askaris who kidnapped him.

The car sped to Vlakplaas, and at an idyllic spot on the bank of the Hennops River, the interrogation of Japie Maponya started. Thirty-six hours later, he would lie in a shallow grave in Swaziland, his skull cleaved open by a spade.

Security police harassment was nothing new to the Maponya family. For many years, members of the family had been detained and their houses searched for any trace of the whereabouts of Odirile Maponya.

Japie Maponya's eldest brother, Daniel, lives in a typical three-roomed township dwelling in Kagiso near Krugersdorp. Against the yellow-painted wall of the tiny living room hangs a photograph of Japie. The rest of the room is decorated by awards and cups that Daniel's church choir have won all over the West Rand.[2]

A priest in the Zionist Church, he is still filled with extreme bitterness and anger against the grey-suited men who took him away, locked him in their little interrogation rooms and tried to force information from him.

'The whole family, from Kagiso to Pretoria to Rustenburg have suffered. They've all suffered. The police came at night, they surrounded the house, knocked down the door, broke windows, asked questions about Odirile. Once, they took my mother away and asked her questions. She didn't know. They took my father away and asked him questions. He was an old man, my father. This thing of the police has created a sickness in my father. When he came back after he was questioned, I had to take him to the doctor. My father is dead today, and he died with that sickness in his heart.'

His father, Joseph Maponya, told his interrogators that Odirile was back in the country and was probably in the former homeland of Bophuthatswana. The security police were convinced that Odirile would have made contact with at least some of his family members. Daniel was the next to be detained and questioned.

'They put my head inside the water. They pulled me out. They said: "Tell us the truth." I said: "Which truth must I tell you? You can do what you want." They said: "We are going to kill you." I said: "Yes, do that." They tied a sack over my head, and put my head in the water. First I was trying to drink that water, but after a while I couldn't any more. I thought I was going to die. I am angry, because they put me in prison for nothing. They never charged me. I suffered for *mahala* – for nothing.'

Daniel said Japie was never interested in politics: 'Everybody loved Japie. He was a church-goer. He was all right in his mind. There was no problem with Japie. That's why we felt it is the right thing for him to marry Maureen. Japie wanted to be a man. He wanted to have a family.'

Maureen Zondi and Japie Maponya had been living together since the birth of their baby girl in 1982. They planned to get married at the end of September 1985 and go on honeymoon in East London where her family lived.

One night in late 1984, Japie Maponya was detained. Maureen said a lot of policemen in camouflaged uniforms burst into their house and took him away. Police had information that he might have known where Odirile was hiding in Bophuthatswana. He came back a day or two later.

And then the young man permanently disappeared on September 25, 1985. 'We searched everywhere. We went to the hospitals, to the police stations, but there was nothing. The police said they think Japie went to Odirile, but I know it was not true and that something terrible must have happened to Japie,' said Daniel.

In May 1995, Maureen Zondi and Daniel Maponya came face to face with the killer of their lover and brother. As Maureen entered the witness stand, she said to Mr Justice van der Merwe: 'I have taken the oath and will tell the truth, but before I proceed with my evidence, I want the court to show me this Mr de Kock. I want to see him.'

'Mr de Kock, will you please stand up.'

Dressed in a grey suit, his hair neatly clipped, De Kock rose. Their eyes met for a moment.

'Thank you,' she said.

Daniel Maponya was sitting in the second row of the public gallery, staring at the accused. 'He was reading the papers, writing, laughing. You know, that is what makes me to think more about that man. When you look at him, he didn't have any sorry. He was not having that shame. If I was not a Christian, inside the court, I would have killed that man, but because of Christianity, I didn't make it like that.'[3]

I asked Maureen how she felt looking at De Kock. 'My heart was so painful when I see De Kock, because I was thinking for Japie.'

'Can you ever forgive him?'

'In my life I won't. I wanted to be a wife who had everything. I wanted to look after our family, a big family. Now I have nothing.'

Neither Maureen nor Daniel could ever have contemplated the agony and pain in which Japie Maponya died.

His suffering started at Vlakplaas when the askaris questioned him. Chris Mosiane described the interrogation in court: 'He was kicked, he was punched, they swore at him. It was a free-for-all. They were like bees attacking a man. They hit Japie until they were tired.'

Moses Nzimande was one of the interrogators: 'Everybody present participated in dealing out blows. He was beaten up thoroughly. He was being asked about his brother. He repeatedly said he did not know where he was.'

While the askaris were beating up Maponya, the white policemen were drinking in the bar. One of them was Eugene Fourie, a security policeman who served in Oshakati in Namibia before coming to Vlakplaas in 1982.

'We first had a few drinks before we went down to the river to see what they were doing with Maponya. We drank rum and Coca-Cola. It was "Boeretôts" – you count one, two, three, four when you pour the rum in the glass. We called it "police coffee". You must stand firm when you swallow it. All of us who came from Ovamboland drank a lot. There was nothing else to do,' Fourie testified.

After about an hour, Fourie went down to the river to see how the interrogation was going. 'Maponya was lying on the ground and Radebe was busy questioning him in their language. It went very wild at one stage. When he didn't want to talk, people would stand closer and kick him from all sides.'

Willie Nortje and Eugene de Kock also arrived on the scene. 'When we got to the farm, the blacks were already assaulting him. He was in the minibus. They were kicking and slapping him. Sometimes they would let him sit upright and then flattened him again. De Kock asked me if I had some teargas with me. He grabbed Japie behind his head, forced his mouth open and sprayed the teargas into his mouth. Japie said he knew nothing about his brother. We then knew that he was not going to speak,' said Nortje.

Willie Nortje seldom looked at Eugene de Kock as he was testifying about his role in, and knowledge of, illegal operations carried out over the nine years he was at Vlakplaas. The murder of Japie Maponya was the first incident that Nortje testified about. He was tense at first, biting his lip and looking down at his feet in the witness box. He was, after all, playing Brutus to Colonel Eugene de Kock's Caesar.

'After the interrogation, De Kock and myself said to one another that there is only one solution now, and that is that we will have to kill him. He was manacled to a bed for the night, and De Kock told the askaris to give him food and pain pills. He said we will have to get rid of him the next day.'

The following day, De Kock spoke to his friend and head of the Security Branch in Piet Retief, Warrant Officer Frederik Pienaar. 'Pienaar said we can bring him, he's got a place where we can get rid of him. I put a spade and an Uzi submachine gun with a silencer into the car.'

For almost a decade, the son of a highly respected judge kept secret his role in the murder of Maponya. When he finally admitted his complicity by taking the witness stand in September 1995, he did so under duress, and only after being told that unless he testified against Eugene de Kock, he would himself face charges relating to the murder.

Dawid van der Walt, a stockbroker with a Johannesburg firm, joined the police in December 1981 and was recruited to the Security Branch while still at college. After two tours of duty in Ovamboland, he was posted to Security Branch head-quarters in Pretoria where he 'sat around doing nothing' before requesting a transfer to Vlakplaas.

Van der Walt said he had witnessed, but not taken part in the assault. However, 24 hours later, he accompanied De Kock, Nortje and Fourie on Maponya's last ride.

'Colonel de Kock said he got permission from higher up to make the man dis-appear. At about seven o'clock, after everybody had left, we took Maponya out and put him in the vehicle. We left for Piet Retief.'

Fourie testified that they spoke openly about how they were going to kill the man. 'Japie could hear the conversation. He knew he was going to die. He never said a word. He was calm. He never asked us to save his life. It's the first time in my life I had ever seen something like that. I was scared. I was not sure we were doing the right thing. My nerves were on edge because although we were carry-ing out an order that came from the top, we were doing something that nobody was ever to know about.'

When they arrived at Piet Retief, they picked Frederik Pienaar up. Pienaar said they must drive in the direction of the Nerston border post of Swaziland. Just before they got to the border post, they turned right onto a dirt road leading next to the border. At some stage, they stopped, climbed over the fence and walked about 50 metres into a plantation. Maponya still had a blanket over his head and Nortje led him.

While the rest of the killers led the blindfolded and handcuffed man across the Swazi border into the plantation to be executed, Dawid van der Walt waited at the car.

'He said he would look after the car. Maybe he couldn't take it,' said Fourie. Minutes later, Van der Walt heard the sound of 'several blows with a heavy ob-ject, bones cracking, and a single shot'.

Ten years after the killing, Eugene Fourie and Willie Nortje recounted the last moments of Japie Maponya. Although their accounts of events differed slightly, nothing could hide the horror of that dark night in a plantation in Swaziland.

Nortje: While we stood in the plantation, De Kock started clearing an area with the spade where we would dig the grave. I was supposed to shoot him. I couldn't get myself to do it, and hit him behind the head with the Uzi. I felt sorry for him. I wanted him to be unconscious before I shot him.

Fourie: Willie Nortje told Maponya to kneel so that he could shoot him in the back of his head. Maponya didn't do it quite right. Willie took the machine gun and hit him against his head. Japie fell. Willie wanted to shoot him, but the gun jammed. He said: 'Oh shit, it doesn't want to fire.'

Nortje: Japie tried to get up, and that was when De Kock hit him with the spade. He hit him about three or four times. I put a sub-sonic round into my pistol and shot him through the head.

Fourie: Maponya was making throaty sounds. We didn't know whether he was dead. De Kock took the spade and cleaved his head open with the sharp end. He did it a few times. Things were coming out of his head. We were very tense because dogs were barking and it seemed as though they were coming closer.

Nortje: I touched the wounds on his head. His brains were coming out. He was still breathing, I could hear it, but he was on his last. Fourie and myself stayed there until he didn't breathe any more. We undressed him completely and covered him with branches.

Nortje said that on the way back to Pretoria they spoke little. 'It was a gruesome story, and it wasn't supposed to have happened like that.'

'Death was nothing new to us. We worked in Namibia with bodies every day. We saw many bodies. Death didn't bother us. The police made a machine out of you,' said Fourie.

Maponya's bag with clothes was taken back to Pretoria where it was burnt a few days later. In the bag was a silver star of the Zionist Christian Church.

In his evidence, Eugene de Kock justified the killing of Maponya by saying: 'Japie Maponya was a supporter of the ANC. He supported his brother.'

Ackermann: There was no evidence that JapieMaponya was ever involved with the ANC.

De Kock: He wasn't a member, but he was a supporter.

Ackermann: He was a law-abiding citizen with a wife and a child.

De Kock: One can be a law-abiding citizen, but still support such an organisation.

De Kock tried to create an image in court of feeling real remorse for his victims. He spoke about children that would never see their fathers again and said he was haunted by the image of those he had killed.

Not so, say his friends. I asked Lieutenant Peter Casselton, who came to Vlakplaas at the end of 1989 and became De Kock's very best friend, how the death squad commander felt about killing.

'Nothing. You can't feel anything. You know, if you treat AIDS patients, you can't feel pain if someone dies. That's part of life. If you feel pain, you can't do the job anymore. Eugene is a soldier, he's a killer. And that's what he was taught by the South African government.'

Former colleague and friend Riaan Stander agrees. 'It was immaterial to him whether it was an enemy or not an enemy. It was a question of doing a job. In a certain sense, he is a cold-blooded killer.'[4]

Talking about the cruelty with which they killed Maponya, a laughing Casselton said: 'Is there a kind way to kill someone? Normally killings happen quickly. You don't have time to go and find a lethal injection and lie the boy down on the bed. If there's a spade handy and you want to kill somebody, you better get on with it with a spade.'[5]

I never met Eugene Fourie, who went on early pension with post-traumatic stress disorder, but I have spent some hours with Willie Nortje and once went to his house in one of Pretoria's upper-class suburbs where I also met his wife, Welma Nortje, a senior officer in the South African Police Services.

I've seen Nortje at home, I've seen him comforting his baby, I've watched his eyes as he spoke about the atrocities he committed. Apart from De Kock, Nortje has probably killed more people than anybody else at Vlakplaas. Colleagues would tell you that this gentle giant could very easily explode into a vicious killing machine. The murders he committed were cruel and merciless.

And yet, every time I see him, I am surprised by how 'normal' the soft-spoken Nortje is. I see real remorse when he speaks about Maponya. A conversation would usually end with: 'I don't know why I did it. I am ashamed of myself.'

I am not alone in my observations of Willie Nortje. Ivor Jenkins and Bea Roberts from the Institute for a Democratic Alternative (Idasa) spent six weeks with him in Denmark at the beginning of 1994 after he decided to talk and was taken into a witness protection programme.

'He's an ordinary person. He's a good person, I think inherently he is good. When I saw Willie, he would be a wonderful brother to have, you know he's like a guy you feel you want to grab and give him a hug and sit around a braai and have a nice chat to him,' says Jenkins.[6]

'I never had a horrible feeling about Willie. I always thought that he was nice and I like him. And it was quite difficult in my mind to reconcile what I knew he had done with the person I had day-to-day interaction with,' says Roberts.

I often think of Willie Nortje playing with his baby, and then of him sitting next to a dead man touching his brains which he had minutes before helped to blow out.

'Why did they do this to Japie?', Daniel Maponya often asked me. I never knew how to answer him, because the murder of his brother had nothing to do with war or crime or politics. He was innocent; his only crime was having a brother who had joined the ANC.[7]

Daniel said his father died as a result of the whole affair. Odirile blew himself up in Pretoria in 1986 when he tried to plant a bomb near a cinema complex. The family never received his remains to give him a proper funeral. The body of Japie has not been found either. Investigators combed the woods in Swaziland, but couldn't find it.

'We are crying about that body of my younger brother. We have told them that they must bring the body of Japie. We just want to bury the body by ourselves. The whole family thinks like that.'

Maponya cannot understand why the other killers like Nortje and Fourie are walking free. They should all be charged and punished.

I look at Maureen Zondi, jobless and still in anguish about Japie. Eugene de Kock, Johan le Roux, Willie Nortje, Eugene Fourie – men who deprived her of being just a mother, a wife, being happy. Daniel has to look after her and the child. How can we ever expect them to simply forgive?

'De Kock is a cruel man, a cruel man. That man, he must suffer. He must suffer. If things go well, they must hang him. He must die, once. And the others as well,' says Daniel.

'Can you ever forgive them?'

'Well, I will, I will. But I know that God is going to punish them. I will forgive them, but God is going to punish them. 'Cause they've done a sin.'

Says Maureen Zondi: 'I don't think I can.'

Chapter Four

Attila and his Huns

'The honeybadger. Its outward cuddly appearance conceals an animal that is proportionally the most ferocious of all. When it loses its temper, it goes into a frenzy. It has never been known to flee from any adversary and will even attack the primary predator, man, without provocation. It is to be treated with the greatest respect.'[1]

This is how Eugene de Kock saw himself and his men. After he took command of Vlakplaas, he designed a unit emblem and chose the honeybadger. The animal was set against a red background of the African continent, which represented all the policemen who had spilled blood in their fight against Communism.

He then drafted a code of conduct and called it 'The Honeybadger – Attrition of War'. He described the animal as invincible and invisible.

When Anton Ackermann discussed the code of conduct with De Kock, he said: 'It sounds like you.'

De Kock: I take exception to the fact that you compare me with an animal. I'm a human being.

Ackermann: Is this how you wanted your unit to be?

De Kock: We were hard and tough. That didn't mean we were murderers. But we could take the best that Umkhonto we Sizwe could throw at us and then do the extra mile.

Ackermann: The frenzy you talk about sounds familiar, doesn't it?

De Kock: I don't know, not me.

Ackermann: With respect, Mr de Kock, I think you were in the Voortrekkers for too long.

Eugene de Kock was a young man when he started reading and studying books on warfare. He based his battle strategies on the philosophies and writings of the Chinese warlord Sun Tzu, who lived around 450 BC, and the Mongolian warrior Attila the Hun, who invaded central Europe 800 years later.

De Kock ordered several of his men to study The Art of War by Sun Tzu, who based his philosophy of warfare on seven essential principles, amongst them: 'Attack him when and where he is unprepared, appear where you are not expected', and 'Learn the art of subtlety and secrecy, be invisible and hold the enemy's fate in your hands.'

The warfare strategy of Attila the Hun was largely based on fear, intimidation and surprise. The Mongolians, armed with bows and arrows, conquered Europe on horseback, and crushed and destroyed any resistance that came their way. Attila was renowned for his cruelty because he spared no-one, women and children included. Attila said he was driven by a 'lust for brutality' and would select only the most 'vicious and ferocious-looking warriors' to accompany him on his bloody missions.

'Brutality has become a powerful force that ignites the spirit of warriors, driving them to commit their talents to any nation that bribed them into service. You as leaders of your tribes and I, the King of Huns, must turn this lust into a mere disciplined distribution of rewards to Huns who will willingly give their services to our nation, either in or out of battle. We must continue to grant unto our warriors their rights of pillage and at the same time provide rewards for acts off the battlefield that we endorse.'

Their nicknames ranged from the quaint and playful – Brood (Bread), Balletjies (Little Balls) and Chappies – to the more manly and warlike Duiwel (Devil) and Snorre (Moustaches).

If Prime Evil saw himself as Attila, they were his Huns, a brotherhood of brutes that was nothing but an official, state-sanctioned mafia bound by a common belief in the 'total onslaught' ideology, adrenaline, money and, above all, blood. And once blood was spilled, it ensured silence and secrecy.

There was a time when they were closer than brothers and incredibly loyal to one another. It was a man's world where women counted for little and humanity and compassion were seen as a weakness. I don't know about a single instance where a Vlakplaas operative shared his darkest secrets with his wife. The same hands that caressed a wife today could have strangled an activist or pulled a trigger yesterday.

This is how Eugene de Kock described his marriage: 'I was suffering from severe stress as a result of my work. My wife was a much more outgoing person than myself. She wanted to go to the State Theatre and that kind of thing. I also wanted to go, but I didn't think it was right. You had shot somebody yesterday and now you were listening to opera. I wanted to withdraw myself from normal society. I couldn't tell her exactly what was going on and it created an anxiety in me.'

The men killed and stole, and had to keep their secrets amongst themselves, so they withdrew into each other's company. There is no stronger bond than that between men who have spilled blood together. If an experience was, above all, secret and illegal, they could only discuss it amongst themselves. The Vlakplaas culture, skills, techniques and methods had much in common with those of the Sicilian Mafia, with one important exception: the Vlakplaas men believed that they were busy with a big and important mission in the interests of national security. Treason was punishable by death. When Dirk Coetzee spoke in November 1989, he was sentenced to death in the Vlakplaas pub.

De Kock had a strategy of compromising his men by involving them as quickly as possible in a killing. When he, for example, murdered Brian Ngqulunga in July 1990, two of his co-conspirators were men he decided to 'contaminate' and, therefore, ensure their silence.

Men had to have been involved in death squad operations to become members of De Kock's 'inner circle'. His closest confidants would drive him around and be privy to the planning of an operation. Nothing would happen at the unit without his personal stamp of approval.

The men did everything together. They preferred to spend an evening of male bonding and drinking in the Vlakplaas pub, a night out in the bush or a fortnight of 'team building' on the Natal north coast. I don't know of any homosexuality amongst them, but it is a revelation to look at photographs of the unit relaxing or playing together. They would wrestle, bury one another in the sand, play tricks and get stone drunk. Always hanging on to and touching one another. It was only within this brotherhood that they could let their masks down and be themselves.

De Kock, however, seldom played along or took part in the fun. He was always at a distance, never smiling; stark and serious. In the early 1990s, some of the men made use of a Military Intelligence brothel in Johannesburg, but De Kock never used the women's services.

De Kock described himself in a police questionnaire as loyal, patriotic, a person with a broad vision, a dynamic commander and a strategist. 'I'm a relentless hunter who stays on the track until the problem is solved. I act without mercy against the country's enemies and criminals. Many criminals shiver when they hear that I am on their track. The ANC-PAC alliance is haunted by me and I am feared.'

He was also feared by his own men. He didn't hesitate to assault them and, if it was necessary to maintain the sinister secrets of his actions, he would kill them. They never questioned his commands and killed at his request.

Let's look at some of the members of his 'inner circle'. For 13 years, Warrant Officer Willie Nortje was Eugene de Kock's confidant, co-conspirator and bosom buddy. They served together in Koevoet, and when De Kock was transferred to Vlakplaas, Nortje followed him a year later. Nortje was party to secrets and murders that implicated him in more than 100 of the 121 charges against De Kock, making him the second most effective assassin of the unit.

They raided houses in Lesotho and Swaziland, ambushed cars and minibuses and executed ANC supporters and policemen who wanted to talk. Together, they were decorated with the Police Star for the killings they performed.

When De Kock's eldest child and namesake was born, he asked Nortje to be the godfather. A similar honour fell to Welma Nortje, Willie's wife, when De Kock's second son, Michael, was born.

In De Kock's own words, Nortje left the unit as 'a man with means'. Over many years, tens of thousands of rands were pilfered from the police secret fund and found their way into Nortje's own pocket.

'We were very close. He gave me money from false claims, he gave me two stands, although he later took one back again when we had our fall-out. He gave me about R10 000 at a time. De Kock's confidants were often his drivers. I drove him around for quite a long time. As soon as he had a fall-out with one person, he would get a new driver.'

Major Chappies Klopper also frequently chauffeured De Kock. He was recruited from the Security Branch at Soweto's Protea police station in 1989. A small man with an obviously big ego, Klopper also became party to corruption and several murders. Over a three-month period in 1992, De Kock, Klopper and a few other confidants stole R240 000 from the police secret fund.

Anton Ackermann asked De Kock in court about the gifts he had given to Klopper and Nortje. 'What gifts did you give to Nortje?'

De Kock: I can't remember everything, but he left the unit as a man of substance.

Ackermann: A stand?

De Kock: Yes.

Ackermann: How much was it worth?

De Kock: About R68 000, R70 000.

Ackermann: What did you give Klopper?

De Kock: A stand with a house, about R50 000.

Ackermann: And this is not even the money you gave to them in cash?

De Kock: That is correct.

Ackermann: Isn't that what Attila the Hun talks of: reward your Huns?

De Kock: Well, the Romans did exactly the same. The hordes of Alexander the Great did the same. We just did it on a more civilised scale.

Judge: But why did they have to get money for killing somebody?

De Kock: It was so that they could look after themselves better. They exposed themselves to a lot of danger. You didn't kill for money. It wasn't a *jolly patrollie* (jolly patrol) we were on. They believed in what they were doing.

Judge: But was it possible for them to have said: I don't want to be a member of Vlakplaas any more. I don't want to be used outside the norms?

De Kock: Yes, it was possible, but they didn't.

Judge: Then I have to accept that they either enjoyed what they did at their normal compensation, or they were satisfied to do it with an additional reward.

Warrant Officer Andries 'Brood' van Heerden was only at Vlakplaas for about two years, but was instrumental in supplying Inkatha with weapons and participating in the killing of an askari who had lost his service pistol. He was described in court as an expert in 'tubing' detainees – suffocating them with the inner section of a car tyre.

These three – Klopper, Nortje and Van Heerden – were very close to De Kock, but were ironically also the first to swear affidavits against him. Chappies Klopper was the first to spill the beans when De Kock assaulted him twice, once when he was found with a black prostitute in a toilet in a seedy hotel in Berea in Johannesburg, and the second time on a car journey between Cape Town and Pretoria.

Ackermann: Why are you testifying against De Kock?

Klopper: I don't like him.

Ackermann: Can you tell us why you don't like him?

Klopper: We were on our way back from the Cape to Pretoria. We drank a lot. Not far from Colesberg, De Kock got very angry and ordered me to stop and get out of the car. He grabbed me and hit me with a pistol in the face. He fired a shot past my head. He said he would kill me. He was like a lunatic. He said he'd leave me in the Karoo for the jackals … My shirt was torn and my mouth bled. Afterwards, I said to General Engelbrecht that De Kock's loyalty towards me lies on the road between Beaufort West and Colesberg.

Ackermann: Were you before then a confidant?

Klopper: We were very close. We moved together.

Ackermann: And then things went wrong?

Klopper: I was very scared of him. I believed he would have shot me.

He said he started fearing for his life when colleagues warned him that De Kock wanted to 'take him out'. The only way out, he said, was to swear an affidavit and get his former commander behind bars.

De Kock's feelings towards Klopper are also less than brotherly. 'He might have been a cute baby, but it stopped there. He is the kind of person that induces involuntary vomiting. He has no problem selling anyone down the river.'

The relationship between De Kock and Nortje also turned sour. 'I was very loyal to him, but at one stage he started pushing me out. He commanded Vlakplaas through a system of "divide and rule". He would give some members more money and benefits to get them to give him information about others. In that way, he knew exactly what was going on. Very few things happened that he didn't know about.'

Of Nortje testifying against him, De Kock simply says: 'I am very disappointed. I can't understand it. But I don't hate him.'

Van Heerden's fall-out with his commander started with something extremely sacrosanct to many Afrikaner hearts: tickets for a rugby test match between the All Blacks and the Springboks. Van Heerden got tickets for the 1992 test at Ellis Park, but instead of inviting De Kock, he asked Nortje and his wife to join them. De Kock, his men told me, wasn't even fond of rugby.

'De Kock is a very dangerous man. He is capable of killing me or any other people who testify against him.'

Several men recall the incredible fear that Van Heerden had of De Kock.

Ronald 'Tokarev' Bezuidenhout, one of only two white askaris in the history of Vlakplaas, shared a room on the farm with Van Heerden. 'If De Kock calls him, Brood will run towards him. "Ja, kolonel", and stand at attention, and then he would start chewing his nails – in front of De Kock. You can look at Brood's finger nails. He used to chew them. So what does it tell you? He was scared of him.'[2]

Most white members initially refused to testify against their former commander, but when the investigators knocked on their doors and gave them a choice between testifying and perhaps spending a lifetime in prison, respect and fear very quickly turned into betrayal, dislike and even hatred.

A handful of men remained loyal till the bitter end. Sergeant Leon Flores, who was involved in the 1988 Piet Retief massacre and helped to dispose of the body of a murdered askari, told investigators he had nothing to tell them.

'Eugene de Kock was a good man, but a very difficult man to work with at times. I had fall-outs with him on various occasions. One night we had a few too many to drink and he slapped me, but fetched me the next morning for breakfast and pretended that nothing had happened.'[3]

Members told me that there were times when he was in such a foul mood and so aggressive that people would hide from him when he arrived on the farm in the mornings. Brood van Heerden gave him the nickname of Fok-Fok (Fuck-Fuck) because of his vile temper.

He got his nickname of 'Prime Evil' when he befriended convicted killer and SADF operative Ferdi Barnard in 1990. 'He was militaristic and maybe like a dictator at times. There was a programme on children's television, the Ninja Turtles or something like that, and there was a bad guy who was Prime Evil. De Kock had a very devious way of putting a thing together that nobody else could think of. But not necessarily in an evil way. It was just a joke, but then everybody started calling him that.'[4]

Of course they only called him Prime Evil behind his back. De Kock accused me in court of having phrased the nickname and said there was no reason why his men would have called him that.

'He's the type of guy that if one of his guys did something wrong, rather than tarnish the man's record and his whole career, De Kock would go and give him a hiding, and physically take him on to make sure that it did not happen again,' says Barnard.

Peter Casselton says: 'He's a hard man, a very hard man. If Eugene de Kock didn't like you, you were out, gone. He's very bad tempered and has always led a life of violence. He's a killer, and that was what he was taught by the South African government. He was ordered to do killings and that's what he did.'[5]

Casselton says there was a party 'full-time' at Vlakplaas. 'It was a lovely life and the men enjoyed themselves. They drank a lot, every day, like all people in that kind of world.'

Vlakplaas concocted its own brew that all new members and visitors to the farm had to drink. This is how Leon Flores describes it: 'It was concocted from various kinds of spirits like cane, brandy and gin that were poured into a five-litre bottle with lots of cloves of garlic. This was topped up with "green mamba", a peppermint green liqueur. We left it in the sun to mature or would speed up the process in the microwave oven. We called the garlic leeutande (lion's teeth). So the glass would contain ten or twelve pieces of leeutande, filled up with this mixture which you had to down. Ninety-eight per cent of the people who drank it ran out and puked immediately. Those who kept it down, had no friends or a wife for a week. Our nickname at head office was the Knoffel Squad (Garlic Squad). You could always identify a Vlakplaas policeman, because he smelled like garlic. We were rum – Red Heart rum – and garlic fanatics.'

Soon after De Kock took command, Vlakplaas was upgraded with false claims from the secret fund. A pub was built, snooker tables installed and an ice machine purchased. De Kock said they only drank the best liquor available. They had the finest wines, and many of the generals and senior officers preferred twelve-year-old Chivas Regal whisky. The generals were regular visitors to Vlakplaas and according to the men, a person like General Basie Smit had his own, personal bottle of Chivas on the farm.

Vlakplaas became such a popular venue for police functions and receptions that a chef was transferred to the farm to prepare potjiekos (meat and vegetables cooked in a heavy metal black pot over a fire). They had to buy four heavy-metal pots, one of them big enough to take two or three sheep in one potjiekos session. 'And then there was still enough space left for the vegetables,' De Kock said.

I asked Peter Casselton to describe a typical day in the life of Vlakplaas. 'Very easy. Drive to work at nine o'clock, park the car, sit around without doing anything really constructive. Lunchtime, buy meat, braai, drink, and go home. The men loved it. We used to go to parties at the Polaris Hotel with hookers and strippers. Eugene paid for everything. It was a good life.'

Leon Flores elaborates: 'One night, for instance, we hired the ladies bar. And it was just our members, no females, just males. We would watch a stripper whom Brood had brought from Johannesburg, and it would become a wild drinking party.'

'Who paid for it?' I asked him.

'Who paid for it? I presume it came from secret funds.'

The police secret fund would also pay for team-building expeditions to the Island Rock police beach resort on the Natal north coast. In most instances, they deterio-rated into nothing more than an orgy of drinking and having fun on the beach.

De Kock said that Volkswagen once donated two four-by-four kombis to the police which were kept at Island Rock. The men drove one of the kombis into the shallow water and couldn't get it out again. When high tide came in, the vehicle virtually disappeared underwater and was in the sea for the whole night. The next morning at low tide, they got the kombi out again, but it had been seriously damaged. Once again, the secret fund was the answer: false claims were submitted to have it fixed and to replace a video camera that had been damaged.

'You know, this was a soldier fraternity. De Kock and many of his men came from Koevoet. You don't play with those people. Sometimes we were not so sober and we would get quite heavy. And one oke would sommer hit another oke. It was a rough world,' says Ferdi Barnard.

Joe Mamasela, who doesn't drink himself, said the men 'drank like fishes. And when they drank, they started beating up the askaris.'[6]

Many operations and killings were preceded by a session of heavy drinking. Some witnesses had difficulty in recalling events because they were simply too drunk at the time. One of the most brutal murders ever committed in the unit's history happened in the Vlakplaas pub when Eugene de Kock and his men, drunk and aggressive, beat up a frail askari who had lost his service pistol.

One night in June or July 1989 Hugh Lugg was woken up by two Vlakplaas men. 'Get dressed and come to the pub,' they ordered him.

'I heard a lot of noise, commotion – you know – people talking and shouting, which sounded to me as if they were under the influence of alcohol. They were not rational.'

Lugg went to sit in the back of the pub behind the snooker table. As a former ANC guerrilla, he was never fully trusted by the other white policemen and was never invited to join the inner circle. That night though, he witnessed a killing that he described six years later in the Pretoria Supreme Court as 'a shark-feeding frenzy'.

British subject Hugh Lugg had joined the ANC in 1981 while living in the United Kingdom. He was sent for military training to Angola, Cuba and the Soviet Union. He entered South Africa in 1987 as a member of the so-called 'Broederstroom cell' which, armed to the teeth, planned a series of explosions and attacks on, amongst others, an SADF installation in Johannesburg and a military tattoo in Durban.

Lugg said he was 'not at all happy' to attack the tattoo, as civilians were to have participated. Personality and political differences started to emerge within the cell and Lugg said he feared he might be eliminated by the ANC. He handed himself over to the Security Branch in May 1988. As a result of his confession, the other members of the Broederstroom cell were arrested. Lugg turned state witness and in early 1989 his former comrades were convicted and sentenced to long-term imprisonment. He was conditionally released and taken to Vlakplaas where he became the first white askari in the unit's history. He stayed on the farm for seven months and shared a room with Sergeant Brood van Heerden.

Van Heerden, a man of six foot three, was one of the men in the pub that night. While Lugg sat in a corner, scared and apprehensive, a black askari was pushed into the room by a group of white policemen. He was Phemelo Moses

Nthehelang, an ANC member arrested by the Soweto Security Branch three months earlier. Nthehelang was small and frail, according to Van Heerden no more than four-and-a-half feet tall. He was accused of having sold his service pistol in a shebeen to get drinking money.

'He was light-skinned, like a Bushman. He had a yellow complexion,' said Van Heerden. The white policemen called him 'Geletjie', Afrikaans for 'Little Yellow One'. His MK name was 'Bruce'.

Sergeant Douw Willemse was also in the pub. He testified that De Kock asked Nthehelang: 'Where is your fucking pistol?' The askari said he had lost it, but De Kock insisted that he was lying.

'De Kock was very aggressive. I knew him well and when he gets like that, few people can stop him. I was scared and knew that something was going to happen and so I walked out.'

This is how Lugg remembered the event: 'They just started hitting the askari and kicking him and soon he was tripped and pushed to the ground. I remember he was in a sort of half-prone position when De Kock took a snooker cue and hit him over the back of the neck and head. It actually broke.'

While all this was happening, the askari pleaded: '*Nee, my baas. Nee. Nee.*' (No, boss. No. No.)

'I must say that I was very upset at the time and I was leaning forward and trying to imagine that I was not even there. I mean, I witnessed a horrific event and these were policemen.'

De Kock's demeanour was a sign to his cohorts to join in. 'The askari was down on the ground and then they took turns hitting and kicking him. It just seemed like it was a shark-feeding frenzy. They tied his legs with a rope. They pushed a sock into his mouth. He was bleeding from his nose, mouth and ears. They twisted his testicles.'

De Kock told Sergeant Steve Bosch to go and fetch some boiling water, 'I think to throw on him', but the kettle wouldn't work. When Bosch returned from the kitchen, Nthehelang was being smothered with the inner tube of a tyre.

It was Van Heerden who got hold of the tube – an old ally in the security police torture arsenal. Van Heerden was one of the 'champion tubers' at Vlakplaas. 'At that time it was a general practice for good policemen. If I had to "tube" a man to get information, I would do it,' Van Heerden said in court.

That is exactly what Van Heerden did that night. In his own words: 'I sat on him while Piet Botha held his hands. I "tubed" him, but at some stage my hands got tired and I wanted to go to the toilet. Piet said he also wanted to "tube". When I came back, there was a rope around the victim's neck and he was lying very still.' Moses Nthehelang was dead. His body was wrapped in a blanket. Douw Willemse said the body was put in the boot of a car and he, De Kock, Leon Flores and Martiens Ras drove in the direction of the Western Transvaal. 'I was very drunk. I must have fallen asleep, because when I woke up, the car was standing at a farm gate,' Willemse testified. They dug a grave, but Willemse said he felt sick and vomited.

The next morning, the bloodstains were washed off the carpet in the pub. The men never spoke about the incident again.

A few months later, Lugg left Vlakplaas and went back to the United Kingdom, where he has been living ever since. He kept his secret for six years, until investigators into the crimes of Eugene de Kock traced him to London and persuaded him to come back and testify.

Eugene de Kock later admitted in his evidence that he and a few of his men drove with the body to a farm in the Western Transvaal where they buried it. Another murdered man had already been buried on the same farm, De Kock said.

Commenting on the practice of torture in the security forces, FW de Klerk said in his evidence before the TRC in May 1997: 'The National Party is not in favour of torture. I reject it, it's wrong. We were given assurances that regular visits were paid to jails. We had reason to believe that there were measures in place to assist in the prevention of this practice. We know that this is a problem throughout the world. It is a problem in each and every justice system that at times detainees are dealt with by security forces in an unacceptable way. It actually forms the theme of almost every fourth American film that one looks at.'[7]

Truth Commissioner: Very high-ranking officers have informed the commission that torture was widespread and that in fact ordinary policemen had their own instruments and their own bags of tricks.

De Klerk: Well, that is terrible, that's terrible. Because of the many rumours, steps were taken [to prevent torture]. With hindsight I have no problem saying that maybe they weren't timeous enough and maybe they weren't strong enough.

Truth Commissioner: You're offering us an explanation that these things were committed by a few individuals and I think in your submission you talk about a few mavericks. But we are faced with insurmountable evidence that in fact torture was widespread within the security forces.

De Klerk: That's why I'm blatantly honest with you when I say that I'm as shocked as you are about these many revelations. We were at times under the impression that claims that torture had taken place were propaganda. We were told that detainees were under orders from the ANC to complain of torture.

Throughout the 1980s, the apartheid government rejected and ignored irrefutable evidence of police torture. Three independent research surveys showed that the vast majority of political and security detainees were tortured by their interrogators. The most comprehensive study was done by the Department of Psychology at the University of Cape Town, which found that 83% of detainees had suffered some form of torture. The most frequent form of torture (75%) was beating, while 25% of detainees said they were subjected to electrical shocks and 18% to strangulation.[8]

People continued to die in detention. On February 3, 1982, the Minister of Police assured Parliament that 'every possible measure was taken to ensure that detainees could not injure themselves and commit suicide'. Yet, two days later, activist Dr Neil Aggett died in detention at John Vorster Square. Human rights lawyer George Bizos coined the term 'induced suicide' during the inquest. Aggett had received no medical attention during nearly three months of detention, despite injuries sustained during interrogation. In a statement before his death, he had described being kept awake and interrogated continuously for 62 hours while he was given electrical shocks. The police sergeant who had recorded Aggett's statement did not request that he be medically examined, later stating in an affidavit: 'The security police were busy with him.' On the day following the sergeant's visit, Aggett's body was found hanging in his cell.[9]

Several months after a state of emergency was declared in July 1985, a young district surgeon, Dr Wendy Orr – today a TRC Commissioner – made an urgent appeal to the Supreme Court to stop the police from torturing hundreds of detainees under her care in the Port Elizabeth prisons. The torture included electrical shocks, being forced to drink petrol, being throttled or nearly suffocated, being slapped, kicked, whipped, punched and beaten all over the body and face.

The most notorious torture case in South Africa's history is that of Black Consciousness leader Steve Biko, who died in September 1977 in police custody in Pretoria, the forty-sixth detainee to die in detention. Evidence given at his inquest by police, doctors and warders revealed that he had been kept naked and manacled for 20 days. He received various blows to his head, some of which caused brain damage. The day before he died, he had been driven from Port Elizabeth to Pretoria naked in the back of a Land Rover.

Who would ever forget the words of the then Minister of Justice, Jimmy Kruger, when he told a congress of the National Party: 'I am not glad and I am not sorry about Mr Biko. It leaves me cold.'[11]

How could De Klerk not have known?

In the training camps of Umkhonto we Sizwe ANC guerrillas had names such as 'Vietnam', 'Confusion', 'Ghost', 'Stalwart' and 'Stretcher', but when they were captured and sent to Vlakplaas as 'rehabilitated terrorists', they were reduced to nothing more than pariahs roaming the townships in search of their former comrades.

Eugene de Kock says he was never driven by racism and would say things like: 'If I was black, I would have been an ANC terrorist myself.' He told the court about an instance in which he had sent his sick black gardener to his general practitioner and even paid for his treatment.

'My race relations were much, much better than those of other security policemen,' De Kock said, and added that he was taught as a child that there was no difference between black and white. He said when he visited the Woman's Monument – honouring the role of Afrikaner women during the Second Boer War nearly a century ago – in Bloemfontein in 1987, he wrote in the visitor's register that more attention and recognition should be given to black people who had also been incarcerated in the British concentration camps.

But let us look at how the askaris were treated. 'The askaris feared him, more so than the white policemen. He ruled by maximum fear. The askaris knew that a black life meant nothing to him,' says Joe Mamasela.

He recalls an event at Vlakplaas, just before he left, where De Kock severely assaulted an askari by the name of Brian Ngqulunga. Five years after the assault, Ngqulunga was murdered by Vlakplaas operatives.

'Brian was a frail, pathetic human being. De Kock took him, he beat him up, and when Brian lost consciousness, he picked him up and threw him up in the sky. When Brian landed with a sickening thud, De Kock jumped on his face several times. This happened because Ngqulunga wanted to leave Vlakplaas.'

Asked about this incident, De Kock said: 'Mamasela had his wires crossed. It was a man by the name of Tshabalala. He went missing for two days during which he threatened people at gunpoint and committed a series of crimes. When I took his weapon away, he was unhappy. I didn't only hit him with my fist, I also hit him with the barrel of an R-5 and that knocked him out. He recovered within two hours and was ready for work again.'

Dirk Coetzee and Jack Cronje had not trained the askaris, but when Eugene de Kock arrived, he introduced formal training in marksmanship and in various forms of combat and other tactics. Some of the askaris even attended a two-month parachuting course at Phalaborwa in the Northern Transvaal.

'De Kock wanted to make us dogs of war. Vlakplaas became a labour camp. We used to work like slaves. We used to dig trenches, build buildings and some-times we had to shoot the whole day. You know, there was this war psychosis that was put into our heads,' says Mamasela.

The general feeling of the askaris towards De Kock was total fear, says Mamasela. 'He had this grip over the minds of the askaris. He instilled fear. Everybody feared him. Even today, the askaris think that they will wake up and find that De Kock is still in charge of Vlakplaas.'

De Kock had a sjambok with which he flogged the askaris. Says Casselton: 'The askaris were very respectful to him because they knew he wouldn't accept slacking in the ranks. If they stepped out of line, he would beat them, physically beat them. The askaris referred to the beatings as "breakdancing", and some of them agreed with it. That was the only language they understood.'

Leon Flores says: 'They were a very difficult bunch of people and he had to be strict to control them. Yes, he used the sjambok, but he never beat them like dogs. He would rather discipline them like you would do with your children. He had to keep that standard of discipline there. The ANC people were not well disciplined.'

To this day, few askaris have returned to a normal life and many are still rejected by their own communities. According to Mamasela, 'It's pathetic. Like in the olden days, they still live amongst one another. They group together and are afraid to go back to their families. Ninety-nine per cent of their existence is still fear. They are not free yet and can't enjoy their lives. They live in their own cocoons.'

The security police used more than 100 askaris, of whom several are dead today. Dirk Coetzee and his gang murdered three: Peter Dlamini, Vuyani Mavuso and Isaac Moema. De Kock killed at least four: Moses Nthehelang, Johannes Maboti, Goodwill Sikhakane and Brian Ngqulunga. Others died mysterious deaths. Petrus Kwagadhi committed suicide, Xolelwa Sosha was assassinated and Silulami Mose and Glory Sidebe died of heart attacks.

In his in camera evidence to the TRC, Joe Mamasela was asked for information on certain askaris. This is how he described some of them:[12]

'Eric Sefadi is a PAC guy, an extremely intelligent young man. He is 100% loyal and devoted to De Kock and refused to testify against him.

'Simon Radebe comes from a police family. His father was a policeman and recruited all of them to the force. He was trusted by De Kock and was involved in many mysterious killings. If De Kock didn't like you, he would go to Simon …

'And then we have Thulo, he is now late (dead). He committed suicide, but before he did so there was a rumour that he had lost his mind.

'Nzimande testified against De Kock, but the whole thing got to his nerves. He went to Durban soon after his testimony and shot his wife and a man he suspected of being her boyfriend. He then shot himself.

'Mfalapitsa was involved in the mine-dump incident where four youths were killed. At the moment he is a pastor of the church. A very eloquent young man, but he is not collaborating with anybody.'

Throughout the existence of Vlakplaas, the unit remained racially segregated and the askaris were always seen as inferior and second-rate policemen. Despite De Kock's efforts in court to portray himself as a non-racist who cared for their well-being, there are two incidents that illustrate his attitude towards them.

The first took place in December 1985 when a Vlakplaas death squad raided a house in Lesotho, killing nine people. Before the raid, De Kock obtained beer with 'knock-out drops' to administer to the activists before the attack. He decided to test the substance.

Ackermann: On whom did you test it?

De Kock: On an askari by the name of Peter Kwagadhi.

Ackermann: Why didn't you test it on a white askari?

De Kock: We didn't have white askaris at that stage.

Judge: Why didn't you test it on a white member?

De Kock: He may sleep too deeply, Your Honour.

Judge: What do you mean by deep sleep?

De Kock: Well, the substance could kill a man.

Judge: Why on an askari and not on a white member? They are both people.

De Kock: The askari's [death] I would have been able to explain, but not that of a white member.

Kwagadhi had to be admitted to hospital, but when De Kock returned to Vlakplaas after the raid, he again tested the substance on him and three other askaris. They all ended up in hospital.

Joe Mamasela said Kwagadhi became mad after the poison was tested on him. 'When he came back from hospital, he went bananas for the whole year.'

The second incident illustrates the depravity and wickedness of Eugene de Kock, Willie Nortje and Brood van Heerden. This incident was never brought up in court, but is described in separate affidavits by Nortje and Van Heerden.[13]

In 1990, four askaris were diagnosed as being HIV positive or suffering from AIDS. Willie Nortje said this was a problem because the other askaris wouldn't drive with them or use the same facilities. Eugene de Kock devised a plan: he instructed Brood van Heerden, who had by then left Vlakplaas and was working for a banking group in Johannesburg, to find work for them in Johannesburg. Van Heerden persuaded the manager of the Chelsea and Little Roseneath Hotels in Hillbrow to employ the men as security guards. The manager didn't know they had AIDS. The four askaris, N'dam, Stretcher, Sebole and Vietnam, were still members of Vlakplaas and were paid by the unit.

'De Kock instructed them to infect black prostitutes in the area with AIDS,' says Nortje, who 'handled' the men and visited them frequently.

'I had to organise for the askaris to get work as security guards at the hotels, but the real reason was so that they could spread AIDS amongst the prostitutes,' says Van Heerden. Nortje says the arrangement didn't last long as they weren't 'disciplined' enough.

Sending black carriers of HIV into the world to infect other black people had nothing to do with the fight against Communism, a belief in the total onslaught ideology or being brought up in an Afrikaner home where his father was a member of the Broederbond and a friend of John Vorster. But De Kock claimed it was simply a lie that he had ever instructed Nortje and Van Heerden to effect such a plan. 'It is a known fact that the most regular clients of black prostitutes are white men. I wouldn't have achieved anything by infecting prostitutes.'

De Kock stressed the fact that he was never a racist and in mitigation he claimed that he had had his askaris regularly tested for AIDS and had demanded good medical treatment for those who were infected. He told me a story of how he once had to carry a wounded AIDS-infected askari out of Swaziland and personally gave him emergency medical treatment. De Kock said he was afterwards covered with blood and even had to wash it out of his mouth.[14]

De Kock said it was not impossible that Van Heerden could have devised such a plan, as he was a hardened racist, but why Nortje would lie about it, he was unable to explain. Whatever the truth, the plan was plain and simple: evil, immoral and vile. And let's not be fooled by Eugene de Kock paying for his black gardener to consult his personal physician or the soft-spoken Willie Nortje cuddling his gurgling baby.

In Koevoet, Eugene de Kock gained a reputation as a fearless soldier because he would track the spoor of Swapo insurgents with his scouts on foot and not take cover behind the thick armour of the Casspir. At Vlakplaas, he enhanced this reputation by spearheading raids into the neighbouring states. He would often be the one to kick the door open and storm into a house, not knowing what was awaiting him. Unlike Dirk Coetzee, who never himself pulled the trigger and used a killer like Joe Mamasela to do his dirty work, De Kock led all operations and killings under his command.

For the South African government, Lesotho in the mid-1980s was perhaps the most worrisome of the ANC's host governments, because it is an enclave in the heart of South Africa and Prime Minister Lebua Jonathan had become quite friendly with the ANC over the years. Several ANC attacks were launched from the organisation's bases and hideouts in the mountain kingdom.

In his evidence to the TRC in May 1997, the former Minister of Defence, General Magnus Malan, submitted the minutes of a meeting of the State Security Council (SSC) held on October 21, 1985. The meeting, chaired by State President PW Botha, recommended 'offensive action' against ANC bases inside Lesotho – even if it meant direct confrontation with government forces – because of the possibility that the ANC was stockpiling arms in the country.

Eugene de Kock launched his most successful operation ever in December 1985 when a Vlakplaas death squad of six men raided two houses in the heart of the capital of Maseru. According to the guidelines set out by the SSC, the raid had to be approved by State President PW Botha.

On the night of December 20, the men smuggled their silenced weapons across the Caledon River. De Kock said it was a suicide operation because Lesotho was politically very tense and everywhere in the streets were trucks full of soldiers. In the middle of the night, under cover of darkness, disguised and camouflaged, the men attacked two houses.

De Kock said his men had instructions not to kill women and children, but a woman by the name of Jackie Quinn opened the door, saw the pistol and grabbed it. She was shot dead. Eight more people were assassinated. Jackie Quinn's baby was also in the house, but she was left uninjured. De Kock claimed that when he got back to Ladybrand, he phoned the Maseru police station to get help for the baby. He said he told them there had been a shoot-out and gave them the address, but there is no record in Maseru of a phone call from a white person in South Africa to report the incident.

By the time De Kock claimed he had made the call, Lesotho police were already on the scene. ANC activist Leon Meyer, also known as Joe, and husband of Jackie, had survived long enough to drag himself to the neighbours and tell them what had happened. All he could say was: 'It was the Boers.'

In a submission to the TRC in 1996, Jane Quinn, sister of Jackie, said: 'This was disgusting, brutal, deceitful, treacherous and cold-blooded murder. I don't care what they [the death squad operatives] have been through or what they've been taught; they were adults who murdered my sister. They made their own choices, and like any other human being, they have to strive to be better than animals.'

The attack was a devastating blow to ANC operations in Lesotho. Amongst those killed were the Umkhonto we Sizwe regional commander, Morris Siabelo, and his chief of staff, Joseph Majose. Siabelo had been sent to Lesotho only two months earlier to consolidate infiltrations into South Africa. In their book *Comrades Against Apartheid*, Stephen Ellis and Tsepo Sechaba write that Siabelo had gained a reputation as an excellent soldier and had been the ANC head of security in Angola before he was posted to Lesotho. Ten days after the raid, the Lesotho/South African border was closed. This led to a coup d'état, masterminded by South African Military Intelligence, on January 20, 1986. The new military government of General Justin Lekhanya expelled leading members of the ANC from Lesotho.[15]

General Johan van der Merwe recommended that the raiding squad be decorated with the Police Star for Outstanding Service. In his submission to the police top command, he said: 'The above-mentioned members of the Security Branch have over a period of two months showed remarkable skill, expertise and ability in the evaluation, investigation, planning and execution of a highly secret and clandestine operation during which the members were exposed to extreme danger. The successful execution of this operation was of the utmost importance for the internal security of the Republic of South Africa. No further details can be provided as it may embarrass the South African government.'

The generals decided that the men should be honoured with an even higher decoration, and during a private ceremony in Van der Merwe's office, they were awarded the Police Star for Bravery.

To Eugene de Kock and his death squads, Swaziland was a playground in which they could operate freely and virtually without interference from the peaceful Swazis. In more than a decade of cross-border violations into Swaziland, the Vlakplaas squads were never challenged by the Swazi authorities. Swaziland was powerless to act against the raiding commandos transgressing its borders. One of the reasons for this was that the border, virtually unpatrolled and badly fenced, was very easy to cross undetected.

But as powerless as the Swazi authorities were to stop South African squads from operating in the country, they were also powerless to stop ANC guerrillas infiltrating South Africa from Mozambique through Swaziland. Officially, Swaziland restricted the ANC by not allowing the organisation to use the country as a springboard for attacks on South Africa, but in practice, many of the ANC attacks carried out in Natal and the Transvaal were planned in that country.

The State Security Council minutes of October 1985 state: 'Relations between South Africa and Swaziland are so good at the moment that no operations should be conducted without the approval or co-operation of the Swaziland government.' Eugene de Kock said in his evidence that the security police operated in Swaziland, while the SADF concentrated on Zimbabwe, Mozambique, Botswana and Zambia. They shared responsibility for Lesotho.

Since 1980, at least 28 ANC members have been assassinated in raids into Swaziland. Several activists were kidnapped and brought to South Africa where they were either killed, prosecuted or became askaris. Vlakplaas was responsible for the majority of killings and kidnappings.[16]

De Kock and his men captured two prize activists in June and August 1986 when they kidnapped Sidney Msibi, a former bodyguard to Oliver Tambo who had been underground in Swaziland since late 1983, and Glory Sedibe, the Military Intelligence chief for the Transvaal, also known as Comrade September. Sedibe was the brother of Jackie Sedibe, today a general in the South African National Defence Force, and who is married to Joe Modise, the Minister of Defence.

Msibi was captured, abducted and taken to South Africa after an ANC double agent made an appointment to see him. De Kock abducted September from a Swazi prison where he was being held because of his ANC activities. Under interrogation by the Security Branch, September decided to co-operate with his captors and became an askari at Vlakplaas. He was probably the most useful askari in the history of the unit and gave unit members sufficient information to enable them to virtually wipe out Umkhonto we Sizwe in Swaziland.[17]

Within 12 hours of September's kidnapping, several ANC safe houses in Swaziland were attacked. In the following year, 11 ANC activists were assassinated as a result of information supplied by Sedibe. Amongst them were Cassius Make, the chief of the ordnance department in the MK High Command and a rising star within the ANC, and Paul Dikaleli, a senior commander for the Transvaal.

When the chairman of the Swaziland Regional Political-Military Council, Ismael Ebrahim, was abducted a few months later and brought to Pretoria, one of his interrogators was Glory Sedibe. Ebrahim was eventually sentenced to 20 years' imprisonment.

In the Ebrahim case Sedibe testified in camera that he had left South Africa in 1977 when he became a member of the ANC in order to further his studies. He was trained in Angola, East Germany and the Soviet Union. He claimed he was freed from the Swazi prison by his own ANC comrades, who arranged for him to cross the border into South Africa. When he entered the country, he thought: 'The only thing I ever wanted to go and do was study. I have landed up being a member of the ANC, the Swazis want to kill me and the Boers want to kill me. I am walking through the bushes and all I want to be is a peaceful man. I want to continue with my studies.'[18]

De Kock arranged for Sedibe's wife and child to come to South Africa to join him. In later years, he became a celebrity by appearing in front of selected police audiences to talk about torture and murder in the ANC camps. He was also used by the South African Broadcasting Corporation to produce propaganda programmes about the cruelty and inhumanity of the ANC. He would conceal his identity on camera by wearing a balaclava.

September said in one programme: 'I'm trained to kill and wreck havoc in South Africa. Cities must go up in flames and innocent people of all races must be killed. But fortunately, I came to other conclusions after spending years in ANC camps.'[19]

In an article in *Beeld* newspaper, published in 1997, an unidentified former security policeman told of how he ate 'vinegar-soaked' fish and chips from the same paper bag as Sedibe, sat around a camp fire braaiing meat with him and philosophised with him about Communism. Sedibe must have been a unique and impressive askari, it seems, for a white policeman to have stuck his hand in the same paper bag to share food with him.[20]

De Kock told the court about various other rather bizarre police operations conducted in Swaziland. Four askaris, armed with stabbing knives, were sent to Swaziland where they had to identify their former comrades and kill them. According to De Kock, they had some success and killed one member of MK and injured another. The plan backfired when one of De Kock's own men, Sipho Ngema, was shot dead in a Swaziland restaurant in January 1988.

The police technical division planted explosives inside silver Parker ball-point pens and sent them to an ANC address in Swaziland. However, by the time the pens arrived at their destination, the four targeted ANC members had already been shot dead by Vlakplaas operatives. The police lost trace of the parcel, until six months later a post office worker opened the parcel and was seriously injured.

The security police have a dismal record of blowing up the wrong people with parcel bombs. Ruth First was killed in 1982 by a bomb probably intended for her husband and leader of the South African Communist Party, Joe Slovo. Two years later, Jeanette and Katryn Schoon were blown up by a bomb intended for Marius Schoon. De Kock said another parcel bomb was sent to an ANC member in Zambia who wanted a copy of the Qur'án. Several teenagers were killed or injured when they stole the parcel and opened it. A few years later, Eugene de Kock sent a parcel bomb to Lusaka in Zambia to kill Dirk Coetzee – but the wrong person opened the parcel, again with fatal results.

Although covert actions in Botswana were the responsibility of the SADF, De Kock and his men killed four people when they blew up an ANC safe house in the 1980s and assassinated a PAC activist, his wife and their two deaf sons in

April 1990. De Kock said that he had had to come to the rescue of the military when they botched a raid into Botswana. The operation referred to was probably an SADF attack on a suspected ANC safe house in March 1988. The raiding commando killed four sleeping people. The SADF claimed afterwards that an ANC military commander had been shot dead in the raid, but the Botswana government said they had all been innocent civilians.

De Kock said that a day or two before the operation there was a function at Vlakplaas, attended by Brigadier Willem Schoon and Generals Kat Liebenberg and Joep Joubert of the SADF. Schoon instructed De Kock to give 46 AK-47s to two security policemen to establish an arms cache near Krugersdorp. The SADF was planning a raid into Botswana, but needed justification to launch the attack. The next day, a shepherd discovered 'an ANC weapons cache'. Twenty-four hours later, the attack was launched.

The army returned with documents and briefcases. De Kock said there was nothing to prove that an ANC safe or transit house had been attacked or that ANC activists had been killed. He said the briefcase he searched belonged to a deputy director of water affairs. In the panic that followed, De Kock had to supply three Makarov pistols, shown at the press conference after the raid. The arms cache supplied by De Kock was also shown to the media.

De Kock said this kind of procedure wasn't unusual; a year or two earlier, Craig Williamson and his men had attacked a target in Botswana and brought back computer disks, but couldn't find anything relating to the ANC on them. De Kock had given them a RPG rocket launcher and night-sight equipment to show at the press conference.

By 1988, Eugene de Kock was the most admired and respected security policeman in the force and Vlakplaas the most prestigious police unit. De Kock and his men continued to roam the country, as well as the neighbouring states, in order to 'solve problems' that other units had difficulty with. The Security Branch at John Vorster Square in Johannesburg had one such 'problem' when they tried to blow up the headquarters of the South African Council of Churches in Khotso House in August 1988.

De Kock said he had been working in the Piet Retief region when he got a phone call from Willie Nortje to come back to blow up Khotso House. The Security Branch at John Vorster Square had tried the previous evening to bomb the building, but one of the plastic bags in which they were carrying a Russian-made landmine had broken and the mine had rolled away. They had decided to withdraw and rather get De Kock and his men to do the operation.

'We took silent weapons with us because there was a suspicion that there might have been ANC members in the building and they could have attacked us. I asked General Erasmus what we should do if other policemen came upon us, and he said we should shoot them,' De Kock said.

On the night of August 31, a John Vorster Square security policeman led De Kock's men into the building. They placed between 80 and 90 kilograms of explosives in the cellar of the building. The explosion occurred some 15 minutes after they had left. The explosion, which shook the whole of central Johannesburg, left a big hole in the basement and blew out all the windows in the building. Valuable documents and cars parked in the building were destroyed. The building was declared unsafe, and repair work continued for years afterwards. Twenty-three people were injured or treated for shock.

At Vlakplaas, a celebration party was laid on, attended by several generals, Johannesburg security policemen and the bombing squad. The guest of honour was the Minister of Law and Order, Adriaan Vlok.

'Vlok congratulated us on the operation and said that all that remained of the building was a pile of rubble. One of the officers made a "shhh" sound to prevent him from saying too much,' said Brood van Heerden.[21]

'The minister thanked us for our services and said that we would fight till the bitter end. We would never give over to the ANC. He said we would fight them for the next thousand years. He wanted to thank us for several operations, but I sent a message to him not to divulge any details. There could have been people who didn't know all the details and I wanted to keep it like that,' De Kock testified. The celebrations continued late into the night.

General Johan van der Merwe said in his submission to the TRC that Adiaan Vlok had ordered him to blow up Khotso House. 'According to Mr Vlok, this instruction had come from President PW Botha personally.'

Vlok admitted his complicity in the bomb attack when he said in his amnesty application that PW Botha ordered the destruction of the building because it had become 'a house of evil'. According to Vlok, Botha said to him: 'I have done everything possible to persuade them [the South African Council of Churches] to come to their senses, but nothing helps. We cannot act against the people. You must render that building unusable.'[22]

Vlok said Botha congratulated him and the police on the success of the operation during a meeting of the State Security Council. Vlok said he believed that all operations launched against the 'enemy' were bona fide, justifiable and authorised. He accepted that apartheid had resulted in pain and suffering, 'but Marxism/Communism's record was more terrible'.

Shortly after Vlok's amnesty application became public, PW Botha denied that he had ever ordered Vlok to plant bombs. Questioned by the Commission about the former government's complicity in blowing up Khotso House, FW de Klerk said: 'I'm not prepared to accept something is true because it is stated in an amnesty application.'

Archbishop Desmond Tutu remarked: 'The Khotso House thing, here you have people who were involved – going up to the cabinet minister level – who have applied for amnesty. Now, we'll have to say they must be very odd people to apply for amnesty for something they have not done.'[23]

Khotso House wasn't the only building blown up by Vlakplaas on orders from Vlok. In May 1987, De Kock was called in by Brigadier Willem Schoon, who instructed him to destroy Cosatu House in Johannesburg, which housed the trade union federation.

'I was speechless, because we were now talking about pure terrorism. I asked him where the instruction came from.'

'From the very top.'

'How high?'

'From the highest authority.'

'From the State President?'

'Yes.'

De Kock and his men, disguised as hoboes, carried out reconnaissance for two weeks before entering the building on the night of May 6. They placed between 60 and 70 kilograms of explosives in the building. Severe structural damage was done and the building was also declared unsafe.

Judge: Any decorations for this, Mr. de Kock?

De Kock: No, your honour, only a handshake and a braaivleis.

This victory celebration went on so long that the next morning at seven, Brigadier Willem Schoon called his superior to tell him he would not be at work, due to 'illness'.

The headquarters of the South African Catholic Bishops' Conference at Khanya House in Pretoria was also targeted by Vlakplaas. On a night in October 1988, De Kock and his men unlocked the doors with special keys made for them by the police technical division. They sprinkled the building with petrol and set it alight.

The police blamed the right wing and the left wing for the bombings and the arson attack. They said the explosions at Khotso House and Cosatu House could have been caused by ANC members who had tried to hide explosives or manufactured bombs in the buildings. At Khanya House, they said they suspected that the supposed leader of the extreme right-wing group *Wit Wolwe* (White Wolves), Barend Strydom, could have been involved.

Van Heerden says that a Warrant Officer Mostert at John Vorster Square was appointed as the investigating officer into the Khotso House explosion and reported weekly to Krappies Engelbrecht and Basie Smit in Pretoria. One day, after a report-back session, Mostert produced a fictitious statement purportedly from a black taxi driver and saying that he had transported a white woman and a white man to Khotso House on the day of the explosion. They had a suitcase with them. False identikits were compiled.[24]

In probably one of the most devious acts ever committed by a National Party cabinet minister, Adriaan Vlok held a press conference in Pretoria in January 1988 and announced a 'breakthrough' in the investigation into the bombing of Khotso House. Four months after Vlok had attended the Khotso House celebration party at Vlakplaas, he said that a 33-year-old ANC activist, Shirley Gunn, was sought in connection with the bombing. Vlok said Gunn, an alleged trained 'ANC terrorist', and two unknown men had entered the building shortly before the explosion. He said they had carried a heavy case, the lid of which was later found in the rubble after the blast. Police suspected that the explosives were destined for a car bomb that had been placed in the parking basement, which had exploded prematurely. Anyone with more information was asked to contact Krappies Engelbrecht at a Pretoria telephone number.[25]

Vlok didn't produce a shred of evidence, but the SABC and Afrikaans newspapers like *Beeld* and *Die Burger* called it a 'shocking revelation' and pounced on Gunn, branding her a 'white ANC woman terrorist'.

On June 25, 1990, Gunn was arrested on a remote Karoo guest farm and detained under Section 29 of the Internal Security Act. Her 16-month-old son, Haron, was incarcerated with her in the Culemborg security police headquarters in Cape Town. Ten days after her detention, her interrogators told her that a magistrate had ordered the removal of her child. 'I was left standing behind a locked gate while a security policeman and the social workers took him away. I will never forget his voice, screaming for me, looking at me in anguish. They hurled abuse at me all the time after they had taken Haron away. "You're a useless mother. A coward, a bitch. How could you allow your child to be taken away from you when all it needed was a bit of co-operation and we could have allowed you to keep him?"'[26]

Nine days later, Haron was returned to his mother and they stayed in prison together until she was released 62 days after her incarceration. She was never charged; the police knew she had nothing to do with the bombing of Khotso House. Talking about her security police interrogators afterwards, Gunn said: 'They're another breed of people altogether. I honestly wonder where they fit in this new South Africa of ours.'

Vlok admitted in his amnesty application that he had falsely implicated Gunn in an 'incorrectly worded' press statement. 'To the extent that it caused her harm, I am sorry and wish to express my sincere regret.'

Gunn has laid criminal charges and instituted a civil claim of R500 000 against Vlok. She says: 'Mr Vlok, I've decided that you will not get away with this.'

The Vlakplaas arsenal that was used so abundantly by other Security Branch units came from Namibia. Willie Nortje says he first travelled to Oshakati in Ovamboland in 1986 to collect a truckload of AK-47s and ammunition, Russianmade hand grenades, explosives, light machine guns and land mines. Another arsenal was moved the following year, and in February 1989, two more loads were brought back to Vlakplaas. In April 1989, as Namibia approached independence and Koevoet was disbanded, a Vlakplaas team drove to Oshakati where they collected an enormous arsenal that included missiles, mortars and rocket launchers.

Brood van Heerden said in his affidavit that one of the trucks his men had to drive back to South Africa contained several farming implements for the Koe-voet commander, General Hans Dreyer, stolen from a state farm in Namibia. They had to unload the implements on his farm, where there was already a bull-dozer, a power generator and several other stolen items.

De Kock admitted that Vlakplaas had become a supplier of illegal weapons to other units. He said he once had a phone call from the head of the Security Branch in Natal, General Bertus Steyn, who said his branch had shot dead four people and needed four AK-47s to plant on them. 'A week, two weeks later, he called again and said he needed another four AKs. Another four people had been shot. After this, I sent him a pick-up truck full of AKs, pistols and rocket launchers.'

And throughout the latter half of the 1980s, the plundering of the police secret fund continued. De Kock said that during 1987 or 1988 he submitted false claims of between R300 000 and R400 000. He said General Nick van Rensburg once told him to get R85 000 for General Bertus Steyn in Durban. 'We submitted false claims and I gave the money to Van Rensburg, who locked it in his safe. Two, three days later, he gave me an envelope with money to take to General Steyn. I opened the envelope, and there was a letter from Van Rensburg: "Bertus, I also have my problems on this side. I take R35 000. Regards, Nick."'

De Kock said three police generals, amongst them Johan van der Merwe, went to Taiwan on an official visit and wanted to take their wives along. The Vlakplaas secret fund provided money for their air tickets and expenses. On another occa-sion, four Vlakplaas members had to sit down and write out false claims for four days to swindle R100 000 from the secret fund in order to send Basie Smit and two or three other policemen on an overseas trip. De Kock had to send his people to shopping centres and supermarkets to collect slips they could submit. Another R40 000 was paid to Colonel Hermanus du Plessis who had to undergo a heart by-pass operation and who also had problems in paying his children's university fees.

Eugene de Kock said in his evidence in court that about three months before the unbanning of the ANC on February 2, 1990, and the subsequent release of Nelson Mandela, the security police knew these events were going to happen. They created great uncertainty within the ranks of the men who had been told previously that they would fight the ANC for another thousand years and never give way to black majority rule in South Africa. But Ian Smith had said the same in Rhodesia and Magnus Malan had promised the troops in Namibia that the Swapo flag would never fly in Windhoek.

'We didn't know any more who was a terrorist and who wasn't. What had we fought for all those years?' asked the Vlakplaas commander.

But as De Kock and his superiors contemplated the implications of FW de Klerk's leap into the future, a new and unexpected threat emerged from within their own ranks. On November 17, 1989, the impossible happened: a former Vlakplaas commander spoke.

Chapter Five

The age of innocence

'The greatest trick the devil ever pulled was convincing the world that he didn't exist.' – from the film *The Usual Suspects*

November 17, 1989, was a dark and sombre day for the South African Police. On that Friday morning, the front page of a small and independent Afrikaans newspaper, *Vrye Weekblad,* carried a larger-than-life portrait of a former Vlakplaas commander with a banner headline in Afrikaans: 'Bloody Trail of the SAP'. It continued: 'Meet Captain Dirk Johannes Coetzee, commander of a police death squad. He exclusively reveals the full sordid tale of political assassinations, poison drinks, letter bombs and attacks in neighbouring states.'[1]

A former police death squad commander had spoken, implicating himself in a series of political killings and blowing the lid off the police counter-insurgency unit at Vlakplaas.

In an office in Security Branch headquarters in Pretoria, Colonel Eugene de Kock and Brigadier Willem Schoon were discussing this news when General Johan le Roux walked into the office. Le Roux, former head of the Security Branch in Krugersdorp, had ordered the killing of Japie Maponya. He told De Kock that he wanted to convey his sympathy as there were obviously tough times lying ahead. De Kock responded: 'One of the allegations in the newspaper concerns a man that you have killed.' Le Roux turned as pale as a corpse, stood up and walked out.[2]

The generals in Security Police headquarters were worried. They were accused of murder and their most secret and covert unit had been exposed. Eugene de Kock was devastated by the expose. He said: 'We all thought that Dirk Coetzee was a traitor, that he was nothing but a white askari. This was the end of my career in the South African Police. It destroyed my self-image and integrity. I knew I would never wear a uniform again.'

At the time, De Kock and Coetzee had never met one another. But from the moment the article appeared, De Kock hated his predecessor as he had never hated before. 'He is nothing but a white askari. A revolting man.'

The first thing Vlakplaas did was to get rid of its enormous arsenal. About 30 steel cases were filled with weapons operatives had earlier that year brought back from Koevoet. The weapons were trucked to Daisy police farm and locked in a safe underneath one of the buildings.

De Kock called his men together and told them that they were facing a difficult period, but that the generals supported them. 'He gave us orders to go out and arrest people, he didn't care what for. We had to show the community and the public that we were not just an anti-terrorist unit. We could do any police work, even if it meant arresting a guy who's pissing in the streets,' recalls Ronald Bezuidenhout.[3]

Documentation at Vlakplaas was destroyed. 'We got rid of all documents, false identity documents and false passports. We got rid of everything. Steve Bosch and I burnt the documents in front of his office in a 210-litre drum,' says Bezuidenhout. According to De Kock, tonnes of police documentation were destroyed. He said that for days on end they burnt documents from eight in the morning till five in the afternoon.

Joe Mamasela, who was then based at the Northern Transvaal Security Branch, says: There were shockwave ripples. Coetzee shook the whole security apparatus to the roots. Generals and brigadiers were running around like beheaded chickens. They kept on having meetings with us, telling us how to lie, that we should stand together, we should hold each other's hands and support one another.'[4]

Each and every grain of dirt which could detract from Dirk Coetzee's credibility was unearthed, polished and presented to the friendly media. At the head of the cover-up was Krappies Engelbrecht.

One of his first tasks was to discredit the allegation that Vlakplaas had kidnapped and murdered Japie Maponya. Willie Nortje says that Engelbrecht came to the farm to take affidavits from the men about the Maponya case. 'Engelbrecht said to me to say as little as possible and to deny that I was in Krugersdorp at the time of the killing. A day or two after my affidavit was taken down, Engelbrecht sent me to Krugersdorp to meet a policeman who gave me a petrol log book dating back to the time that Maponya was kidnapped. Engelbrecht wanted to destroy the book so that there would be no evidence that we were in Krugersdorp at the time. The Krugersdorp security police sent false informant reports to head office that Japie Maponya had been seen in Botswana shortly after he had disappeared.'

False claims were filled in for the period of Maponya's disappearance to make it seem that the Vlakplaas unit was in Jozini in northern Natal at the time. Askaris involved in the abduction and torture of Maponya, who had in the mean time been transferred to other units, were brought back to the farm. All the statements were co-ordinated and 'edited' by Engelbrecht to present a credible web of deceit and lies about the murder.

In his affidavit, Engelbrecht said: 'I am the investigating officer in the Maponya affair. It has been established beyond any doubt that De Kock and his men were not in the vicinity of Krugersdorp at that time. They were doing service in the Jozini region. I am convinced that Japie Maponya was not abducted and killed by Colonel Eugene de Kock and his men. I couldn't find any proof that Maponya was killed. In fact, we suspect that he is still alive and may be in a foreign country.'[5]

In the case of slain ANC lawyer Griffiths Mxenge, evidence was manufactured that Mamasela went to Vlakplaas only in 1982, and thus couldn't have known Coetzee at the time of the Mxenge murder in November 1981.[6]

Coetzee's telephone was tapped by the police technical division in an effort to try and find out where he was. According to Brood van Heerden, he was involved in monitoring conversations between Karin Coetzee, Bheki Mlangeni and myself, in the attempt to locate Coetzee.

In a particularly devious move, a young Pretoria law student and police informant was 'planted' on Karin Coetzee and she started to have an affair with the man. It not only enabled the security police access to Coetzee's bank statements, private documents and letters, but the thought of his wife in bed with another man nearly drove the rogue policeman mad.

'When you do what Coetzee did, the whole might of the state is turned against you and you are completely discredited. And I can assure you it is a formidable machine,' said De Kock. He made no secret of the fact that he himself intended to kill Dirk Coetzee.

Riaan Stander, a former colleague and friend, said De Kock 'was spitting blood' and was looking for the right person to send on this mission.[7] Willie Nortje says they all hated Coetzee and agreed with their commander that he deserved death. But before De Kock could devise any plan, Vlakplaas faced another crisis: State President FW de Klerk appointed the Harms Commission to investigate death squads, unbanned the ANC and released Nelson Mandela from prison.

Six words uttered by FW de Klerk would haunt him for years to come. Days after the exposure of police death squads, he promised: 'I will cut to the bone.'

Addressing policemen at the Police College in Pretoria, he said: 'In recent times, much has been written about so-called police death squads. Allegations by a former policeman have stirred up emotions. I want to give the assurance that no stone will be left unturned to establish the full truth.'[8]

In the end, FW de Klerk didn't even pierce the skin. The Nobel Peace Prize laureate's name will forever be tarnished by his failure to act against his security forces who were killing, torturing and assassinating opponents of the regime. When the truth finally emerged and we discovered that the extent of repression and evil had been worse than we had ever thought, De Klerk still would not accept responsibility for the actions of his men.

FW de Klerk became a member of the Cabinet in 1978 – the year that death squads were unleashed on anti-apartheid activists, starting with the killing of Durban academic Dr Rick Turner. Who did De Klerk think, throughout the late 1970s, 1980s and early 1990s, killed anti-apartheid activists? Did he ever ask questions during Cabinet or State Security Council meetings? Did he never suspect that the security forces might be involved? How come certain journalists, human rights lawyers and opposition politicians knew about the existence of death squads, but De Klerk and many of his colleagues didn't suspect anything?

Who did he think blew up Ruth First in 1982, Katryn and Jeanette Schoon in 1984 and Albie Sachs in 1988? Who assassinated Zweli Nyanda in 1983, Joseph Mayosi in 1985 in Lesotho and Cassius Make in 1987 in Swaziland?

Did he really believe that 'internal strife' in the ANC led to the murders of Griffiths Mxenge in 1981, the Cradock Four in 1985, Fabian and Florence Ribeiro in 1986 and David Webster in 1989? Or that activists had the ability to make people disappear off the face of the earth: Sipiwo Mtimkulu in 1982, the Pebco Three in 1986 and Stanza Bopape in 1988?

And could FW de Klerk, a cunning, clever and crafty politician, have been so naive as to have believed the stories about detainees slipping on soap or diving through the windows of John Vorster Square to their deaths?

In his submission to the TRC in May 1997, De Klerk said he asked four generals, all with knowledge of Vlakplaas, about the murder allegations against De Kock and his unit.

'All four have assured me that they didn't know. I'm convinced that people in superior positions were kept in the dark and they were not being told what was happening. They were getting maybe false reports. One of the generals said that according to the reports that they got, everything was in order; the reports gave no indication whatsoever of these atrocities.'

There were five generals who could report to De Klerk about Vlakplaas: Basie Smit, Johan van der Merwe, Nick van Rensburg, Johan le Roux and Krappies Engelbrecht. Smit, as we have learned from evidence in the Eugene de Kock trial and amnesty applications to the TRC, was a regular visitor to Vlakplaas – the unit even had to keep a personal bottle of Chivas Regal whisky for him. Engelbrecht covered up for Vlakplaas and shared in its illegal profits, while Van der Merwe, Le Roux and Van Rensburg were implicated in killings and death squad activities themselves.

Truth Commissioner: You were given assurances about Vlakplaas by General van der Merwe and you indicated that you believed him. Do you still believe General van der Merwe? That he knew nothing about the operations at Vlakplaas?

De Klerk: Unless I have evidence that he is lying. I found him an honourable man ... I don't question his word just on the basis of rumours.

Truth Commissioner: How reasonable is that explanation that a lowly officer (Eugene de Kock), somewhere below these generals, was responsible for this entire aberration that led to all these things?

De Klerk: There is nothing reasonable in crime. It's unreasonable.

Truth Commissioner: Is it possible in your experience as the president of the country previously that the commander of Vlakplaas would have been able to sustain – taken all the resources he needs, finances, etc. – that situation on his own and keep it secret from everybody higher up?

De Klerk: Yes I think it is possible. It happens every day with theft. For months on end in the banking system with all the precautionary methods. Truth Commissioner: In your view sir, how was it possible that these operatives could behave with such impunity? What made it possible for such aberrations to occur?

De Klerk: They had to fight a revolutionary onslaught that had as its end goal to make South Africa look the way Zaire looks today. And that created a situation where you were not facing a typical military enemy across the barrel of a rifle, but the security forces had to protect the lives and property of all South Africans, to uphold the authority of the State against an onslaught which was underground, which used terrorist methods, which threatened the stability of the state. And the result was: more authority to the security people to fight the war, the very specific war. And across the world where this type of war has occurred there have been these types of aberrations.

A long list of assassinations for which policemen had applied for amnesty was read to De Klerk. 'Whoever authorised that was guilty of a very gruesome and totally unacceptable decision … It was wrong, it wasn't part of the policy … absolutely unacceptable, it falls outside the parameters of what was ever author- ised … I find it as shocking and abhorrent as anybody else … It proves that it was much more widespread and it's a shocking state of affairs and I'm extremely sorry that it has happened.'

'There was never any reference that I can recall in any way whatsoever of our policy being to use terrorist methods. Yes, firm action. Yes, using and applying extraordinary measures. Going underground. Yes, spying. Yes, having covert actions. Having a state of emergency. Putting people in camps without trial. All that, yes. But not murdering people. Not assassinations. It was never part of the policy,' De Klerk said.

It became known as the 'Big Denial', something that the vast majority of South Africans simply don't believe. Desmond Tutu said: 'How can he say he didn't know? When these people were killed, I went and told him about it. It makes me sad. I am really sorry for him.'

The Premier of Mpumalanga province, Mathews Phosa, remarked afterwards that De Klerk, sitting in the Union Buildings in Pretoria, had known everything that went on in the ANC's Quatro camp in faraway Angola, but nothing about Vlakplaas ten kilometres away.

The Vlakplaas unit was only disbanded three-and-a-half years after it was exposed as a death squad. The killing sprees of Eugene de Kock and his men continued into the early 1990s. They stole hundreds of thousands of rands and became embroiled in 'third force' activities by supplying tonnes of weapons to Inkatha impis on the East Rand near Johannesburg. If De Klerk had acted in time, he could have saved probably hundreds of lives.

De Kock believes that Vlakplaas wasn't disbanded in 1990 because the government might have needed the 'sharp edge' of the police should the negotiations with the ANC not have succeeded. He said he asked Engelbrecht to disband the unit shortly after Coetzee's revelations, but the general said the time wasn't ripe yet because the ANC could still withdraw from the negotiating table. 'I was told they could resume the armed struggle and we had to be ready.'

De Klerk's response to Coetzee's allegations in late 1989 was to appoint a judicial commission of inquiry into the existence of police death squads. His chosen instrument to dissect and expose death squads was Mr Justice Louis Harms, who had enjoyed a brilliant legal career and had been appointed a Supreme Court judge at the tender age of 46. He had graduated cum laude from the University of Pretoria and had been offered a professorship at the age of 28. In the late 1970s, he had led the battle to open the Pretoria Bar to all races, succeeding after more than two years of intensive lobbying. He is an expert in patent and copyright law and was much sought after as counsel on these matters.[9]

But the commission he was about to lead had little to do with civil law or muddled legal arguments. This was about deceit, cover-up and murder. And Louis Harms failed to break through the conspiracy of silence that the police presented to him. He should in the first place never have accepted his terms of reference – laid down by De Klerk – which prevented him from investigating operations conducted and atrocities committed outside South Africa's borders. Time and time again, as accounts were given to the commission of the death squads poised at South Africa's borders, the stories of their raids were cut short by Louis Harms.

Orange Free State Attorney General Tim McNally was appointed to lead the State's evidence. Just before his appointment, McNally had led a commission of inquiry into the death squad allegations of Almond Nofemela and Dirk Coetzee. In his report, handed to De Klerk at the end of November 1989 but released only a year later, McNally found that there was no evidence to suggest that either Coetzee or Nofemela had been telling the truth. He made the finding about Coetzee without interviewing him, but simply by making enquiries about his background. Yet the same Tim McNally accepted an assignment to lead evidence to the Harms Commission. In a court of law such prejudice as to the conclusion of the commission could have been used as grounds for demanding a recusal, or even to invalidate the findings of the court.[10]

Most incredible of all was the police team appointed to investigate Vlakplaas. The team was headed by General Ronnie van der Westhuizen, dubbed 'General Fix-It' after he had tried two years earlier to abort a murder investigation against a security policeman. He was assisted by the nimble Krappies Engelbrecht and Colonel Hermanus du Plessis. According to Dirk Coetzee, Du Plessis was involved in the murder of an anti-apartheid activist in 1981 and the disappearance of a student leader in 1982. Suddenly, the death squads had to investigate themselves.

After a decade of disappearances and assassinations, many thought the day of reckoning had finally arrived. But the public's initial perception that Harms and his team would unearth the full story of the death squads soon proved to be an illusion. There followed months of utter frustration as files went missing, death squad operatives appeared in clown-like disguises, documents were not produced and state witnesses bluntly denied any knowledge of death squads.

A veil of secrecy was drawn across the activities of the Vlakplaas squad and Louis Harms was faced with blank and bare denials. De Kock and his men were whitewashed and presented as knights in shining armour.

Says Craig Williamson: 'We were dealing with a system with the most incredible hypocrisy. On one hand we had to pretend that we were all God-fearing Christians who walked round with Bibles under our arms, while on the other hand we were supposed to go around making sure that white apartheid rule wasn't overthrown. And that was done very, very effectively.'[11]

One important fact did emerge at the commission, and that was that Vlakplaas had achieved very little of what it was set up to do – to identify and arrest ANC and PAC insurgents. Brigadier Willem Schoon said he was commander of Section C for eight years and that only about 20 arrests were made in that time. Captain Paul van Dyk spent seven years at Vlakplaas and said that fewer than five arrests were made during his time. Almond Nofemela arrested only one infiltrator during his nine years on the farm, while Brian Ngqulunga was there for nine years and never identified anyone. If they were not arresting activists, what were they doing?[12]

Opposition parties, the ANC, newspapers like the *Weekly Mail* and *Vrye Weekblad* and human rights lawyers warned Harms that he was the victim of a massive cover-up and accused De Klerk of appointing a toothless commission. Louis Harms, in the words of Constitutional Court judge Laurie Ackermann, wielded a blunted scalpel. He could not cut through the tissue of lies.

Joe Mamasela, implicated by Coetzee in virtually all his death squad operations, was one of the main witnesses to appear before the Harms commission. Like all the other security policemen, he denied any complicity in any illegal activity. Today, he admits: 'Oh, I lied. We all lied from Cape to Cairo. It was a shambles. We were told to lie. There was no way that we could compromise the police. We were told, in all certainty, that we should lie. We must just tell the truth about our own backgrounds, because they could find that out easily. We were told to say no, we did not know anything. That was the bottom line.'[13]

This is how Craig Williamson puts it: 'They believed totally the nonsense that was fed to them. The whole Harms Commission was a farce. It was fed manure and it was kept in the dark and it grew the type of mushrooms it was supposed to grow. I think the one important thing in this country we will have to come to terms with is the total lie we all lived with. We often used to talk, or you heard people saying that if you make the lie big enough you can fool all the people all of the time. There was in South Africa a culture of pretending that what was happening wasn't happening at all.'

De Kock said that Joe Mamasela was making excessive financial demands during the sitting of the Harms Commission. He said Engelbrecht asked De Kock to kill Mamasela because he had become a 'nuisance', but the askari overheard the conversation, went to a lawyer and wrote a letter to headquarters.

Peter Casselton says De Kock was despondent and dejected during the early days of the Harms Commission. 'Once upon a time Basie Smit didn't come (to Vlakplaas) one day, he came many days. He had his own bottle of whisky there. So did Krappies Engelbrecht and so did Nick van Rensburg and all the other generals, celebrating and having a party. And when the shit hit the fan, they disappeared. No one came there. Nobody. It hurt Eugene.'[14]

De Kock said it wasn't only the social gatherings that stopped, but his own security police colleagues also started to avoid him as though he had a contagious disease. He said he and his men were 'pushed aside as though we were something dirty'. Some of his men, like Leon Flores, told him they wanted to leave Vlakplaas.

The appointment of the Harms Commission coincided with the unbanning of the ANC and the release of Nelson Mandela, steps which left a bitter taste in De Kock's mouth: 'FW de Klerk abdicated when he unbanned the ANC. He wasn't in control of the country any more. De Klerk is one of the biggest traitors in the history of this country. De Klerk was like a petrified puppy who lay on his back and wet himself. He just gave over. He handed a section of his security forces over to the mercy of the ANC. There were only two factions that kept the National Party in power all those years: the police and the Defence Force. The people who helped him to stay in power, the people who helped him to start this peace process, were the people he threw to the wolves.'

In his testimony before the Harms Commission, De Kock said: 'I was never involved in any assassination outside the borders of South Africa. My duty was restricted to collecting information on the activities of terrorists. The accusations of Almond Nofemela and Dirk Coetzee are untrue. There was never a death squad at Vlakplaas.' He said such allegations were 'devoid of all truth' and described as 'beyond belief' the allegation that he had killed Japie Maponya, saying: 'I know absolutely nothing about it.' He said that 'ANC people are still coming across the border. The idea is now to catch them and take them to court.'[15]

But De Kock appeared before the Harms Commission with his leg in plaster. Only days before, he had broken his knee while leading a Vlakplaas commando on a mission to Botswana to wipe out a PAC stronghold. Despite a judicial commission of inquiry, it was business as usual at Vlakplaas.

April 22, 1990. Vlakplaas operatives crossed the river into Botswana at night. 'There were crocodiles and I was scared,' recalled Captain Wouter Mentz. Transferred to Vlakplaas only a few months earlier, this was his first operation.

De Kock said as they approached the house, which was purported to be a PAC stronghold, a guard suddenly appeared and saw them. 'I shot the man in the head, two, three times. I could see his hair lifted from his head. As I went sideways to get a better angle, I fell into a hole and broke my knee.' Willie Nortje said the guard fell, but started screaming. Douw Willemse finished him off. By then, a PAC activist by the name of Sam Chand (also known as Khan) had started walking around the house with a torch.

According to Nortje, Martiens Ras shot Chand with a silenced pistol through the window, but he ran back into a room. Ras then shot a dog. Two members kicked down the door and stormed into the house. 'When I got to the bedroom, Chand was already lying dead on the bed. Martiens and Douw were busy shooting his wife with Scorpions in her body. They shot her through her head and she fell dead.' Leaving Sam Chand and his wife, Hagera, lying dead in the bedroom, riddled with bullets from the silenced machine pistols, the operatives moved from room to room.[16]

It was dark in the house as Nortje moved through the rooms, looking for PAC activists. As he entered one of the bedrooms, he saw somebody in the bed and shot the person through the head. Before they left, the raiders placed 15 kg of explosives under a bed. Just after they had crossed the border back into South Africa, the bomb exploded, ripping the house apart.

Minutes later, the Botswana police arrived on the scene. They discovered five bodies: the guard outside, and inside, Chand and his wife and their two sons, Redwan and Ameen. The person assassinated in bed by Willie Nortje was not a PAC 'terrorist', but a deaf boy. The person in the other room, shot dead by another operative, was his brother, also deaf. The two boys wouldn't even have heard the raiders kicking down the door and killing their mother and father. If they had been awake, they wouldn't have made a sound.

De Kock said Willie Nortje later spoke to him about the children: 'He was in as much of a state as I was. It is a cross I will have to bear my whole life. I believe it was even worse for Nortje. The people who gave the command don't have to live with the dead. But those you've killed don't go away. Not for a thousand years.'

Wouter Mentz says they didn't know there were children in the house. 'Had I known it, I would probably not have participated in the operation. I still cry about this incident and can't sleep because of it.'[17]

The team had to carry De Kock across the Botswana border. In order to cover their tracks and explain their commander's broken knee, they drove to Richards Bay in Natal, booked into a hotel and took De Kock to a local doctor. The commissioner of the KwaZulu Police, General Jac Buchner, stated in an affidavit that De Kock had hurt his knee during an operation in the Natal mountains while his unit was looking for home-made weapons manufactured by Zulus.

Wouter Mentz said about three or four weeks after the operation, Willie Nortje gave him an envelope with about R6 000, said it was for the Botswana operation and that Security Branch Headquarters had congratulated them. According to De Kock's testimony Sam Chand had been a paid informant for Military Intelligence, but had lost control over PAC cadres infiltrating South Africa through Botswana. According to intelligence, a group of 76 heavily armed activists had infiltrated the country, and set up bases in the Transkei. General Nick van Rensburg had instructed De Kock to attack the house and kill Chand and any other activists in the house. According to De Kock, Harms Commission investigator Krappies Engelbrecht had been present when they discussed the operation and had said that he would have liked to go along.

From a police point of view, it was a commendable performance by the men of Vlakplaas who testified before the Harms Commission. The 'investigators' had found no traces of the unit's crimes and the men were well briefed and coached before appearing before Louis Harms. It was soon clear that Vlakplaas was going to emerge from the inquiry unscathed.

But there was a problem: an askari by the name of Brian Ngqulunga. He joined the ANC in 1977 but later became disaffected and was detained in Maputo. He drank insecticide in an attempt to commit suicide and escaped shortly afterwards. He was held in a maximum security prison for nearly two years before the Mozambican authorities deported him back to South Africa. When he was debriefed by the security police, he volunteered to assist them in tracking down insurgents. He was sent to Vlakplaas and was one of a number of askaris who were eventually appointed as police constables without ever attending police college. He was never held in high regard by De Kock and didn't participate in death squad operations.

However, under Dirk Coetzee he had been a member of the death squad that murdered ANC lawyer Griffiths Mxenge in 1981. Coetzee and Nofemela implicated Ngqulunga in the killing.

Joe Mamasela, who was a good friend of Ngqulunga, said: 'The whole thing shook him to the marrow. It disturbed him. He was a completely devastated person. The whole exposure worked into his mind. He was frail, he drank too much and he was on the verge of a nervous breakdown.'[18]

The generals and Eugene de Kock were concerned that Ngqulunga was going to admit his complicity in the murder of Mxenge. De Kock said he gave Ngqulunga sleeping tablets and the askaris were told to give moral support to him, but after a heavy drinking session he shot his pregnant wife three times. Fortunately, she didn't die and was admitted to hospital.

Ngqulunga was well briefed before his appearance before the commission. He got into the witness box, took the oath and calmly denied that he had participated in the murder of Mxenge.

But he later said to Mamasela that he was contemplating telling the truth. 'He said this thing was eating away at his soul. He wanted to tell the truth. The Friday before I went to testify, there was a meeting in General Engelbrecht's office.

Concern was raised about Brian's behaviour and his drinking problem and that he was becoming progressively agitated and nervous. They were afraid that he might jeopardise the police case at the Harms Commission.'

De Kock said he was instructed by Nick van Rensburg and Krappies Engelbrecht to kill Ngqulunga. The generals said his condition was deteriorating and he had already approached the ANC.

Willie Nortje said De Kock was unhappy about killing the askari as the man had done nothing to him. In the end however, De Kock said he would have to take charge of the operation as it was one of their own people and they knew how to do it.

Ackermann: Was Brian Ngqulunga a perpetrator?

De Kock: Yes, Your Honour, he broke the unwritten rules of the security police.

It was decided to lay the blame for the killing at the ANC's door by shooting him with an AK-47. Simon Radebe was instructed by De Kock to befriend Brian by taking him home in the afternoons and drinking with him. Radebe had to let his colleagues know when the time was right for the killing.

One day in July 1990, Radebe said to them: 'Tomorrow will be the day.'

When De Kock had to pick assassins for the operation, he decided to involve Balletjies Bellingham and Dave Baker in order to 'contaminate' them. He also instructed Wouter Mentz to be part of the team. For once, De Kock didn't lead the squad because he didn't want to be present when Brian was killed.

Captain Wouter Mentz said in his testimony before the TRC that they were wearing balaclavas when they abducted the askari from a township north of Pretoria on the night of July 20, 1990. 'As we grabbed him, he shouted: "No comrades, no comrades, I'm one of you. I'm one of you." We loaded him into the kombi, pushed him against the floor and stuffed something in his mouth. We stopped, dragged him out and threw him on the ground. Bellingham emptied his AK magazine on him. I looked away because I couldn't handle it. I became sick when we left again. It was a shocking experience and I'm permanently scarred as a result of the incident.'

Mission accomplished, the assassins drove to a plot in Pretoria North where they hosed down the inside of the minibus, 'because Ngqulunga had urinated (during the assault on him) and so forth'. They then joined Eugene de Kock at the Holiday Inn in Pretoria for *drankies* (drinks) and a meal.

The post-mortem report showed that Ngqulunga's tongue was missing when his body was found. Mentz insists none of his henchmen cut it out. Pictures of the body after it was found show that part of Ngqulunga's face was blown away by bullets, and this may have severed his tongue.

Ngqulunga's grave is pitched high on a hill overlooking Vlakplaas. De Kock instructed all the Vlakplaas men to attend the funeral, but Mentz said he couldn't be at the graveside of a man he had helped to kill and decided to hide in the pub. While he was there, De Kock and Nortje found him. They said they couldn't go either.

Wouter Mentz is a brawny man with a macho moustache and a swagger typical of the men who worked in the police death squad at Vlakplaas. So it was an unexpectedly poignant moment in the hearing when – during an account of how he and his mates had abducted and battered Brian Ngqulunga, and pumped a magazine full of AK-47 bullets into his body – the captain faltered, sobbed softly and asked for a glass of water before he could continue.

The former Vlakplaas operative is a man haunted and tormented by his memories of death. I spent one evening with him drinking in a Pretoria bar and he twice burst into tears when he spoke about the killings he had been involved in.

Thirty-six years old, he comes from a poor Afrikaner family. According to his psychiatric report, his father, a miner, was a tyrant who frequently hit and kicked him. Mentz was scared to come home from school and he attended nine different schools. He became a policeman at the age of 18, and a few years later he was transferred to the murder and robbery unit in Pretoria. He couldn't sleep, started having nightmares, was aggressive and was always on the look-out for a fight. Mentz's psychological death-knell was his transfer to Vlakplaas in August 1989.[19]

He slept very little, but when he did, he had nightmares and flashbacks. Mentz couldn't be alone and became afraid to sleep. His condition deteriorated and he started drinking more and more. His marriage fell apart in 1991 when his wife decided she couldn't take it any more.

Mentz is still a policeman, but has been suspended pending an investigation into his death squad activities. He has undergone psychological counselling, but isn't getting better. According to his psychiatrist, Professor Jan Robbertze, he is seriously disturbed and suffers from serious post-traumatic stress disorder and depression. He is emotional, cries for no apparent reason and pulls out his moustache and hair. When he talks about his past, he may be laughing at one moment and then unexpectedly burst into tears. He needs to be hospitalised. Wouter Mentz simply doesn't fit into society any more.

On November 13, 1990, after more than 70 days of hearings, FW de Klerk released the findings of the Harms Commission. As we all expected, it had been an exercise in futility. For the people of South Africa whose lives had been touched by the death squads, a deafening silence was all they got. The culprits were untouched and ready to strike again.

Harms exonerated the police and found that no death squads had existed at Vlakplaas. In the end, what was investigated was not police death squads, but the mental state of Dirk Coetzee and Almond Nofemela. While the police miserably failed to produce documents of any substance relating to the police atrocities, they had no problem in finding evidence relating to the personality and conduct of their accusers.

Without a single shred of psychological evidence to support his finding, Harms declared Coetzee to have psychopathic tendencies. It was from the outset of the commission clear that Harms disliked Coetzee immensely – Harms told him during his giving of evidence in London that Coetzee was 'talking crap'.

On the other hand, Harms seems to have been impressed by the blunt denials of Eugene de Kock and his men and even said that the Vlakplaas commander was an 'impressive witness'. Harms found that it was not necessary to disband Vlakplaas. This was his recommendation about the unit: the men should in future keep diaries and records of all their actions and operations. Commenting on the criticism levelled at the composition of the commission and its investigators, Harms said the dedication and conduct of the officials had been exemplary and they had acted fearlessly regardless of who the 'opponent' was.

National Party politicians reacted jubilantly to the report. Adriaan Vlok said: 'We've got the Harms report ... death squads never existed in the South African Police. The police don't kill people, they arrest them.'[21]

De Klerk had obviously hoped that the Harms Commission would be the final words spoken on the actions of his security forces. He said in his reaction: 'The events dealt with in the report took place in an era of serious conflict, now belonging to the past. We should act with a view to our future and take conciliatory steps which are necessary to again create a peaceful South Africa.'[22]

The only action De Klerk took was to promote Louis Harms to judge of appeal and Tim McNally to Attorney General for Natal. Harms remains unrepentant about the failure of his commission and in typical FW de Klerk-fashion, he recently said he was a victim of a police cover-up and could under those circumstances not come to any other conclusion but that Coetzee had lied and that there were no death squads at Vlakplaas.

Asked by the TRC about the failure of Harms, De Klerk said: 'The Harms Commission, it later came out, was up against a wall. It couldn't get to the truth, it was misled. So that effort did not succeed as I had hoped it would succeed ... Once again with hindsight, with everything which is coming out, maybe I should have done more. I'm not saying that I was perfect.'

October 3, 1990, Lusaka, Zambia. I was sitting in the departures hall of Lusaka's international airport waiting for Dirk Coetzee and his two sons. From Lusaka we would board a British Airways flight to London, where the former Vlakplaas commander would spend the next part of his life in exile. After hours of vile coffee and local Mose beer, watching an Ethiopian Airlines Boeing land and an Aeroflot jet taking off, Coetzee, his two sons and his ANC bodyguard arrived. Coetzee was out of breath and excited. The first thing he told me was: 'They've sent me a bomb! I got a bomb in the post!'

After I had calmed him down and shoved a Mose into his hand, he told me that on the way to the airport, he had stopped at the local post office to collect a parcel sent to him from South Africa. Weeks earlier he had been informed by the ANC that there was a parcel for him at the post office, but he had had no transport and was living in a motel 8 kilometres outside town. He said that when he saw the parcel, about the size of a shoe box and wrapped in brown paper, he was suspicious. He refused to pay the high import duty ..on the item and after a heated exchange of words with the post office worker he stormed out of the building, telling the officials to return the parcel. The name of the sender on the parcel was that of Bheki Mlangeni, Coetzee's lawyer in Johannesburg.

'It says on the parcel that Bheki Mlangeni sent it to me. Why would Bheki send me a parcel without informing me? I think it's a bomb that De Kock and Vlakplaas had posted to me. The parcel is now on its way back to Johannesburg. You must warn Bheki. Please, warn him that he mustn't open it.'

I looked at Coetzee, thinking he was paranoid about his own safety (his 'paranoia' later turned out to be completely justified). I didn't believe him because I thought that if Vlakplaas men had wanted to kill him, they would have sent an assassin to shoot him. Coetzee also asked his ANC guard, a man by the name of Stanley, to warn Bheki. Coetzee's warning never reached Bheki.

Over the previous year, Bheki Mlangeni had been investigating death squads and had been appointed one of Coetzee's lawyers. He was a well-known activist and had been chairperson of the Jabulani branch of the ANC since 1990. Bheki was a cheerful, dedicated little man whom I got to know well during our death squad investigations. He also became a good friend of Coetzee's as he had frequently had to fly to Lusaka to interview and question the rogue policeman.

One night in December 1990, Bheki and I chased askari Jeff Bosigo right through the night up to the Botswana border. Our first stop was Bosigo's brother's home in Mmabatho, but he told us the askari had left earlier that afternoon. We drove to his parents' liquor store deep in a rural area close to the Botswana border, but his father said he had probably crossed the border. While we were driving through the dusty village looking for the liquor store, Bheki had said to me: 'Hey man, I hope I survive all this to see where it ends.'

Two months later, it ended for Bheki in the most brutal way possible.

It was early evening on February 15, 1991, when Bheki and Seipati Mlangeni returned home from work. In his hand, he clutched a parcel he had earlier that day received from the post office. The parcel was addressed to Dirk Coetzee, but Bheki's name was given as the sender.

It is still a mystery why Bheki, who had been detained on three different occasions and received telephonic threats to his life, opened the parcel. This is how Seipati remembers the events that night: 'We arrived home, he took off his jacket and opened the small box. On one of those cassettes it was written: evidence, hit squads. He took the earphones, put them on his ears, and switched the walkman on. All that I heard was a big bang. I thought somebody was shooting from outside the window, but then I saw him lying on his back.'[23]

He died instantly when the explosives, hidden inside the earphones of the walkman, exploded and punched two holes into the base of his skull.

'I ran to his mother … all I could say was: "Mama, Bheki …" Catherine Mlangeni entered the room where the explosion had occured to find her son 'in pieces … pieces of him, brains, splattered all over the room. That was the end of Bheki.'

Reconciliation and forgiveness is not a notion the family entertain just now. 'For a person who has never killed anybody, for a person who has been peaceful-ly fighting for his people's dignity and for a person who has never carried a weapon, to be killed like that, was just terrible,' says Seipati Mlangeni.

I won't try to express my own emotions about my failure to warn Bheki, but I think it's true to say that in the end, the death squads touched all of us.

Eugene de Kock and Vlakplaas had to be the masterminds behind the bomb. Who else wanted to kill Coetzee, could get his address in Zambia, knew that everything that was sent to him went through his lawyer, and could manufacture such a sophisticated device? The police immediately denied any complicity and appointed an investigations team to trace the bombers. Of course they found nothing. But as we were about to close the door on another death squad attack, a mad voice spoke from a psychiatric institution.

Chapter Six

A pig's head and a set of earphones

He stared at me, his blue eyes frantic and fierce. He was a small, nervous man, his body covered in scars. When I met him in May 1991, he had already been shot and wounded three times. Since then, he's been shot at least twice.[1]

In the visiting room of the maximum security section of the Weskoppies Psychiatric Hospital in Pretoria I sat looking at a man with not only a body, but a life and mind full of scars. A cough-mixture addict, he had spent more than a decade on the edge of society, in the underworld and on South Africa's secret but official business. Here was a man who had fought on all sides: for the SADF, for the ANC, and finally, for Eugene de Kock's death squad, as one of only two white askaris in the history of Vlakplaas.

I had been called to Weskoppies by Ronald Desmond Bezuidenhout, alias Desmond Barkhuizen, Ronnie Daniels and Duncan Smith. He introduced himself as Tokkie, a nickname he had acquired from being accidentally shot by a Russian-made Tokarev pistol in an ANC training camp in Angola. He was in hospital for assaulting his wife, Marilyn. After his threats to kill her and blow up their house, Marilyn had become so disturbed that she had tried to commit suicide by drinking rat poison. She laid a charge against Bezuidenhout, and he was arrested and sent to Weskoppies for 30 days of mental observation.

Sitting with me in Weskoppies was Marilyn, holding his hand. She had tears in her eyes and was asking for his forgiveness. She promised to withdraw all charges against him. Bezuidenhout, heavily sedated, just stared at her.

He said he wanted to tell me about the parcel bomb that Eugene de Kock and his Vlakplaas operatives had sent to Dirk Coetzee in May 1990, but which had instead blown up Bheki Mlangeni eight months later. Bezuidenhout said he was one of the death squad men who had sat boozing in the Vlakplaas pub and decided to kill Coetzee.

'Hell, we hated that duckfucker of a Dirk Coetzee,' he said.

Bezuidenhout was talking to me in an effort to win Marilyn back because she had told him to break with the past and start a new life. His way of doing it was to spill the beans. He told me he had shaved his beard, dyed his hair and hacked it into a different style.

For the next few hours, behind the high walls of Weskoppies, Bezuidenhout lifted the lid on the death of Bheki Mlangeni. I visited him again a week later, by which time he had written out his life story for me on four sheets of pink writing paper. 'I have been a spy, double agent, killer, mercenary, fugitive, security policeman.

I have been kept in a hole in the ground by the ANC, I have been shot, I have been tortured. I have been in many strange places. I have also been at Vlakplaas.'

Police eventually dismissed Bezuidenhout as merely a police informant who had been issued with a pistol and had spent 18 months at Vlakplaas. He was seen as a liar, alcoholic and drug addict, never trusted by his colleagues because of the time he had spent with the ANC. It took five years before Bezuidenhout's revelations about the murder of Bheki Mlangeni proved to be true. But beyond that, his life story is a testimony to a South Africa where life was cheap, where dignity and humanity were difficult to find.

Bezuidenhout spoke much about his childhood. He grew up, as he called it, 'on the pavements' where he soon learned about 'the other side of life'. His mother was only a teenager when he was born in Port Elizabeth. She was 15 when she married his father, but it didn't last. She was divorced and married again.

According to Bezuidenhout, his stepfather was 'a bastard'. 'I was viciously beaten and hung up in a sack in the garage for hours. I was the scum in the house. My parents were always stuffed with booze.'

It was Bezuidenhout who found the body of his younger brother just after he had shot himself. His sister also committed suicide. Bezuidenhout eventually landed up in reform school, but he ran away, was sent back, and ran away again. He was eventually raised by his grandmother.

'My stepfather died last year. I was the only person who wept at his funeral, but I will never forgive him for my miserable childhood,' Bezuidenhout scribbled on his pink paper.

He joined the SADF in 1973 and became a reconnaissance soldier. 'I soon got the nickname of Short Shit Meany because I was fit and tough and did not take any shit. I was taken up in a special unit and went to Angola to hunt for terrorists. I was dropped by parachute at night into enemy territory where we had to hide and rest during the day and move around silently at night looking for terrorists.

'I never saw bugger all, no Swapo, no terrs, no Angolan soldiers, no Cubans, no Russians, just the bloody bush. It was here, during my training, and as a member of a recce (reconnaissance) unit in northern Namibia at a base called Sodolite, that I learned to hate kaffirs. We were told they're the enemy.'

Bezuidenhout left the army, but soon went back to the bush as a mercenary. Through the magazine *Soldier of Fortune* he landed himself a job as an instructor for the South African-supported Renamo resistance movement in Mozambique. 'I had no concern for Renamo or their war, but the money was good. Most of the people I trained were kids, between 10 and 15. About a thousand went through my hands. One day, a Frelimo spy was brought to us. I handed my unloaded gun to this kid of about 12 and told him to pull the trigger. He couldn't because he wasn't mentally strong enough. I took the gun, put a bullet in the magazine and shot him. He fell and died before my eyes.'

Bezuidenhout returned to South Africa in 1985. He lived in Vryheid in Natal, where the ANC was very active in recruiting members for its military wing. Two men working with him were members of the organisation and Bezuidenhout told them he also wanted to join Umkhonto we Sizwe. He slipped across the border to Swaziland where he was detained at a jail near Matsapa and deported to Lusaka in Zambia.

To this day, I don't understand why Bezuidenhout joined the ANC. It couldn't have been out of political conviction. He claims that he was a security police agent and was instructed to infiltrate the ANC. Yet I find it unlikely that the Security Branch would have dispatched a white agent to the ANC. It would have been just too disastrous.

'I was three years with the ANC and was kept in a hole in the ground on and off for 14 months. I was frequently tortured by a sadist within the ANC's intelligence ranks known as JJ. They said I was a spy, no matter what I said. They wanted me to sign a statement that I was sent by the government. I refused, and I was down, dizzy, being kicked and punched. I was starved on a diet of only water for 29 days, my foot was broken by a rifle butt and I was shot in the left arm.' He showed me the scar where they had removed the bullet without any anaesthesia. A scar across his head was the result of a heavy blow.

The person who saved his life, he said, was 'Mister' Chris Hani, former leader of the South African Communist Party and chief of staff of Umkhonto we Sizwe. 'I was so dizzy and couldn't see out of my eyes when Chris Hani walked in and said: "What are you guys doing? This guy is almost dead and you're still kicking him. Leave him alone."'

Bezuidenhout was eventually sent to the ANC training camp Vienna in Angola, where he underwent guerrilla bush-war training. He said conditions were appalling. 'I got very sick, started vomiting blood and contracted malaria. The ANC still didn't trust me because they were heavily infiltrated by South African agents. A lot of trainees were accused of being agents and tortured from time to time. One of the instructors, thought to be an agent, was shot dead before our eyes.'

From Angola he was transferred to Tetoroff military base in what was then East Germany, where he underwent specialised military training. After completion of his training he went back to the ANC in Lusaka where he was kept under house arrest with other Umkhonto guerrillas.

One day his ANC commanders told him that they would give him an opportunity to prove his allegiance to the ANC by sending him on a military mission to South Africa to sabotage an oil pipeline in Natal. His mission was a failure and he was arrested in Port Elizabeth towards the middle of 1989.

'I was taken out of a cell by Warrant Officer Wolmarans. They took me up to the seventh floor where I was introduced to Eugene de Kock. Anyone could see that this is a cookie you don't play with. He was quiet, well-spoken, but there was something that tells you: don't play with this guy.' Bezuidenhout agreed to cooperate with his captors. He became an askari at Vlakplaas.

As I sat with Bezuidenhout in Weskoppies, he spoke a lot about 'tubing' detainees. He became a very skilful 'tuber' after joining the Vlakplaas unit and at times I got the impression that he probably enjoyed doing it. He said his tube was used so often that it had the indentation of a human face. 'Tubing is actually very simple. You put him down on his stomach, you handcuff him, you put your knees on his back, and you take the tube and put it over his face. In other words you suffocate the person. You normally wait until you see him wet his pants, then you know: he's going through the gates upstairs. Then you leave him, and the minute he inhales, you tube him again.'

Bezuidenhout hated Eugene de Kock with a passion I had seldom seen before. De Kock had assaulted him ('I was too quick for him, I ducked') and wouldn't allow him into the inner circle of Vlakplaas. 'In a very short message, I can tell you: he's a snake. The one minute he can act normal, the next minute he is completely insane.'

Brood van Heerden shared a room with Bezuidenhout. Van Heerden – like most men at Vlakplaas – disliked Bezuidenhout intensely. 'He drank cough mixture and did funny things. He would suddenly take off and for no particular reason run into the hills and mountains behind Vlakplaas.'

Bezuidenhout hated being branded an askari. Some of the white policemen even called him a 'Communist'. He was a lonely man at Vlakplaas and the black askaris didn't trust him either. 'Askaris, when they get drunk, they can't talk normal, they shout at each other. And Eugene had this sjambok, and he used to use this thing plenty times, on the askaris. He used to hammer them with this sjambok.'

Bezuidenhout conducted operations mainly on the East Rand. 'I was goofed out of my mind when we raided the house of the parents of a political detainee who'd escaped from a prison on the East Rand. We knocked at their door late at night and burst into the house. We threatened to kill his mother and tried to force her to admit that her son had phoned her the same day. The family didn't even have a phone, but it did not matter. We slapped the daughter through the face and assaulted another person in the house. We pulled a plastic bag over his face and slapped and kicked him. We hit him with a sewing machine on his back.'

In the course of this period at Vlakplaas, he shot somebody accidentally, 'tubed' a few people, drank heavily, smoked dagga and became addicted to cough mixture. It was also during this time that he met Marilyn, his wife-to-be.

One night in the ladies bar of Stardust Hotel on the East Rand Ronald caught Marilyn's eye. It was love at first sight. 'He was charming, danced well, and I was

attracted to his strange blue eyes. He asked me to marry him. At first I refused.'
But she couldn't when some time later he stopped his car in the traffic, walked
over to her, and putting a handkerchief down, went down on his knees, and asked
her again. He wanted to marry in church: 'It will then be forever,' he said to her.

She soon discovered who he was: explosives and guns in her house, his face
blackened, a body full of scars and bullet wounds, a tube that he pulled over
people's faces, cough mixture and nightmares about months in a hole, the child
he had shot, and a night he had had to spend with a corpse. He would wake up in
the night and shout at Marilyn to duck, hide and get away.

On our way to Weskoppies Marilyn told me what a good man Ronald really
was. After he had left Vlakplaas, he took his torture tube, cut it in pieces and
threw it away. But she was scared of him. He was a man who had been born into,
and lived, a life of violence. He took all his frustrations out on her.

As I sat in Weskoppies listening to him, I knew he was no Eugene de Kock
or Dirk Coetzee or Joe Mamasela. Maybe only because he'd never had the
opportunity to kill so freely and abundantly. He lied about several things. He
was never a fully fledged policeman, hadn't received any medals and was
certainly not the accomplished assassin he claimed to have been. But he had one
incredible story to tell: of a pig's head with a set of earphones.

'Dirk Coetzee was our enemy number one. Coetzee was a traitor and had to die.
We came together one night to decide how we were going to eliminate him. One
of the men volunteered: "I'll go to Lusaka and do the duckfucker." We decided,
no, that would be too risky. There was a discussion, we should poison him
through wine. You know, you take a syringe, fill it with poison, push the syringe
through the cork and then poison him. I said no, you cannot because this man is
a diabetic, he won't drink that wine. So eventually it was decided we are going
to send him a bomb.'

Bezuidenhout said there was an explosives expert at Vlakplaas, a sergeant by
the name of Steve Bosch. 'He had a safe full of explosives and other beautiful
devices. He volunteered to pack the bomb and send it to Coetzee.' One day,
Bezuidenhout said, he had to go with Bosch to a butchery in Pretoria to buy a
pig's head. The bomb was going to be tested on the head. Bezuidenhout said he
wasn't present, but he heard afterwards that the earphones were put on the pig's
head and the walkman was activated.

'There was hardly anything left. Mincemeat. Another walkman bomb was
then sent away to Coetzee.'

I remember sitting in Weskoppies staring at Bezuidenhout. Just a raving lunatic, or was there an element of truth? ANC intelligence confirmed that he had
been an MK Soldier, I knew he was based at Vlakplaas at the time that the bomb
was sent to Coetzee, and I discovered that Vlakplaas had indeed acquired the
services of an explosives expert.

Bezuidenhout signed a statement and we published his story in *Vrye Week-blad*. Police reaction was swift, and this time they had plenty of ammunition to discredit the messenger. The man was after all in a psychiatric institution.

The day after the story was published, Max du Preez and I were visited by none other than General Krappies Engelbrecht. He was heading the investigation into Bezuidenhout's allegations and had to get statements from us. As Engelbrecht was leaving, he put his arm around Max and said to him: 'Old Max, we are in actual fact on the same side. We both serve the truth.'

Of course, nothing came of Engelbrecht's investigation. Bezuidenhout was declared of sound mind by the authorities, but disappeared into obscurity. But five years later in the Pretoria Supreme Court the full story of the walkman bomb emerged.

On an autumn afternoon in May 1990, Warrant Officer Willie Nortje testified, he accompanied a team of police technical experts down to the river at Vlakplaas. They had a walkman cassette player, a set of earphones and a pig's head with them. They were going to test the prototype of a bomb they had built for Dirk Coetzee. Nortje said that Eugene De Kock often spoke about killing Coetzee. All the men hated Coetzee and agreed with their commander. 'There was talk about intercepting his diabetes medicine, or replacing it with poison, or sending him poisoned wine.'

De Kock said in his evidence that the police technical division was listening to telephone conversations between Coetzee and his wife, but that the rogue policeman was very good in maintaining telephone security and never told his wife where he was. Everything that was sent to Coetzee went through Mlangeni. General Nick van Rensburg finally gave De Kock an address for Coetzee.

Nortje said it was De Kock's idea to send a walkman cassette player. Nothing like that had ever been done before. The explosives expert, Steve Bosch, said he was instructed by De Kock to prepare a parcel bomb for Coetzee. Bosch went to the police technical division and said he wanted 'something very special'. A few days later, they told him to get a sheep's head to test the bomb. Bosch said he and Bezuidenhout went 'shopping', but the sheep's head was too expensive. Instead, they bought a 'slightly rotten' pig's head. The head was wrapped in plastic and brown paper and taken back to Vlakplaas on the back seat of Bosch's Volkswagen Golf. Nortje said the technical experts arrived with a walkman and earphones. 'I went with them to the river. The pig's head was put down, the earphones were put on and it was detonated. It blew a hole right through the pig's head.'

Looking at the pig's head afterwards, De Kock remarked how funny it would have looked with a pair of sunglasses on.

A similar kit was packed and wrapped in brown paper. Balletjies Bellingham knew Coetzee's taste in music and had to go and get a tape to send with the walk-man. He chose Neil Diamond's 'Moods'. A short while later, De Kock mentioned to Nortje: 'The parcel is in the post.'

The men waited. Weeks and months passed without anything happening. By October 1990, Coetzee had left Zambia. But on February 16 of the following year, they received the news about a parcel bomb that had exploded in Soweto. On the morning after the explosion, De Kock said to Nortje: 'Coetzee's parcel exploded. It was the walkman and Bheki Mlangeni got killed. It's a pity, but he was anyway a member of the ANC, so it's no loss.'

Seipati Mlangeni says she can never forgive Eugene de Kock. 'I think if I can see him, I can kill him. To me, he is like a vicious animal that won't look twice at its prey. He's a cruel person.'

I didn't see Ronald Bezuidenhout again until a few days before Christmas 1995. He was roaming the streets of Brakpan, east of Johannesburg, jobless, destitute and depressed. He was squatting with a black family in one of the surrounding townships. In the mean time, Marilyn had divorced him and was thinking about marrying another man.

A few weeks before I found him, he had been shot once again, this time in the buttocks. He couldn't quite explain how it had happened, but I suspect the incident was somehow related to criminal activity. Bezuidenhout said that he had quit taking cough mixture and was sober. I booked him into a seedy one-star hotel where he could spend Christmas.

A year later, Ronald and Marilyn were together again. 'I believe in him. He's getting better. We don't do anything without the Bible.'

As we walked through the garden, Marilyn showed me the graves he had made for the dogs. 'He cries when one of his goldfishes dies. He's a good man.'

Chapter Seven

Brotherhood of crime

It is the year 1991. The investigation into the murder of Bheki Mlangeni has been successfully obstructed, the Vlakplaas unit has deceived and survived the Harms Commission and State President FW de Klerk has rejected requests to disband the unit.[1]

In fact, Vlakplaas has been granted a second lease on life – a request by De Kock has been accepted that the unit's name should be changed to Section CIO and that its members will in future concentrate on fighting organised crime and will specialise in tracing illegal weapons and infiltrating smuggling routes.

'The whole unit CIO will from February 1, 1991, not involve themselves with any political aspects, and will concentrate on the maintenance of law and order in the Republic,' De Kock said.

They were not security policemen any more. In April 1991, the Security Branch was disbanded and Vlakplaas became a unit within the Crime Intelligence Service under the command of Krappies Engelbrecht.

Adriaan Vlok said this step would 'remove the police from the political playing field'. The once terrifying Vlakplaas assassins were now just bobbies on the beat – your friendly neighbourhood cops, catching thieves and smugglers and fighting crime.[2]

It was of course ludicrous of the politicians to have believed that Eugene de Kock and his unit could transform themselves into just another police unit.

Eugene de Kock had killed for so long, that it was improbable that he could be stopped by the stroke of a pen. And that is why the unit remained a death squad and killed till the bitter end. Its members continued to rob the secret fund. The Vlakplaas commander became nothing more than a common crook who was unstable, paranoid and irrational.

And yet, when he had to evaluate himself in a police questionnaire in February 1993, he said: 'I would like to stay on in the force and fulfil my ambition to become a major general one day. I am regarded as the best or one of the best counterinsurgents in the Republic and the South African Police. I am loyal, patriotic, a person with a broad vision and a dynamic commander who led very sensitive units with success. I'm a very good strategist with a broad general knowledge and insight. There is great respect for my abilities and upright and honest methods, as well as the human way in which I deal with perpetrators.'

Craig Williamson says De Kock was regarded as a 'very disciplined, loyal, calm and calculated' man. 'A man you could rely on. A man who was not, in any way, unstable or dangerous. A man who obeyed orders. That's why they needed him and continued to misuse him.'[3]

In the years after the exposure of Vlakplaas, De Kock surrounded himself with criminals, some of them within his own unit.

Captain Chappies Klopper may be the size of a rugby scrumhalf and have the appearance of innocence, but according to his own evidence he is a boyish killer with itchy fingers. He is, furthermore, a thief who stole tens of thousands of rands from the police secret fund. According to evidence in court, Klopper was heavily involved in the underworld where he became a drug smuggler and fraudster. And yet, just before his past was revealed in court, Klopper, still a policeman, was promoted to the rank of major. Klopper, once his chieftain's preferred Hun, fell out of favour when De Kock assaulted him twice.

The relationship between the two men ended abruptly in 1992 when they had a quarrel during a car journey from Cape Town to Pretoria. De Kock hit Klopper in the face, fired a shot over his head and threatened to leave his body in the Karoo for the jackals.

Klapper said his commander told him: ' No one can touch me, I'm Eugene de Kock.'

In another incident, De Kock said he had caught Klapper in a 'sexually compromising' position with a black prostitute one night in a seedy hotel in Berea in Johannesburg. De Kock said he was so upset when he found Klopper that he assaulted him.

De Kock: He could at least have gone to a room. It wasn't necessary to
use the toilet.

Judge: Did you treat him heavy-handedly there?

De Kock: I gave him a smack, your honour. I didn't hit him with the fist.

Judge: We heard it was in the bathroom?

De Kock: It was in the toilets, Your Honour.

Judge: We heard it was in the ladies' toilet?

De Kock: That is correct, Your Honour.

Judge: Why did you go to the ladies' toilet?

De Kock: No, Your Honour, I waited.

Judge: I am serious about this.

Klopper denied that he had ever used the services of a prostitute, but said that after the Colesberg incident, he decided to leave the unit and asked for a transfer to the Narcotics Bureau in Johannesburg. Klopper then decided that he was going to expose his commander's involvement in murder and fraud.

'The last words he said to me before I left is that I must watch my back and that I will one day crawl back to him.'

But before his departure from Vlakplaas, Klopper had shared eagerly in the fruits of his nefarious activities. Over a three-month period in 1992, R240 000 from the police secret fund found its way into the pockets of the Vlakplaas men.

In the early 1990s, the government announced that it was going to compensate people for handing in or finding illegal arms. The reward for an AK-47, for example, was R6 000. This gave Vlakplaas a golden opportunity to register bogus informants that had 'discovered' arms caches and to claim money for the weapons. Vlakplaas members took weapons from their own arsenal, treated them with swimming pool acid to make them look old and rusty, handed them in and wrote out claims for the bogus informants.

In April 1992, Klopper registered a bogus informant under the name of Edward Cardosa and drew R30 000 to buy weapons from a gunrunner. Klopper and members of Vlakplaas travelled to Hazyview in the Eastern Transvaal and handed in 27 AK-47s, 26 magazines, one heavy machine gun, an RPG rocket launcher and ammunition at the local police station. They said they had 'bought' the weapons in three different transactions from a gun smuggler.

When they returned to Vlakplaas, Klopper submitted a claim for R70 000 for 'Edward Cordosa', signed by De Kock and endorsed by Engelbrecht. In his motivational statement, Klopper wrote: 'The weapons they smuggle are sold exclusively to people who undertake to shoot members of the police and the Defence Force.'

Klopper said he gave the R70 000 to De Kock, who gave him R10 000 and kept the rest for himself. Klopper said he also handed the R30 000 'purchase money' to De Kock.

Klapper testified for days about false claims he had submitted for bogus informants who delivered 'exceptional services under life-threatening circumstances.' De Kock signed the claims and Engelbrecht approved the payments.

The false claims were not only restricted to weapons. Klopper testified that he received counterfeit American dollars from De Kock, which he had to hand in at the syndicate fraud unit in Pretoria and for which he wrote out a false claim for the informant who had purportedly found the dollars.

In his claim Klopper said: 'The informant, Pat Surat, took an enormous risk when he intercepted the dollars from the smuggling network. The informant saw a cricket bag full of notes, which he is still going to try and get. But to keep him motivated, an amount of R9 500 should be paid to him.'

The money was shared between De Kock, Klopper and Vlakplaas operative Charlie Chate. Another stack of counterfeit dollars was handed in at the fraud unit, and this time compensation of R20 000 was approved for 'Mr. Surat'.

At one stage, De Kock received two rhino horns and 1 743 counterfeit R50 notes from a friend in Military Intelligence. The same procedure was followed: Klopper handed the horns and false money to the fraud unit, Engelbrecht approved the claim for the bogus informant and R8 000 was shared by Klopper and De Kock.

When Klopper was transferred to the Narcotics Bureau in October 1992, he exchanged a twilight world of murder and debauchery for one of drug dealers and hookers. And according to evidence presented in court by De Kock's legal team, his criminal activity never stopped.

He befriended some of South Africa's most notorious drug barons and members of the underworld. They openly boasted that they had a 'tame cop' named Chappies. One of them, Louis John Stevens, who was described as one of the biggest drug lords in the country, was said to be 'untouchable' because 'he's got dozens of cops in his pocket'. Klopper was accused of once carrying a suitcase filled with cocaine from London to Johannesburg for Stevens.

According to evidence in court, among Klopper's underworld friends was a manager of a Johannesburg night club and brothel where Klopper would engage in sexual orgies. The manager supplied the prostitutes and Klopper the cocaine.

In gruelling cross-examination that sometimes bordered on the unethical and had nothing to do with the charges against De Kock, Klopper was accused of having perverted sexual tastes which had resulted in his expulsion from school on three different occasions . He apparently bragged about his 'numerous encounters with prostitutes'.

The fall-out between De Kock and Klopper deteriorated into the idiotic and manic when they plotted to kill one another. Willie Nortje told me that De Kock went to him and asked him to kill Klopper, who he said had become a threat to the unit. Nortje warned Klopper about De Kock's intentions, and Klopper in turn went to see convicted murderer and underworld gangster Ferdi Barnard.

'He said to me I'm one of a few people that can do a thing on my own and not talk about it. He asked me to kill De Kock and offered me R50 000 cash and a kilogram of cocaine. I said to him he's mad,' Barnard told me.[4]

As the distrust within the Vlakplaas unit grew, members started spying on one another. Klopper said they frequently made tape recordings of meetings. He said De Kock made recordings of him and several other people, while he made recordings of De Kock.

Klopper: He was like a crab. He collected everything he could get, with all respect, I don't think he slept with his wife without making a tape. He never walked without a tape. That is how the intelligence world works. Whenever we would go and see somebody, we would prepare a small tape recorder.

Judge : I have a picture in my head. Sometimes a number of people would sit around a table to have a meeting?

Klopper: Correct.

Judge: You are 20 people around the table. Now you started having the meeting.

Klopper: Yes, sometimes it would be like that.

Judge: Now who gave the sign that you should all switch in your tape recordings?

Klopper: No, it didn't work like that.

Judge: But everybody knew the other one had a recorder?

Klopper: That is correct.

Judge: And at one stage everybody is diving to switch on their recordings?

Klopper: You would switch on the machine before you enter the meeting. You could hide the machine on your body.

Judge: You know, it must have been beautiful to see all of you there with dark glasses, with your jackets and hats and everybody knows the other one has switched on his recorder.

De Kock did indeed make tape recordings of many meetings and conversations. Ferdi Barnard says: 'He had certain tape recordings, he played one to me. He's a very wise man and he took out insurance. Everybody in intelligence does that. Generals that are well-known are speaking on the tapes. If De Kock decides to come out of his corner and make it public, there will be things that would make his trial look like Mickey Mouse.'

De Kock said in court that he had two steel cases full of evidence and records he had kept over the years. But he said he destroyed his documentation and records when the investigation against him started. Vossie de Kock says the evidence was stored at his home, but he burnt it on the request of his brother.

During the early 1990s, De Kock registered some of the country's worst criminals as informants and paid them from the secret fund. These gangsters introduced him and his men to the underworld and used the protection they received from Vlakplaas to further their own criminal activity.

The first was Ferdi Barnard, one of the country's most despised and feared killers. A convicted murderer, he worked for the CCB and the Directorate of Covert Collection, both SADF death squad and dirty tricks units, from 1988 until at least the end of 1992. In the process, Barnard befriended De Kock and became his confidant.

But Barnard is not only a former death squad operative and murderer, but also a diamond smuggler, brothel boss and drug addict. Another paid informant was Corrie Goosen, a convicted diamond smuggler and close associate of Barnard. Goosen was a registered informant of Vlakplaas and the Directorate of Covert Collection. Goosen says he earned between R10 000 and R12 000 per month working for the two secret units.

In 1992, Goosen and Barnard managed a brothel for Military Intelligence in the northern suburbs of Johannesburg. The brothel was a front where informants were briefed and contacts entertained. The Vlakplaas men were regular visitors to the brothel. Vlakplaas donated furniture and De Kock provided funds to set up the establishement.[5]

This is how Goosen describes the venture to me: 'We had the best girls, they were recruited from all over South Africa. They were sometimes paid up to R1 000 a night. The Vlakplaas men loved the women. Well, if you see the girls, they were the best.'

Barnard says he frequently invited the Vlakplaas men for a braai at the brothel. What happened there, I asked him? 'Oh, just drink and braai. Tell each other stories of heroism and that, you know what the guys are like.'

Goosen says De Kock 'never touched a woman'. However, some of the Vlakplaas men were regular customers. 'They didn't have to pay. Sometimes they felt that they wanted to give the girls something to make them feel ... but they didn't have to pay. Military was paying for the girls.'

I asked Ferdi Barnard whether it was true that De Kock had also been involved in diamond smuggling, as some of his former men claimed. 'If the right thing comes along I would say to him look, do you have a buyer for this or for that? I'm one of those people who believe that not all the diamonds belong to Mr Harry Oppenheimer. If it comes along, and I don't have to steal it and I can make some money, then I will. I'm not saying that's what we did, but we did things like that.'

Acting on information supplied to them by Barnard and Goosen, Vlakplaas men even swooped on a group of diamond dealers. Barnard was with them: 'De Kock and his team came in there like they were hitting a house of terrorist infiltrators. I just heard people screaming and shouting. There wasn't even a firearm on the premises, but they broke the doors down, and they pushed all of those people to the ground with guns against their heads, pulled their hair out and stuff like that. The poor captain from the Pietersburg Gold and Diamond Branch was like a nervous wreck. He couldn't believe what he was seeing. Things like that happen when an anti-terrorist unit suddenly has to fight ordinary crime. They were completely out of their depth.'

The duo of Barnard and Goosen and their fellow gangsters devised a scheme to steal diamonds and money in what is known as a 'knock'. In many cases, they would act as middlemen and bring diamond dealers, prospectors and potential buyers together, promising huge profits. The buyers usually didn't exist or were fellow gangsters, and as soon as the diamonds were produced, the middlemen or the gangsters stole them. Victims would be threatened afterwards and were usually too scared to testify against them.

Goosen and Barnard used and abused their connections with Vlakplaas to further their criminal exploits. A Pretoria lawyer, Evadne de Jager, became a victim of Barnard and Goosen in June 1992 when a client approached her to help him to exchange seven billion Angolan kwanzas for American dollars. Barnard and Goosen introduced themselves as the security agents for the kwanzas, which were allegedly in storage somewhere in South Africa.[6]

Goosen wore a leather jacket with the emblem of Badger Arms, a close corporation formed by De Kock in January 1991 to deal in firearms and ammunition. The emblem of Badger Arms, a honeybadger against a red silhouette of southern Africa, was the same as that of Vlakplaas.

De Jager was persuaded to hand R200 000 to Goosen and Barnard to get the kwanzas out of storage, but they simply took the money and disappeared. When De Jager laid a complaint against the two, she was arrested on charges of theft from her trust account and detained for four days. She was eventually released on bail of R50 000. More than two years later, the case against her was withdrawn.

De Jager testified before the Goldstone Commission in March 1994 about the countless death threats she had received and said she believed that Eugene de Kock was involved in the scheme and had been paid R10 000. I don't know whether or not De Kock was an accomplice, but what is a fact is that Barnard and Goosen made use of De Kock's company, took the money and disappeared.

Several years ago Goosen was a South African kickboxing champion and was invited to fight in the United States. 'I didn't have expenses and De Kock brought me 15 000 American dollars at the airport. He's a respectable guy, and for me he's like a father.'

When Goosen was arrested in the early 1990s for trying to break into the offices of the Pietersburg Gold and Diamond Branch, Eugene de Kock phoned the local commander. Says Goosen: 'I was caught for dealing in illegal diamonds, and De Kock heard of that, and he was personally involved in solving the case for me. He went to Pietersburg and spoke to the guys there and said I was working for them. I was released.'

Goosen said De Kock often spoke to him to try and persuade him to stop most of his criminal activity. Even Krappies Engelbrecht was involved in trying to rehabilitate him.

'Krappies wanted to see me and Ferdi Barnard, because Ferdi's father (a former police colonel) phoned him and said he must talk to us.'

'About what?' I asked him.

'Well, we also had other activities, like diamond smuggling.'

Riaan Stander says that De Kock and his men were at one stage involved in smuggling unrefined gold. 'Gold pieces came through my office, which they were using at the time.'[7]

A business associate of Goosen and Barnard, an Australian by the name of Bill Douven, said he attended a meeting in Hillbrow in Johannesburg at which Barnard introduced De Kock to him. De Kock said he had money in Mauritius and Switzerland and wanted to buy gold, platinum and diamonds. Douven didn't trust him and told him to 'get stuffed'.[8]

According to Klopper, De Kock was involved in a car theft scheme, but there is no evidence to corroborate this claim. However; De Kock said in court that he was asked by Krappies Engelbrecht and Hermanus du Plessis to 'neutralise' one of his men, Warrant Officer Piet Botha, because he was involved in car smuggling. He said he refused to do it and spoke to Botha about it the following day.

Willie Nortje testified that Botha had been arrested in connection with cross-border car smuggling, but De Kock warned head office that if the case was pursued, Botha might talk about covert operations. General Basie Smit intervened and the charges against Botha were dropped.

De Kock's paranoia was illustrated by the formidable private arsenal he kept at home. He had licenses for two Glock pistols, a .22 revolver, a .308 hunting rifle, two semiautomatic machine pistols, a Draganov sharpshooter rifle, two shotguns, a Tokarev pistol and a .38 revolver. His arms collection included two machine pistols with silencers, a pistol with a silencer, two 40 millimetre grenade launchers with 80 grenades, four RPG rocket launchers, a variety of hand grenades, ten minigrenades and explosives.

'I didn't have that many weapons because you can only handle one at a time,' he said in court. When asked why he had all these weapons, he said: 'I am well acquainted with the history of Africa. I am a veteran of lost ideologies. I went through the whole Rhodesian and Namibian debacle and saw what happened in Mozambique and Angola and thought the same was going to happen here. I decided to arm myself and my people should it later on become necessary to defend myself or form a self-defence unit.'

He said most of his men at Vlakplaas had taken AK-47s, hand grenades and explosives to arm themselves. Many generals had licensed AK-47s and Vlakplaas had had to supply them with ammunition.

De Kock said his marriage had deteriorated to the extent that his wife wanted to leave him. 'She couldn't continue with this type of life. The media never left me alone. I once told her that she should perhaps leave the country. She couldn't understand why. I took her to the bedroom when the children were asleep and told her about Vlakplaas, that it wasn't just a unit for rehabilitated terrorists. I think she then realised what danger there may be for her and the children.'

He said she issued divorce papers against him at one stage because he was more interested in his work than in his family. 'I must say, if I had to choose between my family and my work, I would have chosen my work. I was over-protective towards my family and changed my home into a fort. I phoned my wife in the mornings to make sure she was safe and wasn't being followed. I would phone the school to make sure the kids were safe. One day there were rumours that black children would come and toyi-toyi at the school to demand its opening to all races. I took a heavy machine gun and a grenade launcher and waited in front of the school. If they had tried to take over the school that day, there would have been a bloodbath.'

Despite the new role of Vlakplaas in supposedly fighting organised crime, De Kock knew that at some stage the unit would have to be disbanded and that despite his ambition to become a general, he had no future in a new, post-apartheid police force. He would never be acceptable to an ANC government.

'We spoke about that at length. Sometimes the okes were not sober, you know, and then they would become quite heavy. Certain threats would be made against the upper management and certain politicians. At times De Kock was like a time bomb going off,' says Barnard.

Contrary to evidence in court, Eugene de Kock said he only started enriching himself towards the end of his career at Vlakplaas. 'When it became clear that I had no future left in the police force, Engelbrecht said to me it was time I looked after myself. He became very emotional when he said I should remember him if he was to get into trouble one day. I started writing out false claims for myself for R250 000 from the secret fund. If I hadn't gone on pension in April 1993, I could have withdrawn another R200 000. I felt if I could do it for others, I could do it for myself as well. It could technically be seen as theft, but I wouldn't have done it unless I had permission to do so.'

Judge: 'I want to tell you: I get shivers down my spine if I listen to how you worked with money.'

The pilfering of the secret fund became very much a family affair when De Kock registered his brother, Vossie de Kock, as an informant under the name 'Deon Brink'. A former Vlakplaas operative, Snorre Vermeulen, was registered under the name 'Theo Parker'. At the time both Vossie de Kock and Vermeulen had been retired early on grounds of ill health.

This was how De Kock motivated payments of R2 000 a month to the two men: 'The above-mentioned individuals are well-connected with weapons smuggling from Mozambique via Swaziland to Thokoza. The weapons are sold in Thokoza and Soweto to people who are involved in violence and serious crimes like robberies and murders. These informants have enabled us to trace cocaine, mandrax, counterfeit money, rhino horn, ivory, stolen vehicles and weapons.'

Chappies Klopper said in his evidence that Vermeulen and Vossie de Kock were compensated for the work they had done during the time that De Kock and some of his men engaged in the smuggling and illegal sale of white mealie meal. In 1992, only yellow mealie meal could be sold legally. Zulu people, Klopper said, didn't like the yellow mealie meal and the white meal was sold to them illegally. De Kock used Vlakplaas trucks to transport the meal from a farm in Natal to Pretoria, from where it was sold and distributed.

The secret fund, estimated to have contained R9 million in the early 1990s, also paid for an Indian Ocean island holiday for De Kock and his wife, an untold number of Glock pistols supplied to Vlakplaas members, and a succession of hunting trips and overseas holidays for Chappies Klopper and Willie Nortje.

De Kock looked after his men well. The secret fund paid for Snorre Vermeulen and Lionel Snyman to undergo advanced deep-sea diving courses and for Dougie Holtzhausen to go on a pilot's course.

Nortje said in his evidence that De Kock felt bitter about the way in which the police had treated him and that he had developed an attitude that he and members of his unit 'should take everything we can get'.

Eugene de Kock's hatred for Dirk Coetzee never died and despite the failure of his first attempt to have him killed, he decided in 1992 to try again. At the time, Coetzee was living in an apartment in London with his two sons, Dirkie and Calla.

Former Vlakplaas operative Leon Flores, then working for Military Intelligence, was despatched to London to enlist the support of Irish terrorist groups in the monitoring of Coetzee. Flores had R10 000 in cash with him as a first payment on R100 000 that the London connection had requested as payment for the killing of Coetzee. Flores was accompanied by Pamela du Randt, a bottle-blonde Military Intelligence captain on official business to the United Kingdom to discredit the ANC by leaking information about their links to the Irish Republican Army to the media. She was code-named 'Olga'.[9]

But the two spies proved to be embarrassingly inept. They were double-crossed and outwitted by their British contact, who turned out to be a British intelligence agent. From the moment the 'Bonny-and-Clyde' couple entered the United Kingdom in April 1992, they were monitored by British intelligence, which stayed on their tracks throughout their four-day stay.

Flores and Du Randt met Ulster loyalists in Ireland, with whom they discussed the monitoring of Coetzee with a view to assassinating the dissident policeman. When the luckless pair attempted to leave the United Kingdom, the British antiterrorist unit arrested them at Heathrow Airport. They were searched, medically examined, processed and officially taken into custody for questioning.

Flores admitted his role in the Coetzee affair, which led to a secret British government memorandum to the South African government: 'Flores and Du Randt's involvement with Irish terrorist groups and their planning of a murder to take place on the streets of London is not an issue which Her Majesty's Government can ignore. Our objective is to see the issue fully investigated to our satisfaction.'

The two spies were deported and upon their arrival in South Africa, they were debriefed and interrogated by counter-intelligence operatives of Military Intelligence. Three top-secret Military Intelligence reports, 42 pages in all, were tabled during the inquest into the death of Bheki Mlangeni. Although the documents did not cast any new light on the walkman parcel bomb, they did reveal De Kock's obsession with Coetzee. It also emerged that Military Intelligence had known nothing of the plot to kill Coetzee and that Flores was a rogue who had acted without the sanction of the military.

However, it also emerged from the court documents that De Kock had contacted a National Intelligence agent called 'Kennedy' with an offer to expose a secret network, known as the 'third force', which was fuelling violence in South Africa in order to derail the peace process. De Kock wanted indemnity in return for his information.

De Kock said in evidence in his own trial that he never planned to kill Coetzee and that the money given to Flores was merely for monitoring of Coetzee, which was done on orders from 'higher up'. However, Willie Nortje asserted that De Kock had told him that he wanted to have Coetzee killed in London.

Flores was fired from Military Intelligence for disobeying orders. De Kock said Flores was destitute and that Vlakplaas had to look after him and his family for about a year using the secret fund. De Kock said that he spent about R100 000 on Flores and his family.

Despite the fact that Eugene de Kock had embarrassed the government of FW de Klerk, broken his promise of February 1991 that his unit would only seek to maintain law and order in the Republic, and planned the murder of a South African citizen abroad, no steps were taken against him. It was clear that he acted with as much impunity as ever before and that the Vlakplaas dirty tricks had not stopped.

Chapter Eight

The shooting party

It was a peculiar group of men, armed with semi-automatic rifles, pistols and hand grenades, that assembled at three o'clock on the morning of March 26, 1992, just outside Nelspruit on the road to Komatipoort in the Eastern Transvaal.

One man was portly and balding, another burly and bearded, while a third was small and looked hardly old enough to be out of short trousers. The leader of the unit was a big, stocky man with a thick pair of glasses.

It was a Vlakplaas death squad, led by Colonel Eugene de Kock. The henchmen were all members of his 'inner circle', people who could be trusted and who knew how to kill. Amongst them were Chappies Klapper, Willie Nortje, Rolf Gevers and Dougie Holtzhausen.

The men were about to teach five would-be bank robbers a lesson. The robbers, they believed, were part of an ANC crime syndicate which robbed banks on behalf of Winnie Mandela, former wife of ANC leader Nelson Mandela. In fact, one of the robbers was her former driver.

Some of the men were still slightly intoxicated from heavy drinking sessions the previous two days. But on that early morning, they were tense, their fingers eager to squeeze the triggers of their automatic rifles.

The previous night, the men had already decided not to take any prisoners. They were going to kill the robbers and set their vehicle alight to destroy all evidence. They would say afterwards they had been shot at, had returned fire and that the robbers' minibus had exploded.

At 3.20 a.m. the Vlakplaas men had got the message: the minibus was on its way. Twenty minutes later, the unsuspecting driver drove into an ambush. A small inferno erupted around him as the Vlakplaas men pumped more than 220 bullets into the minibus. Two of the passengers who were still alive following the attack were executed afterwards.

Two hand grenades and two AK-47 assault rifles were thrown into the minibus, it was sprinkled with fuel and set alight, exactly as planned the night before.

One of the Vlakplaas men who was apparently unhappy about the operation knelt down and started praying.

A few minutes after the ambush, all that remained was the burnt-out minibus, pock-marked on all sides with bullet holes, and the bodies of three charred men. One was still at the steering wheel, his eye sockets staring, his hands welded to the steering wheel. Two men lay sprawled behind him, their limbs grotesquely distorted. The body of another man lay in the road, having been flung there by the explosion of hand grenades planted in the vehicle.

It was a perfect operation, except for one small hiccup: the fifth would-be robber was not in the minibus. He was waiting for his accomplices at a nearby filling station. De Kock despatched a team to take care of him.

For the rest of the men, celebrations followed. They drank at the Fig Tree Hotel afterwards, where Chappies Klopper would boast to people in the bar: 'I emptied my whole magazine into the chest of the driver.'

In fact, the night before and the day that followed were nothing but an orgy of murder and booze.

Christiaan Willem Geldenhuys is a balding and portly man who resembles the prop of a small club's fourth rugby team. Geldenhuys was a policeman for 27 years, in a career that included service in the security police, in Koevoet and in the Murder and Robbery Unit. When he left the force, he had reached the rank of captain but was suffering from post-traumatic stress disorder.

From early 1992, the Murder and Robbery Unit in Pretoria and the Vlakplaas unit undertook joint operations, ostensibly acting against criminals who were planning to committ armed robberies.

Geldenhuys was known as a heavy drinker, a 'man's man'. A month before the Nelspruit ambush, there was a similar operation near Pretoria, in which three would-be robbers, two of them unarmed, were mowed down by a team of Vlakplaas operatives and murder and robbery detectives. At a celebration following the Pretoria shootings, Geldenhuys drank so much that he fell into a fire and then got into a fight.

Geldenhuys was a friend of Eugene de Kock, a man he admired, respected and killed with. But as he was getting into the witness box in February 1995, the policeman was changing sides. His demeanour left no doubt that this was not where he wanted to be.

On his right was the presiding judge, Mr Justice Willem van der Merwe, with the big crest bearing the words 'EUV' (unity is strength) above his head.

But Geldenhuys and De Kock were united no more. Once they stood together as a deadly killing squad, but on that day, Geldenhuys turned against his friend.

Geldenhuys was witness number 54 on the list of 163 witnesses the state intended to call to prove the former Vlakplaas commander guilty of, amongst others, murdering the four would-be bank robbers and their accomplice.

Geldenhuys was the first important witness to give an account of the Nelspruit ambush and another murder that followed later that day. He would be followed by a host of state witnesses, many of whom had participated in the killings.

When Geldenhuys entered the witness stand, a muscular, blonde man in row three of the public gallery muttered angrily and audibly.

'That's Rolf Gevers, one of Eugene's men,' somebody told me. I tried to speak to him, but he wouldn't engage in conversation.

At the time, Gevers was still a member of the faithful band of 'old boys' who presented a united front against witnesses like Klopper and Geldenhuys. During recesses, they filed towards the dock to shake the Colonel's hand and bring him hamburgers or hot dogs. But more important, they were always ready to provide De Kock's legal counsel with ammunition to discredit state witnesses.

However, in July 1995, self-preservation triumphed over loyalty when the 'old boys' switched sides and were whisked away into a witness-protection programme. Their empty seats in the public gallery appeared to be an ominous sign for Eugene de Kock.

A day or two before the ambush, the Vlakplaas men started the journey to Nelspruit. Rolf Gevers and a colleague, Charlie Chate, travelled together. They arrived around lunchtime at the historic village of Pilgrims Rest and went to the Royal Hotel for a drink. They sat there until dark and drank beer, rum and brandy.

Soon after they left the hotel, Gevers fell asleep behind the wheel and overturned the car. He spent a night in hospital, but was discharged and declared fit and ready for the operation.

Sergeant Dougie Holtzhausen and Warrant Officer Willie Nortje drove together. On their way, they stopped at a farm where they drank some *mampoer* (peach brandy). Their combi ran out of petrol. Later that day, they arrived at the Drum Rock Hotel in Nelspruit.

Eugene de Kock and Captain Chappies Klopper arrived at the Drum Rock Hotel with 'two typists from Vlakplaas' with whom they disappeared 'for about three hours'.

When Chappies Klopper took the stand, his exceptional youthful looks belied his testimony as he talked of drinking at roadside pubs on the way to a killing. 'We stopped at all the hotels next to the road to have a drink. I can't remember how many places it was, but we stopped basically everywhere for a drink. I was quite drunk when I got to Nelspruit.'

The typists, Klopper said, came along 'as an excuse to get out of the office'. Like a bright schoolboy in a quiz show, Klopper sucked on his lower lip, eagerly awaiting the next question.

'It was a Volkswagen Jetta, Your Honour,' he replied to a question on what kind of car he was driving. Then, after a small pause: 'Sixteen valves.'

It was agreed from the outset that no prisoners would be taken, and on the eve of the operation, which was spent at the Drum Rock Hotel overlooking a valley outside Nelspruit, plans were laid to plant weapons in the minibus carrying the victims before setting it alight to destroy evidence and to deceive investigators.

Geldenhuys said a prime motive for the operation was financial. The policemen would claim reward money for the recovered arms – which they had planted

– and R20 000 as payment to the informer, Ben van Zyl, who would lure the targets to their death.

Ben van Zyl testified that he became involved with the Vlakplaas unit after leaving the South African Police in 1989. While working as a private detective he assisted Holtzhausen in the arrest of a woman for possession of AK-47 rifles. Afterwards, he became a Vlakplaas informant.

Van Zyl met Tiso Leballo, purveyor of cocaine and AK-47s and sometime driver of Winnie Mandela, in 1991. Van Zyl told Vlakplaas that Leballo was part of a gang acting on behalf of Winnie Mandela and which engaged in robbery. In fact, Van Zyl told them he had been personally introduced to her.

Holtzhausen devised a plan to involve Leballo and his accomplices in a robbery at Coin Security in Nelspruit. The plan was aborted when the robbers failed to arrive. But a month later Van Zyl, known to Leballo and the four others only as 'John', persuaded them to try again.

Van Zyl convinced the five robbers to rob Coin Security in Nelspruit on the basis that he had financial problems. His bank had put pressure on him about a R20 000 overdraft, he told them. He nevertheless believed the men were robbers and they should, therefore, be killed.

'I felt these were robbers. They don't ask for or give any mercy. According to our source, they were given military training by the ANC. I still regarded the ANC and the PAC as the enemy. If my adrenalin starts pumping, I want to destroy the enemy,' Holtzhausen testified.

The Vlakplaas men were told that the would-be robbers were previously involved in a robbery in Witbank, in which a white woman was shot through the head. 'Therefore, they had to die, because an innocent white woman died going to the bank. She had to kneel before she was shot,' said Klopper. But by the time of the Vlakplaas operation, Joseph Malinga and seven others had already been arrested in connection with the Witbank murder.

Leballo and his accomplices were told by Van Zyl that he would supply them with a minibus and AK-47s. The minibus, supplied by Vlakplaas, had belonged to a Springs hotel owner and friend of De Kock who was in financial trouble and needed the vehicle stolen to claim insurance.

The ambush was to take place under an overhead bridge on the road between Nelspruit and White River. Alerted by police radio that the minibus was approaching, the policemen took up their pre-arranged positions.

Holtzhausen: 'When the first shot goes off, your adrenalin starts pumping. You act automatically. Somebody can shout at you to stop shooting, but you keep going. You shoot until the enemy lies still and is out of action.'

Klopper: 'I stood in front of the row of people. I had to shoot the driver. I emptied my magazine on him. The minibus stopped. When we got closer, we could hear groaning coming from the bus. I fired shots in the direction of the sounds.

The person who sat on the left-hand side looked as though he was trying to get out of the window of the minibus. We couldn't miss him. We shot him.'

Constable Johannes Swart: 'I moved towards the vehicle, and heard someone moaning in the back. Klopper was right next to me when I heard someone shout: 'Finish up!'. One of the men in the back tried to get up. I fired about five shots into his chest.'

Willie Nortje said one of the victims was lying next to the minibus. 'He was burning and at one stage De Kock said to me I must shoot him. I said to him, no man, in any case he's going to die because he's badly burnt.'

Holtzhausen: 'I ran back to get an AK and a hand grenade. One of the passengers hung out of the window with a wound in his neck. Everybody was quiet by now and looked dead to me. I took the AK and fired shots inside the minibus so that there would be cartridges. Chate was standing next to me with a can of petrol. I threw the AK and two hand grenades, their pins still in place, into the minibus. Chate sprinkled petrol into the minibus and set it alight.'

Vlakplaas operative Jannie Hanekom was unhappy about the operation. He fired only two shots with his nine millimeter pistol, and it was said that he afterwards knelt down and started praying.

Eugene de Kock was not supposed to be involved in the shooting because he had been involved in a similar incident at Piet Retief in June 1988 when nine ANC infiltrators had been killed. But according to evidence, he emptied at least one magazine onto the minibus.

'He just couldn't help himself. He had to shoot,' said Klopper.

Before investigators arrived from Nelspruit, Klopper pulled his car across the road and set up a blue police light on the roof in support of the pre-arranged cover story that the minibus had sped past a police roadblock and that the occupants had opened fire on the police.

Within hours of the shooting, General Krappies Engelbrecht arrived at the scene, and refused to allow the Nelspruit police to take statements from the task force 'until we had talked in Pretoria'.

A few days later, the close-knit cabal met in De Kock's office to collude in preparing their statements, which were then amended 'three or four times' by Engelbrecht. 'I was fired upon from the minibus. Bullets were flying past me. If my life and that of my colleagues were not in mortal danger, I would not have fired on the minibus,' Geldenhuys lied in his affidavit.

'Suddenly there was automatic gunfire from the minibus. We returned fire, whereupon it burst into flames,' swore Chappies Klopper.

'We wanted to prevent a tragedy and decided to arrest the suspects before they could rob a bank,' Holtzhausen lied.

Minutes after the ambush, informant Ben van Zyl said to Eugene de Kock: 'Tiso Leballo was not in the minibus. If we don't get him quickly, I'm a dead man. He will recognise me.'

Leballo had temporarily escaped death by waiting in a separate vehicle at a filling station for his accomplices. De Kock ordered his men to take care of the problem by kidnapping him and 'getting rid of him'.

Captain Rolf Gevers was the senior officer in charge of the killing of Leballo. In August 1995, he also took the witness stand and in a clear, calm voice, recalled an event of unspeakable horror – of how they had killed Tiso Leballo and disposed of his body.

The judge stared at him for long periods of time. Gevers mostly looked straight ahead of him, avoiding the eyes of De Kock.

'You ask no questions, you hear no lies,' he said in court when asked why he followed illegal orders from Eugene de Kock.

Shortly after being instructed by his commander to take care of Leballo, Gevers met two black Vlakplaas policemen outside Nelspruit. They had somebody in the boot of the car. It was Tiso Leballo.

'He was blindfolded. We took him out, tied his hands, and stuffed a piece of cloth into his mouth. We put him back into the boot of our car.'

For the remainder of the day, Gevers and his accomplices drove around with Leballo tied up in the boot. They had to wait for two colleagues to go back to Pretoria to fetch explosives with which to get rid of the body.

They sat drinking for several hours under a tree near Ohrigstad waiting for their colleagues to return, while the car with Leballo in the boot was parked in the sun. It was late summer in the Eastern Transvaal, and Gevers said it was hot, but they never thought about the man's agony in the boot. He was in any event going to die.

They eventually took Leballo to an old open-cast asbestos mine near Penge that was completely deserted. They took their captive to one of the mining ruins where they interrogated him.

'We started questioning the suspect. We were rough with him. We asked him about illegal weapons transactions. We knew he was Winnie Mandela's driver and we asked him about weapons. We hit and kicked him, but he couldn't tell us anything we wanted to know.'

It was then time to kill him. According to Gevers, Warrant Officer Duiwel Brits took him aside and asked him who was going to do the shooting. 'I said I will. He gave me a loaded .38 revolver. I stuck it in my pants.'

Gevers told Leballo that they were satisfied with his answers and were going to release him and take him back.

'We drove back to the vicinity of the open-cast mine. When we got to the edge of the open-cast area, Brits stopped the car and said he saw something interesting and wanted to go and have a look. We said to Tiso he must come with and I took him by the arm. We were friendly with him. We went to the middle of the open-cast mine, where Brits suddenly grabbed Tiso. 'Shoot! Shoot!' he shouted. I took the revolver out, held it against Tiso's heart, pulled the trigger, but the first shot didn't go off.'

Leballo writhed and wriggled, and according to evidence in court, might have wet his pants at that stage. Brits, still holding him, shouted again: 'Shoot! Shoot!'

'I shot him three times in the chest. He fell to the ground,' Gevers said.

Another policeman who was on the scene remembered it slightly differently. 'I saw him being shot in the head as well. The blood splattered on my shoes,' testified Johannes Swart.

They took the dead man's clothes off. 'Warrant Officer Vermeulen and Sergeant Chate had two or three bags with them. There were yellow and blue sausage-like explosives in the bag.'

They put the dead man in a sitting position – which Vlakplaas operatives called the 'Buddha position' – and tied the explosives to him.

'We drove a kilometre away, and detonated the explosives. It was already dark and we went back with torches. There was just a big hole in the ground where he had sat. We went to a nearby ruin where we spent the night. Late that night we burnt his clothes in a big drum. Tiso had brown leather shoes which Brits took because he said they were too nice to destroy,' said Gevers.

The men drank until they fell over. Early the next morning, they went back to the place where they had blown Leballo up.

'For the next three hours, we walked around looking for pieces of human flesh to make certain that we had destroyed all evidence. The biggest piece we got was the size of a finger nail, only about half a kilogram of flesh and bone. We held this in our hands. We put the pieces of flesh in the hole and blew them up. We searched again for pieces of flesh and blew them up again.'

When asked under cross-examination how he felt about the operation, Gevers simply said: 'It's not nice to shoot a person.'

Swart said: 'The whole incident bothered me. It was not a good thing that we had done. It was wrong, and it shocked me.'

The men left and went back to Nelspruit where they bought more liquor for the road. Before they arrived in Pretoria, they stopped again for liquor. When they got back to Vlakplaas, De Kock told them they could claim R2 000 for the next five months 'for a job well done'.

When Gevers testified about the murder of Leballo, it wasn't the first time Mr Justice van der Merwe had heard a tale of how a body was reduced to nothing. Tiso Leballo wasn't the first victim to be blown up by Vlakplaas.

Eugene de Kock testified that long before the death of Leballo, he had taken an askari to Penge mine to blow him up. The askari, Johannes Maboti, escaped from Vlakplaas and allegedly became Winnie Mandela's lover. He was re-arrested by the security police and given to De Kock to kill. 'I shot him dead, but walked away when they blew him up. That wasn't my strong point.'

Earlier in the trial, Chappies Klopper had described how he and three other Vlakplaas men had used 'five or six explosions' to obliterate the corpse of Sweet Sambo, a suspect who had died during interrogation.

After each blast, they scoured the bush for pieces of body and bone, making a pile out of these which was then blown up again. The rest would be speedily removed by ants.

'But how did you collect the pieces?' the judge asked. 'You did it, tell me. Show me how you did it.'

Klopper held out his hands and showed how he had carried the grisly load. He said: 'We picked up pieces until our hands were full.' His voice faltered, his head dropped and he gasped for breath.

When I spoke to Klopper afterwards about Sweet Sambo, he just shook his head and said: 'We did it. We did it for Eugene de Kock. Fuck knows why. But I still suffer from it. You don't forget a handful of human flesh.'

Just after the Nelspruit killings, the Vlakplaas men celebrated the success of the operation. Ferdi Barnard was also there: 'Chappies Klopper and some of the other members told me how they had shot the robbers, and how the one guy got blown out of the minibus. And still in great detail, with a lot of laughing and that, told me the oke was on fire. Another oke was also lying there, and they didn't know if he said bye-bye or whatever, but Klopper told me how he emptied his R-5 into that man. Klopper with his angelic and nice boyish face, he said that to me.'

In comparison with Klopper, Rolf Gevers appeared to be an accomplished and experienced soldier. He became a policeman in 1980 when he was only 18 years old. He spent many years with the Security Branch in Namibia before joining Vlakplaas in 1991.

But by December 1994, he had gone on early retirement at the age of 32. He suffers from post-traumatic stress disorder and severe depression.

Psychologist Dr Nicky Swartz says his disease is 'permanent, it's irreversible, it's chronic. We see depression, we see aggression, we see frustration, we see isolation. The person feels that he does not fit into society any more.'

Gevers saved his own skin by testifying against De Kock. Maybe his punishment will be that he will have to live what psychologists call 'a living hell' for the rest of his life.

Somebody told me later that Gevers has a son of about five. I've since then wondered: what is the boy going to do when he grows up and learns of his father's atrocities? How is Rolf Gevers ever going to explain them to his son?

Several other men who participated in the Nelspruit ambush and murder of Leballo suffer from post-traumatic stress disorder. Christiaan Geldenhuys is one of them. Snorre Vermeulen and Charlie Chate, the men who packed the explosives around Tiso Leballo, also left the force after suffering serious trauma. Johannes Swart, the man with blood on his shoes, suffers from the same illness. So does Duiwel Brits, the policeman who held Leballo.

De Kock said that several of his men had to go for psychiatric treatment. 'Two or three landed in Weskoppies (Psychiatric Hospital) for two or three weeks. But I didn't ask them about their symptoms. It was very sensitive and people didn't want to speak about it.'

Sergeant Dougie Holtzhausen, who supplied the information that led to the ambush, testified against De Kock one day after waking up from yet another session of sleep therapy. He had been hospitalised several times and was also treated for alcohol abuse.

'Our lives have been destroyed. I suffer from aggression against my family. I drink a lot, so much that I sometimes forget about certain things.'

When Holtzhausen testified, he asked the judge for a postponement so that he could take his medication. 'I am not sleeping at the moment, because if I take my pills it takes me a long time in the morning to recuperate. Here where I am sitting, I am under enormous pressure. I feel like a traitor. I don't want to testify against De Kock. I have a problem with that.'

Judge: 'You seem to be close to tears. Is that so? You nod your head. Do you want us to postpone?'

Chapter Nine

A hidden hand

January 12, 1991, and as more than 100 people were praying and mourning at a night vigil organised for a slain ANC member, a gang of raiders hurled a hand grenade into the tent and opened fire with AK-47s. Thirty-eight people were killed and 40 injured in one of the most brutal attacks in the war between ANC comrades and Inkatha impis in and around Johannesburg's strife-torn townships.[1] Twelve Inkatha members were later arrested in connection with the attack. Three of the men were confidants and associates of the Transvaal youth leader of Inkatha, Themba Khoza.

A few months earlier, Khoza and his three confidants had been arrested for the illegal possession of firearms when weapons, including an AK-47, were found in the boot of his car. Khoza was later acquitted because of lack of evidence. Where did Khoza and the Zulu impis get the weapons used in the attack and transported in the boot of his car?

In 1991 and 1992 virtual full-scale civil war raged in Natal, while townships in and around Johannesburg were on fire as ANC comrades and Inkatha impis did battle. At the time, National Party politicians said it was simply 'black-on-black' violence and that most of the weapons had been smuggled into South Africa through Mozambique and Swaziland, and distributed in the townships.

Anyone who watched television news in the two years after the unbanning of the ANC in February 1990, would have been an armchair witness to horrific scenes of blacks murdering blacks in South Africa's townships. Ordinary people could have been forgiven for reacting with despair to the brutality and barbarism in the townships, and for having concluded that it might be best, after all, if whites continued to govern the country.

According to the Human Rights Commission, more than 20 000 people died in political violence in South Africa between the mid 1980s and April 1994. More than 1 200 people died between August 1990 and March 1991 in townships in and around Johannesburg.[2]

People on all sides were both perpetrators and victims. But the conflict was not a matter of acts of spontaneous violence carried out at random by foot soldiers. On the one hand, supporters of the United Democratic Front (UDF) and the ANC were the victims of Inkatha death squads, set up, trained, armed and supported by the apartheid government and its security forces. On the other hand, numerous

Inkatha supporters were the targets of death squad actions launched by elements of Umkhonto we Sizwe, self-defence units and militant comrades.

This 'hidden hand' fomenting violence in South Africa's townships and in Natal became known as the 'third force'. Since his release in February 1990, Nelson Mandela had warned FW de Klerk and his government that rather than stopping the bloodshed, the security forces had become embroiled in the violence through supporting and arming Inkatha.

Commenting on the allegations of a third force, Adriaan Vlok said: 'We are investigating it with vigour, because if there are people behind it, if there is a so-called third force, then ideally we would like to catch them … but so far we have found no evidence.'[3]

Mandela warned that what South Africa was facing was the beginning of a Renamo-style organisation. Here he was referring to the South African-backed rebel movement in Mozambique, at the time trying to overthrow, undermine and destabilise the existing order in Mozambique.

It was only years later that the full picture emerged of how the apartheid government and its security organs had devised a secret and devious strategy to disrupt and wipe out the ANC through the formation of a 'third force'.

Since the early 1990s, Vlakplaas had been one of the units stoking 'black-on-black' violence by supplying Inkatha impis on the East Rand near Johannesburg and in Natal with tonnes of weapons.

Nineteen years ago, a young security guard met an ambitious Zulu handyman at the building society where they both worked. The pair came from different worlds – Brood van Heerden was a former security policeman, and Victor Ndlovu was a member of Inkatha. But they built a long-lasting friendship, founded on their mutual hatred of the ANC. Van Heerden speaks Zulu fluently.

Van Heerden became a policeman in 1971, and served in Namibia and Rhodesia before being transferred to the Security Branch at John Vorster Square. He left the force in 1978 and joined the United Building Society as a security guard. This was where he met Victor Ndlovu.

Van Heerden rejoined the Security Branch in the 1980s, and said that he detonated a bomb in a cinema where the movie *Cry Freedom* was being shown, planted a bomb at a night club in Hillbrow and was a member of Eugene de Kock's team that had blown up Khotso House.[4]

Van Heerden was transferred to Vlakplaas in February 1989, where he participated in the 'tubing' of askari Moses Nthehelang and transported weapons from Namibia back to Vlakplaas. He left the police a few months later and went back to the United Building Society, where he was again in charge of security.

However, he remained in contact with De Kock and his former colleagues at Vlakplaas and one of his first 'freelance' jobs was to try and arrange for HIV-infected askaris to spread HIV amongst Johannesburg's black prostitutes.

By the middle of 1990, the civil strife between Inkatha and the ANC in Natal had spilled over to the Transvaal. A clear pattern emerged. First, Zulu-speaking outsiders would be bussed into the hostels. Second, a bloodbath would take place inside the hostels as the outsiders battled for supremacy with the established residents, many of whom would flee. Third, the hostels having been secured as Inkatha strongholds, the impis would set off on nightly rampages against the communities around them, indiscriminately killing and looting. Large areas around the hostels became desolate no-go areas.[5]

The Inkatha occupation set off a terrible chain of events as ANC comrades who had armed and organised themselves into self-defence units retaliated. They ambushed the hostel inmates as the inmates walked through the streets, shooting them and hacking them to pieces. In the end, there were no guiltless parties, only innocent residents who became engulfed in an orgy of violence.

Van Heerden was visited by his Inkatha friend who introduced him to Themba Khoza. They wanted to know: can you help us with weapons, and why are the police not helping Inkatha in the Transvaal in the same way as in Natal?

In June, Van Heerden paid a visit to his former commander at Vlakplaas and told him about the Inkatha request. A week after Van Heerden's visit, De Kock and Willie Nortje met Khoza and Ndlovu and discussed the supply of weapons to them.

De Kock said he initially refused Khoza's demand for weapons because 'I did not want to get involved in a war', but at an Inkatha funeral in a township near Johannesburg, the ANC threw a hand grenade at the mourners. This event convinced De Kock that the ANC was wiping out Inkatha and he then decided to provide the organisation only with grenades and ammunition, as it already had enough other weapons.

'I was convinced that South Africa was on the verge of a civil war and I knew that the white people would not be prepared to fight for their existence. The only way out was to help Inkatha.'

De Kock met Khoza and senior Inkatha official Victor Ndlovu at Van Heerden's flat. 'Khoza said to me they were being destroyed by the ANC. The Zulus were not trained and armed with only spears and knobkieries.'

Nortje said he had to prepare ten M-26 hand grenades by removing the numbers and cleaning them. A week later, De Kock gave the hand grenades to Van Heerden, who kept them in his office in the bank building for a week before he handed them to Khoza.

'I heard the next day that many people had died and were injured, but Khoza wanted more weapons,' Van Heerden said.

For the the next two and a half years, De Kock and his men would provide AK-47 and SKS assault rifles, belt-fed machine guns, pistols and revolvers, M-26 and Russian-made F1 hand grenades, home-made bombs, home-made shotguns, mortars, rocket launchers and landmines to Inkatha in Johannesburg and Natal.

Van Heerden, De Kock and Nortje became card-carrying members of Inkatha.

They also registered several senior Inkatha officials as informants and paid them monthly allowances from the police secret fund.

A picture of a state-sanctioned, but secret third force emerged from the evidence and affidavits of De Kock, Van Heerden and Nortje. They justified their involvement with Inkatha by claiming that they merely tried to help the movement to defend itself, although this is contradicted by the fact that Inkatha was given bombs, hand grenades and heavy machine guns that could fire between 600 and 1 000 bullets per minute.

Referring to Themba Khoza and Humphrey Ndlovu, Anton Ackermann said: 'These are people that sowed death and destruction here in the Transvaal, isn't it?'

De Kock: In the process of defending themselves, they did sow death and destruction.

Ackermann: And you associated yourself with these people?

De Kock: I back any person trying to defend himself.

Ackermann: These are people you are prepared to walk a road with?

De Kock: I don't know which road. I didn't lead them in their attacks. I gave them advice.

Ackermann: You also provided them with the necessary means?

De Kock: That's all they needed, the rest they had already.

Ackermann: You were friends?

De Kock: No, we weren't. We didn't eat from the same plate.

Ackermann: You had a common enemy?

De Kock: Yes, we had a common enemy. My enemy's enemy was my friend.

He said that the arming of Inkatha took place with the sanction and blessing of the police top command. 'There was a very brotherly relationship between Inkatha and the security police because they had a common enemy.'

FW de Klerk said in his evidence to the TRC: 'There is no basis on which any senior policeman could have been under the impression that it was okay to do this type of thing. One of the first things I did (when I became State President) was to call the top police officers from across the country together and to say that this was the end of the government asking you to be politically involved or to advance any political cause.'[6]

De Kock said he was at first hesitant to supply AK-47s to Inkatha, but one night at a Vlakplaas function, he discussed it with Generals Krappies Engelbrecht and Nick van Rensburg, who 'liked the idea'. They decided, however, that instead of providing AK-47s, they would manufacture shotguns. General Basie Smit agreed to sign a false claim to enable De Kock and his men to buy material for the shotguns. A former Rhodesian friend and engineer helped them to manufacture 150 shotguns, 100 of which were given to Themba Khoza, while the rest were sent to the commissioner of the KwaZulu Police, General Jac Buchner.

'But Inkatha wanted the real thing, and we started supplying them with AKs. Van Rensburg knew about this. We also started providing them with explosives and landmines. At one stage, Inkatha used their ammunition too quickly because they shot on full automatic, and we had to convert the weapons into semi-automatic so that they could fire single shots only and save ammunition. The Zulus were very unhappy about this,' De Kock said.

The Vlakplaas commander provided explosives to Khoza and showed him how to manufacture home-made bombs from empty ice-cream buckets. They became known as 'bucket bombs'.

Van Heerden became the middle man between Khoza and De Kock, who gave him a scrambler to put on his phone whenever they made arrangements for the delivery of weapons. De Kock also gave Van Heerden a police radio to monitor police movements so that he could inform Khoza about police raids on hostels and road blocks. Van Heerden drew up maps of ANC strongholds and areas controlled by them and Vlakplaas paid for the transport of Inkatha supporters between Ulundi and Johannesburg. The funds came from a special slush fund.

In September 1990, Themba Khoza was arrested at a road block with weapons in the boot of his car and was detained. Next day, De Kock and Nortje visited him in jail in Vereeniging, and according to De Kock, Nick van Rensburg authorised De Kock to pay his bail of R10 000. Nortje had to arrange with a friend from ballistics to remove and replace some of the working parts of the rifle so that the weapon could not be connected to acts of violence. Khoza was later acquitted on the charge of illegal possession of firearms because of a lack of evidence.

Nortje said the weapons for Inkatha were initially stored at Special Forces headquarters in Pretoria, but during the Goldstone investigation into military intelligence, De Kock and Snorre Vermeulen had to find another storage facility. The weapons were transported by truck to an arms manufacturer, Mechem, where they were stored in two containers. Heavy weapons like mortars, bombs and RPG rocket launchers were stored at the police college near Pretoria.

Vlakplaas registered Themba Khoza, Humphrey Ndlovu, Victor Ndlovu, James Ndlovu and three other Inkatha officials as informants and paid them between R500 and R1 000 per month. Khoza and Humphrey Ndlovu were given cars. Van Heerden said he was never compensated for his services, but De Kock did give him money for groceries as the Inkatha officials always ate at his home.

Van Heerden said he also had to arrange a meeting between De Kock and KwaZulu minister Celani Mthethwa, who was registered as an informant and who became good friends with De Kock. Mthethwa wanted weapons to distribute to Inkatha impis in the Port Shepstone area of southern Natal.

Nortje and De Kock drove to Ulundi on two occasions on which they delivered AK-47s, ammunition and hand grenades to Mthethwa's ministerial house. De Kock said he also handed him ANC documents on how to set up self-defence units. Van Heerden said Mthethwa twice came to Johannesburg to fetch AK-47s and ammunition which he transported back to Ulundi in his black ministerial car. This was safe because he was never stopped or searched.

De Kock said that Vlakplaas was not the only police unit distributing weapons to Inkatha. He testified that Nick van Rensburg told him one day that he had to submit a false claim for R20 000 because the commissioner wanted to buy spears for Inkatha. He said he also received a 'weapons shopping list' from General Bertus Steyn in Natal.

De Kock said he stopped dealing with Khoza when he was warned that the Inkatha leader was drawing two salaries from the security forces: one from Vlak-plaas and the other from the National Intelligence Service, whom he was also working for. The relationship betweeen them then soured.

The idea of a 'third force' was a brilliant stroke: to use Inkatha as a bulwark against the United Democratic Front and ANC by building up the organisation as a counter-revolutionary force. Its impis would be organised into death squads by training, arming and supporting them. This would allow the architects of this evil plan to foment 'black-on-black' violence, yet shrug their shoulders and tell the world that blacks were simply not capable of ruling.

The idea of forming a 'third force' goes back to the mid-1980s when the struggle against apartheid reached unprecedented levels. The state adopted equally drastic measures to counter these threats, which included the use of terrorism and guerrilla warfare.

According to the minutes of the State Security Council, the formation of a 'third force' was discussed at a meeting on May 12, 1986. 'The third force must be mobile with a well-trained capacity to effectively wipe out terrorists. It must be prepared to be unpopular and even feared, without marring the image of the Defence Force or the police. The security forces must work together in the setting up of the third force in order that those who undermine the state are countered with their own methods.'[7]

FW de Klerk attended the State Security Council meeting, but denied that a third force was ever formed. During his submission to the TRC, he was asked: 'Would a reasonable person – a member of the security forces who is enjoined to use the strongest possible methods to combat the revolution – not interpret that this was said to authorise killings and assassinations?'

De Klerk: As far as I know, not having been directly involved then, there were at all times general rules and guidelines … that we were not above the law. That was the ethos of our approach.

Truth Commissioner: For a member of the security forces, for a member of the Security Branch … when that person is told: develop ways to effectively wipe out terrorists – use their own methods to do so. His reasonable interpretation, Mr De Klerk, is to use the methods he knows so well. No reasonable man cannot foresee that a man would interpret such statements to mean: you can kill, you can assassinate, you can bomb.

De Klerk: We tried to adhere to Christian norms and principles. That was the ethos under which I grew up and under which I served: firstly as an ordinary Member of Parliament, then as a minister and that was the ethos also in the cabinet under my presidency. I reject the implication that there was this almost immoral everything-goes-in-a-state-of-war. That was not the philosophy within which I lived, within which I operated and within which I served.

Two hundred Inkatha soldiers were recruited and secretly trained by Military Intelligence in the Caprivi in northern Namibia in 1986. The training became known as 'Operation Marion', a 'third force' that was armed, financed and directed by the SADF, although the top leadership of Inkatha also knew about the purpose and activities of the group.

The SADF masterminded the Caprivi training and controlled the trainees. After stirring up violence in Natal, the impis were bussed up to theTransvaal in 1990, and Eugene de Kock and the generals saw a golden opportunity to deliver a final blow against the ANC.

June 17, 1992, and in an obscure township 65 kilometres south of Johannesburg, one of the worst massacres in South Africa's political history took place. Inkatha assailants, wearing red headbands and wielding axes, knives, spears and automatic weapons, slaughtered 45 men, women and children.[8]

Hours later, the world witnessed the image of a nine-year-old child impaled by a spear, and grief-stricken families and angry young comrades vowing revenge on the Inkatha inmates of the KwaMadala hostel from which the attack had originated.

Nelson Mandela said 'I can no longer explain to our people why we want to talk to a regime which is murdering our people'. In a ferocious attack on FW de Klerk, he said that the Boipatong killings had been the work of 'faceless murderers who worked closely with the government'. A few days later, the ANC withdrew from constitutional negotiations, plunging the country into a political crisis.

In his response, De Klerk defended the security forces, which he claimed were not involved in the massacre and which, he said, operated with impartiality. The Boipatong massacre happened a day after the ANC's Soweto Day launch of a mass action campaign. The commissioner of police issued a statement declaring the first day of mass action to have passed off peacefully, but then the Minister of Law and Order, Hernus Kriel, put a cynical political spin on the massacre by blaming it on the ANC campaign. His spokesperson, Captain Craig Kotze, said 'the political temperature had been pushed unacceptably high' by the ANC campaign which had 'created a climate making incidents such as these more easily happen'.

A few days after the massacre, De Klerk attempted to visit Boipatong, but was forced away by angry residents. The posters said it all: a picture of De Klerk, his eyes coloured in bright red like a devil's, and the words: 'How many more deaths? De Klerk GET OUT'.

The government's insensitivity to township violence and its refusal to accept any responsibility for the carnage was reiterated by the Minister of Foreign Affairs, Pik Botha, when he addressed a United Nations Security Council meeting a month after the Boipatong massacre and said that to 'accuse the government of fostering violence was an insult'. He maintained that most of the violence was the result of ethnic and political conflict between ANC supporters and Inkatha.

The Goldstone Commission could find no direct evidence of police complicity in the attack, although it was told that all 13 hours of recordings of communications between the operations room of the South African Police internal stability unit and police officers on the day of the massacre had been accidentally erased. The commission heard from seven witnesses who testified that the police had assisted in the massacre.

I asked Eugene de Kock during one of my visits to him in prison whether he knew anything about the Boipatong massacre, but he denied that either he or any of his men were in any way involved.

It is possible that his weapons could have been used in the attack. The massacre took place at a time of increased weapons supply to Inkatha, most of which were distributed to hostel inmates.

According to Brood van Heerden, De Kock had always stressed that the weapons had to be handed to bona fide Inkatha members in the presence of indunas at the hostels.

Riaan Stander says that the Vlakplaas men were involved in the attack. 'The night after Boipatong, or maybe it was a day or two days afterwards, I saw two of the members coming back, reporting back to Eugene, and at that stage they were wearing disguises and you could see that they did not look like normal policemen.'[9]

Stander says they said to him it had been a very successful operation as it was a 'turning point' in the war between Inkatha and the ANC.

A few days after the massacre, Corrie Goosen says, the Vlakplaas 'boys' had a braai at the brothel in Johannesburg. Members of the Directorate of Covert Collection of Military Intelligence were also present.[10]

'We had a party there, and these things were discussed. De Kock and one of the guys of Military Intelligence, whom I only knew as Arthur, discussed Boipatong. They gave the weapons to Inkatha, but as I understood the whole thing, there was not supposed to have been a massacre. They only gave the weapons to Inkatha so that they could defend themselves. I heard De Kock saying that he was sorry that it had happened like that,' says Goosen.

Arthur, I was told afterwards, was the pseudonym for a former Rhodesian called Geoff Price. A former member of the Rhodesian security services and a director of the Zimbabwean Central Intelligence Organisation, he had come to South Africa at the end of 1981 and had joined the security police before becoming a member of the Directorate of Covert Collection.

Goosen, of course, is not a shining example of uprightness and honesty, while

Stander is vague about his knowledge of De Kock's complicity in the Boipatong massacre.

It is impossible to determine how many people have died from bullets fired from Eugene de Kock's guns or how many houses and people were blown apart by his hand grenades and bombs, but his arming of Inkatha may be the greatest legacy left behind by his command of the police counter-insurgency unit at Vlakplaas.

De Kock, his comrades-in-arms and the generals brought South Africa to the brink of an abyss, during the time he was ostensibly responsible for investigating and infiltrating illegal arms routes and arresting arms smugglers.

Brood van Heerden said De Kock never wanted to become involved in train violence, but after several train incidents, Victor Ndlovu and Themba Khoza would say to the Vlakplaas men: 'We hit them again.' There is little doubt that De Kock's weapons must have found their way onto the trains.

Amongst the victims of third force henchman like Eugene de Kock are those within his own ranks: dedicated and upright policemen who battled to find the weapons and to stop the carnage. One such man is Captain Thys du Plessis, the former commander of a Soweto mobile train unit. For several years, he tried in vain to stop the senseless killings on the trains, search the wagons and disarm commuters. He failed, and one day in July 1993, he collapsed. Today he is still a nervous wreck and he will never lead a normal life again.[11]

This is how Du Plessis describes his collapse: 'That Sunday, I said to my wife that things were getting too much and I couldn't handle it any more. She asked me what was wrong, and I said to her I was going "off my trolly". I would take my fire arm and start threatening people. Everything became blurred and the next moment, I woke up in hospital. I sat there and cried like a baby.'

He was diagnosed as suffering from severe depression and post-traumatic stress disorder. His psychologist, Dr. Nicky Swart, says: 'He suffers from extreme, catastrophic stress which broke him down emotionally. He will never be able to work as a policeman again. I think he may at some stage be able to do a few small things that interest him, something like a vegetable garden, but we must remember that the smallest thing is going to set him off again.'[12]

When I met Thys du Plessis shortly after he was forced to take early retirement on medical grounds, he said: 'I often think I should take a pistol and get rid of this problem. But then I think of my family and try to come to terms with what I am. My wife told the children that although their father looks healthy from the outside, he is in fact a very sick man. When I feel this monster building up inside me, I have to warn them to get away. I'm still scared I'm going to hurt them.'

De Kock continued to supply weapons to Inkatha long after he had left the police force in April 1993. He also became involved in training Inkatha impis near the Umfolozi game reserve in Natal.

In October 1993, six KwaZulu administration trucks were loaded by De Kock with arms, explosives and ammunition and driven to an Inkatha base in Natal. De Kock said Inkatha member Phillip Powell asked him for the arms and ammunition in order to train Inkatha self-protection units.

'He once told me with tears in his eyes that he was tired walking amongst the bodies of his people which were mowed down by the ANC. This was only about defence, because they were being destroyed by the ANC.'

The weapons were collected in two consignments. According to evidence produced in court, De Kock and former Vlakplaas operative Snorre Vermeulen collected four truckloads of ammunition and explosives from Mechem on October 1. By then De Kock had already left the police, but he was introduced to Marthinus Gouws, who was in charge of the armoury of Mechem, as a member of the force and he said that the police wanted the explosives for the training of students. Gouws said Mechem had had an enormous amount of arms and ammunition in its armoury and had decided to get rid of the excess.

De Kock claimed that the weapons were to be used for self-defence and training, but this is a list of the arms that were loaded at Mechem: 700 anti-tank mines, 1 000 hand grenades, 1 400 rifle grenades, 14 400 AK-47 rounds, 15 191 R-1 rounds, 182 RPG-7 rockets, 120 mortars, 1 428 rifle grenades, 125 kilograms of explosives, 98 anti-personnel mines and RPG rocket launchers.

Three weeks later, De Kock collected another 395 kilograms of explosives, 188 mortars, 288 hand grenades, 7 500 rounds of ammunition and 200 shrapnel mines from Mechem, also destined for Natal.

De Kock: This was about the survival of Inkatha. They (the ANC) were busy exterminating Inkatha on the East Rand and in parts of KwaZulu, and it was decided to form self-defence units so that they could protect their own people.

Ackermann: How do you defend yourself with a rocket launcher?

De Kock: It's an anti-tank weapon, but is also suitable for taking the enemy out when he is hiding behind ant hills, big trees and rocks.

Ackermann: Tell us more about the mortars.

De Kock: It is very good for defending a kraal [traditional village].

Ackermann: How do you defend your kraal with a mortar?

De Kock: Well, depending on where your enemy is, if they are on a hill or a rock formation, you can take them out with a mortar.

Ackermann: I have a note here that this mortar has a range of up to three kilometres?

De Kock: That is correct.

Ackermann: And your 81 millimetre mortar?

De Kock: It has a range of between five and six kilometres. I have walked into many ambushes and if it wasn't for mortars, we wouldn't have survived without injuries.

Ackermann: We also heard about land mines, I think it was Claymore mines?

De Kock: they contain a thousand pieces of shrapnel ... and are very effective for defending a base against attacking troops. They have a terrible effect on troops storming you.

Phillip Powell asked De Kock to assist him in training Inkatha self-defence units (SDUs) at their secret Mlaba camp near the Umfolozi game reserve, but De Kock said when he arrived there that conditions were atrocious. There were virtually no sanitary services, or running water and some of the people were sick.

He told Powell that he couldn't help him unless conditions were improved. Two weeks later, Powell called him again and said facilities had been upgraded.

One of the Inkatha commanders in the camp was a man with a most remarkable story: Daluxolo Wordsworth Luthuli, grandson of ChiefAlbert Luthuli, former President General of the ANC and Nobel Peace Prize laureate.

Following in the footsteps of his legendary grandfather, Daluxolo Luthuli went into exile in 1963 to join the ANC's armed wing, Umkhonto we Sizwe. He received military training in the Luthuli camp in Tanzania and Odessa in the Soviet Union. He was arrested upon his return to South Africa in 1967 and sentenced to ten years' imprisonment, which he spent on Robben Island in the company of Nelson Mandela, Walter Sisulu and the rest of the incarcerated ANC leadership.[13]

After his release from the island, he joined Inkatha, although he still secretly worked for the ANC and had several meetings with Umkhonto we Sizwe Chief-of-Staff Chris Hani in Lesotho. But by the middle 1980s, he had been drawn into the Natal conflict and found himself increasingly supporting Inkatha. Luthuli eventually became commander of Inkatha's armed wing and was amongst the 200 impis who were secretly trained by Military Intelligence in the Caprivi.

One of the first attacks masterminded by Luthuli and his Military Intelligence handlers and carried out by a team of Caprivi trainees was the massacre of 13 people, mostly women and children, at KwaMakhuta (Natal) in January 1987.

'There were literally hundreds of incidents ... so many that they have blurred my memory. I accept that under my control and direction many lives were lost, many people sustained injuries, hundreds of houses were destroyed or damaged and a huge quantity of personal property was lost.'

Luthuli said he was instructed by the Inkatha leadership in 1993 to train self-protection units for Inkatha at the Mlaba camp. 'The central committee had decided that this was a system whereby the armed wing of Inkatha could be increased.' He said Powell appointed six instructors, two white men and four black men, to assist in the training. 'When these instructors arrived they were accompanied by a third white man who wore thick glasses. He was thick-set in build and quite tall ... Problems arose from the outset. My men were against white involvement ... and did not trust their set-up. Many groups came and went from this camp and they numbered 400 to 600 on each occasion. I last heard that there were 8 000 trained SDUs,' Luthuli said in an affidavit, dated March 1995.

All of Eugene de Kock's arsenal did not find its way to Inkatha. Long before he had left the police on early retirement, he tried to set himself up as an arms dealer and flew around the world trying to enter the armaments business.

He admitted in court that shortly after the expose of Vlakplaas at the end of 1989, he decided to become an arms dealer and subsequently flew to eastern and western Europe, where he made contact with dealers in Serbia, Croatia, Slovenia, Germany and Austria. He imported a hundred Glock pistols and said he was on the verge of clinching a deal to sell South African-manufactured G-5 cannons to Serbia when the United Nations slammed an arms embargo on the Serbs.

It was illegal for any policeman to run a private business venture, especially one that was involved in trading in arms, without the permission of the commissioner of police.

In January 1993, more than three months before De Kock left the force, Ferdi Barnard told me that theVlakplaas commander had become a gun runner and had registered a company by the name of 'Honeybadger Arms and Ammunition'. On business cards carried by De Kock, Honeybadger – which had the same emblem as theVlakplaas unit – said it dealt in 'all arms, local and international'. De Kock frequently flew overseas under the name of 'Lourens de Wet'.[14]

I was also told that some of South Africa's most notorious security forces members, past and present, had banded together in a secret, well-trained and well-armed organisation called the 'Badger Unit'. Its members included former operatives of the CCB, Military Intelligence and the security police. Badger was said to be involved in arms smuggling and providing arms to Inkatha.[15]

The police said the revelations, published in *The Star* newspaper, were 'devoid of all truth' and that Honeybadger was a legitimate police operation created to combat illegal gun-smuggling and that the existence of the Badger Unit would be investigated. It probably never was.

De Kock continued to smuggle arms to Inkatha, offer weapons to arms dealers and arm himself and his men with machine guns, bombs and hand grenades as they awaited the Armageddon they predicted would accompany the coming of the new South Africa.

Democracy meant political freedom for millions of black South Africans, but for Eugene de Kock, the beginning of a life behind bars.

Chapter Ten

Prime time

October 30, 1996, and in the shadow of the monument of Boer President Paul Kruger, perched high on his pedestal in Pretoria's Church Square, civil servants, office workers and business men, clad in suits and armed with lunch boxes and brief cases, flocked to work.[1]

By early morning, as grey clouds hung ominously in the Pretoria sky, Colonel Eugene Alexander de Kock, dressed in grey and white, had been driven from Pretoria's Central Prison to the Supreme Court where he was searched and locked in a cell underneath the court rooms.

For the previous twenty months and ten days, De Kock had travelled the same route and sat in the same bench in court GD where a tale of savagery, so vile it was beyond comprehension, had been spat out by a troupe of former Vlakplaas operatives and then finally, by the accused himself.

In the end, a picture was painted of a killer who went out again and again to slaughter those who opposed the policies of his political masters, who sat on the highest benches and spoke of barbarians who wanted to seize power.

Eugene de Kock had won many battles, but had finally lost his war. Mr Justice Willem van der Merwe had to decide what punishment befitted his crimes and would satisfy society's demand for retribution. Weeks before, the former Vlakplaas commander had been found guilty of six murders, conspiracy to murder, attempted murder, culpable homicide, manslaughter, assault, abduction, defeating the end of justice, illegal possession of arms and ammunition, and fraud.

More than half an hour before proceedings were due to start, the court room had filled up and the corridor of the building swollen with people who had come to catch a last glimpse of the man who had become known as 'Prime Evil'.

Rolf Gevers, the killer who blew Tiso Leballo to nothingness, gave De Kock a cheery thumbs-up sign before settling back in the public gallery to wait for the judgement. Former security policemen and families of the victims were sitting shoulder to shoulder as the historic clock above the Ou Raadsaal (Old Council Hall) on Church Square struck ten times and Van der Merwe entered the court room with his flowing scarlet robes. De Kock sat passively, staring straight ahead of him as the judge started reading out his epic sentencing speech, lasting three hours.

The judge imposed the ultimate sentence under law: life imprisonment with no leave to appeal. He found that the crimes were cold-blooded, cruel, calculated and callous, and that Eugene de Kock should never again be allowed to step out again into a world he almost destroyed.

He sentenced him to altogether two life sentences and 212 years' imprisonment for 'revolting acts planned and executed in cold blood' and committed, condoned and covered up 'by a system rotten to the core'. He said: 'The actions leave one with a chilling feeling … it fills a person with revulsion.'

De Kock showed no emotion as the judge condemned him to a life behind bars. Most journalists who had followed the court case were surprised by the severity of the sentence, but many spectators who sat in the court room and stood with clenched fists outside preferred to imagine De Kock swinging lifeless from the end of a rope.

'He should have been killed,' said Daniel Maponya, who felt his brother's death had not been properly avenged.

'They should bring back the death sentence just for him, then do away with it again,' said an emotional Margaret Nyalende, the mother of Lawrence Nyalende, who was one of the men murdered in the 1992 Nelspruit 'bank-robber' ambush. 'Now he'll be eating fish and chips in jail,' she sneered.

On April 30, 1993, after 25 years of service in the South African Police, Eugene de Kock said he 'was thrown to the wolves' when he went on early retirement – but not before State President FW de Klerk and the Cabinet had authorised a payoff of R1 million to the former Vlakplaas commander. The government approved payment of an amount of R17,5 million to De Kock and 83 Vlakplaas policemen who left the force. Askari Joe Mamasela got more than R400 000 for his 13 years of killing service.[2]

'They gave me too much money, I think it was to shut my big mouth up,' Mamasela says.[3]

De Klerk rejected any insinuation that the payouts were to buy silence from the men. He said in Parliament that many of the Vlakplaas operatives were former ANC and PAC members and that 'the first thing the ANC would have done would have been to immediately get rid of these people. It was, therefore, necessary to disband this unit.'

Mamasela says that after they had received their final packages, De Kock called a meeting of askaris at the Hartebeespoort Dam near Pretoria. 'He said there was a need for the police to arm us with AK-47s, hand grenades and explosives because the ANC was going to eliminate us one by one. He prepared us that should the ANC kill one of us, we should march to Shell House and mow down anything that moves. I was provided with an AK-47, three magazines and five hand grenades.'[4]

De Kock and other policemen made a secret deal with the Commissioner of Police, General Johan van der Merwe, that the state would pay for their legal defence should they be prosecuted for any offence committed as policemen. In the end, the taxpayer had to pay more than R5 million to De Kock's legal team.

Before his departure, De Kock believed he still had a future in the force and he wanted to become a general. But to avoid prosecution, he first had to make a deal with the former enemy. De Kock and Krappies Engelbrecht had a meeting with the head of ANC intelligence, Joe Nhlanhla, and offered him information in exchange for a continued career in the force. Nhlanhla rejected any deal.

De Kock had already had a conversation with a senior ANC official in 1991 about his future in the police when his askaris had accidentally abducted George Nene, today South Africa's High Commissioner in Nigeria.[5]

Nene said he was confronted by about seven askaris who overpowered him, bundled him into a car and drove him to a place near Hillbrow in Johannesburg. They then realised that they had got the wrong man, and De Kock personally arrived to take Nene to where he wanted to be. Ironically, Nene had been an MK commander in Swaziland during the 1980s and a target of De Kock's death squads.

'He apologised profusely and said it was unfortunate that we had to meet in such circumstances. He said it was time for people like me and him to sit down and join hands to form an effective security service for the future. It was clear from what he said that he saw an important role for himself in a new police force. He gave me his telephone number and said I should contact him in order to discuss this. I never did,' says Nene.

De Kock's first strategy for survival was to arm and train Inkatha. Between September 1993 and the election in April 1994, Inkatha trained as many as 8 000 paramilitary fighters in secret bases in KwaZulu. Inkatha, the right wing, the police and former security forces operatives, amongst them Eugene de Kock, hatched an elaborate plan to resist the incorporation of KwaZulu into a democratic South Africa. The top command of the old South African Police, including Generals Basie Smit and Johan van der Merwe, knew of and abetted the plan.[6]

De Kock's other scheme was to throw his weight behind the right wing. Although De Kock claims that he was never a rightwinger, he tried to sell them weapons and was ready to join in a countrywide uprising against an ANC government. Brood van Heerden says that De Kock often discussed the possibility of a coup d'etat and that he had good relations with Irish nationalist organisations.[7]

One of the men who were also training and arming Inkatha was a former SADF officer by the name of Riaan van Rensburg. Before the elections, he was a close confidant of the leader of the Freedom Front, General Constand Viljoen. At the time, Viljoen was trying to unify right-wing organisations in order to form a united front against a black take-over. He had thousands of trained men all around the country, ready to take up arms at his command.

In the winter of 1993, De Kock had a meeting with Viljoen. The former policeman wanted to know how far rightwingers were in their planning to go to war. He said he had an arsenal of arms available in the event of a right-wing uprising.

'He was totally disillusioned with what was going on in the political arena in that he felt that De Klerk was selling out all the white people and that something had to be done to stop a take-over by the ANC. He was bitter in that he had given his life to fight the ANC and was now being persecuted for having done so,' Van Rensburg says.[8]

Just before the April election, De Kock met Viljoen and Van Rensburg again. Van Rensburg says they were taken to De Kock's home, where he was sitting with Snorre Vermeulen and a former operative in the Directorate of Covert Collection, Clive Brink.

'They were drunk. De Kock sat there and told us about his capabilities, the people that he still has on the ground and the literally tonnes of weapons like missiles and explosives that were available to him at short notice. He offered the weapons to us, but at a price.'

Van Rensburg says that he got the impression that De Kock was ready to go to war. 'He suggested that there should be an armed conflict, that we must get our people in place, he will get his in place and we must work together and go into a total war situation.'

Constand Viljoen wasn't interested in dealing with De Kock. 'We weren't in it for the money, and it was quite obvious that he was. And the fact that he was intoxicated, and the fact that he was boasting about how strong and fantastic they are, and using words such as "They get information by tubing people", went against our grain. When we left, General Viljoen turned around to me and said: "This is most definitely one person we will not be working with." And the message was left: don't phone us, we will phone you.'

A month before the election, Eugene de Kock knew that somebody had spilled the beans and that an investigation had been launched against him and that he might be arrested soon.

'Well, he told me he was going to be arrested, but he seemed to be prepared to go to trial and see what happens. He wasn't aggressive or angry. He was resigned. I think at the time he believed promises that were made to him, that the worst won't come to the worst, just stay on the bus,' says Craig Williamson.[9]

Peter Casselton said De Kock also told him that he was going to be arrested, but wasn't worried, because he thought he was going to get the backing from the generals. 'He never thought it was going to become as serious as this.'[10]

Riaan Stander says De Kock was extremely aggressive before his arrest. 'He became very unstable, very paranoid. The one moment he would be calm, the next unreasonable and abusive.'[11]

Ferdi Barnard says his friend was again like a 'time bomb going off'.[12] About a month before his arrest, De Kock started wrapping up his personal and business affairs and sent his family abroad. At the beginning of April, Audrey de Kock and their two sons, Alexander and Michael, left South Africa for Ireland.

He sold his house in Pretoria, cashed in four retirement annuities worth R200 000 and three endowment policies worth R40 000. During the same period, he withdrew R235 000 from his bank account in Pretoria.[13]

At the time, De Kock had various overseas bank accounts in, amongst others, Switzerland, Portugal, the United Kingdom and Jersey. The Swiss account in Zurich contained nearly R1 million in several foreign currencies.

On April 5, De Kock walked into the office of his lawyer and longstanding friend, Wim Cornelius, and brought him a gift. It was a police bow tie that officers wear to official functions. With the bow tie was a letter: 'Wim, I have worn this only once to an official function. You will have more use for it than me. Greetings, Eugene.'[14]

On April 27, 1994, millions of South Africans assembled at voting stations around the country to cast their ballots. The threat from the right wing and Inkatha petered out as General Constand Viljoen and Chief Mangosuthu Buthelezi came on board and participated in the election. De Kock said he didn't vote, and instead, booked himself an air ticket to Portugal. He was due to leave on May 8, two days before the inauguration of Nelson Mandela as South Africa's first democratically elected head of state.

But at nine o'clock on Wednesday, May 4, while he was drinking at the International Police Association club in Pretoria, Eugene de Kock was arrested. He had $1 000 in his purse, and a machine gun, night-sight equipment, $16 000 and R50 000 in his pick-up truck.

Thirteen thousand kilometres away, in the Danish capital of Copenhagen, a group of South Africans were having a party, not to celebrate the coming of democracy to their fatherland, but to mark the arrest of a man they feared, even hated, but had once worshipped.

Amongst the party-goers were a trio of killers who were on a witness protection scheme in Copenhagen. They were accompanied by their families, human rights lawyers, state advocates and policemen. They were on a mission to tell their tale of a decade of murder and destruction perpetrated by them and their colleagues at Vlakplaas.

Willie Nortje, Chappies Klopper and Brood van Heerden blamed their complicity in murder on Eugene de Kock by saying that they had had to carry out his orders and that he was the mastermind behind all operations. The three men were not in Denmark because of a sense of remorse, but were motivated by a mixture of hate, fear and the desire to save their own butts.

The story of how the three men had come to Denmark started in early 1994 when Chappies Klopper, obsessed with hatred of De Kock, decided that he was going to talk. The first step in exposing the criminal activities ofVlakplaas was taken when he made contact with two of the new breed of officers in the South African Police, Majors Eugene van Vuuren and Pieter du Plessis. They in turn arranged a meeting between Klopper, Danish and Dutch diplomats, and the regional director of the Institute for a Democratic Alternative for South Africa (Idasa), Ivor Jenkins. 'I was very surprised by his posture. I suspected somebody having been involved in this would look much more vicious and brutal. But here comes a very nice looking man, almost soft-spoken and with a giggle,' says Jenkins.[15]

They asked Klopper whether he would be willing to speak to Mr Justice Richard Goldstone, at the time heading an inquiry into political violence. Klopper and Goldstone met on a Sunday morning, on which Klopper handed his false passport to the judge and gave him some information about the past activities of Vlakplaas. Goldstone assured Klopper that if he would be willing to testify, he could arrange for protection and indemnity from prosecution. Chappies Klopper testified before Goldstone and his commissioners and became known as 'Mr Q'.[16]

Klopper: It was common knowledge amongst security police units what
their Vlakplaas work entailed.
Commission: What did they do?
Klopper: The elimination of ANC and PAC terrorists.
Commission: By shooting them?
Klopper: Yes.
Commission: What can we nail De Kock with?
Klopper: Lots of things.
Commission: Let's hear it.

Chappies Klopper implicated his former commander in a host of incidents of murder, fraud and gunrunning. But he went much further when he told the commission about the dealings of a senior police general with prostitutes.

Commission: It is of the utmost importance that we cannot continue with
a corrupt police force.
Klopper: No, that is …
Commission: It is in your children's interest.
Klopper: There is a joke amongst the whores, that's now the prostitutes.
Commission: Yes?
Klopper: They call the general 'Half Price'.

Willie Nortje says that in March 1994, Krappies Engelbrecht told him and De Kock that there were problems because the Goldstone Commission was making enquiries at the Department of Internal Affairs about their false passports. Shortly afterwards, De Kock, Nortje, Engelbrecht, Basie Smit and Johan le Roux were subpoenaed by the commission.

'We were in quite a state, because we didn't know what was going on. It seemed as though it was about weapons for the Zulus. I was called in by Goldstone and allegations were put to me. The judge spoke about third-force activities, but I denied everything. Their facts, however, were accurate. They were on the right track and I knew it was just a matter of time before they would discover everything,' says Nortje.

He went home and discussed his dilemma with his wife, Welma Nortje, who said to him he should do what he thought was right. That same night at nine o'clock, he went back to see Goldstone and told him that he would make a statement.

On March 17, Nortje testified before the commission. While Klopper only knew about the weapons for Inkatha, Nortje was more personally involved. But he wouldn't tell the commission everything and was vague.[17]

Commission: This is your chance. It is over, if you don't talk to us you are going to jail. I don't want to threaten you, but this is serious.

Nortje: I understand the seriousness.

Commission: This is damn serious ... You surely have a family as well. We can help you, really, but we want the truth.

Nortje: Sir, I'm telling you, I don't know what they did with those weapons ... I didn't give the weapons to the Zulus.

Commission: You're not playing open cards with us ... Don't you want to tell us the Vlakplaas story? We will not throw you to the wolves.

Nortje: The problem is, I don't know about most of the things. I don't have the facts.

When he was questioned about De Kock, Nortje said: 'We have walked the same road for 12 years and we are friends. Things happened which we didn't agree with, and he manipulated us and put us into this position. I want to know what is going to happen after this.'

Richard Goldstone said to Nortje that he had already discussed the evidence of 'Mr Q' with FW de Klerk and that complete protection was available inside and outside of the country. He said he had also informed Nelson Mandela and that the future ANC government was in favour of granting indemnity to state witnesses.

Goldstone: I can ask the State President tomorrow to suspend Smit, Engelbrecht, Le Roux and the members of the Vlakplaas unit that we are going to name.

Nortje: I would like that, yes.

Commission: Start at the beginning and tell us what you feel like telling us.

Nortje: I arrived at Vlakplaas in 1984 ...

One day later Richard Goldstone released what became known as his 'third-force report', in which he exposed what he called 'a horrible network of criminal activity' of gunrunning, death squad activity and the orchestration of violence to destabilise the country.[18]

The main players in his report were Colonel Eugene de Kock, Generals Krappies Engelbrecht, Basie Smit and Johan Le Roux, several Vlakplaas operatives and Inkatha officials Themba Khoza and Humphrey Ndlovu. In his report, Goldstone referred to his main source of information as 'Mr Q', although by that time, there were two Mr Q's – Willie Nortje and Chappies Klopper. Two days after the report was released, a newspaper identified 'Mr Q' as Klopper.

In the report, mention was made of De Kock's involvement in the 1985 murder of Japie Maponya. Klopper only arrived at Vlakplaas four years after the murder, while Willie Nortje was at the murder scene with his commander. 'I knew then that De Kock would know that I had also spoken. I didn't sleep at home that weekend. I phoned De Kock the Sunday morning and said to him I saw him as responsible for the whole mess. If he hadn't entered into the fight with Klopper, this would never have happened.'

The next morning, the Vlakplaas men met at a coffee shop in Pretoria to discuss the Goldstone report. Nortje said everybody ignored him because they knew that he had spilt the beans. He went home, contacted the Goldstone Commission and said he wanted to leave the country. The next day, Nortje and his family flew to Denmark where Klopper was already under witness protection.

Ivor Jenkins and his wife were at the airport in Copenhagen to receive the Nortje family. It was an ironic meeting. Five years earlier, Jenkins had had to leave South Africa after mysterious raiders shot at his Pretoria home. One of them was Willie Nortje.

At the time, Jenkins had been involved in a disobedience campaign in Pretoria. One night, thirteen shots were fired through his front window. His wife was then eight months' pregnant with their second child. After the baby was born a month later, they left for the United States.

In March 1994, Jenkins and his wife received Willie and Welma Nortje and their one-month-old baby at the airport in Copenhagen. 'They were in total fear and desperate for help,' says Jenkins, who had to 'babysit' the family for six weeks.

Back in South Africa, Brood van Heerden was confronted by Eugene de Kock about his testimony to the Goldstone Commission. 'He is a very dangerous man who will murder potential witnesses. I fear the man. He had threatened to kill Willie Nortje after it became known that he had spoken,' says Van Heerden. Within days, he and his family were also in Denmark.[19]

'They were extremely nervous. They were in a foreign country and they had no idea how long they would have to stay. Ten days or ten years? In their minds, De Kock was always present and they believed that he would come and kill them because they had betrayed him. They almost attached a godlike status to him,' says Jenkins.

The three men had to recount, step by step, the horror of their deeds. Welma Nortje heard for the first time about her husband's involvement in point-blank executions and murders. Brood van Heerden had to describe in graphic detail how he had pulled a tube over Moses Nthehelang's face and 'tubed' him to death.

'For the first time, they had to look at themselves. And it didn't come easy. At times, they giggled when their statements were read back to them. I don't think it was easy for Willie Nortje to hear what he was. The wives were just quiet, as this was mostly new to them,' says Jenkins.

It became known as 'the cell of a thousand delights'. Instead of being incarcerated and treated as an inmate awaiting trial on murder, Eugene de Kock was living in rent-free luxury in the Adriaan Vlok police station in Verwoerdburg, outside of Pretoria. Although shut, the door to De Kock's cell was left unlocked.

His cell resembled a hotel room. When a police captain visited him in December 1994, there was a colour television set, a video recorder and an M-Net decoder. Hidden under a pillow were an empty Klipdrift brandy bottle, a bottle of Red Heart rum, a steak knife, a battery charger and a cell phone.

In a period of six months, De Kock had made more than 900 calls on his cell phone. Among the calls were 25 to police headquarters in Pretoria, 11 to the police in Springs, 5 to Inkatha, 14 to the Eastern Cape, 34 to a police colonel, 105 to his wife in Portugal, 6 to Mozambique and 7 to Parliament in Cape Town.

De Kock made 26 calls to the *Weekly Mail* to try and persuade a journalist to publish information discrediting members of the investigations team. He claimed that Colonel Ivor Human had been involved in indecent assault on a black woman and that Captain Mike Holmes had killed a detainee by 'tubing' him.

Two months after De Kock's arrest, Audrey de Kock and the two boys went to live in the Portuguese town of Evora. In the same month, R915 000 was transferred from De Kock's Swiss bank account to her account at Banco Commercial Portugues in Lisbon.

De Kock, who then still received regular visits from his former colleagues, was even taken on 'outings' and accompanied his guards on a visit to the Verwoerdburg rugby club. The visitor's register at the police station was so badly maintained that visitors had even signed themselves in as 'Eugene de Kock'.

But in December 1994, De Kock's happy sojourn behind bars at the police station came to an end when the Attorney General obtained a court order to have De Kock transferred to Pretoria Central Prison. He was incarcerated in the maximum security section in what had previously been death row.

'For three to four months I was in solitary confinement, alone in my section. Two people were later put with me. One was mad, and the other escaped. Sitting on death row was like being in hell's waiting room. There were physical threats against me in prison and soap bars loaded with blades were twice thrown at me. Jail is a hellhole. For two arms of dagga or R100, a member of the 26s or 27s (two notorious gangs) would kill you,' De Kock said.

He must have realised by then that his situation was getting desperate and that he might have been abandoned by the politicians, the generals and his former colleagues. He said he was told that General Johan van der Merwe had told his colleagues: 'Stay away from De Kock. The generals knew nothing. Everything he did, he did on his own accord. He operated on his own, we know nothing about it.'

On January 11, 1995, De Kock's lawyers wrote a letter to President Mandela: 'We have been instructed by our client to request an audience with you at your earliest convenience … We would appreciate it if you could advise us as soon as possible whether you are prepared to accede to our request.' Mandela's office didn't respond or acknowledge receipt of the letter.

De Kock did receive a letter, from Pretoria Central prisoner no. 38/7097:

Almond Nofemela, the former Vlakplaas killer who had been sentenced to death in 1987 after he had murdered a farmer during a 'private enterprise'. On the eve of his execution in October 1989, De Kock had sent an emissary to death row and told him that there was nothing that could be done, and that he should 'take the pain'. Nofemela got a last-minute stay of execution when he swore an affidavit that De Kock had murdered Japie Maponya. He eventually had his sentence commuted to life imprisonment and may be released soon on parole.

Nofemela wrote to De Kock: 'Those who were on top are now at the bottom and the pain that it was said I should take seems to have been taken by all who were happy about it when my days were dark. You are going to appear before the judge too, as I also did in 1987. I was sentenced to death and I wish you don't go there; unfortunately you are going to prison.

'I'm about to be freed and I promise that I'll visit you, as you did to me. You are going to drink the medicine you let me drink seven years ago. I won't die a prisoner. God be with you.

'Your labourer at Vlakplaas,

Almond'

De Kock's transfer to Pretoria Central Prison was the beginning of the end. His trial started in February 1995, and as the picture of horror unfolded and the litany of evidence against him was presented, his visitors became fewer and fewer. His health also deteriorated, and in April 1995, he was rushed to hospital where he was diagnosed as having a massive blood clot on one lung.

'One morning at about eight I went to the bathroom. I didn't feel well, and when I got out of the bath, I fainted. When I regained consciousness, I was lying on the cement floor. A warden found me and took me to the prison hospital where I got an injection and oxygen. I was taken to HF Verwoerd Hospital. Three members of the Special Task Force guarded me in hospital, two policemen were outside the door and there were a further eight outside the building, all armed with automatic weapons. They chained me to my bed.'

And then in July, the band of 'Vlakplaas old boys' switched sides and became state witnesses. Altogether six new witnesses were moved to hideaways where they swore affidavits against the man whose orders they had once obeyed so faithfully. De Kock was alone and deserted, his visitors mostly limited to Peter Casselton, who took him a chicken every Sunday, and an aunt.

'He wasn't just abandoned by the generals, he was abandoned by the entire political structure. And, therefore, everybody from the top down, when they realised the chips were down and that some unpleasant truths were going to come out, ran for cover. And he was left there, the rabbit in the searchlight,' says Craig Williamson. Casselton, who had spent four years in prison himself, believed that Eugene de Kock was not going to survive his sentence. 'All the killing has wrecked and ruined him, especially because he didn't have any backing from the generals. Prison is going to kill him. He won't do it. It will finish him.'

His conviction became a mere formality, and when he took the stand in September 1996 to testify in mitigation of sentence, he was partly driven by a desire for revenge against those who had left him to bite the bullet. 'Nobody who knows war wants war. Politicians start a war, but we have to end it. In the meantime, they just become fatter and larger. If I look at the last two years, it seems as though I was the only white man who fought against the ANC. Everybody is now a reborn supporter of the ANC.'

De Kock dropped a small bombshell in giving evidence when he said that Craig Williamson was responsible for the murder of Swedish Prime Minister Olaf Palme in January 1986. As it later turned out, there was no substance to his allegation.

Ackermann: You are trying to divert attention from your own criminal deeds.

De Kock: No, that is not correct.

Ackermann: Shouldn't we solve J F Kennedy's murder as well?

De Kock: I was still too young when that happened.

He painted himself as a young Afrikaner boy who had become the knight of the generals and the peerless executioner of apartheid. He had ridden for ever onward into war, first in Rhodesia, then in Namibia, and finally in South Africa. His superiors had flocked to Vlakplaas to pay homage, to shake his hand, to pin yet another medal on his chest and to toast his latest bloody victory. From the comfort of their round tables, they had plotted and given orders and condoned and encouraged their killing machine. And then, as the war had appeared lost, they had disowned their hero.

Finally, a team of four experts debated whether or not De Kock was completely sane and responsible for his actions. A forensic psychologist, Dr Carien du Plessis, could find no sign of severe mental disorder, although he was found to be suffering from anxiety and depression. In fact, he was a pretty normal South African male. He suffers from post-traumatic stress disorder. Almost everyone who had done what he did for so long would have suffered from this disorder, but what was amazing was that he had managed to control himself for so long. He was mistrustful, shy and introverted, said a clinical psychologist, Dr Annemarie Novello.

Evidence was led that he experiences flashbacks of skirmishes in Koevoet and is easily frightened by loud sounds. One day, while his attorney was consulting him in his cell in the Adriaan Vlok police station, a shot went off outside the building. De Kock grabbed his attorney, pushed him behind the door and took out a knife he was hiding underneath his pillow.

However, a forensic psychiatrist who testified for the state, Professor Jan Plomp, questioned the diagnoses of post-traumatic stress disorder and said that De Kock possibly suffers only from war stress. He said only two of the murders committed by De Kock could possibly be linked to post-traumatic stress disorder – the murder of Moses Nthehelang in the Vlakplaas pub in 1989, where he lost his temper and broke a snooker stick over Nthehelang's head, and Japie Mapon-ya, whom he killed with a spade. But even in the case of Maponya, the murder was planned long before the execution of the deed. And so were his other crimes.

The judge seems to have accepted the latter opinion.

I have often been asked about my own feelings towards Eugene de Kock. In many ways, I have lived in his shadow ever since Dirk Coetzee spoke out in November 1989. He was then nothing but a phantom hiding on his death farm outside Pretoria, a man with thick glasses and a lust for blood.

I saw him for the first time when he testified to the Harms Commission in 1990, his leg covered in plaster, his face stark, his voice firm, his demeanour steadfast. Not a smile, not a suggestion of emotion.

And then he disappeared for four years. But he always lurked close by as more testimony to his maleficence started to emerge. I connected him to more murders, exposed him as a weapons smuggler and provided possible evidence of his thirdforce activities. Some of his men spoke out, I wrote more, the state is-sued denials and De Kock kept quiet and survived.

After I exposed 'Honeybadger Arms and Ammunition' and the 'Badger Unit' in January 1993, I met a senior police general, Andre Pruis. I gave him company documents and statements and pleaded with him to investigate Eugene de Kock and to stop his criminal activities. Nothing happened.

Seven months earlier, I had flown to Cape Town to interview the Minister of Law and Order, Hernus Kriel, about a list of 'dirty policemen' I had compiled and presented to him. Eugene de Kock topped the list. When I announced my arrival at the ministry of law and order in the HF Verwoerd Building in Plein Street, I was told that the minister had cancelled the appointment.

All the time, people were dying on the streets of South Africa's townships.

Eugene de Kock was arrested a few days after I had left South Africa for the central African state of Rwanda, where a genocidal orgy by Hutu militias exterminated 800 000 Tutsi civilians and Hutu moderates.

I was sitting in a dark house on the outskirts of the capital of Kigali eating beans and rice with soldiers from the Tutsi-dominated Rwandan Patriotic Front when a British journalist, quietly listening to the BBC World Service, asked me whether I knew a South African policeman by the name of 'Colonel de Kock'.

'Yes,' I said.

'He was arrested last night,' he announced, and added: 'For murder.'

At that very moment, Eugene de Kock meant very little to me, as I was still bewildered and stunned by the horrors of the killing fields surrounding me.

But later that evening, as we crept into our sleeping bags, I took a swig of brandy from the litre of Paarl Rock I had bought at a duty-free shop at Jan Smuts Airport, passed the bottle to my colleague and cameraman Ivan Oberholzer and said to him: 'We drink on Eugene de Kock.'

Seven months later, his trial started in the Pretoria Supreme Court. It was only one Saturday morning, a few days before Christmas 1995, that I walked down the passage to the visitor's section of Pretoria Central Prison. I was then producing a two-hour television documentary on the life and times of Eugene de Kock and had decided to visit him. It was our first face-to-face encounter.

I arrived unannounced, and when he saw me through the bullet-proof glass, he just stared at me.

'Good morning, Colonel de Kock, and how are you?' I asked him.

'Why do you want to know? You must be glad to see me sitting here,' he said and wanted to get up and walk away.

'Please don't,' I asked him. 'I have always wanted to speak to you.'

He stayed, and for the next hour or so, we spoke about the court case, the TRC and life behind bars. Although he had pleaded not guilty to the charges laid against him, he made no secret of the fact that the evidence against him was overwhelming and that he expected a long jail sentence. He was amiable, polite and seemed, like so many of his cohorts, just 'ordinary'.

Before I left the prison, I paged through the visitor's register and realised that he had had very few visitors in the previous weeks. I saw the name of Peter Casselton, but not that of his brother or anybody else I recognised. It was going to be a terribly lonely Christmas for Eugene de Kock.

At that moment, I felt pity for him. He was the man who had sowed so much death and mayhem and who had, according to his men, wanted to kill me, and yet, as I spent that Christmas in the mountains of the eastern Orange Free State, I often thought about the killer behind bars.

I visited him another four or five times, mostly with Peter Casselton and once with Lukas Kalino. I was from then on armed with an extra hot peri-peri Nandos chicken, which, according to Casselton, his friend, he was particularly fond of.

At our second meeting, he asked me to convey a message to the deputy chairman of the TRC, Dr Alex Boraine, that he wanted to apply for amnesty. I delivered a letter to Boraine, not so much because I wanted De Kock to get amnesty, but because we needed to hear his full story and a frank confession.

I remember very little of my meetings with De Kock as we spoke mostly about trivial matters, probably because he didn't trust me. He became upset when a fellow journalist told him that I was looking for his wife and children in Europe (which I wasn't), and he sent a message through Casselton that I shouldn't visit him again. Eugene de Kock now has to spend the rest of his life behind bars. His co-conspirators were indemnified and walked free. Most will carry the scars of their killing sprees forever and will be haunted by memories of their victims, but at least they have been granted a second chance. Some have even been richly rewarded for their testimony.

Chappies Klopper, already a criminal, inexplicably received R90 000 for his testimony before the Goldstone Commission, while Willie Nortje and Brood van

Heerden are today employees of the National Intelligence Agency. When it became clear that they could never be policemen again, they became spies. Not one of the Vlakplaas men had to repay a single cent of the money they had stolen. But neither have De Kock or the generals, for that matter, been ordered to return the goods they stole. When I once spoke to De Kock about amnesty, he wanted to know what the difference was between himself and somebody like Magoos Bar bomber Robert McBride, the ANC guerrilla who killed three innocent white women by detonating a car bomb in 1986. Many white people often ask me the same question.

What McBride did was abhorrent and is difficult to justify. But he grew up in his own country as a second-class citizen when he was classified by law as 'coloured'. He rose up against that system, joined the ANC and became a soldier against apartheid. He fought a just war, but in an immoral way. And remember, he was arrested, prosecuted, convicted and spent some years on death row until his release in 1992.

The night after McBride's bomb exploded, he didn't celebrate a 'victory over the enemy' and drink himself into a stupor as the Vlakplaas men often did. McBride was a junior MK operative and obeyed an order, while De Kock often made unilateral decisions about life and death. Ultimately, De Kock made war until the bitter end. He didn't stop when the ANC was unbanned, but continued to kill, plotted to derail a fragile peace process and tried to uphold an unjust system.

Only Eugene de Kock will know whether or not he really feels remorse for his victims. He had never shown any compassion for any of those he killed or tortured and I have often wondered: did this man enjoy killing people?

I have had mixed emotions about Eugene de Kock. When I started learning more about him in 1990, he was nothing but a political serial killer whom I despised and tried to expose. When I later learnt about his bravery in Koevoet, I couldn't help but feel some admiration for him. But when I spoke to Daniel Maponya and Seipati Mlangeni and saw their anguish and pain, it was easy to share their hate. And on the day he was sentenced, I felt happy, not because he had to spend the rest of his life in prison, but because justice had been done.

I waited with the crowd of onlookers for the silver steel doors of the Pretoria Supreme Court to open and for Eugene de Kock to be driven away in a yellow police van. Amongst the onlookers were Catherine Mlangeni, and she had tears in her eyes.

'He's gone,' said Margaret Nyalende, 'to dance on the bones of our children.'

Chapter Eleven

In the heart of the whore

Both their names will for ever be etched in infamy and be synonymous with murder: Eugene de Kock and Dirk Coetzee, two sides of the same coin.[1]

A security policeman who has served under both describes the one as 'a terrible mamba', the other as 'a monster who suffers from severe war psychosis'.

They grew up in an era in which their white countrymen joined hands and vowed to fight the communist onslaught they believed to be lurking across the country's borders, inside the townships and in the hearts and minds of so many black people.

Dirk Coetzee, the son of a postmaster, and Eugene de Kock, whose father was a magistrate, were raised in typical Afrikaner homes. As children, they both stuttered. The young Coetzee was only interested in sport, while De Kock showed a love for music and the outdoors. They were both poor students: Coetzee failed standard nine at his first attempt and initially passed only four matric subjects, while De Kock failed mathematics in standard ten and barely passed his other subjects. They became policemen several years apart but for the same reasons: a mixture of patriotism and a youthful quest for adventure and action. They were once both blue-eyed boys and favoured by the generals. The one was the best police student of his intake, the other rose swiftly through the ranks. Both received medals for faithful service.

While Coetzee was setting up the security police counter-insurgency unit in South Africa, De Kock was an architect of the unique Koevoet fighting formation in Namibia. They had both previously served in the Rhodesian armed forces.

Coetzee was the first commander of the South African Police death squad at Vlakplaas, De Kock the last. They were united in murder as both waged a campaign of terror against anti-apartheid activists.

They were in the heart of the whore.

On the surface, the two men are worlds apart. Dirk Coetzee is a youthful-looking man of 52 years with a shock of grey hair falling over his forehead. De Kock is four years his junior, but after more than three years in prison, he looks grey and fatigued. Coetzee is outgoing and talks excitedly, while De Kock is quiet and reserved.

Although their paths might have crossed a dozen or more times, the two former commanders first met in December 1993, nine months after the Vlakplaas unit had been disbanded. In a meeting brokered by killer askari Joe Mamasela in a pizza parlour, they courteously drank coffee and broke garlic bread together.

Before the meeting, Coetzee had decided to leave his nine-millimetre Glock pistol at home to show De Kock that he was not scared of him. De Kock had a big black bag with him, probably containing his mini-arsenal of a Glock and a machine pistol and maybe a hand grenade he often carried with him.

But although the two men, both fathers of two sons, share similar backgrounds, they found little common ground.

At the time, Coetzee had just returned after more than three years in exile after he had exposed the existence of police death squads and had had to leave the country. De Kock had twice tried to kill him, once by sending him a parcel bomb, the second time by despatching one of his assassins to London.

At the time of their meeting, De Kock was busy smuggling weapons to Inkatha in an effort to derail the peace process and to prevent the ANC from coming to power.

'I knew it was you who had tried to kill me,' Coetzee told him, and added: 'I know you are busy with third-force activities. Why don't you stop it? Haven't you had enough?'

De Kock said very little and left after half an hour. The next time they came face to face was in January 1996 in the Pretoria Supreme Court. As Coetzee predicted, De Kock's past had caught up with him and he was facing a life behind prison bars. Coetzee was a state witness.

When Dirk Coetzee took the oath, he was about to testify about the deadly par-cel he had received from Eugene de Kock. 'Had circumstances been different, it could have been me who was ordered to kill the accused,' Coetzee told the court. They detest one another. In De Kock's eyes, Coetzee is the ultimate traitor for exposing him in November 1989 as a death squad commander. On that day, De Kock's world fell apart and he then knew that he would never wear a uniform again.

De Kock: 'I find him a very, very unpleasant person, somebody I wouldn't like to be seen with in the street. He was a *hensopper* (traitor), 'n *hanskakie* (renegade), he walked over, he was a traitor. I find him despicable.'[2]

Coetzee found his would-be assassin equally repulsive. 'He's a weak human being, and to make it worse, a useless assassin. I was a sitting duck, but he could not kill me. If I had been hunting him, he would have been a dead man today.'

De Kock: 'Coetzee was one of the worst counter-revolutionaries ever.'

Coetzee: 'I have never been a counter-revolutionary, just a policeman.'

De Kock: 'He's a white askari.'

Coetzee: 'If I had stayed on at Vlakplaas, I would have outclassed Eugene de Kock, I would have been involved in more atrocities than him.'

De Kock: 'I hope he becomes 100 or 200 years old and has to sleep in the bed he has made for himself.'

Coetzee: 'He got what he deserved.'

As commanders, both had a repution for being dedicated killers. De Kock was unflinching and dauntless in the execution of his duties. If he had to kill, he killed. Coetzee, on the other hand, never pulled the trigger himself and would leave the killing to a colleague.

De Kock: 'I didn't murder, I did counter-insurgency. I don't like to compare myself to Coetzee.'

Coetzee: 'We just had different methods. I mean, I burned the remains of my victims to ashes, and got rid of evidence in that way. De Kock blew them up with explosives. or would take them into a foreign country.'

Joe Mamasela: 'Dirk Coetzee is the flipside of Eugene de Kock. They are both devils.'[3]

Coetzee: 'We are both gangsters of Olympic achievements.'

Mamasela: 'The first man to rob me of my God-given innocence was Dirk Coetzee, because my first killing mission was through him. De Kock was just a monster, he had absolutely no feeling for human life.'

Both men have been shunned by the system they once served. The politicians and the generals have abandoned them and left them to fend for themselves.

Ironically, the two criminals find themselves on the same side again, baring their souls to the TRC in an effort to obtain amnesty. 'Please forgive us,' both plead, 'for we have done wrong, but we did so at a time when we were blinded by our belief in the divine rule of apartheid.'

The difference is that Coetzee spoke seven years before De Kock.

November 7, 1989. It was a warm and sunny day on the tropical island of Mauritius. A few metres away children were splashing in the crystal-clear water of the Indian Ocean, while further along the beach, sundrenched holidaymakers looked like multicoloured specks on the snow-white sand.

Sitting cross-legged next to me on the beach under a swaying palm tree, slowly sipping a frosty beer, was Dirk Johannes Coetzee, his handsome face tanned and clean-shaven, a slick of hair falling on his forehead. Two days before, we had booked into a tourist hotel on the southern tip of the island. On the face of it, we were just two ordinary holidaymakers enjoying the ambience of the island which had become a haven for South Africa's sun-seekers.

But this was no holiday. We were booked into the hotel under false names. The trip to Mauritius was the culmination of weeks of secret planning, of late-night meetings, cryptic messages smuggled to the Political-Military Council of the ANC and clandestine visits to the organisation's headquarters in Lusaka in Zambia.

Dirk Coetzee is a former security policeman, holder of a police medal for faithful service, the best student of his police college intake nearly 20 years earlier. But Dirk Coetzee was no ordinary policeman.

'I was the commander of the South African Police death squad. I was in the heart of the whore.'

They were words that would later reverberate around the world as Coetzee became the first white South African security policeman to expose the existence of death squads.

Coetzee admitted his involvement in at least 23 serious crimes committed 'in the line of duty' as a member of the security police. It was a bloodcurdling tale that spanned three countries and included six murders, attempted murder and conspiracy to commit murder, arson, sabotage, kidnapping, assault, housebreaking and car theft. All these crimes had been committed between January 1977 and December 1981. Besides the six murders he 'officially' committed, he was also involved in the murder of a Lesotho national during an abortive illicit diamond deal.

For several years, Coetzee would be branded as a traitor and a liar; scorned and despised by white Afrikaners and his former colleagues for having washed their dirty linen in public.

As we were sitting on the beach in Mauritius, the ANC – the dreaded communists and terrorists he had hated, hunted and fought – were preparing to meet the former death squad commander in London to take him into their protection and to give him sanctuary.

For the next three and a half years, Coetzee would hide in exile in the United Kingdom, Zambia and Zimbabwe. During that time, he would survive two attempts on his life and have to move 38 times to stay ahead of Eugene de Kock's death squads.

Like most former security policemen who had made confession of their deeds, Dirk Coetzee was also motivated by a desire for revenge against the generals whom he believed had abandoned him.

He was at the peak of his career when he was handpicked in August 1980 to set up Vlakplaas with 17 'rehabilitated and turned' terrorists and a handful of white policemen. Of the 17 askaris, three were killed by Coetzee and his men, another by Eugene de Kock, three deserted to the ANC and two landed up in prison for murder.

There were also three former Zapu guerrillas brought from Zimbabwe to work as labourers on the farm, while five Renamo fighters from Mozambique occasionally spent some time at Vlakplaas.

Vlakplaas was never set up as a death squad, but rather as a unit to accommodate askaris and to identify and arrest trained infiltrators. But because of the unit's secret nature and the fact that the askaris were already trained soldiers and were at the mercy of their captors, the unit became the ideal base from which operations against the enemy could be launched.

It took Coetzee a year to build up the farm, organise the askaris into units, obtain illegal and Russian-made weapons and appoint white security policemen to take charge of the askari units.

Four squads were formed, each consisting of black policemen and askaris operating under the command of a white officer. While the askaris would mix with township locals, the whites would remain in the vicinity, out of sight, but ready to make an arrest. No PAC or ANC infiltrators were arrested during Coetzee's 18 months as commander.

Coetzee drove around with enough firepower in the boot of his car to start a small war. There was a 40 kilogram case of explosives, a case of Russian hand grenades, five hand machine guns, Makarov and Tokarev pistols with silencers, and a shotgun. He also had corpse bags and strychnine in his car in case of need.

His official car's registration number was DJC 036 T – his initials and his age when he arrived at Vlakplaas. Security police headquarters had their own printing press and provided Vlakplaas with false registration plates, and third party and license discs. Most of the askaris had false passports.

The farm became 'operational' in September 1981, and in an orgy of violence over the next four months, Coetzee and his men committed four murders, attempted murder, arson, assault and car theft.

'I was prepared to kill as many people as I was instructed to kill. I absolutely felt like a hero. I mean, you were there to please your bosses. It was absolutely your ideal to go back after an operation and say: brigadier, general, I've done the job, successfully.'

But Coetzee had always been a bit of a loose cannon, and was frequently insubordinate. He was caught protecting friends involved in smuggling from police investigators and was accused of undermining the good morals of the police by distributing a pornographic movie amongst his friends.

The first important mission Coetzee undertook at Vlakplaas caused an international diplomatic incident when his team of askaris kidnapped a former ANC activist and teacher from Swaziland. The kidnapping was a noisy affair and eye witnesses noticed the registration number of the car into which the struggling and screaming teacher was bundled. The askaris took their victim to the Oshoek border post, and inspired by their success, returned to Swaziland to look for more activists.

But they were spotted by the Swazi police and a high-speed car chase ensued. The askaris fled into a house and tried to hide in cupboards, but the police tear-gassed them out and arrested them. They were later released on bail and smuggled back to South Africa.

The kidnapping caused an international uproar. The head of the Security Branch, General Johan Coetzee, and an official from the Department of Foreign Affairs had to apologise to Swazi officials and release the teacher immediately.

Dirk Coetzee had defied a golden rule: never get caught. In the security police they refer to it as the 'eleventh commandment'.

Johan Coetzee fumed with rage over the embarrassment the incident caused the police – not the first time that the Vlakplaas commander had put him on the spot. Dirk Coetzee remarked afterwards: 'Success has many fathers, failures are orphans.'

If there is one feature of the Dirk Coetzee reign of Vlakplaas that many would never be able to forget, it was his method of disposing of the bodies of activists that had been captured and murdered. Each security police death squad had to find a way of making people disappear. De Kock blew bodies to smithereens with explosives, while Coetzee burnt the bodies to ashes on a fire of wood and tyres.

But it was the ritual that accompanied the gruesome event that caused a mother to say at a hearing of the TRC: 'They braaied my son while they drank and laughed.'

In October 1981, Brigadier Willem Schoon called Coetzee and told him: 'There is a man in the police cells with the name of Mavuso. He is stubborn and uncooperative. We must get rid of him, we can't let him go free.'

Vuyani Mavuso had been captured nine months earlier when the SADF had raided the Mozambican capital of Maputo, killing at least 13 people. During the attack, known as the Matola raid, the invaders captured ANC guerrillas and brought them back to South Africa. One of the suspects was Mavuso, who admitted under interrogation that he had undergone intensive military training in foreign countries and had been involved in a bomb explosion in Durban.

He was handed to the Security Branch, who could not find enough evidence to bring him to justice. Moreover, he refused to co-operate with his interrogators, making him an unlikely candidate for the police counter-insurgency unit at Vlakplaas. 'Charge me or shoot me,' he challenged. They took him at his word.

When Schoon instructed Coetzee to kill Mavuso, he told Coetzee to use the opportunity to get rid of 'poor Peter' as well. Nkosinathi Peter Dlamini, who was an askari at Vlakplaas, was a frail, timid and pathetic policeman who was always late and could do nothing right. He was loathed by his fellow askaris who frequently assaulted him.

A few days later, Mavuso and Dlamini were taken to a police farm. Dlamini, who was under the impression that he was there to guard the captive, was handcuffed to Mavuso.

Coetzee had decided to poison the two before burning their bodies. The previous day, he had obtained poison from the police forensic laboratory. He slipped the poison into cans of cold drink and gave them to the handcuffed men.

By now the sun had set, and the men were standing around the braaivleis fire with brandy, rum and beer, waiting for the poison to take effect. Mavuso started talking incoherently and fell over, scrabbling at the ground. He carried on like that for much of the night, but by morning seemed normal again.

The next day, Coetzee went back to Pretoria to report that the poison had had no effect on the men. He came back and the dosage was doubled, but it still failed to work.

Joe Mamasela decided to teach Mavuso how to pray before he met his Creator. Mavuso was forced to kneel on two bricks and to recite the Lord's Prayer, to the great amusement of the other squad members. They would joke about whether or not Mamasela himself knew the prayer. Every time Mavuso faltered, Mamasela would kick him. After an hour of this gross entertainment Mavuso's face was bleeding and swollen.

Coetzee decided that the poison would never work and that they would have to resort to bullets. Mavuso must have known by then that he was going to die at the hands of his captors. Yet he never spoke or pleaded for mercy. Peter Dlamini, too, must have realised that he was not there as Mavuso's guard.

It was late afternoon when the two men were brought to the banks of the Komati River, between Komatipoort and the Mozambican border in the Eastern Transvaal. Coetzee administered knock-out drops to their cold drinks, and when Mavuso and Dlamini lapsed into unconsciousness, one of the policemen stepped forward, placed his foot against the neck of one of the captives, pressed the barrel of the Makarov against his head and pulled the trigger. The body gave a slight jerk, then lay still, blood oozing from the wound. Seconds later, the other man was executed in the same manner.

In a dry ditch on the slightly elevated river bank, a shallow grave was dug with bushveld wood and tyres. The two corpses were lifted onto the pyre and as the sun set over the Eastern Transvaal bushveld, two fires were lit, one to burn the bodies to ashes, the other for the security policemen to sit around, drinking and grilling meat.

'Well, during the time we were drinking heavily, all of us, always, every day. It was just another job to be done. In the beginning it smells like a meat braai, in the end like the burning of bones. It takes about seven to nine hours to burn the bodies to ashes. We would have our own little braai and just keep on drinking.'

Every hour or so, one of the policemen had to add a new pile of wood to the fire and turn the bodies over. Early the next morning their remains were dropped into the river. By midday – tired, dirty, hungover – Coetzee and his men had returned to base near Pretoria.

At least two more people were cremated by Coetzee in a similar fashion – the first in an effort to prevent the possibility of a Steve Biko-type incident in the Eastern Cape. In September 1977, Biko had died in detention after being left for two days badly injured on a mat of chains. An inquest magistrate had exonerated the police, but four years later, they dreaded being caught with a detainee's blood on their hands again.

That is exactly the prospect that faced the police when a young Eastern Cape activist, Sizwe Kondile, his hands cuffed behind his back, dived through the window of an interrogation room and fell head-first onto the concrete outside. Although he did not seem to be seriously injured at first, his behaviour became peculiar and the interrogators asked a doctor they could trust to examine him. As they heard his warning that the man had sustained head injuries, the possibility of another Steve Biko incident loomed.

Coetzee was called to the Eastern Cape, and when he walked into the Jeffrey's

Bay police station, he was taken to a room where a slender, bearded black man was handcuffed to a bed.

Kondile was taken to Komatipoort where he was shot, thrown onto the pyre of tyres and wood, and burned to ashes.

At the end of 1981, Coetzee was informed that he had been transferred from Vlakplaas to the Narcotics Bureau. His behaviour in the security police had become unacceptable to his superiors. General Johan Coetzee clearly disliked the Vlakplaas commander, who had not only embarassed him with a pornographic film, but had also caused a diplomatic row with a neighbouring state.

Coetzee's transfer was a devastating blow to his self-esteem – it was, in his words, 'as bad as making the Pope a Dutch Reformed minister at Putsonderwater (a dusty village whose name means empty well)'.

His position would deteriorate further to the point where he would face seven internal charges in 1985, ranging from disrespect towards a superior officer to participating in a smuggling scheme. As a security policeman, Coetzee was a member of a close-knit family and an exclusive club, a clique of men who were elevated above the law and who roamed the country hunting down enemies of the state. They were not bound by legal niceties. For them the country's borders were just fences, and laws and regulations were nothing more than words on worthless pieces of paper.

He turned out to be a rather disastrous narcotics bureau detective. After some half-hearted attempts to discover the odd shebeen (illegal drinking tavern), a few dagga joints and a handful of mandrax pills, he was transferred to head office recruitment where he was put in charge of recruiting white policemen. After sitting for a year and four months in an office writing a few letters, he couldn't take it any more.

By May 1984 he found himself in the flying squad, where he had started his promising police career as an aspiring young constable in 1972. At least then he had had a dog, but by 1984 he had to attend to car accidents, prepare reports, and inspect patrol cars and police stations.

Coetzee realised that he had reached the end of the road. In an attempt to find a new career, he started studying law at the University of South Africa (where he passed his first-year courses with distinctions in Afrikaans and Latin!). This is where he befriended Frans Whelpton, who had once been the private secretary to the former Minister of Manpower and Mineral and Energy Affairs, Fanie Botha. Whelpton had also once been a rising star in the National Party and a confidant and friend of at least two cabinet ministers.

But when Coetzee met Whelpton, the police were investigating charges of extortion and corruption against him. Whelpton and a business associate, Brigadier Jan Blaauw, a legendary South African Air Force pilot and Korean War hero, had discovered that Botha had received millions of rands in bribes for the granting of diamond concessions along the Cape west coast. In turn, the two men black-mailed Botha, in order to get their hands on the diamond concessions. Botha, once the most senior cabinet minister, eventually had to resign in disgrace.

Coetzee and Whelpton had much in common: both were outcasts. Whelpton told Coetzee about his anxiety regarding the police, and soon the policeman started his own investigation. He discovered that Whelpton's phone was being illegally tapped, and was told that the police investigating team had called in the help of the Gold and Diamond Branch to set a trap for Whelpton by offering to sell him illegal diamonds. Coetzee warned his new friend, who refused to buy the diamonds. By now, the police had discovered the friendship between Coetzee and Whelpton and were also tapping Coetzee's telephone! A friend was questioned about Coetzee's sex life, drinking habits and personal life. At one stage, he was followed by the chief of the Criminal Investigation Department, General Jaap Joubert, but Coetzee cornered him in a parking garage and, to the amazement of bystanders, shouted at the cringing general to stop harassing him.

At the end of 1984, police raided Whelpton's attorney's office and found a statement signed by Coetzee in which he gave a detailed description of the illegal telephone tapping. Basie Smit made a visit to Coetzee in December 1984 to tell him that General Johan Coetzee wanted to see him. 'I'm on sick leave, and if the general wants to see me, he can come and do so at my house,' Coetzee told Smit. Coetzee had dared to defy the commissioner, and a day later he was suspended from duty.

It was during this time that I met Whelpton and Coetzee. My colleague Martin Welz was investigating the bribery and corruption allegations against Fanie Botha and was being fed information by Whelpton. I remember sitting in Whelpton's back garden and being shown a psychiatric report he had on his former friend the cabinet minister who was then undergoing treatment for severely assaulting his wife and threatening to commit suicide. One night, the couple's two children, scared and distraught, fled to neighbours while their father was battering their mother. State President PW Botha ordered the minister to obtain psychological treatment.

Whelpton was eventually charged and convicted of extortion and sentenced to five years' imprisonment. As details emerged during the trial of South Africa's procurement of nuclear technology from Israel, the judge ordered the proceedings to be heard behind closed doors. Whelpton served more than a year of his sentence, and is today a professor of law at the University of South Africa.

On first meeting him, Dirk Coetzee struck me as an open-faced Afrikaner, no different from many thousands with whom I would rub shoulders on a daily basis in Pretoria. But he was an angry man who was planning revenge against Basie Smit and Johan Coetzee.

Shortly before I met him, he had discovered that not only Whelpton's, but his own telephone was being tapped by the police. By then, he had already decided to leave the force and he consulted his house doctor, who declared him medically unfit for continued police duty as a result of an 'uncontrolled diabetic condition'.

Coetzee compiled a report about telephone tapping and sent it to the leader of the official opposition in Parliament, Dr Frederik van Zyl Slabbert. The report caused a sensation and was published on the front pages of most newspapers. Louis le Grange denied that the police were illegally listening to telephone conversations.

During my first meeting with Coetzee, he told me that the police were waging a terrible vendetta against him, and that they were not only tapping his telephone, but had also broken into his house to look for official documents. He, therefore, kept a deadly puff-adder in a small backyard storeroom to guard some valuable documents he intended to produce at his internal police trial. He was facing seven charges of misconduct.

To show me the contempt with which he regarded the tapping of his telephone, he picked up the instrument and started swearing. He explained that as soon as he lifted the handset – before even dialling a number – the tape recorder at Security Branch headquarters would start running and the policemen monitoring his calls would then have to listen to his vulgar diatribe.

It gave Coetzee much merriment as he used the tapped phone to tell his colleagues about adultery, wife-swopping and policemen visiting prostitutes. He called a senior general a scoundrel for having a sleazy affair with the wife of a Supreme Court judge. Thirty-five additional charges of using vulgar language over the phone were brought against him, and years later, the tapes were used at a judicial inquiry to discredit him.

This is what he said on the tapes: 'Jaap (a general and the CID chief), you stupid fucking cunt, you must go to Jesus Christ, you dumb cunt. You are dumb and you are going to fall! Johan Coetzee, you and that pig's head of a minister, I am going to sink you both …'

Coetzee was a truly bizarre character. He told me how he and another policeman had tried to lay their hands on an instant fortune. Whelpton had told them that Jan Blaauw had piles of money hidden under the wooden floor of his Northern Transvaal farmhouse, and one night, the two crawled through thorn bushes and down a river bed to steal the money. They broke into the house, demolished the wooden floor, but couldn't find the promised fortune.

A friend of Whelpton asked him whether he could get rid of a poacher on his game farm. Coetzee started making plans, asking the farmer whether there was enough good firewood and a river flowing through the farm. He planned to use his old and trusted recipe to solve the problem. I don't know how serious Coetzee was about killing the poacher and burning his body, but the plan was finally aborted.

As I got to know Coetzee better, he mentioned the name 'Vlakplaas' and told Martin Welz and I that it was a secret police farm which he had commanded. He said Vlakplaas was used as a base for former terrorists and that it was still in use.

One night, the rebel cop was tattling endlessly about his escapades in the police force. I asked him: 'Now come on Dirk, tell me, what did you do when you were at Vlakplaas?'

Coetzee babbled on, but this time, it wasn't about corrupt generals or illegal telephone tapping. It was a tale reminiscent of a political thriller, but one, Coetzee assured me, that was all too real.

He told us about a Durban attorney he had murdered, about a young antiapartheid activist from Port Elizabeth who had mysteriously disappeared after being poisoned by the security police, and how the security police had stolen an Eastern Cape labour union's minibus from a Johannesburg hotel.

At the time I was a journalist with the government-supporting Afrikaans Sunday newspaper *Rapport*, and being an Afrikaner from a fairly conservative Pretoria background, I had no recollection of activists who had disappeared or been murdered in mysterious circumstances.

The morning after Coetzee told me about his activities, I looked at newspaper clippings about assassinations and disappearances of anti-apartheid activists and soon recognised the Durban attorney as being Griffiths Mxenge and the young Eastern Cape activist as Sipiwo Mtimkulu. Their names were new to me.

Given that *Rapport* supported the National Party there was no prospect that the newspaper would ever publish Coetzee's allegations. In any event, the political climate of the middle 1980s was not conducive to the exposure of security force's atrocities. Welz suggested that we should keep the knowledge to ourselves until we had an opportunity to publish them – which would only arise four years later. I later discovered that Coetzee told not only me about Vlakplaas, but that he had revealed his secrets to several politicians. In fact, he was at one stage prepared to tell virtually anybody who asked him. At Whelpton's birthday party, Coetzee would be told: 'Dirk, quickly tell them what thugs the police really are.'

It is difficult to say whether Whelpton's guests believed Coetzee or not. Nobody seemed shocked; neither did anybody say they disbelieved him. They probably shared Coetzee's values and took it for granted that the police killed anti-apartheid activists.

Along with Whelpton, Coetzee saw a National Party MP, Wynand Malan (today a Truth and Reconciliation Commissioner), and gave him some information about Vlakplaas and its activities. Malan said he would discuss the allegations with Chris Heunis, who was then a senior cabinet minister, but Coetzee never heard from him again.

He also briefed the Progressive Federal Party (PFP) spokesperson on police, Tian van der Merwe. Coetzee said he spent two days with Van der Merwe, who died in a car accident some years later, and told him in detail of Vlakplaas operations. Nothing came of the meeting.

At his internal inquiry, Coetzee was found guilty on various charges, and the chairman of the board made a submission to the Minister of Police, Louis le Grange, stating that Coetzee was no longer fit to stay in the police force. However, as a gesture of compassion and in view of mitigating circumstances, his salary should be reduced and he should be allowed to retire on pension as medically unfit.

Le Grange approved the recommendations and Coetzee had to appear before a medical board. Coetzee lied to the physician examining him, exaggerating his diabetic condition. He was discharged with a meagre pension and on January 31, 1986, Coetzee left the force, bitter and filled with vengeance.

For the next three years, Coetzee depended on the charity and goodwill of friends and family. He was on occasion a casual labourer at the Kyalami race track outside Johannesburg, where he put up posters to advertise racing events.

His discharge from the police force was a devastating blow to his self-esteem. His former police friends shunned him and he became an outcast, lonely and disillusioned.

By the end of the 1980s, South Africa had changed substantially. The South Africa of September 1989 was not the South Africa of 1984 or 1985. The repressive and authoritarian rule of State President PW Botha had come to a merciful end and South Africa was slowly moving towards a more open, free and just society.

My own position had changed dramatically. From working for newspapers loyal to the government's policies, I had become a founder member of the independent and free-thinking *Vrye Weekblad*, which was part of the so-called alternative press and the only Afrikaans paper to the left of the government.

From its inception in November 1988, *Vrye Weekblad* had been a controversial newspaper, challenging the government on such issues as conscription, security legislation and state corruption. The government regarded us as a threat to the security of the state and so *Vrye Weekblad* had to pay the highest deposit in South African newspaper history before being allowed to register and publish.

We started the newspaper with only the savings of the five journalists involved and a R10 000 bank overdraft from a friendly but nervous bank manager.

In one of the first editions of *Vrye Weekblad*, we published an interview with the banned leader of the South African Communist Party, Joe Slovo, and the editor, Max du Preez, was promptly charged and convicted under the Internal Security Act.

In the second edition, we exposed the corruption and extortion practices of a well-known Bloemfontein attorney. Next to the article was a photograph of the lawyer presenting a bottle of good red wine to his friend, PW Botha, at a National Party function in Bloemfontein. Hours after the article had been published, the attorney left his office with *Vrye Weekblad* clasped under his arm and gassed himself and his young gay lover in his luxury car.

In one of our first editions, I wrote a story about a secret meeting between PW Botha and a mafia boss who lived in South Africa. Botha threatened to sue for defamation and that night, the State President's intention to take legal action against me and the newspaper was one of the main items on television news.

After the news bulletin had been read, the telephone rang, and I knew that it was my mother. She cried so much on the telephone that she could hardly speak. 'I wonder what your late father would have said of all this?' She asked me to write under a pseudonym to prevent further embarrassment to my relatives, members of a proud and established Afrikaner family. It was only in later years that she would become one of my greatest supporters.

Vrye Weekblad became one of the most prosecuted and persecuted newspapers in South Africa's history, leaving Max du Preez with a long criminal record. Most Afrikaners accused us of being traitors to the cause of Afrikaner nationalism. The offices of *Vrye Weekblad* were bombed and Max and I were threatened at gun-point by religious extremists. We received hate-mail and threatening phone calls on a regular basis.

Since Coetzee's suspension from the police in 1986, I had stayed in regular contact with him. When we started *Vrye Weekblad*, I said to Max that if there was one story we should publish, it was the police death squad story. Two incidents spurred us into action.

The first was the murder of a Namibian advocate and Swapo executive committee member, Anton Lubowski, who was shot dead outside his Windhoek home on September 12, 1989. He was a good friend of Max and I got to know him well during my coverage of the election campaign in Namibia. We were outraged by the killing and had no doubt that a South African death squad was behind the crime. The Monday night after the murder, I had dinner with Dirk Coetzee in a Portuguese restaurant in Pretoria. I asked him who could have killed Lubowski, and he said: 'Vlakplaas'. (It later emerged that Lubowski had actually been assassinated by a SADF death squad.)

I asked the former policeman to tell me more about Vlakplaas and security police killings. For the first time, Coetzee spoke freely about death squads. He said that the parcel bomb that had killed Ruth First, wife of Joe Slovo, in Maputo, Mozambique in 1982 had been sent to her by Major Craig 'Superspy' Williamson and his team of agents at the foreign section of the security police. The foreign section had also blown up Jeanette and Katryn Schoon in Angola in 1984 with a parcel bomb. The bomb had been meant for ANC activist Marius Schoon, but he wasn't home at the time and Jeanette opened the parcel with the eight-year-old Katryn sitting next to her.

Coetzee also described various operations in Swaziland and Botswana – how an ANC member's hand had been blown away when he had opened a post box and how Coetzee had killed an infiltrator and a child with a powerful bomb placed against the wall of a house. In Botswana, a woman had been shot at point-blank range when the death squad had attacked her house in Gaberone.

I asked Coetzee whether he felt any remorse. 'I don't know,' he replied. 'I did it for Volk en Vaderland and I believed then that it was the right thing to do. After

I was kicked out of the force, I realised that I had been used to do their dirty work.'

I also asked him under what circumstances he would be prepared to have his allegations investigated and details published in *Vrye Weekblad*. 'Get me out of the country and find me a safe place where my family and I can live in peace. Then I will tell the whole world what I did and what I know.'

I discussed the conversation with Max the next morning. Our dilemma was simple: what to do with a self-confessed apartheid assassin? Even if we had the money to send him abroad, where to? No country would be willing to accept him, and furthermore, how would we protect him?

There was only one way out: the ANC. If we could get Coetzee to the ANC and the organisation was willing to protect and harbour him, we could expose one of the most important political stories of the decade. Allegations of shadowy death squads had been around for years, but for the first time, we had evidence that could corroborate and substantiate the suspicions. We had a man who was 'in the heart of the whore'.

In October 1989, the ANC was still a banned and outlawed organisation. Handing Coetzee over to 'the enemy' constituted a very serious criminal offence, and according to previous court judgements, furthering the aims of the ANC warranted a long jail sentence.

But how would Coetzee react to such a suggestion? I knew he had voted for the Conservative Party in the previous election, and it was almost impossible to contemplate an apartheid assassin joining ranks with the people he had hunted and killed.

And the ANC? What had the organisation to gain? Would its members be prepared to protect and harbour Coetzee? What if they threw him in a hole in the ground in a training camp in Angola?

Why was it so important to publish this story? It was a hell of a newspaper story, the kind of exposé that every journalist and editor dreams about. But more importantly, the story was at the heart of apartheid's most evil face and struck to the core of government ethics and morality. The murder of Anton Lubowski had proven to us that despite the coming to power of FW de Klerk, people opposed to De Klerk's policies were still dying.

This was our kind of story. This was what *Vrye Weekblad* was all about and why a year earlier we had been prepared to suffer incredible hardships to establish a voice for those Afrikaners who had broken ranks with the establishment.

We had to find a trustworthy go-between to establish whether or not the ANC would be interested in talking to Coetzee. We approached a regional director of the Institute for a Democratic Alternative (Idasa), Andre Zaaiman, whom we knew to have excellent contacts with the ANC and who frequently visited the organisation's headquarters in Lusaka. A courier smuggled messages to the ANC's Political-Military Council in Zambia, but before the organisation could take a final decision, an important incident happened.

On the eve of his execution, a death row prisoner swore an affidavit.

On October 20, 1989, the headline in the *Weekly Mail* read: 'Death-row police-man tells of Special Branch hit squad'.

The night before, a 32-year-old former security policeman, Butana Almond Nofemela, had made a last-minute appeal for clemency to the Minister of Justice to escape the hangman's noose awaiting him early the next morning. In his affidavit, Nofemela said he was a member of a police death squad who had participated in several assassination missions on the orders of senior policeman. Sentenced in September 1987 for murdering a Brits farmer – which was not a political crime, but a cold-blooded murder – Nofemela had hoped that his collea-gues in the security police would save him from the gallows. Senior policemen had sent messages to him in his death cell asking him not to talk about his role in the death squads. They had promised to save his life in return for his silence, but three days before he was due to be hanged, he was visited by a security policeman who told him there was nothing they could do for him. He would have to 'take the pain'.

Nofemela realised that he had been betrayed, called his lawyer and swore an affidavit.

'I am a 32-year-old male presently under sentence of death. My execution is scheduled for tomorrow morning, 20 October 1989, at 07h00. I wish to hereby reveal facts about my past which, I respectfully contend, might very well have had a bearing on my conviction and sentence of death had they been known to the trial court, Appeal Court and the Minister of Justice.

'During the period of my service in the Security Branch, I served under sta-tion commander Brigadier Schoon. In 1981, I was appointed as a member of the Security Branch assassination squad, and I served under Captain Dirk Coetzee, who was my commanding officer in the field.

'Some time during late 1981 I was briefed by Brigadier Schoon and Captain Coetzee to eliminate a certain Durban attorney, Griffiths Mxenge. I was told by these superiors that Mxenge was to be eliminated for his activities within the ANC. They instructed me to travel to Durban in the company of Brian Ngqulunga, David Tshikalanga and Joe Mamasela, colleagues of mine in the assassination squad.

'I was involved in approximately eight other assassinations during my stint in the assassination squad, and also numerous kidnappings. At this stage, I do not recall the names of any of the victims. Some of the assassinations, four in fact, took place in Swaziland, one in Botswana, one in Maseru and one in Krugers-dorp. The victims were all ANC members, except in Krugersdorp where the victim was the brother of an ANC terrorist.'

The fact that Nofemela was on death row reduced the credibility of his allega-tions. From the outside, it was unclear whether the confession was genuine, or merely a cunningly hatched plot to escape the noose.

But for Max du Preez and I, the confessions provided much-needed corroboration. Coetzee had mentioned the name of Almond Nofemela as one of his death squad operatives, and their accounts converged in nearly all aspects.

When I saw the ashen-faced Dirk Coetzee that Friday morning, he said: 'This is it. I think I've had enough. I told them a long time ago to look after Nofemela because he could bring all of us down with him. What are we going to do?'

I told him: 'We've already made contact with the ANC in Lusaka. They are interested in what you have to say. Would you be willing to meet them, talk to them, maybe in the end even join them? They are the only people who can really help you and protect you.'

We discussed his options. He said he could join in the cover-up and discrediting of Nofemela that was certain to follow, but that he thought there was a real risk of being isolated with his former colleague. Even if the security police succeeded in branding Nofemela a liar, how long before another death squad member spilt the beans? He agreed to meet Zaaiman.

Two days later, a series of meetings took place between Coetzee, Zaaiman, Max and me. We met late at night in a small thatched cottage, situated on a smallholding betwen Johannesburg and Pretoria. The smallholding was isolated from other homesteads, with a breathtaking view of the Johannesburg skyline.

After a few meetings, and having secured funds through the ANC underground, Zaaiman travelled via Botswana to Lusaka, where the ANC's chief of intelligence, Jacob Zuma, took personal charge of the project. The ANC undertook to ensure his safety inasfar as it was humanly possible and to give him sanctuary, on condition that he was telling the truth.

On the eve of his departure from South Africa, Coetzee had second thoughts. His almost blind father was very sick and might not survive the shock of his son leaving his fatherland and turning against his own people. He felt he couldn't leave his family behind. The enormity of leaving the country and entrusting his life to the ANC had finally caught up with him.

He said he had to go and speak to his eldest brother, Ben, whom he had always entrusted with the important decisions of his life and who knew about his death squad involvement. Later that evening, I received a call: 'I am ready to go. See you tomorrow morning.'

At six o'clock the next morning Coetzee waited for me outside his house next to two suitcases. His wife Karin embraced him, and he picked up his two poodles and gave each of them a kiss. 'I am going to miss the dogs, I am so fond of them,' he said as he got into the car. On our way to the airport, he said Karin did not know what was happening or where he was going. The previous night, he had taken his two sons, Dirkie and Kalla, to stay with friends because he couldn't face saying goodbye to them. He was too distraught to call his parents and tell them he was going away.

On Sunday morning, November 5, 1989, we boarded a South African Airways flight to Mauritius. The plan was to stay on the island for a few days, do the interviews and take a statement before Coetzee would fly to London to meet the ANC. En route to Mauritius, while Coetzee was speaking non-stop in his manic fashion and slugging away on the complimentary liquor, I had mixed feelings about what we were trying to achieve. In a country so desperately in need of justice, we were helping an apartheid assassin to escape exactly that.

Two weeks later, *Vrye Weekblad* published Dirk Coetzee's story: Coetzee's allegations were simultaneously the lead stories on the front pages of leading European and American newspapers, while other foreign correspondents took note of the interview and sent it around the world.

The police were quick to respond. Police public relations chief General Herman Stadler vehemently denied that there was a death squad, admitted that Vlakplaas did exist but said that the 'rehabilitated terrorists' were only used to find their former ANC and PAC cadres and to arrest them. Ironically, the Minister of Law and Order, Adriaan Vlok, had denied on television the very night before that a police death squad ever existed.

Journalists were taken to Vlakplaas and introduced to some 'rehabilitated' ANC and PAC renegades who told the press contingent that they had seen the error of their ways and were now fighting communism.

Eugene de Kock later said that Stadler had phoned him to warn him of the media's visit and told him to get rid of 'anything strange'. The Vlakplaas weapons arsenal was hastily moved to another police farm.

In the week and months that followed, Coetzee, now a self-confessed murderer, poisoner, arsonist, bomber and thief, was also branded a liar, perjurer, traitor, gangster and psychopath.

The mainstream media, especially the Afrikaans newspapers, played a major role in discrediting Coetzee and thereby allowing De Kock and his men to carry on with their killing missions.

Rapport, for whom I had worked only two years previously, published an unsourced article saying that Coetzee had never left South Africa and was hiding somewhere on a farm outside Pretoria. He was sick, without his medication and in a semiconscious state, stumbling around on the farm. Although Coetzee released a statement from Europe in response to these allegations, the newspaper never published a correction. The National Party mouthpiece *Beeld* said in an editorial that one had to be mad to believe Coetzee.

Coetzee spent three difficult years in exile in the United Kingdom, Zimbabwe and Zambia. Although he became a member of the ANC, he was never fully trusted by certain members of the organisation and was for security reasons not allowed to visit the intelligence offices. He sat for days on end in his hotel room without contact with anybody.

The inefficiency that plagues Zambia led to enormous frustrations and confrontations with the people around him. He could not bear the slow service, the poor telephone lines and the bad food. He would jump over a counter to show an attendant what quality of service he expected or would swear angrily at waiters and civil servants.

Coetzee was enchanted with the ANC and it changed his outlook on life, his political convictions and even his vocabulary. 'Terrorists' became 'freedom fighters', the 'enemy' became the 'movement' and the 'communist onslaught' became the 'liberation struggle'. Amongst his highlights were an hour he spent with Nelson Mandela in London and a personal assurance by Archbishop Desmond Tutu that the people of South Africa had forgiven him because he had expressed his sorrow. While in exile, Coetzee would often tell me that he was going to be a police general upon his return to South Africa, a promise made to him, he said, by the ANC's Jacob Zuma. He desperately wanted to be a policeman again and to weed out the dirty cops from the force.

Six years later, the rebel policeman feels as disillusioned and rejected as he was when he was kicked out of the police force in 1986. Instead of being a high-ranking policeman, he is now regarded as a low-level spy, his victims are unforgiving and he has been unable to reconcile with his people.

Today Dirk Coetzee, his wife Karin, their two sons and 12 dogs live in a barricaded and fortress-like house in a middle-class Pretoria suburb. From their front garden you can see the Presidency, perched high on the Soutpansberg, which President Nelson Mandela and his colleagues have occupied since May 1994.

There are double sets of burglar bars at the windows and iron gates at the doors. De Kock sleeps with his Glock pistol, cocked and ready, next to him on the bedside table. His son Dirkie also has a pistol and always keeps it cocked and ready. When Coetzee goes to the bathroom he takes his pistol with him. When he drives into town, he keeps his Glock cocked and ready on the seat between his legs. Very much like Eugene de Kock used to do when he was still a free man. But now he is in jail, and who is Coetzee afraid of?

'Some Afrikaners hate me and would like to kill me, and there's still too many old Vlakplaas people around. And then there is the family of Griffiths Mxenge, who have threatened to do something if there is not justice.'

Since his return to South Africa at the middle of 1993, Coetzee has become lonely and isolated. He hardly has any contact with members of his family and does not attend weddings or funerals.

Dirk Coetzee has become one of the most interviewed people in post-apartheid South Africa and has turned into something of a confessional junkie, telling his tale to any one who cares to listen.

In 1990, he became an atheist and tore up his Sunday school certificate he had received when he became a member of the Dutch Reformed Church. 'It anyway looked like a Smartie box.'

His religious convictions and foul language have landed him in deep water virtually every time he has appeared before South African judges – most of them conservative and Afrikaans.

Whe he testified in the trial of Eugene de Kock, the defence counsel asked him about a tape recording he had made and sent to his friend Frans Whelpton in South Africa, who passed it on to Krappies Engelbrecht. In the tape, he says: 'There is so many damn thieves and dishonest so-called Christians on this earth that Jesus Christ can't fuck them all up, I have to help him. He can't get to every-body. It is impossible, he can't watch all of them.'

Counsel for De Kock: You said you grew up in a Christian home, but that you lost your faith in around 1990.

Coetzee: That is correct.

Judge: An atheist?

Coetzee: A non-believer ... If there is a good place where good people eventually land, I will also get there.

Judge: You will also get there?

Coetzee: Yes.

Coetzee believes that his two children have also been victims of the campaign waged against him. The children spent three years with him in exile and didn't go to school during that time. When they returned with their father, Coetzee enlisted them at academic colleges.

The youngest son, Kalla, completed standards nine and ten in one year and today studies computer science. Dirk Junior received the trophy for the best student of the year in 1995 and had nearly full marks for all his legal subjects.

'During the award ceremony (to receive the trophy), Karin and I were stand-ing around on our own. Nobody came to congratulate us about the achievement of our son. They all knew that I was Dirk Coetzee and, therefore, contaminated. The conservatives hate me, the more upper-class Afrikaners lift their noses as though they had nothing to do with what I have done. I despise them.'

Dirk Junior wants to be a policeman like his father, but despite his high grades, he has been unable to get admission to the police college. Wherever he applies for a job and introduces himself, people say to him: 'Don't tell me you are Dirk Coetzee's child!' His girlfriend's parents applied pressure to her to choose be-tween them and him, and she now lives with Dirk Junior in the house.

Coetzee's biggest disappointment has been with the ANC. Instead of appoint-ing him as a high-ranking policeman, the organisation found him a job in the National Intelligence Agency (NIA) where he works on the counter-insurgency and terrorism desk. NIA has become a haven for killer policemen and not long after Coetzee started working there, he was joined by Willie Nortje and Brood van Heerden.

If there is one thing Coetzee can never be, it is a spy. Everybody recognises him and he simply talks too much. His desk, he says, is clean and bare, except for a few newspapers lying on it. He has been sent on only one mission – to investigate a former SADF officer suspected of smuggling arms – but the project was soon aborted. He often doesn't even report for work.

It is difficult to persuade Coetzee that he can never be a policeman again, even if he was the first to speak and has done such a lot to expose police murder squads. We simply can't have a former Vlakplaas commander in a police force struggling to earn the respect and trust of different communities.

The character assassination of Coetzee continued after his return to the country. In 1995, newspaper headlines accused Coetzee of spying on the Commissioner of Police, General George Fivaz. A KwaZulu-Natal police colonel, H T Moodley, alleged in a statement that after the investigation into the Mxenge murder was reopened in 1995, he had questioned Coetzee, who had told him that he was bugging the offices of Fivaz and other senior police officers.

Coetzee underwent two lie detector tests to try and prove his innocence. He passed both, while Moodley failed his. It later emerged that Moodley was a former security policeman who had been stationed at the Natal Security Branch during the time that Mxenge was murdered.

Today, Coetzee is convinced that South Africa is going 'the same way' as so many other African states and that the country will eventually be destroyed by crime, corruption and racial strife. He voted for the ANC in 1994, but said he would never do so again.

He is sorry that he spoke out. He said he is still punished for the stand he made and it wasn't worthwhile. He would like to leave country and go and live somewhere that he is not recognised and where he will never have to look his people in the face again.

Many people tend to agree with Louis Harms that Dirk Coetzee is mad. However, he underwent an intensive psychological examination in 1996, and according to the report, there is 'no evidence of neuro-psychological impairment. All functional domains are intact.' The report says that although he is intellec-tually above average, he is emotionally intense, impulsive and has a strong temper. 'He seems to be more in touch with his emotions of anger, loneliness and loss than emotions of love and happiness.'

Coetzee has on numerous occasions told the families of his victims how sorry he is for what he has done. But forgiveness has not been forthcoming. In 1995, he came face to face with Dr Churchill Mxenge, brother of the slain Griffiths Mxenge. The meeting was recorded by British television.[4]

Coetzee: Can I first say, I really feel very sorry and would just like to apol-ogise for the grief and sorrow that I have created as a result of my deeds.
Mxenge: I don't understand why a person like you is walking the streets of South Africa. It does not make sense. Dirk Coetzee is not supposed to be where he is today, he should be behind bars.

Coetzee: I understand your point of view, Dr Mxenge.

Mxenge: We will only be happy about this whole saga when justice is seen to be done. By that I mean we would like to see you arrested, charged and sentenced for what you did. You are a free man now, on talk shows, you are a hero.

Coetzee: I don't think, doctor, that we must see me as a hero.

Mxenge: You are a hero, I am sorry to say that, you have become a folk hero, and that is an insult to us.

Coetzee: I think it is a question of fellow South Africans appreciating the openness and at least someone that could stand up against the system and expose the system.

Mxenge: Oh come on, I don't buy that. I think we should stop this interview. I think we have had enough.

The mother of Sizwe Kondile, Charity Kondile, also finds it impossible to forgive Coetzee. Her son faced a bright future: he had just completed his law studies and fathered his first-born. She searched for nine years for Sizwe, until she heard how the security policemen had gorged themselves on brandy, rum and meat next to the burning body of her son.[5]

In 1996, she went back to the spot where the ashes of her son had been scattered in the Komati River. 'As we were nearing that place I broke down. When we got there, I saluted Sizwe. There were flowers growing next to that place, so I took a stone and put it there and prayed that his soul must rest in peace. I washed my hands and left.'

In May 1997, Dirk Johannes Coetzee stood up in the Durban Supreme Court and was convicted of the murder of Griffiths Mxenge. Almond Nofemela and David Tshikalanga were also found guilty of the murder.

More than seven years after the rogue policeman went into exile to tell the world that the apartheid state was committing murder, he was convicted of murder himself. The whole process was a scurrilous indictment of the judicial process and a blatant disregard of the contribution Coetzee had made in bringing South Africa closer to the truth by exposing the death squads.

When he left South Africa in November 1989, he was called a mad, lying and revengeful policeman. One of those who called him a liar was Orange Free State Attorney General and Harms Commission official Tim McNally.

Seven years on, McNally, now the KwaZulu-Natal Attorney General, decided to prosecute Coetzee. Instead of using the former Vlakplaas commander as a state witness against his superior officers who gave instructions for the killing, Coetzee became accused number one.

The sole state witness was former askari Joe Mamasela, who lied at the Harms Commission about ever being involved in the murder of Mxenge. Mamasela only recently admitted to his complicity in the murder, but became a state witness.

In the end, Coetzee was convicted solely on his admissions before the Harms Commission. He never tried to deny his guilt.

On August 4, 1997, Dirk Coetzee, Almond Nofemela and David Tshikalanga were granted amnesty for the murder of Griffiths Mxenge. The TRC said: 'On the evidence before us, we are satisfied that they did what they did because they regarded it as their duty as policemen who were engaged in the struggle against the ANC and other liberation movements ... Coetzee acted on the advice, command or order of one or more senior members of the Security Branch.'[6]

In the meantime, Coetzee has befriended some of the most notorious Cape Town gangsters implicated in drug smuggling and murder, and spent several weeks with them after he was found guilty of the murder of Griffiths Mxenge. Coetzee acts as a consultant to the gangsters, but denies that he is involved in any illegal acts or that he receives money for his services.

I am often asked by people: how come you already knew so much in 1989 and 1990 and most of what you wrote then has turned out to be true?

My answer is always short and simple: Dirk Coetzee told the truth.

He never lied. And he didn't only confess about his own atrocities, but he already said in 1989 that his former friend and colleague Craig Williamson had sent the parcel bombs which killed Ruth First in 1982 and Katryn and Jeanette Schoon in 1984. He told us how his security police colleagues in the Eastern Cape had kidnapped and killed student leader Sipiwo Mtimkulu in 1982 after they had failed to poison him. He told us how the security police had sent explosives in the South African diplomatic bag to London to blow up the ANC headquarters in the British capital. When Bheki Mlangeni was blown up with the walkman bomb in 1991, Coetzee told us from exile in London that the security police had a 'bomb factory' in Pretoria where explosive devices were manufactured.

Most people didn't believe him, until people like Craig Williamson confessed, Eugene de Kock was convicted and the former Minister of Law and Order, a former Commissioner of Police and security policemen applied for amnesty at the TRC.

I can never be an apologist for Dirk Coetzee and understand the anger of his victims against him, but I reject the animosity of his fellow Afrikaners. They probably despise him for confronting them with something they never wanted to know, see or hear.

He reminded them that they grew fat on the bones and souls of the Griffiths Mxenges and Sizwe Kondiles of this world.

Chapter Twelve

The good soldier Joe

Joseph Mamasela is a flashy man with fleshy lips who could easily be mistaken for a horse punter or a car salesman.[1]

But behind the shiny shoes, three gold chains, florid vocabulary and a red BMW with silver mag wheels lurks the mind of a political serial killer who has shot in cold blood, stabbed at night, thrown petrol bombs and led young boys to their deaths.

Like so many township children who entered adulthood in the political turmoil of the 1970s, Joe Mamasela became a dedicated ANC comrade, went into exile and was trained in intelligence by Umkhonto we Sizwe in Botswana. His abhorrence of apartheid was strengthened when his uncle was shot dead by the security police.

And yet, when he started to kill, it wasn't under the banner ofUmkhonto or the ANC. His bombs and bullets were aimed at his own people – the people he had once vowed to free from apartheid's repression.

In 1979, Joe Mamasela became an informant for the security police. Less than two years later, he was based at Vlakplaas. Five months later, he murdered a lawyer in Durban who was suspected of working for the ANC.

He became an askari, and for more than a decade, he killed, again, and again, and again. His name appears throughout the security police chapters of terror and horror and he was a killing slave, first for Dirk Coetzee and Eugene de Kock at Vlakplaas, and then for Brigadier Jack Cronje in a Northern Transvaal Security Branch death squad.

When he left the police in 1993, he had been involved in the murder of 40 antiapartheid activists, some as young as 15 years. Some he helped to strangle, electrocute or blow up. Others were shot and stabbed. Mamasela said that he and his co-killers threw petrol bombs at the houses of about 350 activists.

For his commendable service, he received more than R400 000 when he retired. Before that, tens of thousands of rands were paid to him to ensure his silence and to persuade him to lie to the Harms Commission.

But Mamasela says he is no common killer. He claims he is also a victim of apartheid, the National Party and the security police, and he has, therefore, refused to apply for amnesty.

When he testified in a criminal court case in Durban in April 1997, he said to a white advocate who was cross-examining him: 'I'm a black person. I was born and brought up in this country. Every black person is a victim of the oppressive regime of the South African Police, of the South African government in the past, and that's a fact. You had a sweet life yourself.'[2]

Advocate: Mr. Mamasela, I know that is a fact.

Mamasela: Thank you very much, if you know. I was a victim and am a double one, of the ANC and the security police.

I have heard Joe Mamasela speak gleefully and without a shred of remorse about the people he has killed, but whenever he is in public, he says: 'No self-respecting human being can feel happy about killing even one person, now if you talk about 30, you will know how I feel. It is terrible. It is a bastard act. It is something that one cannot forgive himself for doing. But under those circumstances, one could do nothing.'

Mamasela says the security police robbed him of his 'God-given innocence' when they forced him to kill. 'We were just turned into political serial killers. We had no respect for human life, and our commanders had no respect for our lives. If you don't do these killings, they kill you. They killed a lot of askaris, more than six askaris we killed.'

It is true: askaris who refused to carry out the orders of their commanders or threatened to expose the secrets of their units were executed. But for many years, Joe Mamasela killed and planted bombs with enthusiasm, and according to his commanders, he never needed any encouragement to draw a knife or to lead schoolchildren to their deaths.

When Mamasela testified in court against Eugene de Kock, he told the court about a secret notebook he had kept about killings carried out by Vlakplaas and the Security Branch. Asked why he had recorded only some of the names of the people he had killed, Mamasela said: 'If I had to write all the names of the victims, I would be having a Bible … I cannot be writing all the deaths. I mean, I will be a mortuary chap or what? I could not do that.'[3]

Dirk Coetzee: 'He was ruthless and had the killer instinct. He was a born killer.'

Mamasela: 'When I went to Vlakplaas, I was just a student. I was extremely innocent. And he (Coetzee) was the first man to turn me into a killer.'

Coetzee: 'Ja, it's true, in a way he was forced into killing. But he never objected and was always willing to do the job. He was an outstanding criminal and a cruel man.'

Mamasela: 'I was forced to kill my own people, the people I devoted my life into liberating.'

Coetzee: 'Oh nonsense, Mamasela hated the ANC as much as we did. He was waging his own war against them.'

Mamasela turned state witness at the end of 1994 and made several affidavits to the Transvaal Attorney General. His confessions have spurred several security policemen into action, and led to the exposure of a death squad within the Northem Transvaal Security Branch based in Pretoria.

In October 1996, three former security policemen took the witness stand at the TRC and applied for amnesty for murdering 40 people, but a few months later, they increased their murder tally to nearly 60. If it wasn't for Mamasela's confessions, they might never have come forward.

Joe Mamasela was only one of more than 100 askaris deployed by the security police to act against and to kill their former comrades. In his own words: 'I was forced to kill my own people, the people I devoted my early life into liberating.'

Mamasela grew up in a typical township family in Soweto. His parents were labourers, and like so many township kids of the 1970s, he became embroiled in student politics whilst a pupil at the famous Morris Isaacson High School in Soweto. He was an executive member of the South African Students Movement. Mamasela became part of the 'Class of '76' when he joined in the Soweto uprising and protested against Bantu education and Afrikaans as the compulsory medium of instruction.

He left school the following year and joined the ANC in Botswana, where he received intelligence training. He was sent back to South Africa to mobilise and organise students' cells in and around Johannesburg.

But in 1979, he was arrested when policemen stormed into the house of a fellow comrade and found him there instead. 'The police asked me who I was, and when I said Joe Mamasela, you could see the excitement written all over their faces.' Mamasela said he was taken for interrogation. A certain Captain Viljoen was especially 'diabolic and satanic' when he ordered his men to strip Mamasela naked and to pour ice cold water over him. 'They put electronic apparatus all over my genitals, my entire body, underneath my toes and all that. But the worst thing that this man did was to take something like an electronic stick that they use to prod cattle with, he stuck it in my anus and that was the most excruciating pain I have experienced in my life. I lost consciousness for a long, long time and when I woke up, I found that every part of my body was bleeding. My nostrils, ears, mouth, my genitals were bleeding. This man kept on repeating this sadistic way of torturing me.'

Mamasela claims that he was arrested because of his involvement in the ANC. However, there is evidence to suggest that he was involved in common crime and that was the real reason for his detention and interrogation. A charge of armed robbery had been opened against him in Randfontein, west of Johannesburg, but according to police records, charges were withdrawn.

What may have happened is that, in an effort to avoid a lengthy jail sentence for robbery, Mamasela could have told his interrogators that he was a member of the ANC and that he would co-operate with the police. He maintains, however, that he became a police informant because he had no other choice.

'There was no way I could resist further, they left no doubt in my mind that they can, and will, and are, eager to kill me. So I said no, I will help you, what do you want?'

Joe Mamasela became police informant number WR465, and was told by his security police handlers to go back to Botswana and to infiltrate the ANC. He became a courier for the organisation, but in May 1981, the ANC discovered who his real masters were. When his cover was blown, his half-brother was with him in Botswana, and both were detained by the ANC.

'My brother was innocent, his mere crime being that he was at the wrong place at the wrong time. They murdered him that same evening, they shot him and burned his body.'

Mamasela escaped, and when he went looking for his half-brother, he found his charred corpse in the police morgue. He could only identify him by means of a ring on his finger. He said something died in him and he decided there and then that he would never rest until he had avenged the death of his half-brother.

He came back to South Africa and reported to his security police masters. 'They said: look what the ANC has done. These people were suppose to liberate you, but they are burning you alive. Feeling like I was feeling at that stage, I said fine, okay, I will help you to belt these people. Little did I know that I was jumping out of the frying pan into the fire.'

Numerous ANC and PAC cadres were 'turned' in a similar way. 'They will physically torture you to the point of death. When you give in, that's when they became nice and tell you about the bad things the ANC did against you and how they are going to use you constructively against these people.'

Mamasela says the police had a technique which the askaris called 'the burning of the bridges'. As soon as an activist had been turned into a security policeman, informants would be sent out into his community to spread the word that he was now working for the 'Boers'. This move would prevent the askari from escaping from Vlakplaas because he would then be hated and despised by his own people.

'I had no alternative. My duty was as an askari, just to do everything illegal or legal that my commanders told me to do. We had no say whatsoever over our lives.'

Durban, November 19, 1981. Prominent human rights lawyer and activist Griffiths Mxenge bade a colleague goodnight and left his Victoria Street law firm. It was almost eight o'clock and a thick blanket of mist and rain slowed his journey home to the township of Umlazi.[4]

Mxenge, a former Robben Island prisoner, had fought a tireless campaign against apartheid and was affectionately known as the 'ANC lawyer'. He was famous for his defence of anti-apartheid activists and hundreds of people arrested, detained and charged with offences under the Suppression of Communism Act, the Group Areas Act, the Terrorism Act, the Police Act and the pass laws legislation.

On that ghostly, grey night in November, the lawyer was a worried man. That morning he had been awakened by the screams of his children: one of the family's bull terriers was found dead on the front lawn, the other writhing in agony next to it. Rushed to the local vet, the second dog died on the examination table. The dog had been poisoned.

'Why might someone want to poison my dogs?' he had asked colleagues at work during tea time.

But his rumination was disturbed on the way home that night by the presence of a grey pick-up van parked in the road ahead with its bonnet open. A man stepped out into the headlights, waving. Mxenge stopped his white Audi and wound his window down as the stranger approached.

'Can you help us? There is something wrong with the bakkie. Don't you have jumper leads or something?'

As Mxenge got out of his car, two more figures loomed out of the shadows. The man drew a gun and pointed it straight at him. 'Do as I say. Get into the back of the car.'

One of the stalkers was Joe Mamasela. With him was another askari, Brian Ngqulunga, and two ordinary security policemen, Almond Nofemela and David 'Spyker' Tshikalanga (his nickname means 'nail' in Afrikaans, and had been given to him because of his amorous adventures).

Mxenge was pushed onto the back seat of his car. One of the men slid in after him, holding a pistol against him, while another got into the driver's seat and started the car. They drove back the way he had come, with the pick-up van following behind.

'Where are you taking me? Please don't kill me. You can take everything I have.

You don't have to shoot me,' Mxenge pleaded. There was no answer.

After a few minutes, the driver turned onto a dirt road and stopped the car. They were at the Umlazi cycle stadium.

'Get out!' – a pistol was jabbed into his ribs. Behind them, the van came to a standstill. The driver emerged with a knife in his hand.

This is how Mamasela recalled the killing when he testified in the Durban Supreme Court in April 1997: 'Nofemela and Tshikalanga started stabbing him … he was trying to stand up. He (Mxenge) had a knife, the long knife lodged in his chest, but he pulled it out. He charged Nofemela with his knife, who had to run for his dear life. I grabbed Tshikalanga's pocket knife, and chased the deceased. I lunged several times, trying to stab him in the back. He fell, and the knife fell next to him. Nofemela won back the knife, and as I was grappling with him, I felt him becoming weak. I felt warm, liquid-like stuff running down my hands, my arms, and when I looked at my hands I saw it was blood and then I got frightened, and I saw Nofemela cutting his neck with the long knife. Nofemela ran towards the bakkie where he grabbed the wheel spanner. He was completely beserk and totally uncontrollable as he hit the deceased.'

The killer pack pounced on Mxenge, hitting, kicking and stabbing. When the job was finished they removed his jacket, watch and wallet and drove off with their victim's brand-new car into the dark. Mamasela took R10 from Mxenge's wallet. Griffiths Mxenge was laid to rest a week after he was slain. From far and near, mourners converged on the tiny hamlet of Rayi, just outside King William's Town, to pay their last respects. Archbishop Desmond Tutu told the crowd of 15 000: 'Our liberation is going to be costly. Many more will be detained. Many more will be banned. But we shall be free.'

As Mxenge's coffin, draped in the colours of the ANC, was lowered into the grave, a black security policeman was found covertly tape recording the proceedings. Desmond Tutu and another priest tried in vain to shield him from a frenzied mob screaming: 'Kill the impimpi (traitor)! Kill the impimpi!'[5]

'Have you come here to bury Griffiths or to kill one another?' shouted the archbishop, his white robes splattered with blood, as the battered policeman lay dying behind the makeshift VIP platform.

At about the same time, Joe Mamasela, Almond Nofemela and David Tshikalanga each received a special cash bonus of R1 000 for a job well done. Brian Ngqulunga got nothing as he was scared and had stood aside when his mates attacked the Durban lawyer.

When Mamasela testified before the Harms Commission in 1990, he denied that he had had any involvement with Vlakplaas before 1982. The police forged documentation to prove that he only went to Vlakplaas after the murders of Griffiths Mxenge, Peter Dlamini and Vuyani Mavuso in 1981. This cover-up was used to discredit Coetzee and to suggest that he was a liar.

Human rights lawyers challenged the police cover-up when they produced immigration documents from the Botswana government which revealed that Mamasela, Coetzee and Nofemela had entered that country on November 26, 1981. It was the same night that raiders had attacked an ANC transit house in Gaberone. Mamasela had lied: he could have been present when Mxenge was murdered.

Mamasela, trying to explain his predicament, said the documents were forged: 'Yes, it is the work of a genius who is very sick in his mind.'

Lawyer: A genius?

Mamasela: It is possible. I said this is the work of a genius with a sick mind because really if you look at this thing it looks so convincing, but if you look at it thoroughly you can see there are flaws, there are genuine flaws … My suspicions are that Dirk Coetzee may have been a double agent for all his life in the police force. I am not a liar. I am prepared to put my head on a guillotine. I am prepared to suffer the dire consequences for the truth.

Mamasela and Eugene de Kock never saw eye to eye, probably because, as the askari puts it: 'Ek was 'n *hardegat kaffir wat niks kak gevat het nie*.' (I was a hard-assed kaffir who took no shit.) He claims that De Kock wanted to kill him, but he managed to escape late at night, saw a lawyer and got a transfer to the Vaal Triangle. 'For the first time in all my life I started to work like a policeman. I would go to work at half past seven and knock off at four. I would operate like all other policemen, go to an activist's house, question him and that kind of thing. But my happiness was short-lived because one day I was told that Brigadier Cronje wanted to see me in Pretoria,' Mamasela says.

Cronje, described by Mamasela as 'a father', was a former commander of Vlakplaas, where he had got to know Mamasela well. When Cronje was instructed to form a death squad within the Northern Transvaal Security Branch, Mamasela was an obvious choice to work with him.

'He told me that I am an askari and not a policeman and cannot do as I please. I knew a lot of secrets of Vlakplaas, and there was no way that the police can leave me to work and operate on my own.'

Once again, Mamasela was drawn into a death squad with Captain Jacques Hechter and Warrant-Officer Paul van Vuuren (see Chapter 13 for further details). The three men operated at night in townships in and around Pretoria. For a period of three years, they fire-bombed hundreds of houses, murdered activists and tortured suspects.

Van Vuuren: 'Hechter was the calculating one. Mamasela and I were more bloodthirsty and enjoyed our work. Mamasela shared our sentiments about the ANC. He hated the ANC and was taking revenge for the necklacing of his brother. Jacques Hechter said about Mamasela and I: 'You are the cruellest cunts I've ever seen.'[6]

Hechter: 'He was cruel, more so than any of us. If we had to go and kill, Mamasela was ready and couldn't wait.'

Van Vuuren: 'Mamasela always wanted money after a killing. One day, before we electrocuted three activists, he took a bank card from one of them and forced the activist to tell him his secret bank number. Afterwards, he withdrew money from the account.'

Mamasela: 'Van Vuuren was with me when we withdrew R500 from his bank account, which was used to have a braaivleis afterwards.'

Van Vuuren: 'Mamasela always wore the most expensive clothes. He would say to me: 'I look like the white man, you look like the kaffir.' I frequently had to submit false claims to keep him happy.'

Mamasela was an expert at infiltrating groups of young activists, and using the name of 'Mike', often presented himself as a trained Umkhonto we Sizwe operative. He lured about 25 activists, some as young as 15 years, to their deaths by promising to take them to the ANC in Botswana for military training. In one case, ten young activists, driven by Mamasela in a minibus towards the Botswana border, were poisoned and murdered. In another case, nine young people were massacred in a house in the homeland of KwaNdebele.

Ferdi Barnard, convicted killer and former member of the CCB and Military Intelligence. To be tried for the murder of anti-apartheid activist David Webster, shot dead in May 1989. (Photo: *Sunday Times*)

Former Vlakplaas commander and convicted killer Dirk Coetzee (*left*) and Transvaal Deputy Attorney General Anton Ackermann leave the Pretoria Supreme Court during the trial of Eugene de Kock. (Photo: *Sunday Times*)

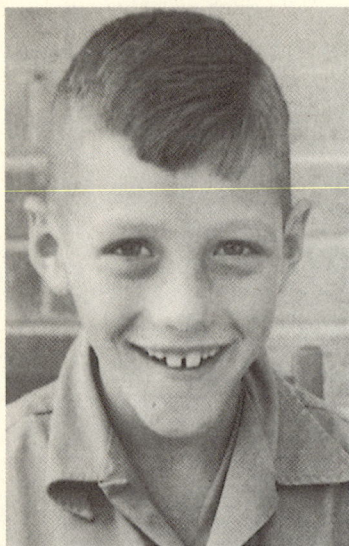

(*Opposite page*) Convicted assassin Eugene de Kock, as a young boy (*top left*); with his brother Vossie de Kock (*right*); the two boys in their Voortrekker uniforms; with their father, Lourens de Kock; a family portrait taken after attending a church service and with an unknown friend.

(*Top*) De Kock with some of his men; an *in loco* inspection at Vlakplaas during his murder trial and in transit from the Pretoria Supreme court in a police vehicle.

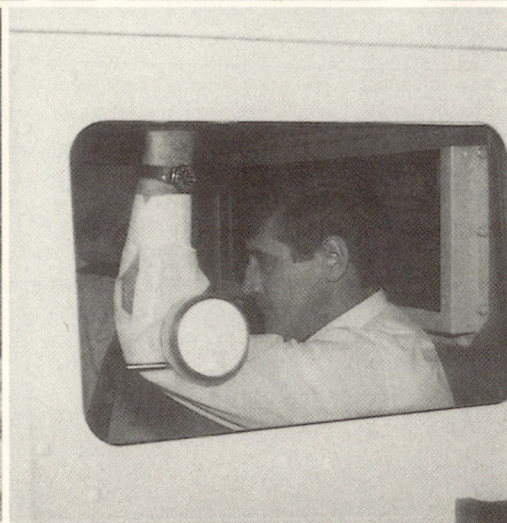

Former Security policeman Paul van Vuuren, who has applied for amnesty for the killing of up to 40 activists during the 1980s. These photographs show him as a young school cadet; during training at the police college with his R-1 rifle (1985); his wedding day and with his baby son.

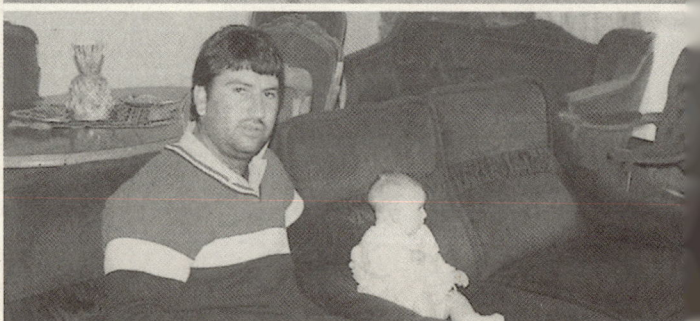

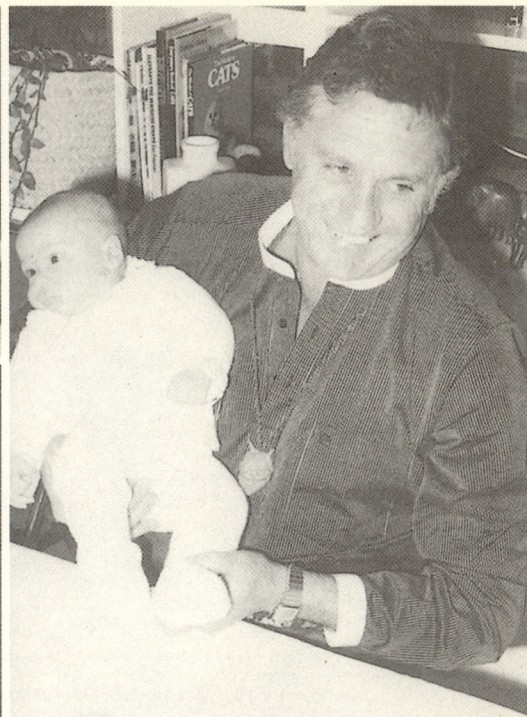

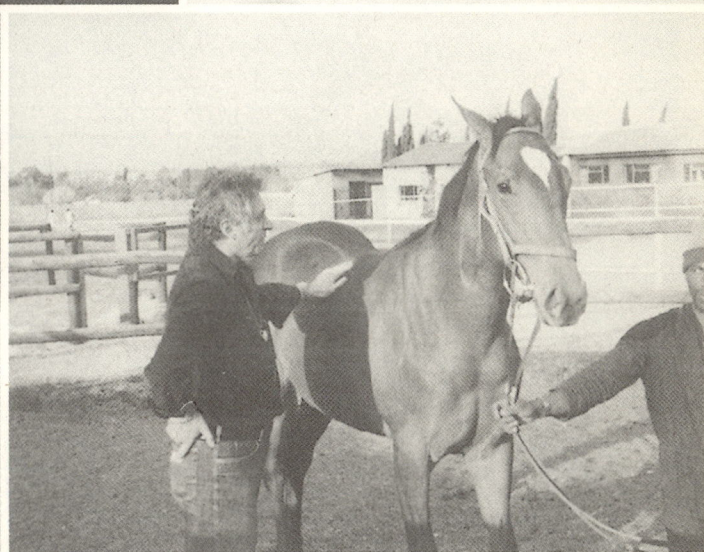

Arms smuggler and self-confessed apartheid assassin Dirk Stoffberg at his marriage to Linda Stoffberg (*top left*); with his first baby son and his race horse. The other three pictures were taken in Switzerland shortly before his arrest for illegal weapons smuggling to Chile and his subsequent incarceration in an American prison.

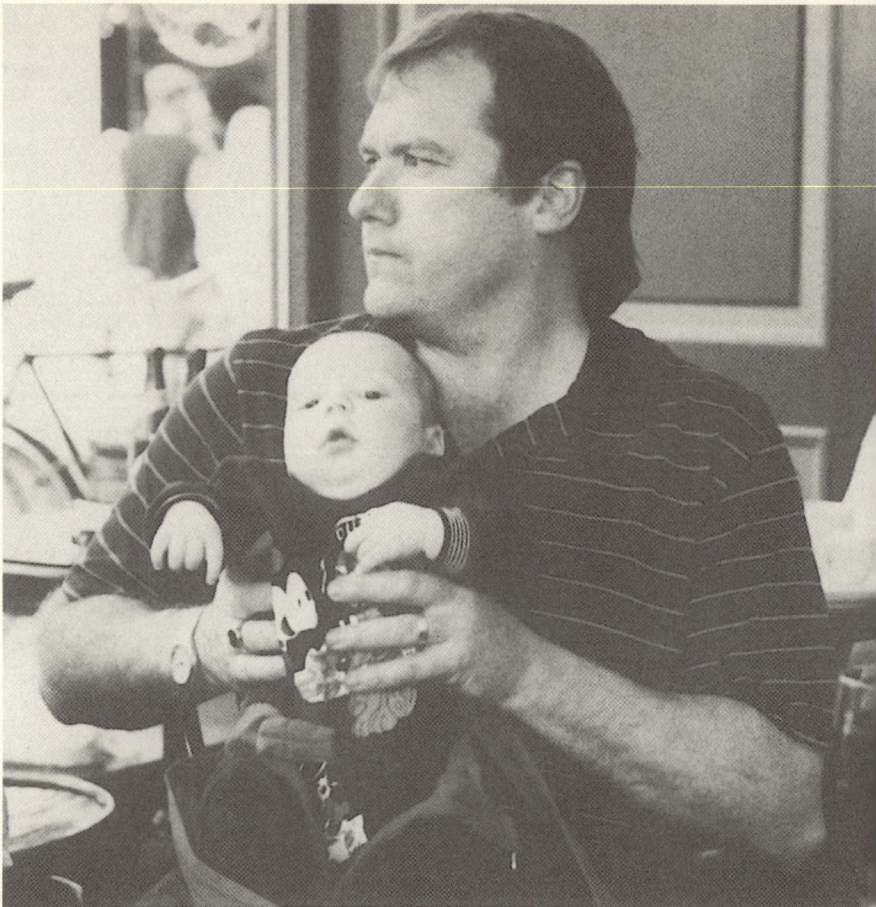

Vlakplaas assassin Willie Nortje with his baby son (*right*). *Bottom*: Eugene de Kock with Willie Nortje (wearing the cap) and Chappies Klopper – once his two closest confidants – who later turned against him and became the main state witnesses in his trial.

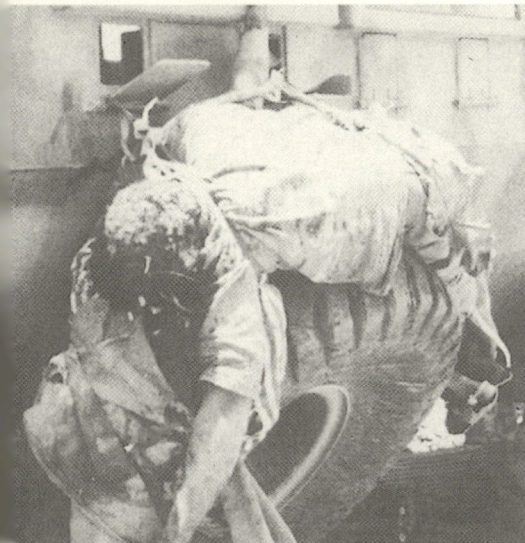

ugene de Kock in the police counter-insurgency unit oevoet during the Namibian bush war. *Top left*: With is brother Vossie de Kock on their way back to South frica. The other pictures show him as a Koevoet commander in action. (*Centre left*) The body of a dead Swapo guerrilla strapped to the spare wheel of a Casspir armoured vehicle. *Bottom right*: De Kock assaulting a Swapo detainee.

Former security police secret agent Peter Casselton, an adventurer who became a close confidant of 'Superspy' Craig Williamson and helped to set up a cell of the Security Branch in London. These pictures show Casselton on a yacht which he co-owned with Williamson in the Mediterranean and which had been purchased with police secret funds; and with his aircraft in which he flew and spied all over southern Africa.

'Superspy' Craig Williamson on his yacht and at a hunting expedition in the Northern Transvaal. *Bottom*: Vlakplaas 'sweeper' General Krappies Engelbrecht (in the striped shirt) with the Vlakplaas men during a 'team building expedition' at the Natal north coast. Engelbrecht was the general responsible for covering up the dirty deeds of Vlakplaas.

The results of a death squad attack by Vlakplaas operatives under the command of Eugene de Kock. In March 1992, four suspected bank robbers were executed in their minibus outside of Nelspruit in the Eastern Transvaal. After the men were shot dead, their vehicle was set alight and blown up. The fifth robber was captured, shot at point-blank range and blown up with explosives. Eugene de Kock was sentenced to life plus 80 years' imprisonment for these five murders.

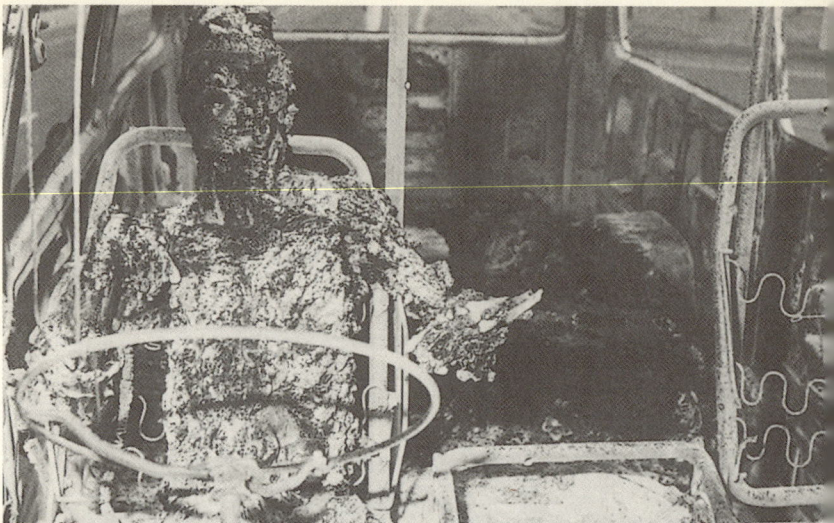

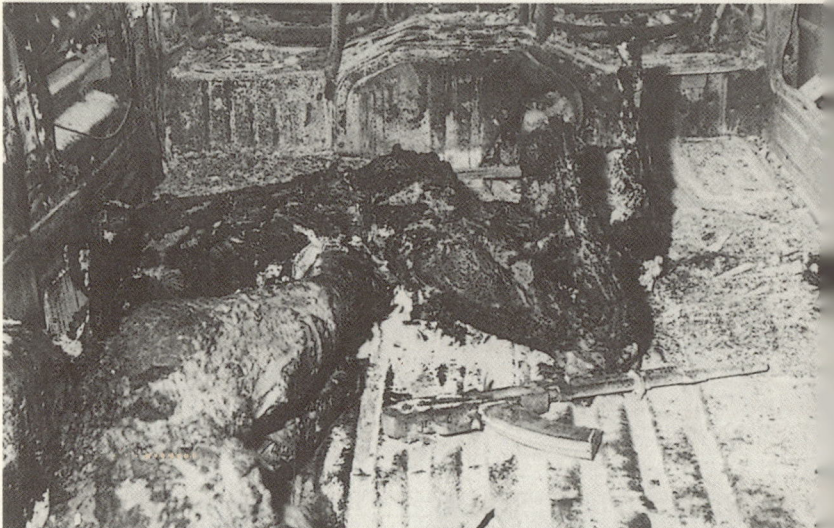

The Vlakplaas men and their friends at play at a police resort on the Natal north coast around 1981. Officially, it was called a 'team building expedition' paid for by the police secret fund. Unofficially, it was nothing but a drunken orgy.

Vlakplaas operatives Willie Nortje (*top left*) and Andries 'Brood' van Heerden (*bottom*) on a witness protection programme in Denmark in 1994. They were two of the most important state witnesses against Eugene de Kock in the trial that led to his conviction and subsequent life imprisonment.

Mabel Malobola was one of those who survived. She testified before the TRC: 'Mamasela tell us when he goes with us, they are going to train us and take us over to exile. And that never happened. Exile was in heaven. I cannot forgive anybody, because I am not God.'

And yet, when Joe Mamasela testified behind closed doors at the TRC in December 1995, he spoke of his 'human compassion' for young people fighting the liberation struggle like he had done many years before.

He said he was once given poisoned T-shirts by Jack Cronje to give to a student leader in Atteridgeville near Pretoria. 'But because I myself was a student, the whole thing did not go well with me, you know with my human compassion. I couldn't deface myself that low to wipe out schoolchildren.'

At the end of his testimony, Mamasela said: 'I was greatly honoured and I would like to express my deepest feelings about the conditions, the cordial humble atmosphere that I got for the first time in my life – I'm 43 years old – for the first time in my life, in my country of birth. I'm a black man myself. I'm prepared to face the firing squad. I'm prepared to die for the truth, that's what I've said and I'm consistent with that. '

Because Joe Mamasela sees himself as a victim, he has refused to apply for amnesty. He has, however, agreed to co-operate with the TRC and has given evidence in secret and behind closed doors. He has never appeared in public to face the families of his victims.

Legina Mabele, a sister of an activist he had shot dead, says: 'I want the truth from Mamasela, because he is the one that performed the killing. I really want him to tell, because that is the truth for us. He's the one who knows what he did. I saw my brother dead, could Mamasela have been so cruel? He must tell, and then I will decide if I can forgive. How can you forgive if you don't know?'

April 15, 1996, and in the East London city hall, 400 people were bewildered and in tears as the arteries of our past bled with the grief of a nation. Archbishop Desmond Tutu, the man who has for so long comforted us with hope and humanity, was weeping for the man in the wheelchair in front of him who had been broken by the brutal arms of his apartheid interrogators.

It was the first week of the South African Truth and Reconciliation Commission, charged with finding out what had happened during the apartheid era. The archbishop had started the process of soul searching by lighting a candle and saying a prayer for healing and repentance.

By the end of day one, people were physically exhausted and mentally frayed. For the first time in this country's history, people could publicly clean their wounds and bare their souls.

Amongst the first who testified were the wives of three men who had disappeared from the face of the earth 11 years earlier. On the morning of May 8, 1985, Sipho Hashe, Qwaqwahuli Godolozi and Champion Galela had left their homes to meet a British diplomat at the airport. They were never seen again.

The three men were leaders of the Port Elizabeth Black Civic Organisation (Pebco) and they had been instrumental in mobilising activists in the Eastern Cape to embark on a consumer boycott. They became known as the Pebco Three.

For many years, the police were suspected of complicity in their disappearance, but police claimed that the men had left the country and were in exile. But after the unbanning of the ANC in 1990, they didn't return to South Africa and nobody had seen them in any of the neighbouring states. They were simply gone.

Rita Galela, Nothembile Hashe and Nqabakazi Godolozi turned to the TRC for answers. 'Please help us to find them. They have been gone now for many years and we are sure they are dead, murdered by the security police. But we have to find their bodies and give them a proper funeral, otherwise their souls can never rest.'

'I am asking for assistance. I'm a proud person, I've never liked doing it. Now I am also asking for the assistance of my enemy. Please tell me what you did to my husband,' said Nothembile Hashe.

Joe Mamasela had the answers. Three months before the start of the TRC, I had done a television interview with the askari in which he had told me: 'The Pebco Three were abducted, they were taken to Cradock, they were brutalised, they were savagely assaulted … they were hit with an iron pipe into their heads, and they died, yes they died, they died one by one.'

'What was your role in the assault?' I asked him.

'My role was to choke them, to strangle them. Just to keep them quiet.'

I had done the interview for a television documentary I was producing about the life and times of Eugene de Kock. At the time Mamasela was still under witness protection and it was his first interview ever. When I first spoke to him, he wanted R100 000 for his story. I later persuaded him that publicity might put him in the limelight and lead to offers from foreign broadcasters. We made an agreement that his interview would only be broadcast after De Kock's conviction, which was five months later.

But after the plea by the Pebco widows, I decided to broadcast Mamasela's confession that same week. I phoned Mamasela and told him I had to use his confession. The Transvaal Attorney General, Dr Jan d'Oliveira, tried to stop me, saying that I was going to interfere with an impending prosecution. At the time, D'Oliveira had already had Mamasela's statement for more than a year, and had done nothing. At the time of the writing of this book, 18 months after Mamasela went public, action had still not been taken.

In 1985 the security police had decided that the Pebco Three were making the Eastern Cape ungovernable and that they had to die. A security policeman phoned the men and pretended to be a British diplomat who was on his way to Port Elizabeth to meet them and to discuss the possibility of foreign funding.

Mamasela was a member of a group of askaris who abducted them at the airport and took them to a deserted police station near Cradock. They were interrogated, and this is how Joe Mamasela described their last hours: 'Nieuwoudt and the other policemen got angry at Hashe, they started hitting and kicking him. He started screaming. We had to keep him quiet, while Warrant Officer Beeslaar took a stick and strangled him. Nieuwoudt hit him with an iron pipe over his head. There was blood coming out of his mouth and ears. He lost consciousness. When he woke up, he started talking. He said he was in possession of 17AKs which were stored at his sister's house. Nieuwoudt quoted passages from the Bible. All the while, there was a braai and drinking. Hashe answered a question in a manner they didn't like, and he was kicked in the face. There was foam coming from his mouth. A policeman went to sit on him and strangled him. Everybody was jumping on him and kicking him. I stood closer and saw that he was dead. Beeslaar took his watch.

'Godolozi was then fetched. He saw the old man, went on his knees and said he would give his full co-operation. Galela was also fetched and questioned, but he didn't know a lot. He was questioned for about three hours and was cruelly assaulted. He was kicked and hit with the iron pipe. Beeslaar squeezed his testicles, and strangled him until he lay still. We put him next to Hashe. Godolozi was pathetically sitting in a corner. The braaiing and drinking continued.

'The next morning, more people arrived. Godolozi was fetched from the garage. The bodies of Sipho and Galela were already stiff. He was assaulted in the same way. After about five or six hours he also died.'

Eugene de Kock said that when Coetzee spoke in 1989, Mamasela had to be paid excessive amounts to keep his mouth shut. 'He received amounts of R18 000, R23 000, R25 000 and R27 000, he got a state vehicle, we had to pay his children's private school fees and install additional security at his house.'[7]

De Kock said Mamasela demanded that the police erect safety lights and had to pave a footpath between his gate and garage to prevent somebody from planting a landmine. The police had to buy him two dogs and provide dog food.

'He kept the police hostage and it was nothing but blackmail. It is in his nature and he would never stop. He's going to suck lots of people dry,' De Kock said.

When I first met Mamasela, he was talking money. He was talking about selling his story for even more to a foreign broadcaster and making money out of writing a book.

When he was taken into a witness protection programme by the Transvaal Attorney General, he demanded money for his 'protection'. At the beginning of 1996, he said he was paid R13 000 per month for his services and he boasted to Dirk Coetzee and his wife that his 'expenses' amounted to R43 000 for a period of two months.

Mamasela invested some of his police payment of R400 000 in a sugar venture in Swaziland. When he testified against former policemen accused of murdering Griffiths Mxenge, he said: 'Every month I was earning between R30 000 and R40 000, now I'm getting a meagre five to six thousand a month (from the Transvaal Attorney General). You call that financial benefit?'

Coetzee says he had seen Mamasela with cash of up to R15 000 at a time, and that he accompanied him to a jeweller in 1994, on which occasion the former askari had bought three gold chains for R31 000 in cash. He frequently gambles at the Marula Sun casino complex outside Pretoria. He would buy his wife, Bongi, a social worker, dresses for as much as R7 000.

I have spent many hours with Joe Mamasela, and never have I detected a shred of remorse for anything he has done. He spoke of ways of making money and would talk about the ANC as 'stupid kaffirs' who 'don't have a chance in hell' of ever getting at him.

Yet, when he testified before the TRC, he said: 'The ANC, more than any other people, they understand that in every war there are casualties, we are the casualties of revolution, we stood up, we tried to pay our humble contribution to the liberation of the emancipation of our people.'

Joe Mamasela, who doesn't smoke or drink, professes to being a reborn Christian. In his house hang two certificates declaring that he has been re-baptised in a charismatic church.

When he speaks about Eugene de Kock, a man he truly hates, he says: 'I think that the only way that De Kock can save and salvage his tattered soul is to go down on his knees and pray to his creator, God. That is the only way that De Kock can be saved.'

Chapter Thirteen

The electrician

It is Sunday lunch on the farm 'Drooglaagte' west of Warmbaths in the Northern Transvaal bushveld. The burly, moustached man at the head of the table takes his wife's hand and asks for grace before tucking into a plate piled high with steak and chops.[1]

As the luncheon guests sip on glasses of sweetish white wine and orange juice, conversation ranges from raised taxes to black people failing to pay their electricity bills. Somebody tells a story of a township dweller who tried to 'steal' electricity and shocked himself to death. People laugh.

'Yes, and now we have our own electrician,' says the woman next to me and looks at the man at the head of the table. More laughter. He grins and demolishes another T-bone steak.

There is nothing out of the ordinary about the scene around me. Ordinary Afrikaner people having Sunday lunch, shrieking children running around on the manicured lawn outside the dining room, plates of braaied meat and debate about Currie Cup rugby.

A copper plate of a storming elephant bull decorates the wall behind me. In the study next door hang two university degree certificates and photographs of prizewinning Brahman bulls.

When only a pile of bones remains of Sunday lunch, a baby about a year old totters into the dining room. The big man picks the boy up and places him next to him on the table. 'Give me a kiss, my beautiful child,' he says and hugs him. Earlier that morning, he had changed the baby's dirty nappy.

I look at his hands comforting the child. The hardy, muscular and beefy hands of a farmer. Hands that have raised award-winning stock. The hands of a hunter that has shot hundreds of buck. The hands of a carnivore par excellence.

But also hands that were made into fists and smashed into the faces of people. Hands that have strangled, aimed guns at people, thrown bombs into houses and pushed electrical wires against living flesh.

Paul Jacobus Jansen van Vuuren was a security policeman during the 1980s. Earlier that day, we had sat down on the pink lounge suite where he had told me that the death squad he served in might have killed more people than any other security police unit. Atthe time, he said, he had enjoyed his work and had been proud of what he had achieved.

He had read about the torture methods of the SS in Nazi Germany and Augusto Pinochet's secret police in Chile. He had tortured more people than he can ever remember.

One of the methods he used was to shock and electrocute people. Hence his luncheon guest's reference to 'the electrician'.

Paul van Vuuren was a master of his craft.

July 1987. In a deserted stretch of open veld north of Pretoria, three men were lying on the ground, their hands and feet tied. Hours before, they had mysteriously disappeared from their homes in townships around Pretoria and Witbank.

They were activists, members of the banned ANC. According to security police files, they were all trained guerrillas and deeply involved in the wave of unrest in the townships.

Standing over the activists were three security policemen, members of a secret death squad within the Northern Transvaal Security Branch. Night after night, the three men, sometimes wearing dark balaclavas, were roaming the townships around Pretoria, killing, bombing and kidnapping activists they regarded as a threat to the security of the apartheid state.

Next to the manacled activists stood a power generator that was utilised to pump water for cattle, but on that day, it was used to extract information from the captured men.

'We put the wire on his hands and feet and shocked it until his body went rigid. We only did it for a second or two,' said Warrant Officer Paul van Vuuren, one of the three security policemen on the scene.

The other two were Captain Jacques Hechter and Warrant Officer Joe Mamasela, the killer askari who had been transferred from Vlakplaas to the Northern Transvaal security police at the end of 1985.

The death squad was playing prosecutor, judge and executioner of the three men when they decided that Andrew Makupe, Jackson Maake and Harold Sefola had to die. But they were worried that they might leave traces of blood behind if they shot them. Another method had to be found. The generator.

The previous day, Maake had been the first to be captured. According to Van Vuuren, he was a security police informant. They had previously instructed him to request the ANC to send him to Botswana to receive military training. He had reported back after three months that he had been trained by Johannes Mnisi, a suspect in the May 1983 Pretoria bomb blast.

But Van Vuuren and Hechter became suspicious of Maake. He started to visit their offices during the day, despite instructions not to do so. Another informant told them they had to watch Maake: he might be a double agent and planning an attack against them.

Jackson Maake was seen for the last time on July 13, 1987. The policeman took the 19-year-old Mamelodi scholar to the stretch of open veld where they interrogated and shocked him with the generator for about three hours.

'We used the generator to send shocks through him to persuade him to talk. He admitted that he was a double agent. He had instructions to eliminate us because we were seen as a danger to the ANC. He told us that the other member of his cell was Andrew Makupe in Mamelodi, who was a courier for the ANC.'

Late that same night, Andrew Makupe was kidnapped as he got into his car. He was taken to the same spot, where his hands and feet were tied and a cloth stuffed in his mouth. The two men, guarded by two black policemen, were left in the open veld on a winter's night.

At dawn the next morning, the security policemen returned and questioned Makupe by starting up the generator and shocking him.

Makupe spoke immediately and told the men his commander was a 'Bra H' in Witbank. The policemen rushed back to security police headquarters where they discovered that 'Bra H' was Harold Sefola, a trained guerrilla and, according to informants, the mastermind behind several bomb explosions, but there had never been enough information to arrest and prosecute him.

That same night, Van Vuuren, Hechter and Mamasela went to Witbank. Hechter and Van Vuuren waited alongside the highway outside the town while Mamasela went to get Sefola. The askari presented himself to the ANC activist as a trained guerrilla who had just entered the country. He said there were other people waiting for him whom he was supposed to meet.

Sefola fell in the trap, and minutes later, Mamasela led him into the waiting hands of Van Vuuren and Hechter. Sefola was taken to the open veld where his comrades were still tied up and awaiting their fate. The generator was started up.

'He admitted that he was a trained terrorist and that he was involved in bomb explosions and planted land mines and limpet mines. We had to force him to talk by shocking him with the generator. At one stage, Mamasela pushed a knife up his nose, after which he gave even more information. He pleaded for his life.'

Van Vuuren said there was something 'different' about Sefola. He was stronger than the other two and believed deeply in his cause.

He asked his interrogators whether he could say anything before he died. Mamasela untied him. He stood up and sang 'Nkosi Sikilel i'Afrika'.

'He said we can kill him, but the ANC would rule one day. He said that apartheid cannot survive and that democracy would be the end of the "Boers". He furthermore said that the security police and Umkhonto we Sizwe are puppets of the politicians.'

As the activist started singing 'Nkosi Sikilel i'Afrika', Joe Mamasela draped an ANC flag over Jackson Maake, who was already dead. As the final notes of Sefola's singing faded away, the wires of the generator were attached to Andrew Makupe and he was electrocuted.

Mamasela said in an affidavit that Van Vuuren ordered Sefola to pray for the other two. He went on his knees, but put his fist in the air and said he saluted his comrades in the name of the struggle.[2] Shortly afterwards, Sefola was also shocked to death. Mamasela said he was shocked until foam and blood came out of his mouth and ears.

'We had to kill them. We had to destroy the whole cell,' said Van Vuuren.

The three hitmen loaded the bodies into a minibus and took them to a dirt road in the homeland of Bophuthatswana, where they blew the bodies up with a landmine.

'We placed the landmine on the ground, put them on top of the landmine, we stood back and detonated the mine,' said Van Vuuren. It had to look as though the three activists tried to plant the mine and accidentally activated the device.

When Sefola had stood in the veld singing 'Nkosi Sikilel i'Afrika' and had told the policemen that the ANC would one day rule the country, Paul van Vuuren had thought he was mad. In fact, Van Vuuren said, he was under the impression that the security police were winning the war. His death squad roamed the townships, killed and tortured activists, and bombed their houses.

It is nine years later. The ANC is ruling the country. Democracy has brought an end to 40 years of apartheid rule. And in the chambers of the TRC, a former security policeman takes the witness stand to plead for amnesty, forgiveness and reconciliation.

'I felt as though I was the one being tortured,' Van Vuuren described the moment he took the oath. Staring at him from the public gallery were the mothers and wives of Andrew Makupe, Jackson Maake and Harold Sefola. They were there to listen to how and why their loved ones had to die.

Elizabeth Maake spoke about the disappearance of her son. 'He left on that Wednesday. That was the last time I saw him. I used to see him coming from school, but that day I didn't see him. I kept asking people whether they'd seen him, but nobody knew where he was. When the sun shines, I think about my child. When the sun sets, I think about my child. This thing is hurting me. They must show me the place where they've killed my son.'[3]

'We didn't like what we did, but we had to stop the killing of innocent women and children,' Van Vuuren defended his actions.

Mabel Makupe's last child was born only a month before her husband disappeared. 'He was a nice guy. He was like a brother to me, like a father, he was everything to me. We were a very happy family, really. We were just looking for him. I kept on asking myself if he's still alive, why doesn't he come home?'[4]

Van Vuuren: 'I would never have done this under normal circumstances. I did it for my country and my people. I was fighting communism.'

Sitting across the commission room from Van Vuuren was Jacques Hechter. He told the commission that he suffered from amnesia and couldn't remember the event. He was, however, also asking for amnesty for the murder, assault and kidnapping of the three activists.

The third member of the death squad, Joe Mamasela, was not there. The former askari said he was also a victim of the security police because they forced him to commit the murders. He, therefore, refused to apply for amnesty.

The former head of the Northern Transvaal Security Branch, Brigadier Jack Cronje, also applied for amnesty. Together, Cronje, Hechter and Van Vuuren applied for amnesty for the killing of more than 40 people during the years 1985 to 1988.

At the time of their amnesty application, murder charges had already been brought against Hechter and Cronje for the killing of ten youths near Nietverdiend not far from the border with Botswana. Van Vuuren attended a cattle auction that day and didn't participate in the killings.

The men were spurred into action not only by the possibility of a lengthy jail sentence, but also by a series of affidavits Mamasela had made to the Transvaal Attorney General. They applied for amnesty for the killings already confessed to by Mamasela.

In no way did their applications constitute a 'full confession' of their death squad activities. Van Vuuren later told me on his farm it was impossible: they had simply tortured, bombed and killed too many people.

June 12, 1986, and the townships are burning. State President PW Botha declares a state of emergency, giving extraordinary powers to his security forces in order to stem the efforts by the ANC, the United Democratic Front and other black resistance organisations to make the townships ungovernable. The state of emergency permits the security forces to detain suspected troublemakers at will without fear of legal recourse. Over 24 000 people are detained between June and December 1986. Some are held uncharged for more than three years. The vast majority are never prosecuted for any offence.[5]

Ten days after the declaration of the state of emergency, ten Mamelodi youths got into a minibus and headed for the Botswana border. They were on their way to receive military training in Botswana to join the 'people's war' against the security forces in the townships.

A few days earlier, the youths had approached a man who said he was an ANC guerrilla and could arrange for them to undergo military training. The young men were eager to do battle and volunteered their services to the ANC. The guerrilla said he would arrange for them to leave the country.

The young activists were typical township comrades who had been involved in resistance activities such as public violence, marches and consumer boycotts. The two youngest members of the group were only 15 years old: Matthews Lerutla and Sipho Sibanyoni, both Mamelodi scholars. Lerutla was once detained, but never charged with any offence.

The 17-year-old Abraham Makulane was a standard eight pupil and had previously been arrested and charged with arson and public violence, but acquitted. The oldest member of the group was the 22-year-old Thomas Phirri, a standard nine pupil who had also been detained, but never charged with any offence.

The comrades were in a buoyant mood as they headed for the Botswana border. The trained MK guerrilla who had recruited them drove the minibus and gave them beer. In the Western Transvaal town of Zeerust, the minibus turned off the main road towards the village of Nietverdiend, the Afrikaans for 'not deserving'. By now, the comrades were drunk and close to the Botswana border.

But a few kilometres further on, their journey ended. The driver was not an ANC member, but a security policeman and a member of a death squad. He was not taking them across the border to join the struggle for liberation, but was driving them to their deaths.

Joe Mamasela turned down a narrow dirt road. A car with Jack Cronje, Jacques Hechter and two other security policemen followed Mamasela, who stopped next to another minibus. By then, the comrades were very drunk.

Four armed men with balaclavas took the ten comrades out of the minibus and injected them 'with something'. They were put back into the minibus and taken to a spot close to the Botswana border.

The kombi was pushed down an incline, filled with explosives and blown up. It had to appear as if trained guerrillas who had infiltrated South Africa had had an accident and blown themselves up. Afterwards, newspaper reports confirmed that 'trained terrorists' had been killed in a car accident.

A decade after the 'accident', Brigadier Jan Hattingh Cronje took the stand at the TRC and confessed: 'We had to eliminate them to prevent them from coming back as trained terrorists and committing acts of terror against innocent women and children. We created the impression that the terrorists blew themselves up because they were not properly trained. The public got the perception that we were effective in combatting and destroying terrorism. It created confidence in the apartheid government and persuaded white people to vote for them.'

Jack Cronje is a 60-year-old police veteran who joined the force in 1956 and served in Namibia and Rhodesia before joining the security police. He was commander of Vlakplaas for two years before becoming the head of the security police in the Northern Transvaal. He retired as a result of ill health in 1987 after undergoing heart surgery.

He told the Commission that the four men in balaclavas who had injected the four activists were all members of the SADF Special Forces unit. He didn't know who they were, and neither did he know who the comrades were.

He said the Commissioner of Police instructed the security police in 1986 to cooperate with Special Forces, which had a special fighting unit to also undertake covert and death squad operations. Cronje said he had had a meeting with Commandant Chari Naude of Special Forces, at which they had discussed and planned the operation to kill the comrades. General Johan Viktor, commander of the police unrest unit, congratulated him afterwards on the killing of the ten youths.

Cronje: I can't remember the specific details, but the youths were

probably involved in school boycotts, consumer boycotts and even arson.
Commission: Were those activities sufficient to justify elimination?
Cronje: No, the fact that they were on their way to military training was in
my view just cause for eliminating them. Were they to return as well-
trained terrorists they could have struck anywhere in the Republic and I
wouldn't have known how to prevent them from doing so.
Commission: You made no attempt to prosecute them?
Cronje: At that time I had no testimony I could use in a case against them.
Counsel for the families of the deceased: I'm speechless in response.

There were several other incidents in which Joe Mamasela recruited activists
for training and led them into the waiting hands of the security police.

In 1987, nine more activists were killed in the homeland of KwaNdebele when
Mamasela infiltrated a group of youths and offered them training in the neighbouring states. A group of Pretoria murder and robbery detectives joined Hechter
and Mamasela in the killing of the youths. They stormed into a house and fired
more than 60 AK-47 bullets into their victims. They then set them alight.

Mamasela promised to take activist Jeffrey Sibiya and another comrade across
the border for military training, but instead, they were handed to Paul van Vuuren
and Jacques Hechter, who strangled them with electrical wire before blowing
their bodies up with a landmine.

Mamasela led another activist to a similar death, but after they had strangled
him, they necklaced their victim by putting a tyre around him, pouring petrol
over him and setting him alight. It had to look like a township necklace murder
performed by the comrades.

In front of the municipal complex in Pretoria known as Munitoria, where most
of the testimony of Jack Cronje and his security policemen was heard, there is a
monument dedicated 'to all victims of terrorism'. The monument, a broken arch
of triumph, was erected during the dying days of apartheid to celebrate the
(mostly) white victims of (mostly) black 'anarchy'.

But for three weeks in February and March 1997, it acquired a new meaning
when a band of police killers lined the chambers of the TRC and confessed to a
season of unparalleled violence and evil. Most white people previously associated the word 'terrorist' with black, riotous and maniacal Communist-inspired
savages who killed innocent women and children by means of necklacing, planting bombs and laying landmines.

But this time, the terrorists were white, all former supporters of the National
Party who considered themselves to be the vanguard of Christian civilisation and
said they were convinced that they alone stood in the way of a Communist
Armageddon. In the process, they committed some of most heinous crimes ever
recounted in the history of the country.

When Eugene de Kock was asked during his testimony in his murder trial whether he was the country's most effective assassin, he said: 'I don't know, we have never had an assasin's conference ... If we look at information I have received about the activities of the Pretoria security police, we may be far back in the line. There were people who were not necessarily more effective in killing people, but maybe more cold-blooded or even sick.'

Seldom before has the word 'eliminate' – a security police euphemism – been heard so often. Never, did they use the word 'murder' to describe their actions.

'We are gathered here today in a spirit of peace and reconciliation. The Afrikaner has struggled for freedom from British imperialism. The African people have struggled for freedom. It is now time for all South Africans to be free, free of the past and free of conflict. We have decided to come forward in the spirit of this new country, in the spirit of trust in the new government and the Truth Commission in particular, and with a purpose of cleansing our souls from the darkness of the past, and to let the truth be spoken about our deeds.'

Not the words of a hypocritical National Party politician, but the opening statement by Jack Cronje and his killer policemen at the start of their testimony before the TRC. I am convinced that they were not the architects of these words, but as they sat there, their faces were stern and unmoving.

'We, as proud Afrikaners, are part of this country, and shall be part of this country in the future. We are prepared to forgive those who have sinned against us in the past. We have forgiven the concentration camps of the Boer War where innocent women and children had died. We are prepared to forgive those who have waged war during the struggle, also on innocent women and children. We similarly ask forgiveness for those who lost their lives, and those who were injured, and we share the grief of those family members of victims.'

Looking at them, I thought about the words of former newspaper editor Donald Woods when he described the Eastern Cape security policemen testifying at the inquest into the death of Steve Biko in September 1977.

'We at the inquest could see their faces, could watch their demeanour under cross examination, and could hear their words – their version of the story. For the first time, these men, products and inheritors of the Afrikaner Nationalist tradition, were flushed out of their police stations and their little interrogation rooms. For once they were in the position of having to account for themselves. These men displayed symptoms of extreme insularity. They are people whose upbringing has impressed upon them the divine right to retain power, and in that sense they are innocent men – incapable of thinking or acting differently. On top of that they have gravitated to an occupation that has given them all the scope they need to express their rigid personalities. They have been protected for years by the laws of the country. They have been able to carry out all their imaginative torture practices quite undisturbed in cells and rooms all over the country, with tacit official sanction, and they have been given tremendous status by the government as the men who 'protect the State from subversion'.'[6]

Nearly 20 years later, the disciples of death had changed very little. Steve Biko died naked, manacled and in pain. So did some of Paul van Vuuren and Jacques Hechter's victims. Donald Woods could see death in the eyes of Biko's torturers; there were times when I could see death in the eyes of Cronje, Hechter and Van Vuuren.

But the difference is that the security policemen at the Biko inquest were protected and guarded by the apartheid powers. A horrifying picture of cruelty and brutality emerged, but the policemen who struck the final blows were defiant and undaunted. On the bench was a conservative Afrikaner magistrate, PJ Prins, who shielded them: 'The available evidence does not prove that the death was brought about by any act or admission involving or amounting to an offence on the part of any person.'

The policemen at the TRC were on their own, abandoned and deserted by the politicians and many of the generals on whose behalf they had killed, in a situation very similar to that of Eugene de Kock.

'We have, so to speak, been thrown away in the gutter, where we now have to take the responsibility on our shoulders to deal with our past, to motivate our actions and to present our view of the conflict. We call upon the previous government, and our superiors, to explain certain orders given to us. We ask. Do not desert us further. Do not turn your backs on us. Help us.'

They said that former State President FW de Klerk was lying when he said in his submission to the TRC: 'In dealing with the unconventional strategies from the side of the government I want to make it clear from the outset that, within my knowledge and experience, they never included the authorisation of assassination, murder, torture, rape, assault or the like. I have never been part of any decision taken by Cabinet, the State Security Council or any committee authorising or instructing the commission of such gross violations of human rights.'[7]

The men end their opening statement with a poem from the Afrikaans poet C Louis Leipoldt:

'Give peace and rest to those of us who are tired of roaming,

'Courage and patience to those of us who are scared of dying.'

Hours later, Paul van Vuuren told the commission how Andrew Makupe, Jackson Maake and Harold Sefola had pleaded for mercy in the face of death.

Is this the face of evil, I wondered as I looked at Paul van Vuuren, dressed in khaki clothes and stretched out on the pink couch in the lounge of the farmhouse.

'How does it feel to shoot a human being?' I asked him.

'To shoot a human being and a buck are basically the same.'

Silence. Then he continued: 'It was exciting days, those years. At times I could not wait to do it. They say to kill is like sleeping with a woman. It's true.'

I didn't answer him.

'Do you understand?' he asked me.

I just looked at him. There were many things I didn't understand. The joy of murder and torture, for one, but above all, why this man had chosen to become a killer and inflict pain and suffering on others.

I have spoken to many death squad killers. Most, if not all, have expressed a deep regret for what they had done and said how sorry they were. In most cases, they were lying.

At least Paul van Vuuren was straight and honest. He looked me squarely in the eyes and admitted that he had a task, which was to kill apartheid's opponents. He did it, he did it with conviction, and isn't sorry. The faces and memories of his victims and his killings don't seem to haunt him. The only thing he regrets is that he had lost the war, was exposed and has had to confess.

In Tom Stoppard's *Rosencrantz and Guildenstern are Dead*, a play on the meaninglessness of the lives of the two minor characters sent to spy on Hamlet, Guildenstem says to Rosencrantz on the eve of their execution: 'There must be a moment at the beginning, where we all could have said no. But somehow we missed it.'

Paul van Vuuren is no different from many white Afrikaners who grew up during the era of apartheid and were subjected to propaganda about the ugliness and evil of black and the beauty and holiness of white. Yet, many embarked on a different road.

Van Vuuren is only two years younger than I am, we both grew up in a typical Afrikaner family and went to the same university. I know what he means when he talks about the effect that the total onslaught ideology had on him.

In many ways, Paul van Vuuren is only a petty offender in the scale of apartheid repression. The real killer is the system of the time. The French philosopher Victor Hugo said: 'If a man sins because of darkness, the guilty one is not he who sins, but he who causes the darkness.'

Paul van Vuuren's defence is that he sinned in darkness.

He was born in Odendaalsrus in the Orange Free State, but grew up on the farm near Warmbaths. It was a National Party home. His mother was once the secretary of Prime Minister John Vorster and the family were members of the all-white Dutch Reformed Church. His father was a heavy drinker, and Van Vuuren said he 'drank himself out of his farms'. He had to find work in a nearby cement factory and start all over again.

According to his psychiatric report, Van Vuuren was extremely aggressive as a young boy. A much older kid once smacked him. The young Van Vuuren picked up a stone, and threw it against his head. The older boy was bleeding, and when the stone thrower saw it, he fainted, fell forwards and broke his front teeth.

Van Vuuren says his father was a policeman at Sharpeville on March 21, 1960 when 69 people were shot dead and 180 wounded as police opened fire on a crowd of 5 000 people engaged in a peaceful protest against the pass laws. Nearly all the victims were shot in the back.

'He told me how they shot the kaffirs who didn't want to listen. I thought it was right, and I think he thought so as well.'

His father was an active member of the local commando and did military service in northern Namibia, where he was badly injured in a landmine explosion. His only brother went to war in Rhodesia and became a member of the Rhodesian Light Infantry.

'There was always talk of war and communism and the *swart gevaar* (black danger) and that we have to stand together to combat the onslaught. I didn't really listen, but it must have made an impression on me. In those days, a kaffir was a kaffir. But we were not racists, you know what I mean?'

I do understand. I also grew up in a house where we spoke of kaffirs, but I also like to think that my parents were not racists. I also remember hearing about Communists hiding behind every bush and the threat of the *swart gevaar*. As kids, we didn't play cowboys and crooks, but *grensvegters* (frontier soldiers) and terrorists. There was a photo book hero by the name of 'Captain Caprivi', and he really knew how to deal with black terrorists, always called something like 'Comrade Lenin' and their white Russian KGB officers, with names such as 'Colonel Petrachoff'. During cadet periods at school, as we stood in our brown uniforms on the parade ground, our platoon sergeant, a teacher who was a former permanent force army officer, told us stories about the border war in Namibia. He once told us how he and his men had rescued school children, no older than us, that had been kidnapped by Swapo terrorists. He said when they had found the children, some had been dying of exhaustion as they were being driven towards the Angolan border, while others were weak and hungry. When I was 16 years old and in standard nine, I had to register as a conscript for two years of national service in the SADF. Most of my friends couldn't wait to get to the Angolan border, where they thought an exhilarating and wonderful experience was awaiting them. In those days, most white people saw conscription as a form of initiation: you had to go in order to become a man.

In 1976, Soweto exploded when black children came out on to the streets to protest against the use of Afrikaans in school. This was the first wave in what would eventually become the storm that obliterated apartheid.

Van Vuuren was at the time in standard seven at the Warmbad High School. 'I thought they should shoot the fucking kids if they didn't want to listen and burn down their schools, which we had built them. I was told the communists were using the black people because they were stupid. But I couldn't be bothered by the whole thing.'

The Soweto uprising was also very far removed from my privileged suburban existence in Pretoria. At the time, the New Zealand All Black rugby team was touring South Africa, and on June 16, 1976, they played a match at the Loftus Versfeld stadium. My father and I attended the game, and when we drove back home, we listened to the radio news and heard about the uprising. It made no impression on me, and I couldn't understand either how children could burn down their own schools. Prime Minister John Vorster assured us that there was no reason for panic and that the security forces had the situation under control.

Van Vuuren was an exemplary high school student. He was a prefect, obtained provincial colours for athletics and played centre for his school's first rugby team. He also had a black belt in karate.

'I was just an Afrikaner boy. I was in standard six or seven when we attended the wedding of the daughter of a local chief. I remember how amazed I was when she got married in white because I didn't know that they also got married in that way.'

The principal of the Warmbad High School, N J J van Rensburg, described Van Vuuren in a reference as follows: 'Paul's way of life is a testimony to a religious and humane person. He is spontaneous and pleasant and is always willing to be of service. He would be an asset to any society or organisation that would want to employ his services.'

Van Vuuren always wanted to be a soldier or a policeman. After school he decided to go to university to prepare himself for a career in the police and he studied criminology at the University of Pretoria. He is one of the only police death squad killers I knew who has a university degree.

I studied political science at the same university. Van Vuuren was in standard nine when I started my first year there. The University of Pretoria was at the time an all-white, conservative and racist institution.

One of my fellow political science students was blind. He had a guide, a black boy of about 15, who escorted him around the campus and sat in the lecture rooms with him. Instead of asking why the boy wasn't in school, some students complained about his presence in the lecture rooms and he was eventually asked to wait outside.

My anthropology professor became one of the architects of the policy of the Conservative Party, while another lecturer, Koos Botha, was in later years involved in a series of right-wing bomb explosions, for which he asked (and received) amnesty. Van Vuuren, who arrived at the university in 1981, said he was never involved in student politics and attended only one political meeting on campus: that of the leader of the neo-Nazi Afrikaner Weestandsbeweging (AWB), Eugene TerreBlanche. 'I thought he was a baboon.'

He voted for the first time in the 1981 general election. 'I voted for the National Party. I believed in them and thought that their policy towards black people was fair and just.'

In the same election, I voted for the more liberal Progressive Party. My family thought I was quite radical.

Paul van Vuuren met his wife-to-be, Cathryn, an attractive blonde girl, during his third year at university while she was a first-year student studying for a BSc degree. She was an orphan.

While Van Vuuren was preparing himself at university for a career in the police, I had to go to the army. I was called up to 4 Infantry Battalion, a fighting unit that would almost certainly have landed me on the Angolan border to do battle with Swapo.

I was not prepared to shoot or to be shot at. I faked a lung disease, was classified as medically unfit to do active duty, and was assigned to the army magazine as a journalist. Make no mistake, I never carried a rifle, but I wrote horrendous propaganda about the 'iron fist of the SADF landing another fatal blow against the communist-inspired and bloodied terrorists of Swapo'. Most of us did our bit for apartheid.

Van Vuuren joined the South African Police in 1984. He said that day after day he and other recruits heard about communism and the total onslaught. As we know from the evidence of Eugene de Kock and Dirk Coetzee, young recruits were subjected to the most blatant form of brainwashing and disinformation.

While Van Vuuren was still at college, a mounting tide of black anger engulfed the townships. Widespread resistance to rent increases exploded in the townships around Johannesburg, and quickly spread to the Eastern Cape. The comrades were threatening to make the townships ungovernable. 'People's courts' were set up to try alleged collaborators and many local councillors were killed, forced to resign or to move out of the townships. Death by the necklacing method became commonplace: a rubber tyre was placed around the neck of the victim, filled with petrol and then set alight. Large numbers of police and then troops were sent into the townships to restore law and order. Daily scenes of violent confrontation between the security forces and the comrades became commonplace. Sticks, stones and petrol bombs were met with armoured cars, tear gas, shotguns and automatic weapons.

Van Vuuren was sent to Port Elizabeth to carry out riot control and was absorbed into Platoon 26. 'I saw dead people every day. I saw people being necklaced and smelled burning tyres and burning flesh. I had a shotgun and we had orders to shoot into crowds of people. I don't know if I killed anybody, but it is possible. I then knew that you could never give power to black people.

'While we were on patrol, a policeman was shot through the legs. The next day, a comrade was arrested by the security police. They were wearing civilian clothes and I could see that everybody was treating them with respect. They interrogated the suspect. They kicked him and beat him and fucked him up. I then got the impression that you have to beat the shit out of a suspect to get information from him. I could see that if it wasn't for the security police, this country wouldn't last for two days and I then decided I wanted to become a security policeman as well.'

The riot police in their Casspir armoured cars and the security policemen in their small interrogation rooms were only one face of the apartheid machinery of the 1980s.

Many of us participated either willingly or unwillingly in creating the incredible darkness that embraced South Africa during that time.

While Van Vuuren was fighting the comrades in the townships, I became a journalist at the government-supporting Afrikaans newspaper *Rapport*.

On June 28, 1984, the ANC activist Jeanette Schoon and her six-year-old daughter, Katryn, were blown up by a letter bomb in Lubango in Angola. The bomb had been intended for Marius Schoon, but he wasn't home at the time and his wife opened the letter. A day after the explosion, my news editor sent me to do an interview with the Commissioner of Police, General Johan Coetzee.

Coetzee told me that the security police had information that Jeanette and Katryn had been killed by the ANC as a result of an internal struggle within the organisation. I wrote a story, quoting Coetzee, and it was published. I forgot about the article, until six years later when Marius Schoon returned from exile, made an appointment with me and said that nothing had hurt him more after his wife and daughter's deaths than the article I had written.

Today, we know that the security police had manufactured and sent the letter bomb. I could say nothing to Marius other than how sorry I was and that I had been totally misled at the time. It is the same argument used by Paul van Vuuren today. But the year 1984 is perhaps the watershed year, during which our paths diverged.

That was the time when Van Vuuren should have said no and turned back, but instead, by the end of that year, he had requested a transfer to the Security Branch. He chose to became a killer.

I continued to work for *Rapport*, but four years later, became a co-founder of an anti-apartheid newspaper, refused to do any further military service and exposed the existence of police death squads.

Quoting again from *Rosencrantz and Guildenstern are Dead*, Guildenstern says: 'We cross our bridges when we come to them and burn them behind us, with nothing to show for our progress except a memory of the smell of smoke, and a presumption that once our eyes watered.'

When Van Vuuren reported for service at the Northern Transvaal Security Branch, he was called in by Brigadier Jack Cronje.

'Yes, you duckfucker, where do you come from?'

'I grew up on a farm near Warmbaths, Brigadier.'

'So can you work with kaffirs?'

'Yes, Brigadier.'

'Well, report to Section B.'

Section B was the unit dealing with black activists. The unit had a network of about 100 informants in the townships who would provide the security police with information about the movement, activities and strategies of ANC and United Democratic Front (UDF) activists and comrades. Files would be compiled on activists and 'troublemakers' who needed the unit's 'attention'.

Van Vuuren said that when he arrived at the Security Branch in April 1985, a formal death squad had not yet been founded. But there was already a great deal of talk that a special unit was needed to counter unrest in the townships.

'One day, Captain Flip Loots said: 'If we can only kill these bastards, the unrest would stop.'

Security Branch headquarters had the same thinking. In his evidence before the TRC, Jack Cronje described how the death squad in his region came into being. 'The ANC, UDF and other black organisations were waging a war against us, and it became necessary to eliminate terrorists and activists. The legal system could not handle the situation and detention under the state of emergency proved to not be effective.'

Cronje said early in 1986 he had had a meeting with General Johan Viktor, who was second-in-command of the police counter-insurgency unit. 'He said we had to bring the situation in the Pretoria area under control. It didn't matter how. He said that Pretoria was burning and the country was burning. Activists had to be eliminated before they could commit acts of terror. From that point on, we waged a fullscale guerrilla war against activists.'

Cronje said the same methods were applied by security branches in other regions. 'It was done everywhere and we were never repudiated by the Commissioner of Police, the State Security Council, the Cabinet or the government.'

In his evidence before the TRC, FW de Klerk rejected Cronje's submission that the security police had then fought terror with terror: 'There was a fight to be fought against those activists which were part of the revolutionary onslaught aimed at making South Africa ungovernable, aimed at overthrowing the state. But to get people to kill other people, to get people to commit murder, was not part of the policy.'

Cronje also revealed the existence of a secret security police unit called the Counter Revolutionary Information Target Centre, better known by its Afrikaans acronym of Trewits. It was founded in 1985 to identify human targets for removal. Each month, representatives of the security police, Military Intelligence, Special Forces and the National Intelligence Service would hold meetings at which intelligence information would be exchanged and targets identified.

'All our actions were contained in situation reports that were sent to Security Branch headquarters. Further reports about our actions were sent to the State Security Council, and, therefore, the Council had to know about the actions of my men.'

FW de Klerk said of Trewits: 'What they were doing, if they actually did it, would defnitely have been unauthorised. It was never part of the policy and I totally distanced myself from that. They were not acting within the framework or anything that comes near a reasonable interpretation of the policies of the government.'

Captain Jacques Hechter was the first to be selected as a member of Cronje's death squad. He was a highly experienced policeman with 15 years of service in the Security Branch, the Special Riot Unit and various detective units.

In turn, he recruited Paul van Vuuren. 'He called me aside and said to me he wanted me to join him and form a death squad that would act against political activists. I felt it was an honour and the right thing to do. I immediately accepted and could not wait to get going.'

Joe Mamasela became the third member of the squad. Van Vuuren said there was a very close friendship between the three killers. 'Mamasela would sometimes sleep in my flat and we would have braais together.'

Jack Cronje gave the three men complete carte blanche to act against activists. 'We could do as we wished. When we had to kill somebody, we would say: "We are going to steal him tonight". He was as good as dead.'

Hechter told the TRC that they would never act upon only a single report or fact. They tried to verify the accuracy of their information. 'I only eliminated people that were involved in numerous acts of violence. We didn't eliminate innocent people.'

The problem with Hechter's statement is that the three men acted as prosecutors, judges and executioners – and relied on untested information supplied by informants. In his psychiatric report, Hechter said that he couldn't inflict pain on others. That is why he didn't shoot people, he told a psychiatrist, but killed them with his bare hands and blew up the bodies afterwards. He sees himself as a fair and righteous man who gave an activist the opportunity to sing 'Nkosi Sikilel i' Afrika' before killing him.

Hechter suffers from what a psychiatrist called 'voluntary memory loss'. He had simply forgotten about many of the murders he had committed. The human psyche, it seems, plays tricks after one has electrocuted and arranged to inject poison into, and blow up, ten others.

Van Vuuren is more honest about what the men did. 'In the beginning we only intimidated people. If activists burnt down a house, we would get reports from informants who they were. We would go that night and burn their houses. If they burn, we burn. After a while, the comrades were not sleeping in their houses any more. We would throw petrol bombs through windows. I suppose people, maybe women and children, could have died in the attacks. In the beginning I was scared, but after a while I couldn't wait to go out at night. It was like sleeping with a woman,' said Van Vuuren.

Joe Mamasela said they fire-bombed about 350 houses in and around Pretoria. Jacques Hechter underwent a crash course in explosives, and when he came back, he introduced 'bucket bombs' to his death squad compatriots.

Van Vuuren said a typical day would start at half past seven in the morning when they would go out for a cup of coffee. Later the same morning, they would ask Flip Loots which names had surfaced in the informant reports. He would tell them who was politically 'active and who needed attention'. They would read through the files and have to decide: did he only 'need a hiding'? Or did they need to 'steal him'? They had complete access to 'terrorist' weapons such as AK-47s and Makarovs and could obtain explosives whenever they needed them. They had a .22 pistol with a silencer which they used to shoot noisy and aggressive dogs.

'We went on operations about every second night. We would use stolen cars and would sometimes wear balaclavas. I must have conducted at least 200 operations, but it could have been 500.'

The squad usually recruited informants from activists they abducted. They would drive around in a minibus and when they came alongside an activist, they would open the door, grab him and pull him in. In other cases, Mamasela would infiltrate activist cells or units and lure activists into Van Vuuren and Hechter's waiting hands.

During interrogation, the men would evaluate the activist and decide if he might be worth recruiting as an informant. They would offer him money, up to R1 000 a month. Once he had given his first report, he was hooked.

Interrogation and torture went hand in hand. Van Vuuren said they would always take a suspect to a remote place where he knew nobody could hear him. 'We were very good at torturing people. I quickly learned that if you don't hit him half-dead, he's not going to tell you everything.'

Each unit and every security policeman had his own method of torturing people. Vlakplaas, for example, was fond of 'tubing' people: pulling the inner tube of a car tyre over a detainee's face to smother him.

'I found that to "tube" a person was not always that effective. You got tired because you had to use both hands and pull hard. We had various methods. We would tie a detainee very tightly to a chair. We had a gas mask which we would put over his face. We would close the air supply with a plug. While the activist would struggle and gasp for air, we could sit back and have coffee. It was much easier than tubing. I read books about the torture methods of the SS in Germany and Pinochet's secret police in Chile. I learned that the best way to interrogate a person was to take all his clothes off to strip him of his dignity. Nobody could last more than five minutes. There was one very important factor when I tortured somebody, and that was that I felt fuck-all for life. I would have killed anybody. A detainee knew he was dead if he didn't co-operate. If you wanted to be a political activist, you had to be able to take the pain.'

'How did you feel about killing people?' I asked him.

'It didn't bother me, because it was the enemy.'

'Did you enjoy what you were doing?'

'Yes, I enjoyed what I was doing, because I thought it was the right thing to do. It was the enemy we were killing. I felt I was busy with big and important things. We always used to say: 'We are reducing the files.'

'Were you an effective death squad?'

'Hechter and myself have killed more people than any other security policemen. We killed many more than those for whom we are applying for amnesty. It is just that we cannot remember everything. We were more effective than Vlakplaas. We never drank during an operation and never stole money. I never made a cent.'

'Do you never feel guilty about anything you did?'

'Harold Sefola disturbed me, because he wasn't scared of dying. He died with dignity. The other two I didn't care about. They were like all the others. I do feel bad about innocent women and children that might have died. But I never have any nightmares.'

'Do you think it was worthwhile?'

'At the time I was proud of fighting Communism, but if I think back about it today, we didn't make any difference. We wasted our time.'

'Are you in any way sorry for what you did?'

'I can't say to the victims or their families that I'm sorry. They're empty words. I would rather say nothing, because it's too easy to say you have remorse.'

The amnesty submissions of the killer commando at the Northern Transvaal Security Branch consisted of several hundred pages. Together, Jack Cronje, Paul van Vuuren and Jacques Hechter applied for amnesty for more than 40 murders. Hechter applied for amnesty for 26 incidents, Paul van Vuuren for 18.

But they were only confessing to incidents already made public by Joe Mamasela. Before their testimony had ended, Van Vuuren told me that they had to prepare amnesty applications for about 15 more murders as a result of information given to the TRC by other policemen who were applying for amnesty.

Van Vuuren said there were several more incidents that he was not going to talk about. 'Sometimes only Jacques Hechter and I went on operations. We are not going to split on each other and it will remain our secret. Nobody will ever know.'

Van Vuuren said to me that to sit and confess to the TRC was the most difficult thing he had ever done in his life.

'More difficult than killing people?'

'That was easy after a while. The Commission are messing around with our souls. It isn't fair. They are making me responsible for the deeds of the politicians.'

He said he became extremely agitated during the hearings. When Chris Ribeiro testified about the assassination of his mother and father, Van Vuuren said he could see the hatred in his eyes. 'I looked at him and thought: 'I'll kill you as well.'

Dr Fabian Ribeiro, a much-loved general practitioner in Mamelodi, was shot and killed at his home on December 1, 1986. His wife, Florence, died in his arms.

Chris Ribeiro testified: 'My father went about his normal work as a doctor. His contact with comrades was to treat their injuries. He would document their injuries and give them advice regarding their right to lay charges and he would then forward the documented evidence. My mother went about her daily chores as a mother and a housewife.'

Van Vuuren said to me that Fabian Ribeiro 'was an old drunkard and not as innocent as everyone thought. He was an instigator in the townships. But his wife wasn't suppose to die. We would have killed him in his surgery with a sharpened screw driver and made it look like a robbery. We waited for him, but he didn't arrive.'

Jack Cronje's death squad applied for amnesty for conspiring to kill Fabian Ribeiro. The men argued that Ribeiro was a 'high-profile terrorist' who assisted comrades financially to leave the country for military training. But as in all other cases, they couldn't substantiate their allegations, as all documentation had been destroyed. But they said they hadn't killed the couple. SADF Special Forces had requested his file and assassinated him and his wife. Cronje said the murders had been carried out by two Angolans flown in from Namibia by Special Forces.

One of Van Vuuren's more bizarre amnesty applications concerned an activist, an aspiring Dutch Reformed Church dominee (minister), a professor and an 'indecent sexual act'.

One night in 1987, Van Vuuren burst into the house of an activist by the name of Sandy Lebisi. He found the activist in bed with the dominee, both naked. Van Vuuren said there was a black policeman, probably Joe Mamasela, with him. He instructed Mamasela to assault the dominee. Mamasela then assaulted him. They then loaded the dominee into their car and took him back to their offices.

Jacques Hechter wanted to do a semen test on the dominee, probably to establish whether sexual intercourse had indeed taken place between the two men. At the time, sex between men was still a criminal offence. The test wasn't done, but the dominee was kept in police custody overnight.

The next day, General Basie Smit told them that Professor Johan Heyns, then moderator of the Dutch Reformed Church, would fetch Hofmeyer. When Heyns saw Van Vuuren, he told him that he was a 'devil policeman'.

Van Vuuren said Heyns tried to justify the dominee's deed. 'He said that the dominee only wanted to feel what it was like to be in bed with a black person.' The security policeman drew out Lebisi's file and showed Heyns that the activist was a homosexual. Heyns wouldn't believe it. Van Vuuren accompanied them to the lift, where the dominee insulted him.

'I stopped the lift, and grabbed him by the throat. I said to him I didn't want to involve myself with people like him. Heyns looked down at his feet. I asked him what he was looking at, and sent the lift down to the ground floor with Heyns and the dominee.'

Although nobody was injured in the whole furore, Van Vuuren asked for amnesty for kidnapping and assault relating to this incident.

They became known as the 'unknown victims' – nameless and unidentified people who had been murdered and tortured by the killer policemen. For example, Jacques Hechter and Paul van Vuuren applied for amnesty for the killing of a 'Hammanskraal policeman and his wife in or around 1987'. They said they couldn't remember who the couple were.

Van Vuuren and Hechter said: 'General Ras told us that a policeman who lived in Hammanskraal north of Pretoria was a member of the ANC. We had to eliminate him because he was dangerous and posed a threat to the security forces.'

General Marthinus Ras, at the time a colonel and acting head of the Northern Transvaal Security Branch, took the witness stand and told the commission that he had ordered the 'elimination' of the policeman after the divisional commissioner of police had told him to order the Hechter-Van Vuuren-Mamasela trio to kill him. He admitted that he gave the order to 'eliminate' on purely hearsay evidence and and didn't so much as shuffle the paper on his desk, or look in a file to see why the policeman had to be killed. And when the policeman's wife was killed as well, he didn't even ask why.

The commission identified the victims as Sergeant Tumelo Richard Motasi and his wife, Irene Motasi, both gunned down in their Hammanskraal home on the night of November 30, 1987.

Brian Currin, the lawyer acting for the Motasi family, put it to Ras: 'You were a police officer, not a judge and not an executioner.'

Ras: That is so, but we did not live in normal circumstances.

Mr Justice Andrew Wilson: You get asked on a flimsy bit of information to provide a hit squad and kill a man. No written instructions, no other information. How is it that a policeman of your standing can act in this way?

Ras: Such snippets of information often came to the Security Branch, and I saw this piece as one ...

Wilson: You gave the instruction to kill this man. You are responsible for the death of this man and his wife.

Ras: That is so, Mr. Chairman. I'm responsible because I said to them that there's a request from the divisional commissioner that this man must be killed and they must do the job.

The policemen tried to convince the commission that the killing of Motasi fell within the framework of their secret war against the ANC. They had to protect innocent women and children from being murdered by 'trained terrorists' and activists.

Each and every person they killed, they claimed, was involved in acts of terror. They said they were never involved in the killing of any person who was not a terrorist or an activist. This is simply a lie.

The policemen couldn't provide evidence that Motasi was ever a member of the ANC or posed any threat to national security. He was nothing more, it seems, than a dutiful policeman with 11 years of service and an unblemished record. Why then kill him?

The answer may lie in the refusal of a black policeman to subjugate himself to the autocratic rule of a white superior officer who had allegedly called him a 'kaffir', said he was stupid and then hit him against the side of his head. Richard Motasi might have signed his own death warrant when he insisted that his superior officer was wrong for assaulting him and should be punished.

On a rainy night in November 1987, he arrived home with a box of Kentucky fried chicken under his arm. When he opened the door, he was met by three men who had been lying in wait inside his home. They were wearing balaclavas and were armed with AK-47s.

The three men were Jacques Hechter, Paul van Vuuren and Flip Loots. Joe Mamasela was in the bedroom keeping Irene Motasi silent.

This is how Van Vuuren described the killing: 'When he opened the door, Jacques Hechter grabbed him by the throat. A struggle ensued. We punched him with our fists, Captain Loots hit him with the butt of an AK-47 and I throttled him. He became unconscious after Hechter kicked him on the chest. We put a pillow over his head and I shot him four times in the head. I went to the bedroom to fetch Mamasela. When I got to the room, I heard shots. Mamasela told me he had had to shoot the woman because she had seen his face.'

In an affidavit made to the Transvaal Attorney General, Joe Mamasela gave a completely different version of the killing of Irene Motasi. 'I didn't kill her,' he said. 'Hechter shot her, and what is more, is that he wanted me to kill the Motasi's young son, who had just passed babyhood, who was asleep in the room next door.' Mamasela said they had entered the house after he had identified himself as a policeman. He said to Irene they were investigating a case of armed robbery against her husband and would wait for his return. He held her captive until her husband returned.

'A big noise broke out in the lounge. The woman wanted to know what was going on, and I said to her Motasi was probably resisting arrest. I heard several shots being fired. The woman was angry and wanted to know what was going on. Hechter came into the room and said to me I should have shot the woman a long time ago. He instructed her to get into bed. He took my revolver and shot her a few times in the head.

'Hechter gave the pistol back to me and said I must go and shoot the child in the other room. I couldn't get myself to shoot him. I went back to the room where the woman was and shot twice in the direction of the bed. My ammunition was finished. When I left the house, I saw the body of a man on the floor. He was lying on his back and there was blood on his face and chest. When we drove back, Hechter once again accused me of not shooting the woman. He asked if I had shot the child and I said: "Yes". He inspected my revolver and saw that it was empty. He was satisfied.'

It was important for the policemen to distance themselves from the death of Irene Motasi. At least they could claim they had instructions to kill Richard Motasi, but his wife was never supposed to have died. They, therefore, put the blame on one another.

When Gloria Hlabangane, the mother of Irene Motasi, arrived at the home the next morning, police were carrying the body of her daughter out of the house.

'They were taking her to the mortuary, so I opened her. She had a big hole on her forehead.'[8]

She found Richard in the lounge with pieces of his brain and skull spread around the room. She then started looking for five-year-old Tshidiso Motasi. She heard him saying behind her: 'They have killed them.'

'I asked him: "Who killed them?".'

"The police, they have killed my mother and my father."

'I said: "How do you know?"'

'"They were wearing the same jersey as my father," he said to me.'

Gloria Hlabangane says the child has suffered a lot as a result of losing his parents: 'It's when other children talk about their moms and dads and we talk about their deaths that he takes their pictures and sleeps with them under his pillow. He's got this memory and he misses them.'

Brian Currin handed documents to the commission showing that Motasi might have been killed because of the criminal charge he had laid and civil claim he had instituted against Colonel W P van Zyl, his superior officer at the Police Training College at Hammanskraal. Currin said Motasi had told him about his fear that the police would murder him.

In an affidavit, Motasi said he was on duty in September 1984 when Van Zyl had insulted him by saying: 'You kaffir, we struggle to overcome your stupidness and I should have killed you a long time ago.'

Motasi said he saluted the colonel, who hit him on his left ear with his open hand. Van Zyl followed him into his office. 'He hit me with his clenched fist on the left hand side of my head just slightly above the left ear. I fell and he kicked me on my buttocks.' The blows perforated his eardrum and left him with permanent disability.

He then laid a charge against Van Zyl. Several of his colleagues visited Motasi and asked him to withdraw the charge. A brigadier threatened to transfer him and said he wanted to know nothing of this 'nonsense story'.

In August 1985, Motasi wrote a letter to the State President, the Minister of Police and the Commissioner of Police. By then, he was desperate for redress and had already undergone three ear operations. He suffered from headaches and was on permanent medication.

'I love my career, but for the sake of my future and success in the force I am compelled to make a humble and urgent request for an investigation before it is too late.'

But his plea to the politicians and the commissioner fell on deaf ears and the intimidation directed against him didn't stop. In another affidavit, Motasi said that in April 1986 he was doing shopping in Hammanskraal. 'I was off duty and went to fill a gas bottle. I suffer from severe headaches as a result of the assault, and therefore removed my police cap.'

When he came out of the shop, he was called by a Captain Kotze who said to him: 'Motasi, I'm speaking to you. Where is your cap? Why aren't you wearing it? My little kaffir, don't you believe that I will fuck you up?'

In May 1987, Richard Motasi sued Van Zyl for R50 000. Six months later, he lay dead on the floor of his house with four bullet wounds in his head.

On June 6, 1997, the fourteen-year-old Tshidiso Motasi came face to face with one of the killers of his parents when Paul van Vuuren agreed to meet him in his lawyer's office in Pretoria. Since the death of his parents, Tshidiso had been living with his grandparents in Soweto.[9]

On the one hand, it was a public relations exercise for Van Vuuren. The meeting was going to be filmed by television cameras and would show the policeman stretching out a hand of reconciliation to a young boy he had orphaned.

On the other hand, Tshidiso Motasi had questions and wanted answers: 'What happened there? Why did you think my father was a spy? What is going to happen to me?'

For many years, Tshidiso has been haunted by the memories of the killing. 'All that I remember is that in the morning the neighbours came to the house and picked me up. And when I saw my mother there, she was shot in the head. My father, he was shot in the head. I didn't know that they were dead. I just said: "Father wake up, father wake up."'

The young boy attended the TRC hearing and listened to the evidence of the killers. 'I thought of taking a glass, breaking it and killing him. When they said my father jumped like a tiger, he laughed, that guy. It was very painful to me because they make it like a joke.'

Across the shining table in the plush lawyer's office, Tshidiso, dressed in his school uniform, took Van Vuuren's hand.

Van Vuuren: How are you?

Tshidiso: I'm fine.

Van Vuuren: I'm sorry what happened to your parents and you, because it was a waste of human life. I'm sorry for that. You must just remember that in those days there was a war in the country. People were dying on both sides of the struggle. The ANC was banned and I was a security policeman. I'm sorry about the way you lost your parents. All that we did was a waste of human life.

Tshidiso: You did something very bad. I can't forgive you, I can't. It is very hard for me.

Van Vuuren: I know that you must hate me. I know that if somebody had taken my parents, I would have felt much more hateful than you.

Tshidiso: I don't have parents. My granny can die any day, because she's gone old now. If she dies, who is going to take care of me?

Van Vuuren: That's a difficult question. You can come and live with me. I'll look after you. If something happens to your granny, you can phone me, I will try and help you.

The meeting ended, they shook hands and parted: the young boy went back to the five-roomed house he shares with his grandparents in Jabulani in Soweto, and Van Vuuren returned to his cattle ranch near Warmbaths.

A public relations stunt it might have been for Van Vuuren, but the young Motasi, tears in his eyes, said afterwards: 'This is my day. A person who killed my parents came to me and said he was sorry. It means something to me.'

I don't know whether Van Vuuren meant what he said when he undertook to help the boy if something should happen to his grandparents.

He will in any event have to live with his memory of the boy for the rest of his life.

Paul van Vuuren said the killing had had a devastating effect on the personal lives of the men involved. 'Hechter's wife left him because of what he was doing. He wanted to shoot himself, but I took the pistol from him and calmed him down. I was very aggressive. If somebody hassled me, I wanted to kill him. We would play 'chicken' by driving at 200 kilometres per hour up a one-way street. I don't know how we survived. We drank a lot, maybe because subconsciously we felt guilty.' Van Vuuren's marriage to Cathryn survived the upheavals of his killer existence, although she also wanted to leave him at one stage. He said he couldn't live with both the hate in his heart for the 'enemy' and his love for her. During his death squad activities, she frequently asked him what he was busy with, but he told her she must not worry. Today, she says she supports him and understands why he did it.

Hechter and Van Vuuren's death squad careers came to an end towards the end of 1988 when a police general instructed them to kill an anti-apartheid activist with an overdose of mandrax tablets. They told the general he was crazy and shortly afterwards Hechter and Van Vuuren were transferred to different units.

According to security police files, Father Smangaliso Mkhatshwa was a Communist and an agitator in the Pretoria townships. Hechter testified: 'It was striking to me that the bishop kept in his room, next to his bed, a very small Bible. And behind a curtain on the wall he had a bookrack in which he had Communist books by Lenin.'

Mkhatshwa had to be eliminated. Two assassination rifles with silencers were specially assembled for the operation. Van Vuuren and Hechter planned to shoot him at Durban airport.

'Van Vuuren, who grew up on a farm, would do the shooting. We parked the combi in the parking area so that we could have a clear view of the main exit. We saw him leaving, but there were one or two people between us all the time. We could not fire on him,' Hechter testified.

Mkhatshwa, today the deputy minister of education, said he was frequently harassed during the 1980s. In August 1986, he was abducted, driven to an unknown place and tortured. The policemen said they were not responsible for the incident. Military Intelligence kidnapped and tortured him.

In 1988, they were once again instructed to kill Mkhatshwa. They said that after General Basie Smit became commander of the Northern Transvaal Security Branch in that year, he requested them to kill Mkatshwa with an overdose of mandrax tablets. Hechter said to Smit it wouldn't work and that, anyway, they didn't trust Smit.

Mkhatshwa and Hechter have had run-ins in the past. 'The last time that Captain Hechter and I met, he had a gun in his hand, pointed at my forehead. Doors were broken down and that is how he, Captain Loots and others gained entry. But because of my deep-felt belief, not only as a Christian but also because of the policy of reconciliation of the government, my sentiments immediately said to me: stretch out your hand and meet Jacques Hechter and Paul van Vuuren.'

And so, in a moment of silence, Mkhatshwa and his would-be assassins shook hands in the chambers of the TRC.

'I'm glad we didn't kill him,' Van Vuuren said afterwards.

After their fall-out with Smit, the death squad was disbanded. Hechter was transferred to police intelligence and Van Vuuren became Smit's personal assistant. 'I was his driver, I had to transport convicts to his house to work in his garden.'

Van Vuuren left the police force in 1989 and went farming, and Hechter retired after a motor car accident in 1991 on grounds of ill health.

According to Pretoria psychiatrist Professor Jan Robbertze, Jack Cronje suffers from serious post-traumatic stress disorder. He still experiences nightmares, amnesia and 'flashbacks' of his experiences. Robbertze describes him as an 'empty' person.

Jacques Hechter suffers from serious amnesia, perhaps as a result of heavy drinking and alcohol poisoning. There are certain murders he simply couldn't remember and he had to rely on the memories of Van Vuuren and Cronje.

Van Vuuren comes from a family with a history of severe aggression, but the psychiatrist couldn't find evidence of any psychiatric disorder. 'He left the police force, came back from the war and continued a normal life,' says Robbertze.

It was on his game farm near Ellisras in the Northern Transvaal that Paul van Vuuren had to come to terms with his frustration of being just a farmer again. 'I was very frustrated after I had left the force. In 1992, I shot 2 000 impala buck. I had to keep my mind occupied and find an outlet for my adrenalin.'

He said he was very strict with his workers. If they didn't listen, he would 'fuck them up'. He would sometimes get so angry that he would get heart palpitations and go to bed.

Van Vuuren says he is religious, but he refuses to go to church. 'The Dutch Reformed Church is racist. I don't pray that much any more. Maybe what I did is going to cost me my place in heaven, and maybe there isn't forgiveness for people like me.'

He is adamant that he is no racist and that he didn't wage a war against black people. He says that before the April 1994 election he was approached by right-wingers who wanted him to join them in planning a possible uprising against an ANC government. 'I told them to bugger off. I'm not a racist.'

He had a fall-out with the Ellisras Farmer's Association because he told them that they want to 'fuck up the kaffirs on the one hand, but sleep with black women on the other'. He eventually left Ellisras and settled on his cattle farm near Warmbaths.

Van Vuuren says he had always voted for the National Party and believed in the reform process started by FW de Klerk. 'Today, I would chase De Klerk like a dog from my farm if he ever set foot here. He sold us out. I have lots of respect for Nelson Mandela, because he came out of jail and didn't hate white people. But Peter Mokaba with his "One settler, one bullet" slogan – I would like to show him a thing or two.'

In May 1996, Van Vuuren received a visit from the Transvaal Attorney General who was investigating charges of murder against him after Mamasela had spoken. 'They asked me to make a statement against Jack Cronje and Jacques Hechter. I refused. We are still closer than brothers and would rather go to jail than testify against one another.'

The only option then was for the three men to do the previously unthinkable: to confess. And so, for more than a month, the bloodbrothers of the Northern Transvaal Security Branch told their tale of death.

'I've never had a problem with labour on the farm. Now, for the first time, people don't want to work for me any more. They see me on television and are scared. People recognise me in the streets. Some see me as a hero, but the higher-class Afrikaner looks down on me with contempt. It isn't fair, because I also killed for them.'

The policemen said in their opening statement that they had decided to confess 'with a purpose of cleansing our souls from the darkness of the past, and to let the truth be spoken about our deeds'.

Paul van Vuuren was not trying to cleanse his soul, he was simply trying to escape justice.

When I first saw and listened to Paul van Vuuren at the TRC, I thought that every movement he made, every blink of his eye, every twist in his face, the clenched fists, all spoke of evil.

I then watched him on his farm, cuddling his baby and hugging his wife and I thought again: see how normal this man is. Where is the face of evil now?

Chapter Fourteen

Once were warriors

Peter Casselton loved poodles. French poodles meant more to him than people. His first poodle was called Liza, and he named his yacht after her. Then came Bubas, who became a regular face in the drinking taverns of Pretoria where the outcasts of apartheid's secret wars hung out. Bubas was abducted and disappeared. It almost broke his heart, but then followed poodle number three, which he named Peppie.[1]

Sitting upright in the front row of the St Saviours Presbyterian Church in Randjiesfontein, halfway between Pretoria and Johannesburg, was Peppie, quaffed and groomed with a red ribbon in his hair. On Peppie's left hand side, a few metres away, stood a coffin with the remains of Peter John Casselton, the former spymaster who had died a few days earlier when he was crushed to death against a wall by a truck he was working on.

In the pulpit was a police chaplain, saying: 'Why, do many people ask, did he have to go now that he's given such good service to his country? Maybe he has been taken from us because God needs him now. Maybe God has prepared his place for him in heaven.'

The chaplain, a grey man who spoke poor English, was clearly a leftover from the former regime and had probably conducted similar funerals for several police criminals. I don't know whether he was aware that the man whose soul he was praying for was a criminal, no Christian at all, and believed in neither heaven nor hell. Sitting behind Peppie were Casselton's friends: amongst them two former Vlakplaas operatives and a host of former Rhodesians, their cherubic faces gone florid from years of hard living and enormous quantities of alcohol.

Many of them were former members of Ian Smith's Rhodesian armed forces who had fought with Casselton against liberation. One, dressed in his Scottish gear, played *Amazing Grace* on his pipes as a last tribute to his fallen comrade.

Their eyes, which had witnessed so much death and mayhem, were wet when the grey-and-black hearse drove Casselton's body away to be cremated. His ashes, friends said, would be cast over the ocean off the Mozambican coast.

His close friend and confidant, Eugene de Kock, could not be at the funeral. He must have been sitting in his maximum security cell in Pretoria Central Prison thinking about the man who, for two years, had so faithfully brought him a hot peri-peri chicken every Sunday.

No family members attended the funeral. The last time Casselton saw his sister, who lives in Australia, was when he was a teenager. He hadn't had contact with his aged mother in London for more than a decade and he had no children and had had no contact with his previous two wives for some time.

His coffin was draped in white flowers. Amongst them was a card from a mysterious admirer who said: 'Peter, my darling friend, my protector. You have been my life, my heart for 35 years. You are my indescribable loss. I will love you for evermore.'

Peter Casselton died a lonely man. Less than three months before he died, I spent a few days with him in Beira in Mozambique and he often said he had nothing and nobody to live for. That's maybe why his poodles were so important to him.

What he took with him to his grave on February 20, 1997, were many of the secrets of the years he spied for the apartheid government. He lived at Vlakplaas and was a confidant of not only Eugene de Kock, but also of 'superspy' Craig Williamson.

Casselton has probably done enough evil, says colleague Phillip van Niekerk, to have booked his place in hell. But I also agree with Phillip that the man had a softness to him that was often difficult to equate with the more diabolical side of his life.[2]

For most of his 53 years, Peter Casselton had led a life that many would envy. There was a time of beautiful woman, flying adventures all over Africa and the Middle East, and years spent on a yacht in the Mediterranean with an unlimited expense account paid for by the South African taxpayer.

Two months after his death, I sat in a Johannesburg restaurant with a journalist friend and told her that I missed Peter Casselton. He had a flamboyance and a flair which made it so much easier to deal with him than with the Eugene de Kocks and the Dirk Coetzees of this world. He was no common killer and thug.

And he certainly had a story to tell.

My first encounter with Peter Casselton was rather disastrous. When Dirk Coetzee spoke out towards the end of 1989, he implicated Casselton in the bombing of the ANC office in London in April 1982. Coetzee identified Casselton as a Security Branch spymaster in London who handled a network of secret agents all over Europe.

Casselton, a qualified commercial pilot and British citizen, was at the time doing crop-spraying in Mozambique, but when he heard of Coetzee's allegations, he hastily returned to South Africa for fear of being extradited to the United Kingdom. Scotland Yard issued a statement saying that it would like to question him about the explosion. Casselton went to stay at Vlakplaas, where Eugene de Kock looked after him.

Casselton later told me that Vlakplaas was at the time desperately trying to establish the whereabouts of Coetzee in order to find and kill him. The Vlakplaas men bugged Karin Coetzee's telephone, but couldn't establish where Coetzee was. De Kock finally turned to Casselton and asked him to contact Karin as the Coetzees and Casselton had been the best of friends in the early 1980s.

Casselton phoned Karin Coetzee and arranged to meet her at a Pretoria restaurant. Karin then phoned me and we talked about the meeting, but Vlakplaas policemen were listening in on the conversation and therefore knew that Max du Preez and I were going to be there to attempt to talk to Casselton.

When Karin arrived at the rendezvous, it was swarming with Vlakplaas policemen. What we didn't know then was that Eugene de Kock and his wife, Audrey, were sitting in a corner of the same restaurant. De Kock, Casselton told me later, feared that Max and I would attempt to kidnap Casselton!

The Vlakplaas policemen were very conspicuous. There were three police vehicles, including a minibus full of suspicious-looking black men who had to be askaris.

Casselton was wired with the most modern listening devices – which later turned out to not have worked! We armed Karin Coetzee with a micro-cassette taperecorder – which didn't work either! There we were, two journalists and a gang of police killers, playing spy-spy!

Casselton, obviously well-briefed by De Kock, told Karin that he was no longer working for the security police and that he wanted to establish contact with her husband. He said that he feared for his life and that he had to find a way of leaving the country. 'I'm stuffed,' he lamented, 'I'm stuffed. Why did Dirk do it to me? I'll rot away in jail for 25 years. I was in jail before: I do not want to go back.'

While Max du Preez and I were monitoring the meeting between Casselton and Karin Coetzee, we were called out of the restaurant by a black security guard who told us that men in a pick-up van had tried to break into our car.

We walked to the van parked some distance away. Inside were two bearded, safari-suited men. One had a two-way radio on his lap and the other held a file. They didn't see us coming until Max roared at them: 'Were you trying to break into our car?'

The one with the file threw it on the floor, while the other tried desperately to hide the two-way radio under the seat.

'Negative,' the one with the radio answered.

Max: 'Were you never near our car?'

Policeman: 'Negative. Was something stolen? Do you have any witnesses? Are there any fingerprints?'

Max: 'Sir, what is your name?'

Policeman: 'Gert Prinsloo.'

Max: 'Are you a policeman?'

Policeman: 'Negative.'

Max: 'You talk like one.'

Policeman: 'Negative.'

After Karin Coetzee had left, we found Casselton still sitting in the restaurant. We walked up to him and and asked if we could talk to him. He denied that he was Peter Casselton and asked us to leave.

As Casselton stood up and walked out to the parking garage, we followed him. He turned around and threatened us: 'Leave me alone. Just leave me alone. I'm very nervous. I'm an old hand at this. Just turn around and walk away. Don't talk to me. You'll have to get up much earlier in the morning if you're dealing with me.'

Casselton sat in his car for an hour, and then roared out of the parking garage. He was followed by the three vehicles in a high-speed car chase through Pretoria. We lost them.

Years later, he told me that while driving back to Vlakplaas, he got tired of 'all this spy shit'. He turned off the road to Irene outside of Pretoria, lost the Vlakplaas vehicles which were pursuing him and booked himself into a hotel for the night. Eugene de Kock, he later learned, then became very anxious as he thought Casselton might have been abducted! For the next 16 hours, teams of Vlakplaas policemen and askaris were sent out to look for him.

Casselton nonchalantly arrived back at the farm the next morning, unperturbed by the furore he had caused.

A few days later, a man approached me saying that Casselton had asked him to arrange a meeting with us. The go-between was a giant of a man who introduced himself as 'Twiggy'. He said that Casselton wanted to talk about the London bomb, weapons he had hidden in bushes just outside the British capital and his falling out with Craig Williamson. We arranged a meeting with Casselton, but he never turned up.

I met 'Twiggy' again after Casselton's funeral – an ex-Rhodesian by the name of Peter Dunnwoodie. He said that Casselton had indeed been worried and had wanted to know whether there was a possibility that he would be extradited to the United Kingdom. He said that Casselton had wanted our conversation recorded and had given him a tape recorder to hide under his clothes. Instead of activating the 'record' button when he had seen me, he had pushed the 'pause' button.[3]

November 16, 1996. Beira, Mozambique. Sitting on the balcony on the third floor of a shabby block of flats on the beachfront, Peter Casselton was emptying a bottle of whisky, while sweat rolled off his paunch and his half-naked body.

The sun was setting over a city struggling to regain its former glory after more than three decades of war. Years before, Beira had been cut off from the outside world when the Renamo resistance movement had sabotaged most of its essential services. The city is today still without running water, sewerage or proper sanitation.

On that hot and humid summer's day, a terrible stench hung over Beira. Casselton hated the place. He had lived there in the early 1970s when it was still under Portuguese rule and had been a playground and holiday haven for white Rhodesians.

He spoke about the Grand Hotel with its Edwardian furniture and magnificent views over the bay, and the Portuguese Club, which boasted a marble staircase and crystal chandeliers.

Today, the Grand Hotel is a squatter camp and the Portuguese Club a ruin. Everything fell apart, he said, when Frelimo won the war of independence and took power in 1975. Confirmation, he said, that blacks can't govern.

'There are two things a kaffir can do well: make a fire anywhere, and fuck.' There was no use in arguing with Casselton that it was his former masters in Rhodesia that had created Renamo in order to to destabilise the Frelimo government in Mozambique. When Rhodesia became Zimbabwe in 1980, South Africa had continued to arm, train and fund the resistance movement, enabling Renamo to destroy Mozambique and to turn it into one of the world's poorest nations.

Casselton was a horrible racist, but he hated Afrikaners even more than blacks. 'No moral fibre, no fucking backbone,' he would say, referring to Eugene de Kock's men who had turned their backs on their former commander and had testified against him.

There wasn't many people or places Peter Casselton liked. 'I'm finished. I'm old. Who's going to employ a bum like me? That's why I'm sitting in this dump fixing old aeroplanes.'

During his last days, Casselton was a pathetic sight, often drunk and close to tears. He lived off the charity of a dwindling group of old drinking buddies. For two years, he had been squatting around Pretoria, often sleeping on mattresses on the ground with sometimes little to eat. Everything he had, he said, could be fitted into the boot of his old Peugeot car.

And then, one night in 1996, his dog, Bubas, was abducted during a pub brawl with a group of Afrikaners in a Pretoria bar. Years before, Casselton had buried a Makarov pistol near Pretoria and he was ready to dig it up and start a war over his dog. For two months, Casselton and a friend combed the streets of Pretoria hunting for the black French poodle or its abductors. He never found Bubas.

When I met him Casselton was in Beira to repair an ancient Dakota aircraft. He showed us his 'Dak', parked on the tarmac at the Mozambican Air Force base just outside of Beira. The base had become a graveyard for old MiG fighters and was almost deserted. Heaps of scrap metal which were the remnants of aircraft cut up after the war were lying all over the airbase. There were two MiG-24s parked in a hangar next to the Dakota which were still capable of flying, but the Mozambican Air Force had no pilots to fly them. Casselton had spoken to the air base commander who had agreed in principle that he could fly one of them. 'I still want to fly a MiG before I die,' he said.

Casselton was always coming up with new and unsuccessful schemes to make money – for example, he tried to buy Russian helicopters as scrap from the same air base in order to repair and sell them to a theme park in Nevada in the United States.

When we arrived in Beira, Casselton was penniless and he was compelled to borrow money from us and from an old Rhodesian army friend, but had to hand over his passport to the friend until he had repaid the loan.

'How am I ever going to do it? No, I'm telling you, I'm over fifty and I'm finished.'

It was difficult to believe that Peter Casselton had once controlled a security police secret fund of more than a million United States dollars.

Peter Casselton was born in Kent in the United Kingdom, but grew up in Southern Rhodesia. He was very young when his parents got divorced and he described his father as a 'bastard'. In fact, when Casselton saw his father again, it was 40 years later when his father visited him in prison in the United Kingdom. Casselton chased his father away and told him to never come back again.

He left school when he was 14 years old and said he could hardly read or write. He worked for some time on tobacco farms in Southern Rhodesia, saved money and eventually obtained his commercial pilot's licence.

Armed with a British passport, he flew all over Africa and the Middle East, mostly doing crop-spraying. When he died, he had done 24 000 hours of flying in countries like Somalia, Egypt, Sudan, Libya, Saudi Arabia, Uganda, Tanzania, Kenya, and all over southern Africa.

He was involved in only one aircraft 'accident', and that was two years before his death when he took part in an insurance scam. A Johannesburg businessman promised him R50 000 if he would crash the man's eight-seater aircraft somewhere in Africa. Casselton flew the plane to Malawi, and 70 metres above Lake Malawi and five kilometres from the shore, simply dropped it into the lake. Fishermen rescued him. Casselton was eventually charged with insurance fraud, but was acquitted when he lied in court under oath, saying that an engine had caught fire. However, by the time he came to collect his reward money for staging the accident, the owner had died in a car collision!

When Casselton spoke about his adventures in Africa, his eyes would light up. 'I once had to fly a child's corpse from Dar Es Salaam in Tanzania to Zanzibar island to deliver the remains to the parents. The people were Muslims and the body was put into a carton box tied with tape. As I arrived on Zanzibar, a Gulf Air Boeing filled with holidaymakers landed next to me. I got out of the aircraft with the carton under my arm. The parents were waiting in the airport building for their dead child. The next moment, in front of all the tourists, the body slipped out of the box and fell on the tarmac! People started screaming and running away, while others froze and stared at the body. I grabbed the corpse, a girl of about eight, and tried to stuff her back into the box. She slipped out of the other side and fell on the tarmac again. The parents saw what was going on and were hysterical. I couldn't get the kid back into the box, and in the end picked her up and ran back to my aircraft. The airport was in complete pandemonium.'

Casselton never tired of telling stories of his adventures. He beheaded an Arab on a camel when he miscalculated his flying height while crop-spraying in Egypt. On another occasion, when he was in Jedda in Saudi Arabia, he had to convert to Islam in order to obtain a business contract.

Casselton was then wealthy, popular and handsome. He married a former Miss Rhodesia and bought his own aircraft. But like most young, white Rhodesians at the time, he was eventually drawn into the army to fight the guerrilla armies of Joshua Nkomo and Robert Mugabe.

Peter 'Twiggy' Dunnwoodie met Casselton in the Rhodesian bush in 1972. Dunnwoodie was a medical orderly with the Rhodesian Light Infantry and Casselton was working for Rhodesian military intelligence. Casselton flew around in civilian clothes in a civilian aircraft and posed as a Portuguese businessman. He could speak Portuguese fluently and stayed in Beira. From time to time, he would also fly for the Portuguese army, which was fighting a war against the Frelimo guerrilla army.

Dunnwoodie said that Casselton was fearless. He would often do low-level reconnaissance flying over Mozambique, trying to locate guerrilla bases. His aircraft was frequently shot at.

'He was the coolest guy I've ever known. He once assisted me when I was forced to do a knee operation on a wounded soldier. Instead of handing me operational instruments, he fed me cold beers and Texan cigarettes. Somehow, we sewed the soldier up and by God's grace, he survived.'

Casselton told me how he used to transport wounded and captured Frelimo guerillas from the battlefield back to Beira. 'I would land just before Beira where Portuguese soldiers would decide which guerrillas were going to be worth anything to them. The rest would be executed. One day, I had a senior Frelimo officer by the name of Keiros in the aircraft. He was wounded in the stomach and was dying. Before we got to Beira, he took out a Makarov pistol and asked me to shoot him. I did. Sometimes, I had to drop Frelimo prisoners from the aircraft into the ocean. The Portuguese were much worse and more cruel than either the Rhodesians or the South Africans.'

'What is the worst thing you've ever done?' I asked him.

'Chimoio, 1977,' he said immediately.

On the morning of November 23, 1977, the Rhodesian Air Force and special forces attacked Chimoio in Mozambique, believing it to be a military base and stronghold of Robert Mugabe's Zimbabwe African National Liberation Army (Zanla).

General Ron Reid-Daly, commander of the Selous Scouts during the Rhodesian war, said afterwards: 'The raid was a great success: 2 000 terrorists were killed, while only two Rhodesians were killed and eight wounded.'[4]

The intelligence for the operation was provided mainly by Peter Casselton. After a low-level reconnaissance flight over the area, he had informed his commanders in Salisbury that Zanla fighters had moved into the camp. Aerial photographs confirmed his intelligence report.

News about the impending attack must have been leaked to Zanla and the night before the bombing, the Zanla guerrillas left the camp. Hours after the attack, Casselton landed his Cessna at Chimoio to assess its effects.

'It was a sight I would never forget. I walked in the camp amongst the hundreds of bodies and all I could see were women and children. There were very few terrorists. It was a miserable failure and I was at least partly responsible for it.'

Writing about Casselton after his death, Phillip van Niekerk said: 'There was reason to despise Casselton. The way he bragged about his intelligence role in the Chimoio massacre was enough to book his place in hell.'

Like many white Rhodesians who couldn't face the dawn of democracy and black majority rule in their country, Casselton came to South Africa in 1979. As a British subject, he needed a work permit and had problems with his immigration papers. A friend introduced him to a Security Branch agent.

Police were at the time setting up a foreign section (Section A) within the Security Branch. The section head was the infamous Brigadier Piet 'Biko' Goosen, the security police officer in charge of Steve Biko's interrogation in the Eastern Cape four years earlier. He was promoted to the rank of brigadier just after the activist's death.

Craig Williamson was the second-in-command of the section. He had earned the nickname of 'Superspy' when he had returned to South Africa in 1979 after infiltrating the International University Exchange Fund (IUEF) in Geneva, Switzerland, becoming its assistant director. He made contact with senior ANC officials in Europe and, according to the police, provided the South African security services with invaluable information about the organisation. According to the IUEF, Williamson took R50 000 with him when he left Europe after discovering that his cover was about to be blown. Section A bought their own secret police farm, Daisy, with the money that Williamson brought back to South Africa.

Goosen, Williamson and their agents would in later years become involved in some of the most notorious assassinations: that of Ruth First in Mozambique in 1982, and Katryn and Jeanette Schoon in Angola in 1984.

Casselton had all the right credentials for an overseas agent: he was British, had served the Rhodesian intelligence services with distinction and was fiercely anti-Communist. He was introduced to the head of the Security Branch, General Johan Coetzee.

'I was never motivated by National Party politics, I don't even speak Afrikaans. I was at the time earning $10 000 per month as a crop-spraying pilot and I asked Coetzee why I should become a South African policeman. I told him that if he wanted to employ me, he would have to pay for it. I was getting a higher salary than the commissioner.'

Casselton was sent to Daisy, where he was trained for six months in surveillance, gathering information, intelligence and counter-intelligence. After his training, he was sent to London to set up a network of agents. Casselton said he handled 10 full-time and about 25 part-time agents all over Europe.

He claimed that he put an ANC cabinet minister through Oxford, while one of his snitches in the Netherlands was a Dutch policeman, a former bodyguard to Prince Bernhard.

'I had a Spanish professor working for me, who was a lecturer at Wits University in Johannesburg. He fell foul of the law, but Section A made him an offer he couldn't refuse: either go to jail, or go back to Spain and work for us. So he worked for me in Spain.'

Casselton had a bank account on the Isle of Man which he called a 'bottomless pit'. At one stage, the account had $2 million in it. 'There was no way of checking how the money was spent. My agents couldn't sign receipts for money paid to them and, therefore, my bosses in Pretoria had to take my word for it. Millions of rands were misappropriated from this fund.'

Towards the end of 1981, Casselton received an instruction from Piet Goosen to collect three sealed metal boxes from the South African Embassy in London. He received them from Sergeant Major Joseph Klue, defence attaché. Klue was recalled to Pretoria in 1982 after the British government threatened to expel him for 'activities incompatible with his office'.

In the three metal boxes were explosives and detonators. Section A was planning an attack on the ANC headquarters in London. Casselton said he took the boxes back to his London flat and put them under the bed.[5]

With nostalgia Casselton would recall the women he had brought back to his flat: 'If they had only known that I was fucking them on top of a bomb.'

A week before the planned explosion, Casselton received more diplomatic post: false passports, details of emergency escape routes out of the United Kingdom, and arms and ammunition. He buried the weapons in the woods just outside of London.

Then the rest of the team, headed by Piet Goosen and Craig Williamson, arrived in London. Other members of the bombing team included Eugene de Kock, Vic McPherson and explosives expert Jerry Raven, who assembled the explosive device.

'The day before the bombing, Brigadier Goosen informed me that the operation had been approved by the Minister of Foreign Affairs, Pik Botha,' Casselton said in an affidavit submitted to the TRC just before his death.

Early on a Sunday morning in March 1982, the bomb ripped through the ANC headquarters at 27 Patten Street in London. It was the first South African military attack on European territory. The bomb did enormous structural damage and a person who was sleeping in the building at the time was slightly injured.

The bombers were later decorated by the Minister of Police, Louis le Grange, at a private medal parade in his office. Casselton never received his Police Star for Outstanding Service as his commanders didn't want to risk blowing his cover.

Casselton said that while he was in London he located the leader of the South African Communist Party and former chief of staff of Umkhonto we Sizwe, Joe Slovo. Slovo, labelled as a 'KGB colonel' by the apartheid government, was for many years enemy number one.

'I followed him around for weeks. I had a sniper's rifle and asked permission from Piet Goosen to assassinate him. It would have been easy, but Goosen told me that the Cabinet wouldn't approve the operation.'

Peter Dunnwoodie said Casselton recruited him for a special operation: to abduct Joe Slovo from London. 'I was a medic in Rhodesia and Peter wanted to know whether I could still do intravenous injections and things like that. He wanted to kidnap Slovo, sedate him, and bring him back to South Africa.'

Dunnwoodie said they had various meetings planning the abduction, but like so many other extravagant security police plots, nothing came of it.

In 1983 and 1984, Casselton broke into the offices of the ANC, the PAC and Swapo in London. 'When I entered the Swapo office, there was a dog who started barking and wanted to attack me. I had to kill him with an iron pipe. I was distraught, because I really love animals.'

The ANC office had a sophisticated alarm system. Casselton said that in order to practise for the break-in, he looked for a building with an identical alarm system.

'One night, I was walking around in Kensington, and there suddenly, was an art gallery with the same burglar alarm. I went back late that night and broke into the gallery. The alarm didn't go off. While I was standing in the gallery, I saw a painting of a Boer general on his white horse, and I decided to take the painting.'

Some time later, the painting was wrapped in cloth, sent back to South Africa and presented to the Commissioner of Police, General Johan Coetzee. It was placed in the commissioner's lounge and it became one of the best in-jokes in Section A of the Security Branch.

But Casselton's life of adventure and luxury in London was about to come to an end. A criminal he had hired to help him to break into the ANC, PAC and Swapo offices was arrested for drunken driving, made a deal with the police and told them about the burglaries.

Casselton was arrested and interrogated by the anti-terrorist squad at Scotland Yard. 'Listen, it's not only our police that batter and torture detainees. Scotland Yard did it to me as well. They knew I was involved in the London bombing and was a South African agent, but couldn't prove it and tried to get me to admit it. I didn't say a thing.'

Casselton held his tongue and never disclosed the identity of his agents or his handlers. He was charged with robbery and tried in the Old Bailey in London.

Just before sentence was passed, the judge asked Casselton whether he had anything to say. 'Yes, Your Honour, I definitely have. As far as I am concerned, the ANC is operating in London under the protection of the British government. I want to ask the South African government to bestow the same generosity on the Irish Republican Army and to provide them with facilities from which they can plan and launch their attacks on the people of Britain.'

'The judge didn't like it and was obviously upset. He looked at me for a long time and sentenced me to four years and six months' imprisonment. It was a hell of a shock, because I thought I would get a year or 18 months.'

Some of his black fellow-prisoners were delighted to discover an agent of the apartheid regime in their midst. 'I was always in maximum security prisons with the hardest of criminals because I was seen as a terrorist. I had to fight for my life. Look at the scars on my arms, that's where I was slashed with razor blades. I once threw an inmate from the third floor of the prison, and he fell on a snooker table and broke his neck. I said it was an accident.'

Casselton worked in the prison dentist's rooms, where he manufactured two cell keys out of parts of a stretcher, but a warder discovered the keys and he spent the Christmas of 1985 in solitary confinement.

While in prison, Casselton was promoted to the rank of lieutenant. He said his only visitors for the nearly three years he spent in prison were a secret agent he had once handled, a shipbuilder who was busy building him a yacht and his long-lost father, whom he chased away.

In order to qualify for early parole, Casselton married 'a broad I once met in a pub' at the Wandsworth prison registry office. Her name was Claire, and all Casselton knew about her was that her father was an artist who painted equestrian portraits for the Queen Mother. In return for her hand in marriage, Claire acquired Casselton's Mercedes 450 car, which had been bought with secret funds. He never saw her again, and may have been legally married to her till the day he died.

After his release from prison, Casselton came back to South Africa. 'I had become an embarrassment to the security establishment and they wanted me out of the way. Craig Williamson negotiated a payment of R100 000, which I was given in cash, and I was told to disappear.'

Casselton was extremely bitter towards Williamson when he found out that he had lost his pilot's licence, his identity as a secret agent had been blown and his savings account had been plundered.

He and Williamson had also created a business, Beach Port, on the Channel Islands and had built a yacht together. They named it the 'Two Lizas' in memory of Williamson's sister, Liza, a lecturer at the spy school in Pretoria, and Casselton's beloved poodle, also Liza, who had died together in a car accident. When Casselton tried to sell the yacht after his release from prison, a check through the books and a visit to St Heliers revealed that the company had become a conduit for all sorts of illegal activities, and was under surveillance by various authorities. It was eventually seized by Interpol. Casselton never got a cent from his investment in the business, which represented a lifetime of savings from crop-spraying and various illicit operations.

Casselton returned to South Africa, penniless and destitute. 'That was the end of me. I was left to fend for myself, which was a battle. The biggest mistake of my life was to have ever joined the South African Police. It turned out to be a complete fiasco.'

Eugene de Kock took care of Casselton and gave him a place at Vlakplaas to stay and sleep. He stayed there for 18 months and became one of De Kock's very best friends.

De Kock said that after Dirk Coetzee's revelations, he was asked to accommodate Casselton at Vlakplaas. He said the man was living in poverty on a smallholding near Johannesburg. He fetched Casselton, registered him as an informant and paid him R3 500 per month.

Casselton commented: 'I did nothing. General Basie Smit came to Vlakplaas one day and said I have to work. I told him to fuck off and said, 'I'm not a labourer, I'm a pilot''. These Dutchmen did nothing to help me to renew my pilot's licence and I wouldn't work for them.'

Shortly after Dirk Coetzee had spoken out, Craig Williamson visited De Kock at Vlakplaas. The 'Superspy' was worried that Casselton drank too much and that he would talk. He asked De Kock to take Casselton to Swaziland and to 'make a plan with him'. De Kock said to Williamson to do it himself.

'As soon as Williamson left, De Kock called me and told me that Williamson wanted me killed. Why would I talk? I was given the "third degree" by Scotland Yard and never revealed names and rotted in prison for three years. I think Williamson wanted me killed because he owed me so much money and was looking for a way to get rid of me. I really hate him. If it wasn't for his kids and his wife, he might not have been as healthy as he is today.'[6]

Casselton enjoyed life at Vlakplaas. 'There was a full-time party there. Three times a week, all the generals were there, celebrating. There was plenty of booze, no problem.'

He said while he was staying at Vlakplaas, he became involved in a scheme to smuggle emeralds. He had several meetings with the smuggler, a Zimbabwean, who told him one day that he had been a Zipra guerrilla during the Rhodesian bush war. The smuggler proudly told Casselton that he had been involved in the shooting down of a civilian Viscount aircraft over Matabeleland in 1978 in which 13 people had been killed.

'I killed him. I took him and I shot him. I buried him afterwards on Vlakplaas,' Casselton said. While we were in Beira, he promised me that he would take me to Vlakplaas and show me the grave of the smuggler.

He was also involved in a rather bizarre plot to steal minibusses, pack the bumpers full of explosives and detonators, and re-sell them again to taxi-owners driving to and from Zimbabwe – obviously in the belief that the taxis were going to cause accidents and to explode. Again, nothing ever came of it.

As the closure of Vlakplaas became imminent, Casselton and his dog Bubas had to move on and they squatted with another drinking buddy. Peter Dunnwoodie said he found Casselton over Christmas 1995 sleeping on the floor in a dilapidated house in Pretoria. There was no running water and he was dirty. 'I was shocked and could not believe it. I took him in and he stayed with me for a while.'

Everybody I spoke to described Casselton as an 'unguided missile', undisciplined and obstreperous. He never invested any of his money and he had no pension. His racist remarks were horrifying and death meant nothing to him. But he had one exceptional attribute: loyalty towards his friends. And nowhere was it more evident than in his friendship with, and admiration for, Eugene de Kock.

The first time I met Casselton again after our brief squabble in 1989, was one Sunday morning in January 1996 at Pretoria Central Prison where we were both waiting to visit Eugene de Kock. In his right hand he clutched a brown paper bag with a roast chicken.

I went with Casselton down to the cells where De Kock was waiting for us behind the thick, bullet-proof glass. The two men, both outcasts, obviously adored one another.

'Howzit, Gene.'

'Howzit, Pete.'

'No, okay man, and you?'

'I'm fine. Glad to see you.'

'Gene, I brought you a roast chicken.'

'No, Pete man, you shouldn't. It costs a lot of money.'

'No, you know me, Gene, I always make a plan. And I know how you like your chicken.'

Every Sunday morning, Casselton would cook De Kock a hot chicken peri-peri in the kitchen of the Brass Bell restaurant in Pretoria. He said he once had to sell his watch to obtain money to buy a chicken.

When Casselton's dog Bubas went missing, De Kock pinned up a note on the prison's notice board offering a R500 reward for the return of the French poodle. Casselton was already in Beira when Eugene de Kock was sentenced to imprisonment of two life terms and a total of 212 years in jail. He didn't visit him on the Sunday before the final verdict was passed – only the third time in two and a half years that Casselton wasn't there. He said he couldn't have faced De Kock, because he knew his friend was going to be put away for ever and there was no way he could have comforted him.

'Prison life is hell. What do you tell somebody who was going to stay there for ever?'

When a spy suddenly dies, one is always left with suspicion that he may have been a victim of his own craft. Two months before Casselton died, he submitted an application for amnesty to the TRC. He would have confessed his complicity in the London bombing and was contemplating telling even more.

Eugene de Kock, a man who had been driven by a belief in conspiracies for most of his life, does not believe that his friend's death was an accident. He said Casselton knew too much and would have told the TRC about the millions of rands that were pilfered from the police secret fund.

But fate for Casselton appeared in the garb of liquor rather than assassination. He was working on a truck when it suddenly started moving and squashed him against a wall. Friends said that he had been drinking since early that morning, but that he wasn't drunk.

Pinned against the wall, his last words were: 'I'm dying. I'm going to die', before slipping into unconsciousness. His body was crushed and he died a few days later.

Dunnwoodie believe that had Casselton not died by accident, he would have taken his own life. 'He would not have died an old man.'

It was only after his death that friends discovered that he might not have been as penniless as everyone had thought. He owned property near Bulawayo in Zimbabwe, along the Mozambican coast and 15 hectares of land on Pemba island off the Tanzanian coast. He made a will before his death and left everything to the son of an old girlfriend.

When I think of Peter Casselton sitting on the balcony of his flat in Beira, gushing forth resentment and bitterness, it was clear that he had reached the end of the road. He had lost all his wars, his friends, his chance to have a family and above all, his dignity and self-respect as he sat in the heat in a smelly city fixing an old aircraft.

Writing about the human relics of apartheid, Phillip van Niekerk said: 'In a sense they were kindred spirits. The evil that accompanied white rule has passed with defeat into history, but the individuals who were corrupted by it are fated to live out their days like misfits, beached whales on the shore.'

Chapter Fifteen

The man who made mincemeat out of a judge's arm

There were two things that Pieter Botes liked to boast about. The one was how he 'stuffed up the enemy' in Mozambique; the other was the 'mincemeat' he made out of Albie Sachs's right arm.[1]

Today Albie Sachs is a Constitutional Court judge, but on April 7, 1988, he was an ANC activist and law professor at the Eduardo Mondlane University in Maputo, capital of Mozambique and on his way to the Costa Do Sol beach to jog.

It was a public holiday – Women's Day – and there were many people strolling the streets of the capital as a cheerful Sachs, dressed in bathing trunks, walked out of his Polana apartment towards his red Honda car. He had packed a frosty beer to drink after his run.

Earlier that morning, a bomber had attached a five-litre tin, filled with plastic explosives and connected to a tilt switch, beneath the Honda. The bomb, powerful enough to blow up a small house, was supposed to detonate as soon as somebody started the car and tried to drive away.

Weeks earlier, a team of black defence force operatives had infiltrated Mozambique to do surveillance on the ANC activist. Within days, they knew his daily routine, the layout of his house, his political and personal history, and his weak and strong points. A few days before the attack, the explosives were delivered to the operative in Mozambique, where the bomb was assembled.

As Sachs opened the door of the car, the Avenida Julio Vinti Quatro was engulfed in an inferno. For many seconds after the blast, the only sound audible was that of burning metal. Then people started screaming. All that remained of the car was a heap of crumpled metal with two beach chairs protruding from the back.

For Sachs, everything suddenly went dark. He said he felt arms coming from behind him, pulling at him under his shoulders. On that bright and sunny day in Maputo, Albie Sachs refused to die. His book, *The Soft Vengeance of a Freedom Fighter*, is the testimony of a survivor.

'Oh shit … I am feeling strange and cannot see anything … I must have banged my head. The darkness is not clearing, this is something serious, a terrible thing is happening … I cannot steady myself as I wait for consciousness to return and light to return … I am being kidnapped, they have come from Pretoria to drag me over the border and interrogate me and lock me up. This is the moment we have all been waiting for, the few ANC members still working in Mozambique.[2]

'I feel a sudden surge of elation and strength as I struggle, making an immense muscular effort to pull myself free. I might be an intellectual but at this critical moment without time to plan or think I am fighting bravely and with the courage of the youth of Soweto even though the only physical violence I have personally known in my life was as a schoolboy being tackled carrying a rugby ball ... But I am unable to struggle any more, I just have to go along and accept what happens, my life has gone.'

A Mozambican journalist with a video camera was near the scene of the blast, and moments after the explosion his camera started rolling. It remains one of the most harrowing and haunting moments in the documentation of South Africa's history – a war scene reminiscent of the film *Apocalypse Now* as Sachs, surrounded by a heap of crumpled metal and his right arm dangling from his shoulder, tried to push himself up from the scorched tarmac.

As doctors fought for Sachs's life in the Maputo Central Hospital, the bomber made a phone call to Pretoria to tell his handler, Pieter Botes, that the ANC academic had been blown up. He said to Botes that Sachs would not survive the blast and that there had been panic and chaos in the streets of Maputo as people had realised that South African forces had struck once again.

But Sachs did not die. Apart from his mutilated right arm, he had four broken ribs, a fractured right heel, a severed nerve in his left leg, a lacerated liver, scores of shrapnel wounds and ruptured eardrums.

He described his ordeal: 'I am wrapped in complete darkness and tranquility. If I am dead, I am not aware of it. If I am alive, I am not aware of it, I have no awareness at all, not of myself, not of my surroundings, not of anyone or anything.'

Sachs remembered a friend, surgeon Ivo Garrido, speaking to him: 'Albie ... you are in the Maputo Central Hospital. Your arm is lamentable ... we are going to operate and you must face the future with courage.'

The operation lasted seven hours as a team of Soviet doctors took out scores of pieces of shrapnel from all over his body and head. Regaining consciousness in the intensive care unit, he discovered that his right arm was missing: 'Watch ... my hand creeps over my shoulder and slides down my upper arm, and suddenly there is nothing ... so I have lost an arm ... that's all, they tried to kill me, to extinguish me completely, but I have only lost an arm. I came close to death and survived.'

The operative who planted the bomb was paid R4 000. When Sachs returned to South Africa after the unbanning of the ANC and was told who had maimed him, his reaction was wry: 'Only R4 000? I don't know if that's because he was black or because it was only an arm.'

'Ek het 'n sousie van Albie se armpie gemaak.' (I made mincemeat out of Albie's arm.)

Gleeful. Triumphant. Smug.

I was looking at the man sitting across from me in a Pretoria restaurant gorging himself on a rump steak and beer. He called himself Marius and he said that he was a senior member of a secret and mysterious death squad within the SADF that was called the CCB.

'Why did you blow Sachs up?'

'I have never met Albie and have nothing personal against him, but we knew he was working for Umkhonto. It was war and soldiers shouldn't cry.'

'He wasn't a soldier, he was an academic?'

'I was a soldier and Albie was a soldier, no matter what he said.'

'Are you proud of it?'

'It was a huge success. It was a professional job by a group of highly skilled and dedicated soldiers.'

'Why was it a success?'

'You know, in a war it is sometimes better to maim than to kill the enemy. We knew that everywhere Sachs went in Maputo, people would see the stump where his arm once was and say: "Look, the Boers blew it off", knowing that we can do the same to anybody we choose.'

'How many assassinations were you involved in?' I asked him.

'Six,' came the matter-of-fact reply.

He added: 'Ons het hulle geroer.' (We shook them up.)

It was towards the end of 1988 that a small group of South Africa's best-trained and most feared soldiers joined hands to work out a masterplan for a very special SADF unit. The group of soldiers studied the structures of the CIA, KGB and Mossad (the American, Russian and Israeli secret services). Their intention was to structure their organisation in such a way that it could function and survive completely independently of the SADF.[3]

It had to be able to generate its own funds, buy its own weapons and gather its own intelligence. It had to be so secretive that it could never be exposed. No member should know the identity of any other; even the top echelons should not know all the members who worked for them. There also had to be members who did not know for whom they were working.

The unit had to consist of the very best the South African armed forces could muster: brave and fearless men who had earned their decorations not by being mere 'pen-pushers', battle-hardened men who could destroy, disrupt or intimidate the enemy at any place or any time, using any method. It was an organisation that took upon itself the right to charge, try, condemn and even execute people regarded as enemies of the state. The enemy was not only the ANC and PAC in their military camps in southern Africa or armed cadres trying to infiltrate South Africa, it was also those people inside the Republic who supported 'leftist' organisations, fought against apartheid and struggled for a non-racial society.

There was only one rule for members to follow in conducting their operations: their tracks should never be traced back to the SADF. Therefore, a bizarre organisation with a civilian facade was formed.

It was established along the lines of a private company, in which the government was called the 'Controlling Trust', the overall commander the 'Chairman' and the commanding officer the 'Managing Director', with 'shareholders', 'clients' and 'suppliers'. The managing director had to submit a budget to a 'Board of Directors'.

The organisation was eventually called the Civil Co-operation Bureau (CCB), a sinister-sounding name for a deadly group of men, acting as if they had complete immunity from the law. Although it formed part of the SADF's Special Forces, there was no public indication that it was part and parcel of the military. At Special Forces it functioned under the codename 'Triplane'.

The CCB started life in the early 1980s under the name D40 (D stood for Delta and 40 for the number of people who first joined the organisation) and consisted of operatives and former members of the Rhodesian security forces who had come to South Africa after they had lost the war which led to black majority rule and the birth of the state of Zimbabwe in 1980. D40 transmuted, in turn, into Barnacle, 3 Reconnaissance Regiment and eventually into the CCB. The CCB was set up in April 1986 and in 1988 it became a 'civilian organisation'.

In his submission to the TRC in May 1997, the former Minister of Defence, General Magnus Malan, admitted that he had approved the formation of the CCB. 'The role envisaged for the CCB was the infiltration and penetration of the enemy, the gathering of information and the disruption of the enemy.'

Truth Commissioner: What did you have in mind by the disruption?

Malan: Well sir, you can disrupt the enemy in various ways. You can throw sugar in its petrol.

Truth Commissioner: Absolutely, but what did you have in mind.

Malan: That's disruption. The situation would dictate [what to do].

It was, of course, absurd for Malan to suggest that one could take a team of battle-hardened soldiers, band them together in a special and secret unit, order them to 'disrupt the enemy' and then expect them to throw sugar in petrol tanks, break windows or steal potplants.

The CCB was the creation of Malan and his securocrats, obsessed with retaining power and blinded by the delusion of a Communist plot to expel the white man from South Africa and to create a classless, Marxist society. It became a sinister monster.

In its final form the CCB's tentacles stretched from South Africa all over southern Africa to Europe. The CCB operated in nine active regions: South Africa, Swaziland and Mozambique, Namibia, Botswana, Zimbabwe, Lesotho, Angola, Zambia and Europe. Each 'region' had a 'manager' and a 'co-ordinator' who reported to the 'managing director'. There were also 'regions' that dealt with logistics and administration.

The CCB spent millions of rands of taxpayers' money on establishing a network of agents who spied on anti-apartheid activists, acquired Russian and foreign manufactured weaponry on the black market, bribed African business-men and government officials, hired professional assassins and criminals to execute the South African state's enemies, tried to buy an island off the Mozambican coast and sponsored operatives who had fled South Africa to avoid persecution or extradition for the atrocities they had committed.

In line with Malan's philosophy regarding the 'disruption of the enemy', the South African region of the CCB (region six) decided in 1988 that a monkey foetus should be hung up at Archbishop Desmond Tutu's official residence in Cape Town.

A CCB operative by the name of Abram 'Slang' (Snake) van Zyl told the Harms Commission in 1990: 'I just received an instruction from the managing director who told me that the foetus of an ape would be made available ... It was a very sensitive case and there was no discussion about the reason for placing the foetus.'

Van Zyl climbed over the wall of Tutu's residence and hung the foetus in a tree. The foetus was inside a bottle and it had to be hung in such a way that although not too conspicuous, it would eventually be found. The nails had previously been treated by a witchdoctor to ensure the success of the operation.

The CCB also decided that lawyer Dullah Omar – today the Minister of Justice – should be killed for defending 'terrorists' and for being a member of Lawyers for Human Rights. They hired a Cape Town gangster by the name of Peaches Gordon and ordered him to steal Omar's heart pills so that they could be substituted with poison pills. The gangster took two pills from his sister-in-law, who also had a heart condition, and handed them to his CCB handler, who in turn gave him poison. On his way to Cape Town, the gangster threw the poison out of the window. It later turned out that he admired Omar too much to kill him. When Gordon was instructed to monitor Tutu and ANC activist and theologian Dr Allan Boesak, he looked their addresses up in the telephone directory and wrote false reports.

By this time, Gordon had taken R15 000 from the CCB for nothing but confidence tricks and lies. But he probably overplayed his hand: in January 1991, his body was found on a highway near Cape Town.

But the CCB was not only a mixture of absurdity and gullibility. It left a bloody trail of death across the subcontinent: David Webster in South Africa, Anton Lubowski in Windhoek, sabotage and bomb explosions in Zimbabwe, and Albie Sachs and poisoning in Mozambique.

And yet, we know very little about the organisation. When I met Botes, the CCB had already been exposed and was under investigation by the Harms Com-mission. We had become used to nameless soldiers with false beards, sunglasses and wigs floating through the commission room bluntly denying responsibility for any actions, refusing to answer questions on grounds of self-incrimination and hiding vital project files. Because of the commission's terms of reference, which prevented it from investigating cross-border operations, only a small part of the CCB's work could be scrutinised.

The rest of the organisation, officially disbanded in 1990, is still shrouded in a veil of secrecy.

Pieter Botes was one of the men which gave the CCB its 'civilian character'. For two years he was one of the CCB's elite, entrusted with some of its inner secrets.

He was a captain in the elite Special Forces or 'recces' and held the rank of major in the Citizen Force. The recces can be described as South Africa's Special Air Service (SAS) and were used to fight apartheid's secret and unconventional wars on the subcontinent. They were highly-trained, hand-picked and fearless.

Botes left the SADF to become an apple farmer and was down and out when he was approached to join the ranks of a secret intelligence unit. At first, he did not know whom he was working for or exactly what the work entailed. At first, people spoke simply of 'the organisation' and it was only a month later that it was explained to him that was in fact the CCB and that his task would be the disruption and elimination of the 'enemy' in Mozambique. He took an oath under the Official Secrets Act not to disclose any information about the CCB. At the time, he was committed heart and soul to its objectives.

Yet it was a disillusioned Pieter Botes that I met one Friday afternoon in April 1990. On the surface, the chubby and ruddy-faced Botes seems like a gentle and mild-mannered person, an everyday family man who owned a personnel agency and lived on a smallholding outside Pretoria, where he also raised sheep.

He was extremely nervous and spoke softly, glancing around him. 'I think I'm being watched.' He kept quiet for long periods as he fidgeted and fiddled with his pen.

Botes remains the most senior member of the CCB to have spoken openly about the organisation. As co-ordinator and at times regional manager for the Mozambican region (region two), he was in military terms probably equal to a major.

Botes was driven to confession by hatred of the managing director of the CCB, Joe Verster, who was once one of the most powerful military leaders in South Africa. As the organisation's commander Verster had the power to charge, try and order the assassination of activists he regarded as a threat to national security.

Verster received a general's salary and his military status and power were far superior to the rank of colonel which he held when he officially resigned from the SADF. Verster started his path to military glory as a parachute instructor at 1 Parachute Battalion in Bloemfontein before undergoing specialised training as a reconnaissance soldier. He also attended a warfare school in the Republic of China (Taiwan) and received further training with the Rhodesian Selous Scouts. Before joining the CCB in 1985, he attended further military courses in Beirut and Israel. Verster had been a founder commander of 5 Reconnaissance Regiment and gained extensive battle experience in Namibia and Angola.

When FW de Klerk ordered that the CCB be investigated Joe Verster put an emergency plan into operation to make the project files disappear. When a Harms

Commission investigator jumped over the eight-foot wall of CCB headquarters on a smallholding outside Pretoria to seize the organisation's files, he found an empty safe. CCB members boldly refused to return the files and ignored instructions by the Chief of the Defence Force and Malan to produce the relevant documentation.

Verster was one of the CCB men who appeared before the Harms Commission with a false grey beard and a wig and Louis Harms ordered that no photographs of him might be published. Botes and I shared one common view: that Joe Verster did not deserve the protection that the commission had bestowed on him. Botes gave me a passport photograph of Verster which we immediately published in *Vrye Weekblad*.

Harms blamed Verster in his final report for the disappearance of the files, and said that the CCB had arrogated to itself the power 'to try, sentence and punish people without the persons knowing of the allegations against them or having the opportunity to defend themselves'.

Although the CCB murdered, planted bombs, conspired to kill, disobeyed military orders and wasted and stole millions of rands of taxpayers' money, no steps have ever been taken in South Africa against a single member of the organisation.

A quarrel between Botes and Verster had taken place in August 1989 when Verster accused him of the mismanagement of funds totalling R200 000. 'I had just returned from Namibia where we made plans to disrupt Swapo before the elections. When I walked into Verster's office to report back to him, he accused me of virtually stealing money. He threatened to kill me.'

Six days after the falling-out, a bomb exploded outside Botes's Verwoerdburg office. 'The bomb exploded late at night and was not intended to harm anybody. It was a warning from Verster. If he wanted to kill me, he could have done so.'

Six months later, Botes decided to talk. With him was a pile of papers and documents setting out the working and the structures of the CCB. Not only was Botes about to commit a criminal offence under the Official Secrets Act by revealing highly classified information, he was also setting out to betray his former comrades and fellow soldiers. 'They haven't paid me or my men. Ek gaan hulle roer ... en jou vertel hoe ons a sousie van Albie se armpie gemaak het.' (I am going to shake them up, and tell you how we made mincemeat out of Albie's arm.)

Verster owed Botes and 18 of his operatives an amount of R1,45 million. According to his accounts, the CCB owed agents 11 and 12 amounts of R300 000 each. One of the amounts of R300 000 had been set aside for three senior Mozambican government officials who had sold a fishing quota to a front company of the CCB. According to Botes, the CCB needed the quota in order to give the organisation's members easier access via the sea to Mozambique. For the same reason, the CCB also had plans to buy an island off the Mozambican coast.

Botes showed me the official guidelines of the CCB. According to directives, the CCB could make use of any technique to discredit, manipulate or disrupt targets. This could be done through hidden tape recorders or cameras, planting false evidence, threatening calls or letters to family members, bribery, prostitution, or the exploitation of 'skeletons in the cupboard'.

All new recruits to the CCB had to resign from either the SADF or their previous employer. The CCB personnel file would state only pseudonyms: real names would be revealed to no one. Even inside the organisation itself agents were instructed to address each other only by their pseudonyms. The directives instructed CCB members to wear false beards, wigs and sunglasses when they talked to 'indirect' members.

There was a very sophisticated code language that operatives had to use over the telephone or whenever they exchanged sensitive information. During the spresentation of projects telephones were unplugged, curtains drawn and a radio turned on to play in the background. A writing pad was used from the back to make identification by means of indentation more difficult. All operations had to be undertaken using foreign weapons and explosives, and weapons were loaded using gloves to prevent leaving fingerprints on ammunition.

I spent two days with Botes as he unravelled the deepest secrets of the CCB. Reading through his documents and listening to him made it difficult to believe that the organisation had been conceived and run by apparently intelligent and mature people.

Botes himself made a mockery of the belief that the CCB was professional and that assassinations were planned down to the finest detail. Their cataclysmic scheme to obliterate the ANC turned into a circus: there was little or no control over the actions of operatives, targets were badly selected and many operations were so extravagent or idiotic that they couldn't possibly succeed.

The men of the CCB probably thought of themselves as living out a John le Carré novel, while they were in fact nothing but the losers, liars, psychos and killers of *Pulp Fiction*. Pieter Botes could have walked straight off a Quentin Tarantino film set.

Like all South African security force death squads, the CCB also plotted the death of Joe Slovo. According to Botes, they had information that every year on August 17 – the anniversary of the death in Maputo of his wife Ruth First – Slovo visited her grave.

'It was a brilliant plan,' Botes told me. A few days before the anniversary, a CCB operative planted a bomb underneath the tombstone, consisting of plastic explosives and a detonator in a tin can. On the day of the anniversary, the agent who was to detonate the bomb waited for Slovo at the grave, 100 metres away, kneeling with a bunch of flowers in his hand. The electronic mechanism to detonate the bomb was hidden in the flowers.

The operative was arrested by Mozambican intelligence, still kneeling next to a grave awaiting the arrival of the Slovo.

Poisoned razor blades were among the bizarre assassination methods conceived by the CCB. Botes said he was contacted by a CCB spy handler who wanted him to help with the murder of Durban lawyer Kwenza Mlaba. According to a CCB document, Mlaba was a senior member of the ANC who provided funds to military members for operations.

A CCB assassination plan was launched, in which an agent would pretend to be a client and consult Mlaba in his office. The agent would then leave a shopping bag with a new razor and blades behind when he left. The CCB hoped that Mlaba would use the razor and blades to shave and thereby the poison would penetrate his skin, with fatal results.

The plan was eventually dropped. When told of the assassination plot, the bearded Mlaba said: 'This goes to show how poorly informed these guys are. I don't shave, and I have never used a razor, let alone one given to me by a stranger.'

In March 1990, Namibia became independent after just over seven decades of South African rule. Since the early 1960s, a bitter bush war had been fought between South Africa and the South West African People's Organisation (Swapo), which was recognised by the United Nations as the official representative of the people of Namibia. For many white South Africans, it was a bitter pill to swallow when the South African government announced that it had reached an agreement with the international community on the independence of Namibia. White South Africans feared that after the UN-supervised elections the former enemy would become the new government and members of its armed wing the new military rulers of the territory.

Botes was called to Verster's office in May 1989 to be briefed on a master plan to disrupt Swapo's functioning before the November elections. Three different CCB regions would be deployed in Namibia: Botes's region two, the internal region under the command of regional manager Staal (Steel) Burger and the Namibian region under the command of Roelf van der Westhuizen. The Namibian operation was codenamed *Doopdag* (baptism day).

The three regional commanders were briefed separately. The one was not to know what the others had to do. Botes received instructions to assassinate senior Swapo officials Hidipo Hamutenya and Danny Tsjongerero. The murders had to look as if they were committed by radical Swapo members unhappy with the 'soft-line approach' of Hamutenya and Tsjongerero, in order to cause dissension within Swapo.

Botes was instructed to plant bombs at Swapo meetings and to throw hand grenades among the crowds. The CCB devised a plan to put cholera bacteria and the yellow fever virus – provided by an army doctor – into the drinking water of Swapo refugee camps in northern Namibia. A printing press ordered by Swapo and awaiting delivery at Walvis Bay and 54 Swapo motor vehicles were identified for sabotage. Botes said the CCB was to use a special oil that would cause the engines to seize.

Not even Untag – the United Nations (UN) peacekeeping force overseeing the independence process – was to be spared, although Botes was instructed not to harm officials. The cars of the UN's Special Representative and chief administrator were to be fire-bombed, however.

A few days after receiving the plan, Botes deployed his team of agents in Namibia. An operative who could speak Kwanyama, one of the local languages, infiltrated the Swapo camps. Tsjongerero was removed from the CCB's death list after he became ill, but the plans for Hamutenya's assassination were to go ahead. Botes decided to have him shot with a Russian-made pistol outside the Namibian Nights night club in Windhoek, which was frequented by Hamutenya and other Swapo members.

A consignment of weapons arrived in Namibia, consisting of ten hand grenades, 31 blocks of TNT explosives and an RPG rocket launcher with nine rockets and four limpet mines. Botes stored the weapons in a cache outside Windhoek. In the meantime, three Swapo members were recruited to assassinate Hamutenya. The assassins did not know who they were working for or why they had to murder the Swapo leader, but they were promised huge sums of money.

Three days after Botes had received the weapons, he returned to Pretoria to report back to his superiors about the feasibility and progress of the project. He had to submit a final draft to Verster three days later. 'As soon as I walked in, he accused me of mismanagement and the argument started. I stormed out of his office and my participation in the Namibian project ended. I withdrew, and in the end, nothing materialised,' Botes told me.

Four days later, Botes received news that an agent had infected the drinking water at the refugee camp at Dobra with cholera. The bacteria did not survive, Botes explained, because the chlorine content of the water was too high. So yet another CCB project had failed.

At the judicial inquest into the death of David Webster in the Johannesburg Supreme Court in 1992, CCB co-ordinator Wouter Basson confirmed the evidence of Botes and testified that Joe Verster had authorised plans to 'distribute disease in the camps', disrupt meetings and burn buildings.

The whole Namibian project once again illustrates the debauchery of the CCB and its leaders. Did they honestly think that by poisoning refugees, assassinating Swapo leaders or causing car engines to seize, they could stop Swapo from winning a democratic election? The CCB obviously did, and so went ahead with the project. The result was indeed calamitous – but did nothing to enhance the CCB's own political or military objectives.

When Pieter Botes stormed out of Verster's office the entire disruption campaign in Namibia threatened to collapse. According to the CCB plan, a Swapo leader had to die in order to create discord in the run-up to the elections. It was no longer possible to kill Hidipo Hamutenya as Botes had withdrawn his men. Another leader had to be killed, and the CCB's attention turned towards Swapo's 'white boy', for long regarded in South Africa as a traitor and a renegade Afrikaner.

At the bedside of Molly Lubowski lies her son Anton's Bible. On top of it is a handmade, heart-shaped card. 'This was the last Mother's Day card I got from Anton,' she says, pointing to the inscription: 'I love you.' Inside are two locks of hair in almost identical shades of brown. 'This one I managed to cut off before Anton's father got rid of his baby curls. And this one I took from Anton's head as he lay in his coffin.'[4]

Anton, his parents say, expected to be killed one day. 'When he came to visit us in Cape Town and we went out for dinner he would always sit with his back to the wall. If they shot him he wanted to see them; he didn't want to be shot in the back like a dog,' says Wilfried Lubowski.

Anton Lubowski died in exactly the manner he feared. He never saw his assassins in the dark of night, pumping 11 high-velocity AK-47 bullets into him in front of his Windhoek home.

At twenty past eight on the night of September 12, 1989, Swapo's so-called 'white son' parked his car in front of his home in Sanderburg Road to pick up his lover, human rights lawyer Michaela Clayton. The street lights were switched off, giving perfect cover to the assassins. Lubowski pushed the buzzer at the security gate to summon Clayton. She heard a sharp crackle and thought somebody had thrown fire-crackers into the garden. Instead, Lubowski lay dead outside the gate. His murderers were seen speeding away in a red car.[5]

The previous night, Lubowski had been seen on South African television as he greeted Swapo exiles at Windhoek Airport. He was six inches taller than anybody else around him as he embraced Swapo leader Andimba Toivo ja Toivo, welcoming him back on Namibian soil. Two days later, Lubowski appeared on the front page of *The Star* in a photo of policemen putting his corpse into a body bag.

Anton Lubowski, known as Lubof by his friends, posed no threat to the South African government and played no role in Swapo's military structures. In a tribute to him, Max du Preez, an old-time friend, wrote: 'My friend Lubof … of all the people I knew, he was the one who adored and loved life the most. Anton was no revolutionary. Unless there is such a thing as a humanitarian revolutionary who can party until the early hours of the morning, who is partial to tailor-made trousers, silk shirts and fast cars, who cries openly when he speaks about his children who no longer live with him and who has a sense of humour.[6]

'Five years ago Anton and I were drinking beer in the garden of the old Kaiser Krone Hotel when a couple of rough boys at the table shouted out at him: "White kaffir!"

'I remember as if it was yesterday the way his face lit up. "It's true," he said to me, "I am a white kaffir."'

'He was too.'

Lubowski was once a model Afrikaner. His mother was of good Afrikaner stock and his father was a respected German Namibian. He went to school at the elite Paul Roos Gymnasium, attended the University of Stellenbosch and became an SADF officer when he was conscripted into the army.

But in March 1984, Lubowski declared his allegiance to Swapo. A month later, State President PW Botha said in a letter to him that he had become a disgrace to the SADF and withdrew his officer's commission. After that, he was detained six times by the South African authorities and on the last occasion was locked up in solitary confinement in a corrugated iron hut with only his underpants and a Bible.[7]

His membership of Swapo, which condemned him in the eyes of many Afrikaners, started a five-year campaign of terror and harassment which ended brutally in his death. He received countless death threats and survived an attempt on his life when his car was sprayed with bullets one evening while returning to Windhoek from Katatura township. Poison letters arrived daily and his advocate's practice was boycotted.

The morning after Lubowski's assassination, a woman called the police and informed them that a man staying in one of her flats had acted suspiciously the previous day. In the politically charged atmosphere of Namibia the police were under immense pressure to get their man, and later that day, an Irish criminal and hitman by the name of Donald 'The Cleaner' Acheson was arrested.

It soon appeared that Acheson worked for a secret organisation in South Africa which had, amongst others, offered him $200 000 to kill a prominent liberal newspaper editor by putting poison into her personal sanitary towels or her toothpaste. He was also told to obtain a car, hire a flat and keep an AK-47 handy in case he should need it.[8]

Acheson soon led his investigators to his CCB handlers – Ferdi Barnard, Calla Botha and Chappies Maree – in Johannesburg. Barnard and Botha were detained and they then revealed the existence of the CCB.

Despite the fact that the conspiracy to kill Lubowski occurred in South Africa and that he was gunned down before Namibian independence, Mr Justice Louis Harms refused to hear evidence on his murder as the commission was precluded from investigating 'external' CCB operations.

Yet, the killer's tracks clearly pointed to the CCB. Slang van Zyl admitted in his evidence to the Harms Commission that he was told to monitor the human rights lawyer less than three weeks before his death. 'I was monitoring Mr Lubowski and the people he contacted, but I was not advised why he was being monitored.' He revealed that at a CCB meeting at the Rosebank Hotel in Johannesburg on September 1, the Lubowski project was discussed. He said Staal Burger and Chappies Maree were present, but told him and Calla Botha to leave as they were not directly involved in the project.

It was further established that Staal Burger had flown to Windhoek on September 12 in a seat booked in the name of Gagiano. Burger left Windhoek again on September 13, the day after the murder. Chappies Maree was also in Windhoek, while Donald Acheson had flown into the Namibian capital on September 10.

Louis Harms stopped the advocates for the Lubowski family dead in their tracks every time they tried to obtain more information about the killing. The judge said he had fully considered the question of hearing evidence: 'If I can assist, I shall assist. If the commission stumbles upon evidence, it shall provide that evidence to the relevant authorities. I'm afraid I cannot change my decision.'

Even after his death, Anton Lubowski remained a victim: he was finally made a victim of the Minister of Defence, General Magnus Malan. After the revelations about the CCB's complicity in the murder of Lubowski, Malan was embroiled in a battle for his political life: both the left and the right of the political spectrum demanded his immediate resignation.

February 26, 1990. Magnus Malan made an astounding disclosure in Parliament: 'I want to disclose today that Lubowski was a paid agent of Military Intelligence. I am assured that he did good work for the SADF. The Chief of Staff Intelligence, General Rudolph Badenhorst, would, therefore, never have approved actions against Lubowski.'[9]

Malan's claim was met with shock and outrage. 'You have besmirched a hero. Not a single black person in South Africa or Namibia believes you,' Democratic Party co-leader Denis Worrall told Malan. Swapo's Theo-Ben Gurirab, who became Namibia's Minister of Foreign Affairs after independence, said: 'Malan's allegations were a cheap shot by a drowning man clutching at the smallest straw. You know as well as I do that Anton was harassed over the years by these people. Why would he work for them?'[10]

As pressure mounted on Malan to furnish evidence to prove his allegation that Lubowski was a paid agent, FW de Klerk came to his rescue, broadening the terms of reference of the Harms Commission by instructing the judge to investigate whether or not the Namibian advocate had worked for Military Intelligence. He did not, however, authorise Harms to find the murderers.

I am still at a loss to understand why FW de Klerk instructed Louis Harms to investigate the allegations of spying against Anton Lubowski instead of finding and acting against suspected murderers within his own ranks. What did De Klerk hope to gain? Did he hope to divert attention from the bloody campaign by the SADF to disrupt elections in Namibia? Whatever his reason, his weren't the actions of a man who wanted to know the truth.

Louis Harms played along. Rudolph Badenhorst persuaded Harms that the hearing about whether or not Harms was a spy could jeopardise the lives of certain people and the security of the state. The judge ordered an *in camera* hearing. The legal team for the Lubowski family protested, but the judge ruled that they could not be present. The SADF issued a decree under Section 118 of the Defence Act that prevented the Lubowski family from investigating his bank account.

With only the judge and one official of the commission present, the SADF presented evidence supporting Malan's claim. Harms heard that three payments totalling R100 000 had been paid through an intermediary by the name of Global Capital Investments into Lubowski's account. Global, in turn, received three payments from Military Intelligence.

All that the evidence proved was that a civilian company – not known to be a Military Intelligence front – paid money into Anton Lubowski's account. He could have been paid for normal consultancy or legal work he had performed for a client in South Africa. We still don't know what proof was presented to Harms about the work which Lubowski had allegedly done for the SADF or the motivation for his alleged recruitment.

More so: how do we know that the evidence presented to Harms was authentic? Harms convicted and sentenced Lubowski on one-sided and untested evidence. Surely the commission should have accepted nothing it heard from Military Intelligence on face value? Agents were taught to lie, deceive, fabricate and forge – an art they skillfully illustrated at the Harms Commission.

In his final report to the State President, Harms explained that the allegation that Lubowski had been paid by Military Intelligence was undeniable. 'Cross-examination would have made no difference,' he said.

Molly and Wilfried Lubowski reacted with anger and bitterness: 'We reject with repugnance the Commission's finding that that Anton received R100 000 as an agent of Military Intelligence. The Commission's decision to hear evidence in camera resulted in a secret, one-sided character assassination of Anton. On the other hand, the security establishment, who we have no doubt is responsible for his murder, was protected.'

The allegations against the CCB did not go away. A maroon leather-bound diary embossed with gold was handed in at the David Webster inquest in the Johannesburg Supreme Court in 1992. The owner of the 1989 diary was CCB co-ordinator Wouter Basson, who was questioned about torn-out pages from the diary – one of them being for September 12, the day on which Lubowski was murdered.[11]

Police forensic experts, deciphering indentations on the next page of the diary, have been able to ascertain the contents of the missing entry. The vanished page included the cryptic phrases: 'disguise/don't phone', 'change clothes', 'don't use pager', 'no personal contact after job' and 'Zambia – stay for two days'.

Basson conceded that the notes appeared to be instructions for an assassin after completion of an assignment, but denied that the CCB had killed Lubowski. He said it was coincidental that the words appeared on that day and that the page had been torn out. Entries in the diary also referred to 'Client 1' being made to 'fall before the end of August' and 'Client 2' by the middle of September.

In a judicial inquest into the death of Lubowski, Mr Justice Harold Levy found in the Windhoek Supreme Court in June 1994 that the fatal shots that ended Lubowski's life had been fired by Irish mercenary Donald Acheson, but that the killing had been orchestrated and sponsored by the CCB. Levy said prima facie accomplices to the killing were amongst others Joe Verster, Staal Burger, Ferdi Barnard, Slang van Zyl, Calla Botha, Wouter Basson and Chappie Maree.[12]

When asked about the Namibian judgement at his appearance before the TRC in 1997, Magnus Malan said: 'I did not even see the judgement, or hear about it.'

During a conversation with Ferdi Barnard at the beginning of 1993, he told me that he had originally been assigned to shoot Anton Lubowski. Barnard said he was armed with an AK-47 and twice tried to assassinate Lubowski while Lubowski was on a visit to South Africa. He said, however, that he couldn't get a clear view of him and had had to abandon the project. His colleagues then flew to Windhoek to 'finish him off'.

Rich Verster is a former senior operative of the Directorate of Covert Collection, a secret dirty tricks unit within Military Intelligence. In May 1997, I interviewed Verster in Her Majesty's Prison in Dorchester, England, where he was awaiting trial on attempted drug smuggling (see Chapter 19).

Verster was despatched to Namibia in 1989 to disrupt the elections and to recruit Swapo agents. One of the Swapo leaders he was asked to recruit was Anton Lubowski. He said he hired a house in Windhoek and recruited officials from the post office to bug the telephones of three Swapo leaders, including Lubowski, as well as the United Nations peacekeeping force.

He said he sat for hours listening to Anton's conversations, but failed to detect a 'weakness' which could have 'opened' him for possible recruitment. All the tapes, he said, were sent to a secret underground facility of Army Intelligence in Pretoria, known as 'Blenny', from which the dirty tricks campaign in Namibia was co-ordinated.

Verster succeeded in recruiting two people, one a well-known journalist in Windhoek, who were close to Lubowski. He said he was at the Safari Motel just outside of Windhoek when one of the agents phoned him. 'He was hysterical and asked me: "You bastards, why the fuck did you kill Anton?"'

'Which Anton?'

'Anton Lubowski, and you killed him!'

'I said there were never plans to kill him, because he was a target for me to recruit.'

Verster said he immediately phoned his superior, a former Rhodesian by the name of Geoff Price, in Pretoria. 'He already knew about it and said there was a mixup. I must get in my car and drive back to South Africa as quickly as possible. I drove back the same night.'

He said Lubowski was framed by Military Intelligence at the Harms Commission. 'I worked with Lubowski's file, and I would have known if he was a Military Intelligence agent. We were desperate to recruit him, but failed. His signature was faked and documents forged. We had to get the heat off the CCB, who made a terrible mistake by killing the wrong man.'

Verster has in the meantime been interviewed by a team of investigators from the TRC and Transvaal Deputy Attorney General Anton Ackermann.

Pieter Botes could have provided the Harms Commission with invaluable information about the assassination of Anton Lubowski, the CCB disruption campaign in Namibia and operations in Mozambique, but he wasn't allowed to testify about 'external' operations.

In fighting the 'enemy', Botes and his men had blown up telephone installations, sabotaged railway lines, bribed officials, and cut off water and electricity supplies. In the end, Botes claimed, he had planned and carried out six successful assassinations in Mozambique.

The day before *Vrye Weekblad* was due to publish Botes's revelations, Botes phoned and said he wanted to see me and Max du Preez as he was uncertain whether we should go ahead with publication. In order to persuade Botes of the importance of his story, we initiated a night of heavy drinking. After many double brandies and coke, he lifted his glass and announced: 'Ek gaan hulle roer.' (I will shake them up.)

Over his half-empty glass Botes confessed that he was a born soldier and needed the excitement of hunting the enemy down. He said he still believed in the concept of the CCB and that the thrill of secret warfare was still in his blood.

'I miss the war and I need the action. I have asked friends what I can do to put some excitement back into my life. Somebody suggested that I should go for flying lessons. He said the sensation of freedom would still my urge for action. But what do I do when I get back on the ground and I still haven't stuffed anybody up?'

Late that night Botes took us to his house because he had a bottle of pear *mampoer* (a very strong traditional liqueur), which he wanted us to taste. By that time, Max and I were extremely drunk. Botes, on the other hand, showed few signs of intoxication. We sat around his dinner table gulping down the burning liquid. After two or three tots, we told him that we could not possibly swallow another one.

'I will show you what I do to people who refuse to drink my *mampoer*', he said. He left the room and came back with a grain bag, from which he drew a Russian-manufactured RPG rocket launcher. He put the launcher against the wall and said: 'Now you will drink my pear *mampoer*.'

Max maintains that there was a rocket in the launcher, while I simply can't remember. Whatever was true, we finished the bottle. On the way back to Johannesburg, Du Preez was overcome by temporary blindness and had to stop in the middle of the road.

A few days later, Botes' sheep were poisoned.

It was dangerous times for CCB operatives to speak out. At about the same time I was speaking to Pieter Botes, I flew to London to meet a man by the name of Tony Adams in a London pub. He said he was a member of the CCB and Special Forces and that he had been involved in various operations outside South Africa and had information about two murders committed by the SADF inside the country.

Adams was in a desperate financial predicament: his housing business in Bophuthatswana was on the verge of bankrupcy, he feared for his life and he needed money to make a new beginning elsewhere. He said his jacket with all his money had been stolen from him. He asked me whether I could arrange a meeting with the ANC as he had valuable information about the training of Inkatha soldiers by the SADF. He said his information would implicate Mangosothu Buthelezi in atrocities committed in Natal and was so important that it might affect the negotiations between the ANC and the National Party. He wanted R250 000 for his information.

After more meetings, he admitted that his name was actually Willie van Deventer. He said he had not been involved in the murder of the Ribeiro couple, but had been present when SADF agents had planned the assassination. He also claimed he had been present when a car bomb had been built to blow up Piet Ntuli, a cabinet minister and ANC activist in the homeland of KwaNdebele, in July 1986.[13]

Van Deventer said he had left a tape recording of all these details with his lawyer in Pretoria and that he was in possession of documents that would prove his allegations. He had two meetings with a senior representative of the ANC in London and also tried to sell his story to various British newspapers and television networks. When he failed, he had to return to South Africa and after *Vrye Weekblad* had published his allegations, he was subpoenaed to testify before the Harms Commission.

Van Deventer retreated behind a curtain of secrecy and refused nine times to answer questions on the grounds that he could incriminate himself. He also claimed to have lost his memory between the time he had made the claims in London and when he was called to give testimony before the Harms Commission.

Van Deventer came close to death afterwards when he mysteriously fell from a building. His Pretoria lawyer disappeared.

Brigadier Jack Cronje and his Northern Transvaal Security Branch death squad said in their amnesty applications that they had conspired to murder Fabian and Florence Ribeiro, but that Special Forces had requested their files and had murdered them instead. They also asked for amnesty for the killing of Piet Ntuli, whom they admitted to having blown up. They said, however, that Special Forces had built the bomb.

The Inkatha soldiers that Van Deventer spoke about must have been the 200 Zulus trained by Military Intelligence and Special Forces in the Caprivi in

Namibia in 1986. At the time that Van Deventer had spoken to me, the Caprivi trainees, backed and armed by Military Intelligence, were waging a campaign of terror in Natal and the Transvaal as the dispute between Inkatha and the ANC threatened to plunge the country into full-scale civil war.

The legacy left behind by people like Pieter Botes embraces not only the maimed and the dead on the 'enemy' side. Within the CCB's own ranks were also victims – people mangled and marred by a dirty war and by ruthless people. None more so than a middle-aged Bloemfontein bricklayer and shebeen keeper who woke one day to find himself an apartheid assassin.

Chapter Sixteen

The shebeen keeper who had a dream

This is the story of a man who had a dream.[1]

Of a middle-aged black bricklayer and shebeen keeper who wanted to start a performing arts school for township kids.

But in this tale of betrayal, manipulation and deceit, an ordinary man woke one day to find himself a bomber and a poisoner – in the name of apartheid.

Leslie Lesia was once a colourful, chirpy little man. Known and loved by all. But when I met him towards the end of 1990, he was a broken and bitter man.

He could hardly walk, his face was deeply lined, his brown eyes were lifeless and speckled.

He eventually died alone, deserted, abandoned. Even hated.

Botshabelo township outside Bloemfontein is nothing more than an endless collection of four-roomed matchbox houses and shacks divided by unmarked dirt roads.

Leslie Lesia lived at number 4205, a brightly painted four-roomed house. The first time I visited him, he proudly paraded me around the home and showed me the wondrous ceiling of the dining room – a mixture of wood and draped red satin decorated with golden buttons and chains – which he had put together himself.

His house had once been a beehive of activity as township dwellers had flocked to the shebeen (township tavern) he kept in his backyard. Lesia was a legend in Botshabelo. His wife Miriam remembers the times he would wear a white baseball cap and white trousers and play the trumpet in the shebeen. People would sing and dance and laugh. Lesia was also the township's boxing champion. Also, I later discovered, probably something of a gangster who had spent several years in jail for theft and fraud.

It was in his shebeen that Leslie first spoke of his dream of starting a performing arts school. In December 1985 he established 'Leslie's Performing Arts and Cultural Institute' and distributed leaflets throughout Botshabelo.

'YOUR ROAD TO FAME STARTS HERE!

'IT'S MUSIC ... SONG ... DANCE ... POP ... JAZZ ... INSTRUMENTS ... BALLET ... TAP DANCE ... DISCO ... TRAMPOLINE ... GYMNASTICS ... ART AND PAINTING ... MODELLING ... STAY FIT AND WEIGHT TRAINING GYM ... DRAMA AND CLASSIC ... WE TEACH READING AND WRITING OF MUSIC.

'YOU COULD BE A STAR!'

Within months he had received hundreds of applications from parents who wanted their children to enrol at the school. He held auditions in the Batho Community Hall and soon had more than 500 children on the school's books. Lesia then realised that unless he received financial aid for his project, the school would not survive. Botshabelo is a poor township of mostly domestics and workers who cannot afford the luxury of art classes for their children.

Lesia wrote a letter to the United States Information Service in Johannesburg: 'It is of vital importance that I first introduce the existence of this institute which is the first of its kind in this province, the Orange Free State, for black youngsters. Our main object is to promote and foster goodwill and understanding among them and young whites by forging cultural links, to build and create the right frame of mind on the basis of common interest.' He signed the letter 'Tiger Lesia', which had been his nickname for many years.

He soon received a letter from the American Consul General asking him to fill out an application form for a development grant. Two American diplomats visited his institute to make sure it was a non-profit scheme and non-political. They assured him that they would provide the finance for the school on condition that he set up a steering committee and found an attorney to handle all financial aspects.

Then, suddenly, Lesia received a phone call that would change his life for ever. It was his sister-in-law, bringing news that his late brother's son, Tebogo Lesia, had been killed in a car accident in Tanzania. Tebogo had gone into exile many years before to become a member of Umkhonto we Sizwe and to receive military training. The family had never heard of Tebogo again. Lesia's sister-in-law, who had been under constant surveillance since Tebogo had left the country, asked him to accompany her to Tanzania for the funeral.

Leslie, who had never been politically active, thought it wise to be on the safe side of the law and went to see a security policeman to ask for permission to attend the funeral. The policeman said there would be no problem.

Lesia and his sister-in-law flew to Swaziland in September 1986 and were met by an ANC official called Joseph. He took them to Maputo where they stayed for a week waiting for their northbound flight to Dar es Salaam. During their stay, they were introduced to the leadership of the ANC in both Mozambique and Tanzania. In Dar es Salaam the ANC, who regarded the Lesia family as friends and allies, gave them a couple of letters to deliver to ANC officials in Maputo. One of the letters was addressed to the chief representative of the ANC in Mozambique, Jacob Zuma, today head of the ANC in KwaZulu/Natal.

Two days after their return to South Africa, the Bloemfontein Security Branch questioned Lesia about Tebogo's death. They wanted to know whether he had a death certificate, which he produced for the police to make a copy of. Lesia said he co-operated and told them what they wanted to know. He didn't want any trouble.

A week later, Lesia received a call from a 'Mr Becker' at the American Embassy who asked him to immediately fly to Johannesburg to discuss his arts school. Everything was arranged and paid for. Ernie Becker met Lesia at the airport and took him to a nearby hotel where he was introduced to a 'Mr Brown'. Although Becker spoke with an Afrikaans accent, Lesia was not suspicious as he knew embassies often employed local people.

A few days after this meeting, money was deposited into the school's trust account and a company started delivering milk for the kids. The next night, Lesia held a meeting with township parents, informing them that the school was now funded by the generous contributions of the people of the United States of America. More money was on its way. Lesia immediately ordered musical instruments and gym equipment to be bought.

Lesia never suspected that he was slowly being drawn into a deadly web he could never escape from. 'Mr Becker' was no American diplomat, but Ernie Becker, a former SADF reconnaissance soldier who had become a co-ordinator of region two of the CCB. Throughout the 1980s, the South African security forces had used this unit to wage a ruthless campaign to drive the ANC out of Mozambique.

The United States Information Service has a record of their very first correspondence with Lesia, but after requesting him to fill out an application form for a grant, they never heard from him again. It is now clear that after his visit to Mozambique and Tanzania, his mail had been intercepted and his telephone tapped by the security forces.

After Lesia's visit to the ANC in Mozambique and Tanzania, he must have been a prime target for recruitment. The ANC trusted him and he had access to senior officials. Furthermore, he was extremely naive – with only one obsession in life – his arts school.

The next time Lesia saw Brown and Becker, they introduced two other men whom they said were South African businessmen willing to assist his school project. The two men, who said they were keen to invest in Mozambique and Tanzania, asked Lesia questions about the presence of the ANC in those countries.

'That puzzled me. I couldn't understand how the Americans knew about my trip to the ANC. It was known only to my family, some friends and the security police. Eventually I gave them a brief account of what happened there. They threatened me that unless I co-operated there would be no money for the school. I have greatly suffered to get funds and had promised the children. I could not let the project die.'

Mr Becker produced an album with photographs of ANC members and asked Lesia whether he recognised anyone. Lesia also had to describe Joseph, who had met him and his sister at the airport in Swaziland and had taken them to Maputo. He gave the men information about where Joseph stayed, his friends and his movements.

Mr Brown then revealed himself to Lesia: 'We are not diplomats; we work for

the military. We will continue to give you money, but you must give us something in return. We want you to keep in touch with the ANC in Mozambique and
Swaziland. There are no risks and we will look after you.' Becker gave Lesia a
pager number through which he could reach the agents.

'I was a confused person at that time,' Lesia confessed. 'I didn't know what
to do as I have never done anything pertaining to that. I fed them with what
I thought was innocuous information.'

A while later he was instructed to make contact with Joseph, his ANC contact in
Swaziland. They told him that in order not to raise any suspicions he should make
it a family trip to Swaziland and take Miriam and his mother-in-law with him. When
Lesia got to Joseph's flat in Swaziland, he was not there. The next day he went back
but Joseph was still not there. He knocked at the flat next door to enquire about
Joseph's whereabouts, but the person who answered the door just stood there
wide-eyed without saying a word. He slammed the door in Lesia's face.

Perturbed and apprehensive, Lesia rushed back to Johannesburg, called Becker and arranged a meeting. He told his handler that he couldn't understand why
the people had not wanted to give him any information about Joseph. Brown
laughed and told Lesia: 'Don't worry, we have taken care of him.'

Joseph Medulla had been assassinated on the strength of the information supplied by Lesia. The ANC man was shot dead in front of his flat. 'It frightened me
really and I started realising that every bit of information I give to these people they
act upon. In fact they had sent me on the mission to Swaziland to let me know
I was in their power. They later told me I had been under surveillance all the time.'

Lesia had reached the point of no return. He was already implicated in the murder of an ANC member in Swaziland. Becker told him that should he refuse to
co-operate, they would destroy his school by withdrawing his registration of the
school and exposing him to the Botshabelo community as a military agent.

Lesia had to take an oath under the Official Secrets Act. He was paid a
monthly allowance of R1 600. Becker told him that he would work one week out
of every month for the military. The rest of the time he could spent building up
his school.

Miriam Lesia never knew for whom Leslie worked. In fact, she thought he had
joined the ANC and was involved in underground activities for the organisation.
Should Mr Becker find out about his ANC activities, she warned him, the
Americans might withdraw his funding.

And the school was doing so well. The 1986 year-end concert was a huge
success. Leslie's youth orchestra welcomed the township residents as they
packed the community hall. The children sang and danced, did ballet and
presented gymnastics, presented a short play. Lesia was dressed in a white suit.
He received a standing ovation at the end of the concert.

In January 1987 Lesia undertook his first trip as an SADF agent to Maputo to gather information on the ANC. 'I did not try very hard, and just sat around trying not to attract attention. But I did visit Jacob Zuma and offered my services to the ANC. I was confused and didn't know what to do. The ANC people were friendly to me and I thought of them as my friends.'

Becker was clearly delighted with Lesia's progress. He informed him that he was to undergo a training course in the use of explosives and poison. 'What for?' Lesia protested, 'That was never part of the deal.'

In a hotel room he was shown how to handle and set up an explosives device to booby-trap a door. The device was to be placed on the outside of a door and a wire with a hook attached to the key hole. The device detonated as soon as the door was opened. Becker also brought a selection of poisons with him. One, a yellowish liquid in a small glass bottle with an aluminium and rubber top, would kill within a week or two and would be very difficult to trace in a post-mortem examination.

Becker gave Lesia a poison ring with a hollow top in which the poison could be kept and then surreptitiously slipped into a victim's drink. Lesia was instructed to poison any senior ANC official he came across.

Lesia was given four detonators, four bottles of poison and a nine-millimetre pistol with a silencer. 'I didn't know how to handle a firearm and didn't know what to do with this thing.'

His handler had a secret compartment built into the dashboard of Lesia's car and the engine was modified to provide more power. The poison, explosives and the pistol were hidden inside the secret compartment.

In March 1987, Lesia accompanied Becker to a building in Pretoria where they obtained a case of brandy, a case of vodka and three cases of beer which had been spiked with poison. Later in his hotel room Becker showed Lesia how the beers had been doctored. He said that the tab of the beer could be lifted just enough to insert a syringe needle to inject the poison into the beer.

'There was nothing else I could do. Becker was a dangerous and ruthless person. I felt there was no place I could hide from them. And then there was the children – I couldn't disappoint them.'

Lesia fitted some of the poisoned liquor into his car's secret compartment and left for Maputo. When he arrived in the Mozambican capital he gave some of the liquor to a senior ANC official called Sipho. Invited to a party in Maputo, Lesia saw a young man by the name of Gibson Ncube walking into the room drinking from a can of South African beer.

'It gave me a shock, you know, to see that man drinking the poisoned liquor because I can assure you at that time in Maputo you couldn't just get that kind of beer. Mostly they were drinking locally made beer, and I couldn't do anything to stop him because while he was talking he was just finishing the beer and he had thrown the can away.'

On April 5, 1987, Gibson Ncube died a horrible and painful death. Shortly after drinking the poisoned beer, his feet had become paralysed. The paralysis had gradually spread through his body and he died eight days later in Maputo's Central Hospital. Doctors could do nothing for him.

The assistant chief representative of the ANC in Maputo, Herbert Thabo, phoned Lesia in Botshabelo, informing him that the young activist had died and asking him to assist with the funeral arrangements. Lesia helped to trace the dead man's family in Johannesburg and informed them by phone that their child had died. He travelled with them to Maputo to attend the funeral. Lesia was paid a 'bonus' of R1 000 by the CCB.

After Lesia's return, Becker and Brown told him they had contrived a new plot to get to the ANC: to take booby-trapped television sets as gifts to the ANC in Maputo.

Lesia had to tell his ANC friends that he had connections with gangs who stole television sets and that he would in due course deliver some of them as gifts. Herbert Thabo asked Lesia to find a television set he could send to his girlfriend in Zambia.

Lesia travelled to Mozambique through Swaziland and once he was in the capital, he activated the bomb so it could be set off from a distance by radio. Becker had told him earlier that another agent, whom Lesia did not know, would set off the bomb in the television set.

But the television set never reached Thabo. A senior ANC official, Mhlope, asked Lesia whether he could have the television set. Lesia explained that it was intended for Thabo, but Mhlope said he would pay Lesia well. Lesia sold the set to Mhlope, but before he handed it to him, he defused the bomb.

On his return to South Africa, Lesia lied to Becker and said he had given the set to Thabo. A week later Becker summoned Lesia to Johannesburg and questioned him about why the bomb had not exploded yet. He ordered Lesia to return to Maputo and reclaim the set. Lesia returned to Mozambique on the pretext that he was on a business trip to import seafood.

By the time Lesia arrived in Maputo, the television set had already been taken to Zimbabwe. An ANC member who attended Gibson Ncube's funeral, Frank Chiliza, had been asked by Mhlope to take the set with him back to Zimbabwe as a gift for the ANC's chief representative in that country, Reddy Mzimba.

When Chiliza arrived in Harare, he moved the set into his flat. When he left for work, his wife, Tsitsi, decided to switch it on.

In the early morning of May 11, 1987, an explosion ripped through Harare's northern surburbs. Tsitsi Chiliza, a mother of two, was blown apart and the flat destroyed.

The same day, the Zimbabwean Minister of State for Security, Emmerson Mnangagwa, said in a statement that the bomb had been an electronically detonated device which had blown up when the set was switched on.

'It is quite clear that agents of the South African regime had devised a plot to kill the chief representative of the ANC, which misfired with disastrous results.'

South Africa denied complicity in the attack. Foreign Affairs Minister Pik Botha mouthed his usual rhetoric, saying that countries that allowed insurgents into their territories were 'playing with fire'.[2]

The SADF said in a statement: 'It is no more than an absurd attempt to yet again try to use South Africa as a scapegoat for their (Zimbabwe's) own deteriorating internal security situation.'

In Zimbabwe, the Central Intelligence Organisation (CIO) went to work. Within a day, the bomb was traced back to Mhlope and eventually to Leslie Lesia. At the time, Lesia was still in a hotel in Maputo, waiting for instructions from Becker. He couldn't find the television set, and was unaware that the set had exploded in Harare.

Four days after the explosion, there was a knock on Lesia's hotel door in Maputo and when he opened it, four CIO agents in civilian clothes burst in and started searching his room. They told Lesia to pack his clothes and warned him: 'Keep your mouth shut or we'll shoot you.'

The men took Lesia to his car, blindfolded him and took him to an airfield, from which he was flown to Lusaka. Once there, he was taken to a room where a dozen men were waiting for him. He recognised one of them as an ANC official called Pat.

'Why am I here?' Lesia asked his interrogators.

'Just tell us the truth. Who recruited you? Who are your bosses in the Defence Force? What information did you give to the Boers?' his interrogators demanded.

A defiant Lesia told them: 'Fuck you, gentlemen. I have been gathering information for the ANC. I am one of you.'

Lesia tried to assure his interrogators that he was dedicated to the ANC and gave them Jacob Zuma's name as a reference. But the men knew he was lying. 'You're talking bullshit. We know you're a South African spy and you're going to pay for it.'

It was only on the next day that Lesia was told that the television set he had given to Mhlope had been transported to Harare where it had exploded and killed a woman. He was kept for three days in Lusaka before being blindfolded again and driven to Harare, where he was taken to a police station and charged with murder.

'It was a great shock to me that this woman had died. First Joseph, then Gibson, and now the woman. And here I was in Zimbabwe at the mercy of men I knew were going to torture me until I told them the truth.'

Lesia was taken to the notorious Goromonzi detention centre, where he was stripped naked and thrown into cell number one, known as the 'Robert Mugabe cell' – the Zimbabwean Prime Minister had once been detained in the same cell by the Ian Smith regime.

'My hands were manacled behind my back and attached to an iron ring on the wet cement floor. I lay on my back and could not move. I was left for three days without food or water. I forced my mouth to the cement floor to lick up the wetness to try and quench my thirst.'

On the third day the warders carried Lesia out of his cell and threw him onto the gravel yard. His interrogators took two pick handles and thrashed him on the soles of his feet until he could take the pain no longer and passed out. He was then carried back to his cell and thrown on the wet floor, where he regained consciousness. The same torture was repeated day after day until Lesia's legs had swollen up so much that he could no longer walk and passed blood in his urine.

On June 16, 1987, Lesia could no longer endure the pain. On that day, his fifty-third birthday and also the commemoration of the Soweto uprising of 1976, he confessed. Later that day, he was taken to his white Mazda 626 with the 'I Love Bloemfontein' bumper sticker on it.

He showed his interrogators the secret compartment, in which they found the pistol with the silencer, the explosives and the poison. He told them about his recruitment, his handlers and the murders of Joseph and Gibson.

'Now they knew I was guilty and they became really vicious. I was given electric shocks on my private parts and they hit me with a Coke bottle against my head.'

As a result of his torture, Lesia would never walk normally again and he suffered from pain till the day he died.

There was overwhelming evidence against Lesia, but the State was eventually forced to withdraw the murder charge against him – he had been tortured too badly. The Zimbabwean Supreme Court had a proud record of dismissing confessions made under duress or as a result of torture. During the 1980s torture by the CIO has allowed various South African agents to be either acquitted or to escape being charged.

Minutes after the murder charge against Lesia had been withdrawn, he was redetained under the Zimbabwe state of emergency and taken to the Chikurubi Maximum Security Prison outside of Harare. For the next three years, he would be prisoner number 387/87.

While in detention Lesia met other SouthAfrican agents and assassins being held or having been convicted by the Zimbabwean authorities. Amongst them were Phillip Conjwayo, Kevin Woods and Michael Smith, all three on death row awaiting execution for murder and sabotage; Barry Bawden, sentenced to 40 years' imprisonment for sabotage; Odile Harrington, sentenced to 25 years' imprisonment for spying; and Guy Bawden, who was held with Lesia under the state of emergency regulations.

Guy Bawden had been involved in the blowing up of anti-apartheid activist Jeremy Brickhill by a bomb in October 1987, but had been so severely tortured that he couldn't be charged. 'My stomach lining was split, which caused me to bleed for two full years in prison. I was in a bad state, but Leslie was even worse. Although he couldn't walk, they continued to beat him,' Guy commented.[3]

Miriam Lesia was only informed of her husband's fate weeks after his arrest.

'He told me he was going to Mozambique to see the ANC. Then he disappeared. I thought it had something to do with the ANC. Then they told me he was in Zimbabwe and that he was a spy for the government. I didn't believe it. It was impossible.'[4]

Lesia's detention meant the end of his arts school. As news reached the community of Botshabelo that their teacher was an assassin, people withdrew their children. No more money was paid into the school's bank account.

'It was a great shock to the community. Leslie was trusted. Some of the kids came to our house, where they sat and cried with me. Not only were their dreams shattered, but a man they loved was a spy,' said Miriam Lesia.

Lesia became Zimbabwe's longest-serving black detainee. In protest against his detention and the refusal of the authorities to allow Miriam to visit him, he embarked upon two hunger strikes.

'I could take the pain they inflicted on me, but I worried most about my wife back home. By then, my arts school had been closed down and the family had very little money. From that day I was abducted from Maputo, the South African Defence Force stopped paying me my monthly allowance. My wife never got a cent while I was in jail. They just did not care.'

Miriam was never permitted to visit her husband and their only means of communication became the monthly exchange of letters. Lesia's letters, written on jail paper and heavily censored by the warders, depict a man in dire need and in extreme pain.

In August 1988, he wrote: 'Hi there love, I beg of you to keep on fighting until the dust has settled down, love. I am sorry if what I am telling you right now is going to shock you. My love, I am semi-paralysed in both legs from the hips downwards. I feel somewhat that you don't or rather, yet realizes in full the seriousness of my situation (sic). Love, I want you to pause and think.

'Love, I want you to go to the university and insist that you want to see Colonel Steyl (Lesia's Military Intelligence contact in Bloemfontein) and explain to him my predicament and that I have insisted that he must personally introduce you to the office of the Minister of Justice or Foreign Affairs ... I am afraid for my life.

'Gee my love, have you any idea what they have done to me? It's barbaric – and I mean that in the full ugliness of the word. Otherwise, my love, I am a believer and I hope and trust that my faith in God will never desert me. Though I must admit your letter made me a worried man when you mention your weight loss. But again I remember that you once told me that *letswai* turns women into fatties, remember? Let's hope, my love, that you are not going to fall into a trap like Mopapi. Don't forget to kiss yourself for me. Bye now my love.

'And remember, tigers don't cry.'

The military refused to accept any responsibility for Lesia. They simply told Miriam that they didn't know who he was and that he had never worked for them.

In July 1990, Robert Mugabe lifted the state of emergency in Zimbabwe. For

Leslie Lesia and Guy Bawden it meant freedom as the authorities had no legal means of detaining them any longer. They boarded a South African Airways flight from Harare and flew back to Johannesburg.

Lesia had been detained for altogether 39 months. He was met at the airport by Colonel Ludwig Kemper of the SADF and taken to 1 Military Hospital at Voortrekkerhoogte, where he was treated for ten days. He was debriefed by a colonel, three majors and a captain of Military Intelligence who wanted to know how he had been arrested in Maputo, what kind of treatment he had received in Zimbabwe, and who his interrogators had been. He was also interviewed by military psychologists.

And then they dumped him. After Lesia had spent two weeks in hospital, Military Intelligence booked him and Miriam into a dingy Johannesburg hotel. After a few days he received a phone call from the military: 'Mr. Lesia, we are sorry, but we can only pay for your accommodation. You will have to pay for food yourself. We are sorry, but that is all we can do.'

Not only did the SADF dump Leslie Lesia in a backstreet Johannesburg hotel, they also deserted a sick man in desperate need of further medical care. A doctor later diagnosed cancer of the testicles, probably contracted as a result of the continual electrical shocks. He could not afford to pay for treatment himself. Most of his medical expenses were paid for by Guy Bawden.

To Military Intelligence, Leslie Lesia was an expendable commodity: gullible, naive, badly trained and black. His handlers must have known it was madness to send him back to Maputo after he had delivered the booby-trapped television set and the poisoned liquor. And yet, when he was arrested, they denied his existence. The fact that he had lost his life's dream, undergone unimaginable suffering at the hands of his interrogators and became an outcast in his own community, meant nothing. They had no more use for Leslie Lesia.

Shortly after Lesia was released, Odile Harrington arrived back in South Africa after being detained in Chikurubi Prison for two years. The frail-looking arts graduate had been sentenced to a 25-year jail term in 1987 by a Zimbabwean judge who had said she was unrepentant and that she deserved the death penalty. She had been arrested by Zimbabwe's CIO and that she had been tortured, starved and sexually assaulted for 11 months while being held in solitary confinement.

While the homecoming of Lesia hardly attracted any attention in the media, Harrington received a heroine's welcome from Pik Botha and later had tea with State President FW de Klerk. She was immediately offered employment as a librarian in the Department of Foreign Affairs.

I met Leslie Lesia three months later in his Johannesburg hotel. He was hungry and I took him to a Chinese restaurant. By then, I knew who he was. Shortly after his release, Pieter Botes had phoned me and said that Lesia, known in the CCB as 'Tiger', was back in South Africa. Guy Bawden arranged the meeting.

The man sitting in front of me was desperate, bitter and filled with hatred. He wanted money for his story, lots of money, to start a new life and a new arts school. Since his release from Zimbabwe he had been unable to return to Bloemfontein for fear of reprisals from ANC comrades.

Vrye Weekblad was at the time involved in a defamation case against police forensic chief General Lothar Neethling. Lesia claimed he had vital information about the poisoning of activists. He said that towards the end of January 1987 Becker had called him to Johannesburg and taken him to Jan Smuts Airport where he had been asked to try and identify anti-apartheid activists arriving in Johannesburg from the United Kingdom.

While they were sitting at the airport hotel Becker had pointed at a man having a meal and said to Lesia: 'Do you see that man there? He's the big boss of the police. He is the man helping us to get the stuff.' Becker had pointed at Lothar Neethling. The 'stuff' he had referred to was the poisoned liquor that Lesia had had to take to Maputo.

We needed Lesia's evidence, but we wouldn't pay him. 'Your only chance of ever returning to Botshabelo would be to stand up in court, confess what you have done and testify against the South African government. I am sure the ANC would forgive you for betraying them,' I said to him.

Lesia agreed, but said that before he would get into the witness box, he wanted an assurance from the ANC that he would be forgiven and that he would not be harmed. That night, I met with the ANC's chief of foreign affairs (today Deputy President), Thabo Mbeki, who sent Lesia a personal note saying that the organisation was not looking for revenge and that it would welcome him back in its ranks should he testify against Neethling.

Mbeki's message was like a second lease on life. Lesia's eyes were sparkling when he said: 'Well, let's get to work.' He said his greatest ambition in life would be to start his arts school again when he had regained the trust of the people of Botshabelo.

It was a stroke of luck that he had never thrown anything away. He had an enormous collection of old air tickets, hotel vouchers, notes and diaries to corroborate his evidence.

Lesia and I had to travel to Bloemfontein to search for documentation and to fetch his white suit to wear in court. On our way, we stopped in Soweto at the home of his sister to collect some more evidence. His brother-in-law refused him entry into the house and threatened to kill him if he ever saw him again. Lesia was unmoved. 'He has always hated me.'

It was the first time since his fateful visit to Maputo that he had returned home. After his exposure as an agent, activists in Bloemfontein had sent messages to Miriam that they would kill the traitor should he ever return. As we climbed out of the car, his mother-in-law, who did not know he was coming home, curiously opened the front door of his green-painted house. She embraced him with tears rolling down her cheeks while his kids stared wide-eyed at their father's sudden homecoming.

After a few minutes, friends and relatives arrived with beer and food. As we sat down under the red satin ceiling in the dining room, Lesia spoke non-stop. He was happy, I think, for the first time in many years.

Later that day, Lesia put on his baseball cap and ventured out into the streets to face the residents of Botshabelo. We stopped at a shebeen he used to frequent. There was a stunned silence when Lesia walked in, took off his baseball cap and simply announced: 'I am back.'

A woman rushed forward and pressed his face against her breasts. A few old friends and drinking acquaintances shook his hand. Others just looked at him. Someone ordered him a drink. He told them that he was going to rectify his wrongdoings and that they should watch television and read the newspapers.

'I think they have forgiven me,' Lesia said as we left Bloemfontein later that day.

I also thought so. How wrong we were.

Lesia provided us with a whole bag full of old air tickets, hotel vouchers and his diary. Among his documents were a number of notes he had made during his briefings by Becker and Brown.

According to the notes: 'All big fishes in the Communist Party must be exposed and be destroyed inside and outside the Republic of South Africa. Thus we will have a meeting once or twice a month for briefing and instructions.'

Two days before Lesia was due to give evidence, we chartered an aircraft to Zimbabwe to try and obtain more evidence to corroborate his story. Lesia's lawyer in Harare, who had been paid for years by the SADF to represent its imprisoned agents, handed over his passport and the brass-plated poison ring that had been found in his car.

The CIO gave us the photographs that had been taken when Lesia had shown them his secret compartment and had uncovered the pistol and silencer, the poison, the explosives and the poison ring. The bottle of poison could not be found and it was only after Lesia had given evidence that we were informed that it had been traced. According to forensic tests conducted in Harare, the bottle contained an anaesthetic substance.

Leslie Lesia rose from obscurity to short-lived fame as his death squad story unfolded in the Johannesburg Supreme Court. His revelations were the main news in the biggest newspapers. The night after his first day in the witness box, Lesia looked at himself on television and said: 'I have really shown them a thing or two, haven't I?'

On the second day, as we walked out of the court building, Lesia came face to face with an ANC member he had known and betrayed in Mozambique. The man smiled at him, lifted his fist and shouted: 'Amandla!' It was a gesture for Lesia that he had been forgiven and accepted back into the ranks of the ANC.

The next day, Lesia returned to Botshabelo. I was convinced that he would be accepted back into the community and could start a new life. Even revive his arts school, who knows?

Mr Justice Johan Kriegler later said in his judgement that he was convinced that Lesia had been recruited and used by the CCB to undertake clandestine operations in the neighbouring states and that he had been responsible for the poisoning of Gibson Ncube and the booby-trapped television set that had exploded in Zimbabwe.

I never heard from Leslie Lesia again, but in March 1995 I was in Bloemfontein and decided to look him up. Botshabelo had changed very little. Still the same unkept dirt road that took me to the green-painted house at number 4205.

Miriam opened the door, invited me in and said: 'Leslie died a few months ago. He had cancer. He always complained about his testicles. It was his manhood, you see, although at times he was functioning well,' she said, and smiled.[5]

After Lesia came back, he had joined the ANC and wanted to work for the organisation. 'The problem was that he gave exiles poison. It was his downfall, because people thought he killed their children in exile. He was very disturbed, because they wouldn't forgive him. He had lots of nightmares, he would go out at night, smoke a lot and try to think how to build himself up. But he never had any answers. People who were his friends were told not to speak to him. They did not understand what happened to him in Zimbabwe. He couldn't go to shebeens any more or walk the streets. He tried to lead a normal life, but couldn't. It didn't help to confess. He should never have said anything.'

Lesia was alone when he died, with only Miriam next to him. 'He was a good man. Had he known what the result would be, he would never have done it.'

I was horribly naive to have believed that Lesia could have returned to his community and started where he had left off. For many people, he had simply perpetrated too much evil. Forgiveness and reconciliation is a long and painful process.

When I think of Leslie Lesia, I think of the words of former Minister of Defence Magnus Malan after his acquittal on charges of conspiracy to murder in the Durban Supreme Court in 1996: 'God is my witness that I have never done anything wrong.'

And of the famous black journalist Nat Nakasa who wrote in the 1950s in *Drum* magazine: 'God does not have enough tears to wash South Africa clean.'

Chapter Seventeen

'Keep the pot boiling'

July 1983, and somewhere in the operational area in northern Namibia, South Africa's supreme leaders met to plot and determine the fate of millions of people around the country's borders.

The chairman of the meeting was bald and spectacled, a securocrat who for 11 years had been at the helm of one the most contemptible governments ever put together. His name: PW Botha, a hawk with a wagging finger and an iron fist.

He was surrounded by 12 of his most trusted and senior cabinet ministers, amongst them the Minister of Foreign Affairs, Pik Botha; the Minister of Defence, Magnus Malan; the Minister of Police, Louis le Grange; and the Minister of Justice, Kobie Coetsee.

Also at the table were the Minister of Co-operation and Development, Piet Koornhof, who in later years would shame his former colleagues by fathering children with a 'coloured' escort girl; the Minister of Manpower, Fanie Botha, who would have to resign after accepting money for bribes; the Minister of Mineral and Energy Affairs, Pietie du Plessis, who would go to jail for fraud; and the Minister of Transport, Hendrik Schoeman, who would commit suicide.

And then there was the youthful Minister of Mineral and Energy Affairs, FW de Klerk, a rising star in the National Party and the son of a former President of the Senate. In 1989 FW de Klerk would topple PW Botha from power to become South Africa's sixth National Party head of state. Seven years on, he would appear before the TRC and deny that it had ever been the policy of the National Party to kill, torture or assassinate or that he had ever been privy to any such decisions.

Botha and his ministers were joined by the heads of the three arms of the security forces: the Commissioner of Police, General Johan Coetzee; the Chief of the Defence Force, General Constand Viljoen; and the Director General of the National Intelligence Service, Dr Niel Barnard.

This was an extraordinary meeting of the State Security Council (SCC), a secretive cabinet committee that met at least once a week to co-ordinate the state's security policy. According to many political analysts, this became Botha's 'inner cabinet' and the seat of real power during his period of office.[1]

On that day in Namibia, discussion focussed on the government's security policy towards its neighbours. The SSC decided: 'As far as the conventional build-up of arms in neighbouring states is concerned, it should be prevented, and in regard to the extent of danger it holds for the RSA, it should be destroyed/ neutralised. This method is legally an act of war and should, therefore, be carried out in an indirect way.

'Actions against Lesotho should be intensified in regard to the extermination of terrorist bases and a change of government. The establishment of Marxist surrogate forces in Lesotho must be prevented.

'Botswana must be tempted into the South African camp in an attempt to counter the Marxist threat. The leadership dialogue with Zambia must be continued, without jeopardising actions against the ANC in that country.

'The pot of internal conflict in Zimbabwe must subtly be kept boiling.'

The minutes of the meeting, number SVR 12/83, were marked 'Top Secret' and only 62 copies were printed and distributed. Copy number 59 got into the hands of the TRC.

If we look beyond the political jargon, the SSC decided on that day in 1983 to sabotage, kill, organise a coup d'etat and stir up a civil war.

The decisions of the SSC were followed by several cross-border raids into Lesotho, including the attack in December 1985 in which Eugene de Kock and his men killed nine people, a coup d'etat masterminded in Lesotho by Military Intelligence in January 1986, and an extensive destabilisation campaign in Zimbabwe.

In his second submission to the TRC in May 1997, De Klerk said: 'I am not aware of any initiative "to support any other movements or organisations in other countries that sought to overthrow or influence the policies of those countries". I can imagine that South Africa during this period may have tried to use organisations to influence the policies of other governments in the course of its legitimate international diplomatic activities and in its efforts to bypass sanctions – but you would have to approach the Department of Foreign Affairs for further information in this regard.'

Speaking about his participation in the SSC, FW de Klerk said in his evidence to the TRC: 'I was there as an ordinary minister of education and leader of the National Party in the Transvaal. I can just say that this type of planning, this type of "It's okay" has never been discussed, it was not the atmosphere in which discussions took place on the Council. It was broad strategies ... policy decisions which cannot be interpreted in any way whatsoever as authorising these unlawful acts resulting in these atrocious violations of human rights.'[2]

It is absurd of the former State President to allege that he didn't know what his colleagues were talking about. He was part of a conspiracy to commit acts of terror against legitimate, independent and internationally recognised states. There is no indication in the minutes that he questioned any of the decisions made.

FW de Klerk said further: 'I've never been fearful, not of PW Botha or anyone to put forth my view. I haven't been a yes-man or in any position where I served. And I'm telling this commission and the country, that I have not been part of a decision which authorises that (murder). I could not live with such a decision.'

Magnus Malan admitted in his submission to the TRC that he had ordered several cross-border raids. 'I authorised numerous cross-border raids against enemy targets in southern Africa. Cross-border raids caused bloodshed. As a Christian I regret the loss of lives ... [but] I consider these operations to be legal.[3]

'The government's policy was clear: stop the perpetrator of violence at all costs. The carrier of the car bomb, landmine, limpet mine from the neighbouring states had to be destroyed, outside our borders or inside the country before he could commit his atrocity. The destruction of the terrorist, his base and his capability was the mission of every soldier in the South African Defence Force and was also the policy of the government of the day. In this way the killing of innocent civilians could be prevented.'

'This is a photo of Barry when he was in the anti-tank support group and these are all photographs of him in the Rhodesian Light Infantry. And this was a certificate that he was given when they finished their tour of duty.'

An image of a smiling young man in a brown army uniform, a beret over his short-cropped hair, hanging against a white wall and starting to turn yellow.

'He was always a wonderful young man. He was always very open and honest. He served in the Rhodesian Light Infantry for three years. I wouldn't say he enjoyed the war – it was a nightmare. Most wars are.'

The elderly woman continued her tour down the wall. More photographs, more army uniforms, another certificate. Tears as she spoke of him, a wet tissue clutched in her hand. Many of his mates were now dead, she said, 'but at least he is alive.'[4]

She took a step back in time and pointed to a photograph of him as a boy. Another uniform, this time the Cecil Rhodes Preparatory School in Bulawayo. More mates, more smiles, all of them white.

'He went to boarding school from six, seven years old. I think that did him a lot of good, boarding school. He was always a very happy youngster. I don't really know what else to say.'

Photographs of the boy amongst cattle, surrounded by the African bush, holding a hunting rifle. He was entering adulthood, living a carefree adventure in a land of leopards, witchdoctors and ancient African ruins.

I was on the farm 'Albany' of Des and Irene Bawden in the southern Zimbabwean province of Matabeleland. The Bawdens are cattlemen and have worked this land for more than a century. The farm is a stone's throw from the Matopos – the last resting place of Cecil John Rhodes, the colonialist and founder of the settler state that became known as Rhodesia.

When Barry Bawden was growing up, the once prosperous colony was rapidly collapsing into chaos, a tragedy created by the adults around him who had made a Unilateral Declaration of Independence in 1965 to ensure their continued life of special privilege, denied to their countrymen of colour. Like their southern neighbours across the Limpopo River, they said their actions were in the interests of the survival of Christianity and civilisation.

Barry's age of innocence ended when he left school and he was conscripted into the Rhodesian army to fight the forces of majority rule knocking at the door of his fatherland. At the time, the guerrilla forces of Robert Mugabe and Joshua Nkomo had surrounded and infiltrated Rhodesia from the north, east and west, and international economic sanctions against the country were in place.

The war ended in 1980 and gave birth to Zimbabwe. However, instead of embracing the policy of national reconciliation and nation building preached by Robert Mugabe, Barry Bawden and many of his former comrades-in-arms turned their back on the newly founded state and tried to destroy the infant democracy.

That is why Barry Bawden has to sit in the Chikurubi Maximum Security Prison outside Harare for 40 years. Three of his co-conspirators have been sentenced to serve 70 years each.

In 1988, Bawden was taken away by the Zimbabwean Central Intelligence Organisation (CIO), and charged and convicted of sabotage. Michael Anthony Smith, Phillip Masiza Conjwayo and Kevin John Woods were convicted of murder and sabotage and sentenced to death. Their sentences were later commuted to 70 years' imprisonment.

The four men were secret members of the South Defence Force, a cell of the CCB that murdered and masterminded a series of bomb attacks in Zimbabwe. After independence, they offered their services to the South African state which used them as tools in its destablisation campaign.

They were used, in the words of PW Botha's State Security Council, to keep the pot in Zimbabwe boiling.

For many years South Africa waged a war to uphold apartheid far beyond its own borders. Death squads played a significant role in the government's use of the neighbouring states as buffer zones against the ANC's influence. Operatives like Pieter Botes, Leslie Lesia and the Zimbabwean agents mentioned above were vital elements in the disruption and destabilisation of southern Africa. The ANC had to be kept as far away as possible by forcing neighbouring states to expel South African refugees, making pre-emptive strikes against the ANC, setting up surrogate forces, and in some cases, even establishing a military presence in other countries.

Since 1980, says Dr Joseph Hanlon in his book *Beggar Your Neighbours,* South Africa has invaded three southern African capitals – Maseru, Gabarone and Maputo, and four other countries in the region – Angola, Swaziland, Zambia and Zimbabwe; sent death squads to attempt to assassinate two prime ministers – Robert Mugabe of Zimbabwe and Lebua Jonathan of Lesotho; supported dissident groups that have brought chaos to two countries – namely Unita in Angola and Renamo in Mozambique, and less serious disorder in two others – namely, antigovernment forces in Zimbabwe and the Lesotho Liberation Army in Lesotho; disrupted the oil supplies of six countries – Angola, Botswana, Lesotho,

Malawi, Mozambique and Zimbabwe; and destroyed railway lines in seven countries – Angola, Botswana, Lesotho, Malawi, Mozambique, Zambia and Zimbabwe.[5]

More than one million people in southern Africa have been displaced and
virtually all the states have had to care for refugees of South African attempts at
destabilisation. South Africa itself has had to cope with a refugee influx from
Mozambique as a result of its destabilisation policy against that country. More
than 120 000 people have been killed in the region, most of them starved to death
in Mozambique, at least partly as a result of South African-backed rebels having
prevented drought relief from getting to the starving.

Destabilisation helped the South African government to foster the myth
amongst the white electorate that blacks could not rule themselves. To this end it
was important to create turmoil around South Africa. How many times have we
heard white South Africans say: 'Look around you and see what's happening on
our doorstep. We don't want something similar to happen here.'

Nowhere in the region has the role of the death squads been more clearly
illustrated than in Zimbabwe, which held the greatest threat to South African
dominance of the region. Zimbabwe has always been the pivot of the transport
network of southern Africa and, as the most developed state besides its southern
neighbour, it has always had the potential to prosper and develop independently
of South Africa.

The new government of Robert Mugabe posed a bizarre political threat: his
policy of pragmatism and reconciliation after independence raised the prospect
of a flourishing non-racial state that would further expose the ills and wrongdoings of apartheid. By early 1981, South Africa had clearly decided to attack
Mugabe and to destabilise his country. To white South Africans, Mugabe was
portrayed as a Marxist intent on establishing one-party rule in his country and on
leading the campaign to enforce a similar system on the white man down south.

Although South Africa was more constrained in dealing with Zimbabwe than
it was with some other states in the region, it established a highly sophisticated
and well-trained death squad for operations against Zimbabwe.

At independence, at least 5 000 Rhodesians with military and security
connections crossed the border into South Africa. Some sold their military skills
to the South Africans and became the soldiers of destabilisation. Many of the
highly trained Rhodesians were absorbed into D40, Barnacle, 3 Reconnaissance
Regiment and, eventually, the CCB.

However, many former white Rhodesian soldiers stayed on to work for the new
Zimbabwean government. One of them was Geoff Price, who became director of
close security in the CIO after independence. Price exploited Mugabe's policy of
reconciliation and rose from his pre-independence position as Abel Muzorewa's
campaign manager to the officer personally responsible for Mugabe's safety.

Price had a long history of co-operating with South African security officers.
In promoting Muzorewa, he had made use of South African funds to hire

helicopters, to print pamphlets and to organise rallies. But the new government in Zimbabwe thought that Price was a good example of a professional soldier and that he would serve whatever government was in power.[6]

They were wrong. By the time Robert Mugabe assumed power, Price had already been recruited by South African Military Intelligence.

On December 18, 1981, a bomb explosion ripped through the headquarters of the Zimbabwe African National Union (ZANU) in downtown Harare, killing seven people and injuring 125. The bomb went off above the third-floor conference room where the ZANU Central Committee under the chairmanship of Robert Mugabe had been meeting. The lives of the prime minister and his cabinet were probably saved by a delay in starting their meeting. The people killed were mostly innocent bystanders in a bakery next door while the injured were mostly Christmas shoppers on the packed street outside.[7]

Price was not initially suspected of complicity in the explosion, but as investigators proceeded two other white security officers were detained. Before they could be interrogated, Price took urgent leave to visit relatives in the United Kingdom. A few days later, the two officers admitted to being part of a spy ring under his command.

Price then came to South Africa, where he first worked for the Security Branch and then in later years became a senior officer in the Directorate of Covert Collection of Military Intelligence, where he worked under the codename of 'Arthur Wiltshire'.

It later turned out that he had established and controlled one of the first South African spy cells inside Zimbabwe even before independence. The cell had carried out surveillance of the ANC's chief representative in Zimbabwe, Joe Gqabi, before he had been assassinated in Harare in July 1981. Gqabi had been shot and killed as he had come out of his house.[8]

South Africa was also implicated in an explosion in August 1981 that had rocked the Inkomo barracks outside Harare. The Inkomo site was a major weapons armoury and arms and ammunition worth $25 million were destroyed in a blast that could be felt 30 kilometres away in the capital.

The CIO detained an engineer and bomb expert, Captain Patrick Gericke, claiming he had had free access to the armoury and was working for South Africa. Gericke was then sprung from jail in an incredible cloak-and-dagger operation by South African agents.[9]

The operatives freed Gericke by kidnapping the wife and children of the investigating officer in the case, Fred Varkevisser, who was forced to release Gericke. In a hazardous landing on the streets of a Harare suburb, Gericke was picked up by a light aircraft flown probably by none other than Peter Casselton, who took off towards the South African border. (Casselton told me how he had once had to pick up an agent in Harare – who must have been Gericke – and had skimmed the trees on his way back to South Africa. He said a Russian-manufactured MiG fighter had overshot him just before he had entered South African air space.)

South Africa was also held responsible for the destruction of a third of Zimbabwe's military air power. In July 1982, saboteurs planted explosives in 13 fighters at the Thornhill Air Base near Gweru in central Zimbabwe, wiping out the country's strike and jet interception capabilities.

South Africa was, however, caught with its pants down in August 1982 when three SADF soldiers were killed infiltrating Zimbabwe to sabotage the railway line that runs to Maputo. Pretoria admitted that the men were members of its armed forces and that they were former Rhodesian soldiers, but claimed that they had been on a private and unauthorised mission.[10]

The most damaging legacy left behind by apartheid's secret war in Zimbabwe was the civil war instigated in the southern province of Matabeleland. Dissident activity in Matabeleland began in 1982, but it had its roots in the integration of the three pre-independent military forces – Robert Mugabe's Zimbabwean National Liberation Army (ZANLA), Joshua Nkomo's Zimbabwean People's Revolutionary Army (ZIPRA) and the Rhodesian forces – into a new national army of reconciliation. Towards the end of 1981 there were clashes between ZANLA and ZIPRA in which several hundred people died. South African agents took advantage of the civil unrest and started sowing the seeds of a low-scale civil war in which an estimated 6 000 people died.[11]

One of the architects and masterminds behind the civil unrest was Malcolm 'Matt' Calloway, a former member of the Rhodesian Selous Scouts who stayed in Zimbabwe after independence and became a local commander of the CIO. He left Zimbabwe in 1982 and joined 5 Reconnaissance Regiment in Phalaborwa, where the SADF was training former Rhodesian soldiers and Renamo guerrillas to destabilise Zimbabwe and Mozambique.[12]

Calloway and other former Rhodesians set up an organisation comprising a small group of former Zimbabwean guerrillas recruited by South African agents known as 'Super-ZAPU'. Many came from the Dukwe refugee camp in Botswana, to which they had fled to escape the violence in Zimbabwe. They were brought back to 5 Recce, where they were trained, armed and sent back to Matabeleland to foment the violence.

The main role of 'Super-ZAPU' was to create chaos and disruption. The dissidents attacked shops, schools, busses, villages and farms. Amongst the thousands that died were 30 white farmers.

Clear evidence of South African involvement in the civil unrest in Matabeleland emerged in December 1983 when a former guerrilla, Hillary Vincent, was arrested in Botswana and turned over to Zimbabwe. Vincent admitted that he had met Calloway in Francistown in Botswana in January 1983 to talk about training and arms. Three loads of arms were brought across the border from South Africa to Botswana, from where they were distributed to Zimbabwean dissidents. Among the weapons were 70 AK-47 assault rifles, ammunition, mines, rocket launchers and 258 kilograms of plastic explosives.[13]

South Africa even established a radio station for the dissidents, Radio Truth, which beamed its anti-Mugabe messages accross the border into Matabeleland. South Africa repeatedly denied that that it was in any way involved in the broadcasts, but on November 25, 1983, the station mixed up two tapes: the vernacular broadcast of Radio Truth began with the introductory music of 'Voz da Africa Livre' – the South African-sponsored Renamo radio station that broadcast its messages from the same location.

In response to the growing wave of unrest in Matabeleland, Robert Mugabe sent in the undisciplined and ill-trained Fifth Brigade to quell the violence. There were immediate reports of brutalities and the killing of civilians. The situation deteriorated until the signing of the unity agreement between Mugabe and Joshua Nkomo in 1987.

But even then, the pot had to be kept boiling.

Jeremy Brickhill grew up in Matabeleland in Zimbabwe. His family were mostly farmers – old-fashioned Rhodesians with a love of the land but a reluctance to change. He went to Cecil Rhodes Preparatory School in Bulawayo, where the Bawden boys were his school mates and classmates.[14]

When he left school, he was, like all white Rhodesian boys, conscripted into the Rhodesian army. Unlike his classmates, he refused to serve and instead, supported majority rule and became a member of Joshua Nkomo's Zimbabwe African People's Union (ZAPU). Brickhill left Rhodesia for Zambia and became the only white soldier to serve in Nkomo's military forces.

After the war and with the dawn of democracy Brickhill returned to Zimbabwe. Those who were with him at Cecil Rhodes Preparatory School couldn't forget and wouldn't reconcile with him. His classmates became his would-be assassins.

On October 13, 1987, Jeremy Brickhill was the target of a car bomb explosion in Harare's Avondale shopping centre. He was severely burnt by petrol, he lost his spleen, several ribs were broken and his left leg was badly damaged and left full of shrapnel wounds. Brickhill was in and out of hospital for more than a year and it took eight months before he could walk again.

The mastermind behind the attack on Brickhill's life was Kitt Bawden, today still one of Zimbabwe's most wanted men, assisted by Guy and Barry.

Guy Bawden, who lives in Johannesburg today, says that Brickhill was blown up after Kitt Bawden had discovered that he was taking limpet mines into South Africa and 'because his wife was Russian'.[15]

'There was R70 000 on Jeremy's head. But Kitt wasn't paid out because he did not die. He said afterwards to me that he couldn't believe that a person could survive a blast like that.'

The operation was another CCB cock-up. Brickhill denies that he has ever been a member of the ANC or transported limpet mines to South Africa, and besides that, his wife is not a Russian – she's a South African citizen from Durban. How difficult could that have been to confirm?

Three months later, Bawden and his cell of CCB operatives had tried to blow up an ANC transit house in Bulawayo. An unemployed man, Obert Mwanza, was hired by Kevin Woods and Kitt Bawden and paid R10 to drive the car and to park it in front of the house. Bawden sat in another vehicle some distance away and detonated a bomb in the car as Mwanza parked the vehicle. Mwanza was blown to pieces and two ANC members were also killed.

A few days after the blast, Kitt Bawden fled to South Africa, but Kevin Woods, Michael Smith, Barry Bawden, Guy Bawden and Philip Conjwayo were arrested. Altogether, 23 Zimbabweans were arrested, including the fathers and wives of the suspected bombers. Des Bawden was amongst those who were detained.

'We had no idea at all that they were involved in anything like this. The soldiers came at about six o'clock in the morning. Des was at the dip sorting out the cattle. They already had Barry, they had my brother-in-law John. They had Greg, my nephew. And they took Des off,' tells Irene Bawden.

Des Bawden spent four months in detention before he and the other farmers were released. Barry Bawden, Smith, Woods and Conjwayo were charged with sabotage, murder and the illegal possession of firearms. Guy Bawden could not be brought before the court as he had been too badly tortured.

Smith said during his trial that he had been a member of the SADF since 1980, that Kitt Bawden was his commander and that his first allegiance was to South Africa. The men refused to divulge any information about other operations they had been involved in. Woods, for example, was one of the South African agents who had manipulated the violence in Matabeleland. He had been a former administrator of the CIO before being recruited for South African Military Intelligence in 1983.[16]

The South African military desperately tried to free their imprisoned operatives. A jailbreak operation was planned and codenamed 'Direction 1 and 2' and the price tag for the rescue attempt was R6 million. A former Rhodesian mercenary, Sammy Beehan, was hired to carry out the operation. A Zimbabwean Air Force pilot, Gary Kane, was recruited to steal a military Agusta Bell helicopter and to fly the imprisoned men back to South Africa.[17]

Fifteen South African agents were standing by on the day in June 1988 that the accused were due to appear in court in Harare for a monthly remand hearing. The SADF commando planned to free them on their way from prison to court, but the operation turned into a disaster when Beehan was caught with an arsenal of weapons as he tried to enter Zimbabwe.

It later turned out that the Zimbabwean security authorities had come to know of the plot in advance. The jailbreak had to be aborted and Kane fled to South Africa in a stolen light aircraft. He shot an 11-year-old girl in the stomach during his escape. Beehan was charged along with the other agents and sentenced in absentia to 40 years' imprisonment. The 'Zimbabwean Four'became the 'Zimbabwean Five'.

On November 19, 1988, the Zimbabwean judge president ordered that Woods, Smith and Conjwayo should hang and that Bawden should spend 40 years in jail. Robert Mugabe later commuted their death sentences to life imprisonment.

The families have been split apart by the arrest and incarceration of the men. Guy Bawden believes that the men could have evaded their arrest, but his brother Kitt failed to warn them and fled Zimbabwe on his own. 'He's a traitor, and as long as I don't see him or have contact with him, that's good enough for me.'

The SADF paid out R250 000 to Kitt Bawden when he returned to South Africa. In March 1995, I tracked him down in Cape Town and arranged a meeting with him – ironically, at the Rhodes Memorial at the foot of Table Mountain.

The bearded and steely-eyed Bawden admitted that he was a field commander of the Zimbabwean region of the CCB. He refused to discuss any covert operations he had been involved in, but admitted that he had killed people. 'I think we were good soldiers. We were professionals. Innocent people get killed in war situations. That's the nasty thing about war.'[18]

Zimbabwe's most wanted man said he had been recruited by the SADF in 1981. 'At the time it seemed the right thing to do. We'd just come out of the Rhodesian war, and it was an emotional period. But it was a waste of time. I lost my inheritance in Zimbabwe and still get homesick when I think about the farm. I destroyed my life.'

None of the men in prison are still married today. Eileen Smith divorced her husband to start a new life. 'How can you love somebody if you haven't seen that person for seven years? I respect him, I admire him, I will always be there for him, but you cannot define an emotion like that when you haven't seen somebody for many years. Families have gone through an awful lot. Little Casey Bawden was born the day after her father was arrested and hasn't seen him yet. Mike's dad passed away two years ago and he couldn't go to the funeral.'[19]

The attitude of the men in Chikurubi has not been conducive to their own release. They have yet to apologise to their victims and show no signs of remorse. More than five years after he was injured by the bomb explosion, Jeremy Brickhill visited the men in prison and asked them: 'who did you work for and who ordered my bombing?' The conversations were recorded.[20]

Barry Bawden: 'It's hard to say here, I can't put my head on the block. That's unfair here … but I'm pleased to see that you've recovered. I've become a Christian and I have been praying for you as well.'

Michael Smith: 'I was asked to help, and I felt it was the right thing to do at the time.'

Kevin Woods: 'If I've been dropped like a dead rat, well, that's just my tough luck.'

'Where do I have to look if I want to find the answers for why I was attacked?'

'In a crystal ball … You're not going to get the answers from me.'

Jeremy Brickhill said his encounter left him with a feeling of emptiness, and that he had expected at least an explanation of why he had become a target. 'If they stubbornly refuse to give any sort of an account of what happened, they will be forgotten people.'

It was ironically Guy Bawden, a free man with no obligation to justify anything, who a few months later apologised to Brickhill and explained to him why he had become a target of attack.

March 1995, and in an Anglican church in Cape Town, I came face to face with a man without hands. I had met Albie Sachs once before, but at least he had had a hand left that he could offer to me. Father Michael Lapsley had nothing; where once were hands, are now metal clasps. We couldn't shake hands, but in the hour that followed, this remarkable man embraced me with his compassion and faith.[21]

In April 1990, Lapsley, then an ANC chaplain based in Harare, received a large envelope. 'Inside were two religious magazines, one in English, one in Afrikaans. When I opened one magazine, the act of opening it was the detonating device for a bomb which then exploded. I didn't lose consciousness, but I went into darkness, and in the process I lost both my hands, an eye, my eardrums and [I had] a range of other injuries.'

Michael Lapsley was a chaplain. His work in the ANC was pastoral and theological and he could, therefore, never have been a military threat to the apartheid forces. 'I've been saying all over the world that apartheid is an option for death carried out in the name of the gospel of life.'

Three years before the attack, Lapsley had been warned by the Zimbabwean authorities that he was on a South African death list and he had armed police guards.

I don't know who sent the parcel bomb, but it has the hallmarks of yet another death squad attack. Lapsley received the envelope a few months after the official disbanding of the CCB, but at the time the Directorate of Covert Collection of Military Intelligence still planned and executed attacks on anti-apartheid activists far beyond South Africa's borders. I believe the Directorate planned the attack.

Michael Lapsley is reminded of his disability every moment of every day. And yet, he says: 'I realised shortly after the bombing that if I was filled with hatred, bitterness and a desire for revenge, they would also have killed my soul. People around the world, through their love, support and prayer enabled me to make my bombing redemptive. I was able to grow in faith, grow in hope, grow in compassion. I have become a victor. Those who bombed will have to live with their guilt for ever or come to terms with their deed at some point in their lives.'

In early 1995, Guy Bawden received a letter from his cousin, Barry Bawden, written from the Chikurubi Maximum Security Prison near Harare. For the first time in more than six years, the young man was optimistic, even cheerful. He wrote:

'They say we will be out soon! President Mandela says we will be out soon! Guy, I have a South African passport now and am ready to travel. They say soon, Guy, but it could still be a month. So please carry on trying for all of us.'

A month earlier, Eileen Smith had received a letter from Michael Smith: 'Last night I saw the moon and the stars for the first time in six years. That's incredible.'

At the time, the men were in a buoyant mood. State President Nelson Mandela had in a spirit of reconciliation requested his Zimbabwean counterpart to release the men and South Africa had awarded South African citizenship to them. The Zimbabwean prisoners were the last members of the apartheid security forces anywhere in the world who were incarcerated.

The government of FW de Klerk had refused to accept any responsibility for the men or admit that they had planted bombs and killed on behalf of the apartheid forces. They had been completely abandoned by their former masters.

And yet, according to the records of the SADF, Michael Smith was given South Africa's highest decoration for bravery when he was awarded the Honoris Crux in the early 1980s. The SADF appointed and paid for a lawyer in Harare to represent the men. And that was all. The families were then left to fend for themselves.

'The National Party government military, I would say they're a bunch of cowards. Traitors, if anything. They've left their people there, they've done nothing to help them. They've got rubber necks. That's what it is. The generals have taken their money and run. The fat cats,' says Guy Bawden.

It was ironically the coming of democracy and black majority rule in South Africa – which the men had fought to prevent – that brought new hope of an early release.

Just after the ANC came to power in May 1994, Mandela received the families of the imprisoned men. 'He came out of his office to greet us and take us in and said he would get in touch with his friend Mugabe and do his utmost to get the prisoners released. And I know he has tried,' says Irene Bawden.

In 1995, the Zimbabwean government itself was making positive noises about the release of the men. One of the most senior Zimbabwean cabinet ministers, Dumiso Dabengwa, said: 'They must tell the entire story of their activities in Zimbabwe, like the bombings that took place and the attempt on our president's life. When the nation is informed of that, and the people of Zimbabwe feel yes, we think that we now know and understand why they did these things, we probably should accept a request for their release.'[22]

The South African Deputy Minister of Foreign Affairs, Aziz Pahad, said that Nelson Mandela has repeatedly asked Robert Mugabe to release the men. Other governments in the region – those of Angola, Botswana, Mozambique and Zambia – have all freed South African agents. It is only Robert Mugabe who has stubbornly held on to his prisoners.

The year 1995 passed, and the men were not released. 'Every day, we were told that something was in the pipeline. And then it just seems to peter out, nothing comes of it. It just fades. It's bad enough for us, but it is even worse for them, because they built up their hopes and then nothing happens,' says Irene Bawden.

In the meantime, the parents of Barry Bawden continued to visit their son every second or third month. 'Well, he's always so thrilled to see us. You get to Chikurubi and you stand waiting for him to come down and you just see this lovely smile at this little window. He's always so thrilled to see us.'

In 1996, the men appointed a Pretoria lawyer to approach the TRC to investigate the possibility of appearing before the commission to tell their stories. Dumiso Dabengwa said that the Zimbabwean government would make it possible for them to testify in Zimbabwe. Although the TRC cannot grant amnesty for deeds committed in other countries, it can give the men the opportunity to confess, ask for forgiveness, and plead for leniency and compassion.

But at the cut-off date for applications for amnesty in May 1997, only Kevin Woods had approached the Commission. The others, it seems, have chosen to remain silent.

At the end of May, President Robert Mugabe said in an interview with a Zimbabwean newspaper that he had rejected requests from the South African government for the release of the men. 'We will keep these people in prison until such time that we are satisfied we should release them, if at all we will release them.'[23]

Mugabe said the fact that South Africa had granted them new citizenship meant nothing to him. 'I don't know how they can become South African citizens through remote control. These are Zimbabweans who violated Zimbabwean laws and should be punished as such.'

Barry Bawden and Sammy Beehan may be released on parole some time in the future, but for Kevin Woods, Michael Smith and Phillip Conjwayo, prospects are bleak.

The 'Zimbabwean Five' have become apartheid South Africa's 'forgotten ones'.

Chapter Eighteen

Desperado

Desperado (n.) A man who commits dangerous, especially criminal, acts without worrying about himself or other people: a gang of armed desperadoes (*Oxford Dictionary*)

The venue and the name might have changed, but it was still the same seedy opulence, the same red-mouthed girls in orange and red miniskirts with black fishnet stockings serving middle-aged customers arriving in Mercedes Benzes and BMWs.[1]

Classified ads in Johannesburg newspapers describe Club 69 as an 'erotic exploration', a place to 'live out your orgasm in our famous fantasy suite' and offering the 'deep throat dome, porn palace and pool room'.

Club 69 is on the doorstep of Johannesburg's affluent northern suburbs and boasts one of the best locations in the city: 92 Oxford Road in Rosebank. When I arrived there one Tuesday night in June 1997, I was whisked past three well-heeled customers glued to a television set on which a blonde aerobics instructor was peeling off her gymsuit and flexing her pelvic muscles. A few metres away, a row of female flesh, miniskirts drawn up and legs seductively crossed, awaited the arrival of new clients.

In the illegal casino at the back of the brothel, Ferdi Barnard was in deep conversation with a man who he later told me represented one of the gangs on the Cape flats and wanted to buy weapons from him.

Since my previous meeting with Barnard, he had moved his brothel to a new address in Oxford Road and The Palace (previously known as Yub Yum) had become Club 69.

I wanted to see him before his arrest for the murder of anti-apartheid activist Dr David Webster, shot dead on 1 May 1989. As I was speaking to Barnard, the Transvaal Deputy Attorney General, Anton Ackermann – the state prosecutor who had led the team which had put Eugene de Kock behind bars for life – was finalising an indictment against Barnard that included charges for the murders of Webster and a Johannesburg drug dealer, an attempt to assassinate Minister of Justice Dullah Omar, and various incidents of fraud, robbery and the illegal possession of firearms. The might of the state, previously mustered against Eugene de Kock, is now to do battle with Ferdi Barnard.

The former policeman knew about the investigation, but was fighting back. The state temporarily lost one of its prime witnesses when Barnard traced his former lover and mother of his child, Amor Badenhorst, to where she had been placed under police guard under a witness protection programme in the Western Cape and lured her back to him. He laughed when he told me how incompetent the state's protection programme was and how easy it had been to trace her.

Barnard offered Amor a cash amount, a house and a new car. She simply could not refuse his offer and informed Ackermann that she no longer wished to testify against her former lover. There was clearly a leak in the Attorney General's office, as Barnard had not only found out where Amor was in hiding, but knew the exact details of the indictment and investigation against him.

However, when Badenhorst arrived back in Johannesburg to claim her compensation from Barnard, he had been unable to deliver on his promise and within days she was back in Ackermann's camp.

For months, the noose of justice had been slowly tightening around Barnard and he could no longer operate with the impunity he had enjoyed during the apartheid years. When I visited him in Club 69, he knew he was going to be arrested and that his final battle would be fought in the Supreme Court. Barnard is already a convicted killer and if pronounced guilty again, he will face life imprisonment in the maximum security section of Pretoria Central Prison.

'They've got fuck all. I'm waiting for them!'

When I arrived at Club 69, Barnard said he had been drinking since the previous day when he had appeared in the Klerksdorp Magistrate's Court on charges of stealing more than R10 million's worth of diamonds from a family of prospectors in the Western Transvaal.

Barnard's friend and fellow gangster Corrie Goosen was accused number one in the Klerksdorp case, but when Barnard had stepped into the dock to face the magistrate, the place next to him had been empty.

On May 31, 1997, Goosen died when he crashed his Honda Blackbird 1100cc motorcycle while racing at a speed of more than 300 kilometres per hour on a highway near Port Elizabeth in the Eastern Cape. Goosen's face was mutilated beyond identification in the accident, and police hastily ran fingerprint tests to determine that it was in fact his corpse. His brother Johan Goosen, also a diamond smuggler, had faked his own death in 1992 to obtain a R172 000 insurance claim, but had been arrested two years later and convicted of fraud. He actually died in August 1995 – also in a high-speed motorcycle accident. At the time of his death, Johan Goosen had also been charged for illegal diamond dealing.[2]

Barnard benefitted at least temporarily from his friend's death: he told the magistrate that Corrie's accident had left him without legal counsel and he could not continue until he had consulted a new lawyer. He said he was busy selling his double-storey house in Roodepoort in order to obtain money to pay his lawyers. He had arrived at court earlier that morning in an old Toyota – probably to give the impression that he had financial problems. He told me that he had not long ago bought himself a luxurious Audi A6, but had had to borrow the Toyota because his car was in the garage for repairs.

Corrie Goosen was the latest in a series of Barnard's friends and fellow obsters who had died a violent death. Three years earlier, another gangster and Military Intelligence agent, Eugene Riley, who had been very close to Barnard, had been murdered in his Johannesburg home. Barnard had also arrived late for a court hearing in February 1997 when one of his friends had been shot dead in a night club brawl in Johannesburg. According to his lawyer, Barnard was in a state of fear and suffered from concussion.

Barnard is a reminder of the years when hoodlums and gangsters flourished under apartheid by offering their services to the apartheid forces. In return, they continued their mafiosi schemes without fear of prosecution as long as they could further the cause of their political masters.

Ferdi Barnard had his heyday when he drove around with a shotgun, which he aimed at political activists. He also plotted grandiose schemes to annihilate the ANC. But the Ferdi Barnard I saw in Melville in October 1996, holding on to his crack pipe as though it was a lifeline, and the man I saw in Club 69 six months later was a sorry sight; at 38 years of age he is in the twilight of his life.

In December 1996, two months after he had confessed that he had murdered David Webster, Barnard said he had stopped using cocaine and crack. He looked healthy and in much better shape.

But a few months later, he was back on cocaine. While we were talking into the night at Club 69, he would often disappear, saying that he had to go and snort 'two lines to sober up'. He was rather drunk and confessed that he had been drinking rum and coke since the previous day.

Barnard maintained that he would never use crack again. He said most of his money had gone 'up in smoke' and that he was struggling financially. At the height of his addiction, he said, he had bought up to R50 000 of cocaine and crack every month. He had sometimes smoked crack with prostitutes at The Palace, but two girls took an overdose of the drug and he had to give one mouth-to-mouth resuscitation. She bit his lip open and he had to get stitches. Amor Badenhorst also took an overdose. Her heart stopped beating and Barnard had to rush her to the emergency unit of Ontdekkers Hospital in Roodepoort.

'I was dying of all the crack,' he said. 'I once had four television sets in my house, but they are gone, sold to get crack. Some nights I was too scared to go to sleep in case I would OD (overdose). I would walk up and down the street at night and couldn't control the muscles in my face.'

Crack is formed when cocaine is mixed with baking powder and then cooked, usually in a teaspoon over an open flame. The name comes from the crackling sound it makes while it is cooking. Barnard professes to be an 'expert' in the manufacture of crack.

At the age of 38, Barnard is grey and gaunt, the result of too much crack and cocaine and a year or three too many in the sleaze and degradation of the Johannesburg underworld.

'I cannot plan my life, because I know they are going to arrest me. There is nothing I can offer any woman. What do I say to her? I have lost two women and two children. I will never get another job,' he said. More rum and coke, another line of cocaine. 'Just to sober up,' he would say every time he returned.

As Barnard stood there, his 1,9-metre frame rocking back and forth, he said: 'I will go to prison, but I will fight them till the bitter end.'

He said he wasn't the menace he was made out to be and blamed the media for the fact that everywhere he went, people cast surreptitious glances in his direction – hints of fear, awe, suspicion and curiosity in each quick look.

'It's sometimes good for business, but it has destroyed my personal life,' he said. Drug barons and criminals approached him to perform 'hits' or to buy weapons. Even the *Ystergarde* (Iron Guard) of the fascist Afrikaner Weerstand-beweging had asked him to speak to them about the art of secret and covert war.

'I told them to piss off. You know me, I've never hated the kaffir. That is not the way I was brought up. I fought terrorists and communists, not black people … There was a time when I thought you were a communist, you and that *Kaffer* du Preez. Both of you were targets, but I've watched you over the years, and you were right. Apartheid was stupid. It wasn't right.'

He said he was an agent of the police organised crime unit and that he had helped them to uncover Cuban and Colombian drug lords. 'I can have a hundred ecstasy pills delivered within a hour – at a special price.'

Ferdi Barnard has an incredible ability to survive and to avoid justice. In the process, however, he has bribed policemen, lied under oath, killed and dominated others through fear. There are few people prepared to stand up in a court of law and testify against him.

He is extremely canny and clever, but has one weak spot: he often shoots his mouth off, which is ultimately going to lead to his downfall. He has told too many people about the assassination of David Webster.

While we were sitting in Club 69, he told me: 'I have told you many things in the past, and you have never dropped me.

'If you do, I will kill you.'

December 1984, and facing Mr Justice Gert Coetzee in the dock in the Johannesburg Supreme Court was a 25-year-old Narcotics Bureau sergeant by the name of Ferdinand Barnard. The judge, an imposing man with a sergeant major's moustache, had to sentence the young policeman on conviction of murder and attempted murder.

There was a time when Barnard had had everything going for him. The son of a former police colonel, he joined the force, excelled at the Police College and became a Narcotics Bureau detective on the West Rand near Johannesburg. According to evidence in court, he became disillusioned with crime and the state's inability to deal with criminality. He took the law into his own hands and executed two drug dealers who had been set up to rob a Roodepoort pharmacy. He was also found guilty of stealing a car linked to the set-up and of attempting to murder a drug addict.

Despite the callousness of the crime, the judge decided to pass a lenient sentence on the killer to give him a second chance in life and in the hope that he would rehabilitate himself. As he sentenced Barnard to six years' imprisonment, he said: 'I will give you a chance. It depends on what you make of it.'[3]

After serving just more than half his sentence in Pretoria Central Prison, Barnard was released on parole in 1988 and was given a job at the Roodepoort insurance company of former Springbok sprinter Willie Smit. He found his duties as a claims assessor boring, resigned after three months and told Smit that he had been offered a job with the security police, and that he would be monitoring political activists.

Barnard was drawn into the twilight world of the CCB as a freelance agent, paid a monthly salary of R5 000 and given a car. He started living a life in accordance with the total strategy of no rules and no tales.

Calla Botha is a man that can clearly take care of himself – a former Transvaal rugby forward of Herculean proportions with a frame that resembles a century-old tree trunk. In 1988, Sergeant Botha was one of a group of Brixton Murder and Robbery Squad policemen who suddenly resigned from the unit and left the South African Police.

Among them was one of South Africa's most famous policemen: Lieutenant Colonel Daniel 'Staal' Burger, whose nickname, which literally means 'steel', was taken from a popular radio comedy series about an invincible cop. During his 24 years in the police, Burger gained a reputation as a fearless and ruthless detective who always got his man.

Burger's shock departure from the Brixton unit was followed by two more resignations, those of Lieutenant Abram 'Slang' van Zyl and Warrant Officer Chappies Maree. Van Zyl, once a rising star in the police, had been given his nickname by fellow police officers who thought his eyes look snake-like.

The resignation of the four policemen followed shortly after a controversial court case during which two of their colleagues, Sergeant Robert van der Merwe and Captain Jack la Grange, had been convicted of murder and sentenced to death. The media speculated that the resignation of Burger and his men was connected to the court case, but it turned out later that there was a much more sinister reason.

The four men were recruited to form the core of the internal region of the CCB, an elite Special Forces unit within the SADF. When Slang van Zyl, a tall and softly spoken man with a wild quiff, testified before the Harms Commission of Inquiry in 1990 about the activities and nature of the CCB, he said: 'We were advised that the disruption of the enemy could, for instance, be anything from the breaking of a window to the killing of a person. The managing director told us that we would be indemnified against prosecution for acts of violence that we committed during the execution of authorised projects.'[4]

Working for the CCB gave both Van Zyl and Botha the opportunity to combine patriotism with profit. They earned much more than they had done previously in the police and were given a housing subsidy, a telephone subsidy, a pension scheme, a travel allowance and a car.

The CCB claimed to operate against all 'enemies' of the state, from the left and right of the political spectrum. Van Zyl said he had a soft spot for right-wingers: 'Personally, I must say, I preferred leftists as targets rather than rightists.' However, he conceded, the decision to murder people had never been easy. It had to be avoided at all costs, but unfortunately circumstances demanded that such action had to be taken from time to time. The action of the CCB, he said, was 'for me, for you, I'm talking about the whole South Africa.'

Botha and Barnard, a former first-league rugby player himself, had gone down in the same scrum many times before, and in 1988, they found themselves on the same side again as they plotted the destruction of the ANC and its supporters.

Because of their bulk and size, Ferdi Barnard and Calla Botha were hardly a duo who could disappear into obscurity and melt into their surroundings – as spies are supposed to do.

When activist Roland White, a founder member of the End Conscription Campaign, saw two very noticeable men hanging around his office in June 1989, he phoned the police. They were picked up and detained for questioning. They told the police that they were debt collectors and were after a white car, 'not a Mr White', Their details were taken and they were released.

When Irish hitman Donald Acheson was detained a day after the murder of Swapo advocate Anton Lubowski, he told the Namibian investigating officer, Colonel Jan 'Jumbo' Smith, that he was in Windhoek on a 'secret mission'. He said he worked for a shoplifting syndicate in South Africa and intended to set up one in Namibia. A radio page number in Acheson's name was traced back to Ferdi Barnard and Acheson identified the killer policeman as his handler.[5]

The murder trial led Smith to South Africa, where he exchanged the information he had obtained with Brigadier Floris Mostert, who was investigating the murder of David Webster. Mostert's knowledge of Barnard was linked to the Roland White incident, and it soon emerged that the actions of the two 'debt collectors' were less innocent than the pair had claimed. On October 31, 1989, Floris Mostert pounced on Ferdi Barnard and detained him under Section 29 of the Internal Security Act. Shortly afterwards, he detained Calla Botha as well.[6]

Barnard provided Mostert with invaluable information. He claimed that he was a member of a secret organisation committed to a strategy of violently intimidating the radical left. As a result of Barnard's information, the CCB's cover was blown wide open.

Ferdi Barnard had bungled in failing to follow all the regulations and security instructions of the CCB. Acheson was not supposed to have known whom he had worked for, but because Barnard was careless, he left a trail that led back to him. As a result, Barnard was detested by many senior members of the CCB. Managing director Joe Verster said that he was a criminal and that he had never wanted Barnard to work for the organisation.

In turn, Barnard described Verster to one of the Webster investigators as a 'mad fucking fanatic' with a 'plastic beard hanging to his stomach'. When Verster appeared before the Harms Commission, Barnard said, he was nothing more than a 'glug' with hair and dark glasses.

A transcript of a conversation between Barnard and the investigator in question was handed in as evidence to the judicial inquest into the death of David Webster in 1992. The conversation had taken place in July 1990, after the testimony of Verster and most of the CCB operatives before the Harms Commission. Inquest lawyers had a difficult time quoting from the transcript – each and every sentence of Barnard's was spiced with a wide variety of expletives. During a conversation of an hour, he used the word 'fuck' more than 300 times.

He referred to a campaign the CCB was waging against Slang van Zyl, the member who admitted to the Harms Commission that he had participated in violence and attempted assassinations. According to Barnard, the CCB spray-painted slogans on Van Zyl's walls and put an advert in a newspaper in his name, saying that he wanted to sell a fat white pig sow and her piglet. The sow, Barnard said, referred to Van Zyl's wife and the piglet to his child. It was a warning to the former operative. 'They see him as the fucking root of all evil. They are going to get him.'

Barnard said he was sure that the CCB was going to try and kill him for exposing the organisation during his detention. 'Those guys will fucking shoot you. They don't play with you. Some nights I fucking get up 15 times in one night to see what is going on outside. I cannot fucking rest man ... They fucking tamper with vehicles and those sort of things. You just have a horrible accident. You can't fucking beat them.'

October, 1992, and Calla Botha and Ferdi Barnard found themselves shoulder to shoulder again – this time in courtroom 4F of the Johannesburg Supreme Court at the judicial inquest into the death of Dr David Webster, gunned down on Workers' Day in May 1989.

The two occupied the same corner of the courtroom every day and became the star attraction of the inquest as lawyers acting for the family of the slain human rights activist tried to clear away the web of lies and deceit that had been spun around his death.

The inquest into the death of Webster was one of the most important events in South African legal history, and came more than two years after the Harms Commission had failed to find his killers. Although the assassination bore all the hallmarks of a CCB killing, Harms had found that there was only a suspicion that the CCB might have been involved in the murder of Webster. 'The CCB has done nothing to allay this suspicion,' he said.

Harms was exasperated by the refusal of the CCB operatives to hand over their project files to the commission. At one stage, he threatened to order a court martial if his requests were not met. 'The commission has, since its inception, tried to obtain documentation through subpoenas, threats of dire consequences and consultation … Unless we call witnesses one by one, we will not be able to ascertain where those documents may be … What should I do, have them shot? My patience is wearing thin.'

The organisation's administrative manager, Braam Cilliers (a pseudonym), was told outright that he had lied when he had said he did not know where the files were. 'I am not that dense. If Joe Verster did not know where the documents are, you have to know … It is an absolute lie.'

And yet, Harms allowed the CCB operatives to get away with lies and denials instead of compelling them to hand over their files in order to get to the truth. Even more so, he bestowed a mantle of protection on them which they had never deserved. Operative after operative appeared in comic disguise and was allowed to use a pseudonym.

If it was indeed Joe Verster behind the long, false grey beard down to his chest and the equally wild wig, nobody really knew. He complained that he and his men had been 'contaminated' and branded as terrorists.

'People got a fright and we don't know which way this thing is going … There are people who don't sleep at their houses. At the moment we have cases where wives with little kids go to their husbands to introduce the kids to them and then go away again at night … If it was possible for me to get the files, I would have done so. But at this stage I cannot.'

Verster admitted that a CCB member could have murdered David Webster but denied that the CCB had been officially responsible for the murder. Webster had never been a CCB 'project' and the organisation did not have a file on him.

In 1989 a cloak of silence had been drawn around the Webster assassination, but two years later, on the eve of the inquest, evidence appeared to implicate Barnard in the killing. A colleague and I at the *Sunday Star* discovered that a few days after the murder, Barnard had confessed his complicity in the murder to his CCB handler, who had passed the information on to Joe Verster. We were also told that Barnard had told his former employer, Willie Smit, how he had shot Webster.

On the Thursday night before we published the allegations, we drove to Barnard's house in De Wet Street in Roodepoort to obtain his comment. The property was enclosed by a high white security wall and without an intercom or bell, so I started shouting his name to attract attention over the barking of a ferocious guard dog.

The next moment, a white Volkswagen Jetta came skidding to a halt next to us and a fuming Barnard leapt from the car and headed straight for me. 'I'm going to send you on sick leave,' he barked as he leaned over me like an oak tree over an acorn. It was a most frightening moment as I tried to back off and calm him down. 'If there is incriminating evidence, they can charge me,' he said and sent us off again.

On a Wednesday in October 1992, Willie Smit, his black moustache neatly trimmed, took the witness stand in courtroom 4F of the Johannesburg Supreme Court. He looked nothing like the Springbok sprinter who had once run the 100 metres in a record time of 10,27 seconds.[7]

Smit had all the reason in the world to feel uncomfortable. His eyes were fixed on the microphone in front of him, but every now and then he, too, glanced at Barnard and Botha staring at him. For an entire day, he told the inquest court details of how Ferdi Barnard had confessed to him that he was the man who had shot David Webster. He said Barnard had described how the dead man 'flew up into the air as the shot hit him'.

Smit testified that on numerous occasions Barnard had intimated his involvement in Webster's murder, and had told Smit and Smit's mother that the police considered Barnard to be the most accurate shot from a moving vehicle. The former policeman had shown him an album with photographs of at least 22 men that he'd killed, Smit said. 'He said that to kill again was nothing because it would be just another person.'

In cross-examination, the lawyer acting for Barnard and Botha told Smit: 'You would make a very good fiction writer, but as a liar you are hopeless ... Take the point and admit the lie ... As fiction this reads fantastically, but as a statement it is totally false.'

By tea break the next morning, Smit had made a complete about-turn and had withdrawn his evidence. His lawyer told the court that his client had 'spoken to somebody' during tea, and that he no longer wished to continue with his testimony. In a short statement, Smit said that every shred of his evidence was a lie.

Sitting shoulder to shoulder at the back of the court, Barnard and Botha, their faces a picture of innocence, feasted their eyes upon the former sprinter making a fool of himself.

A potentially damaging witness was out of the way, but several other witnesses also implicated Barnard in the murder. In April 1989, less than a month before the killing of Webster, Barnard had borrowed a sawn-off shotgun from a former Military Intelligence operative. George Mitchell testified that Barnard had said of the weapon: 'It is so short, it will shoot nicely from a moving vehicle.'

When Barnard testified, he said he had meant nothing more by this observation

than 'you can shoot guinea fowl when they fly up – just like out of a pick-up.'
He denied that he had confessed to anybody or had had anything to do with the
murder and said he believed that there was a conspiracy to make him the fall guy.

Willie Smit's mother, Johanna Smit, confirmed her son's discredited evidence
when she said Barnard had confessed the killing to her. 'I told him it was terrible
that they are killing people like dogs in the street.' According to her, his response
was: 'But he is a dog, *tannie* (aunt) ... You should have seen how he flew through
the air – five yards high.'

Barnard's CCB handler, Lafras Luitingh, told the court that Barnard had confessed to the Webster murder three days after it had happened. 'Barnard paged
me to go to see him. I expected that he was going to ask for money, but he said
he had killed Dr Webster. I asked whether it was a CCB project and he said no.'

Luitingh testified that he had told the former head of Military Intelligence,
General Rudolph 'Witkop' (white head) Badenhorst about Barnard's involvement, but said that the general had threatened him: *'As jy nie ophou om te lol met
hierdie Barnard-storie nie, gaan ek jou opdônner.'* (If you don't stop messing
about with this Barnard story I'm going to beat you up.)

Badenhorst was at the time of this conversation conducting an internal SADF
investigation into the murder of Webster. Luitingh said he had told Badenhorst
of Barnard's confession in the presence of Krappies Engelbrecht, who was the
Harms Commission investigator into Webster's death.

Badenhorst and Engelbrecht denied in their evidence that they were part of a
cover-up or that they had been informed of Barnard's confession. Joe Verster and
CCB intelligence officer Derrick Louw (a pseudonym) told the court that they
had also said to Badenhorst that Barnard had confessed about 'flooring' Webster.
If Badenhorst had indeed been told of the suspicions regarding Barnard, he
hadn't told the Harms Commission.

Engelbrecht, accused of telling Ferdi Barnard and Calla Botha 'to keep quiet'
while they were in detention, appeared to be upset by the allegations that he
could have been involved in a cover-up and told the court that he had always
been respected for his honesty and lack of bias. He claimed to have been
complimented for exactly those qualities by several judicial officials in cases in
which he had testified.

In a near-repetition of the farce which had taken place at the Harms Commission, Mr Justice Michael Stegmann ruled that most of the former CCB operatives, including Joe Verster, could testify *in camera* and that no photographs and
sketches of them could be published. The judge ruled, however, that Verster
could not arrive at court in a disguise.

Verster said in an affidavit that he was afraid of being identified as he had ordered several violent operations against 'South Africa's enemies'. Stegmann
said he accepted that Verster's safety rested in his hands and ordered that evidence be heard behind closed doors.

I still find it inexplicably absurd that this country's highest judicial officers have accorded special protection to a man who ran a death squad and ordered acts of violence against his countrymen simply because they opposed apartheid.

Verster was ferried into the basement of the court building by his lawyer every day and entered the court room through a side door. One day, I saw them driving out of the building, and as they stopped at a traffic light, ran towards the Mercedes Benz. There he was, a highly decorated reconnaissance soldier and once one of the most powerful commanders in the SADF, diving for cover on the back seat of the car, his suit jacket drawn over his face as he tried to shield himself from me.

Joe Verster said in his *in camera* evidence that when Badenhorst was appointed to lead the internal investigation, Verster had told him: 'General, you must know this: I don't trust you.'

He said Badenhorst had lost his temper because Verster didn't want to 'play along' with the general's inquiry. 'Because I didn't want to play along, Badenhorst tried to chase me out of the office. I said that it was my office, and I stayed seated. He then got up and, in front of Krappies Engelbrecht and (CCB administrative officer) Christo Brits, assaulted me. I did nothing – I just left him.'

Verster confirmed in his evidence that Lafras Luitingh had told him of Barnard's confession. Verster said he had fired Barnard just before the murder because of a security breach on a Zimbabwean operation, but believed Barnard had killed Webster to prove his worth to the CCB so that he would be rehired.

Verster said he not only told Badenhorst about Barnard's confession, but had informed Magnus Malan in a meeting in July 1990 that Barnard had admitted to the killing, although he said that it was only hearsay. Malan said in a statement that the meeting Verster referred to dealt with retrenchment packages for Verster and his men and that CCB activities had never been discussed.

In a letter to State President FW de Klerk, dated May 5, 1992, Verster alleged that four generals, including SADF Chief, General Kat Liebenberg, had influenced their subordinates in the CCB to make documentation 'change' and 'disappear'. In a further letter dated October 6 the same year, Verster warned De Klerk of serious discontent among members of the security forces, and should they band together, he said, they would be vastly superior to Umkhonto we Sizwe.

Who lied? Verster? Luitingh? Badenhorst? Engelbrecht? Or the host of CCB operatives who testified at the inquest? This was Mr Justice Michael Stegmann's dilemma as he evaluated seven weeks of testimony. As he removed one diaphanous strand of evidence, another, just as diaphanous, would take its place. In the end, there was nothing to see.

He delivered his judgement: 'The truth has not been told.'

In the words of Stegmann, many of the witnesses were 'professional liars who make their living in deception' and who were 'unblushingly resourceful' in building up tissues of 'conflicting falsehoods'. Luitingh, he said, was a disinformation expert who was accustomed to lying. Verster had contradicted himself and his evidence had to be treated with caution, the judge found.

There was enough prima facie evidence to bring Ferdi Barnard to court on a murder charge, but if those responsible had to be identified 'beyond a reasonable doubt', he could not do so. 'In my judgement, Ferdi Barnard is at this stage entitled to the benefit of the doubt … This inquest will not be content with any of the sacrificial lambs which have been thrown to it.'

The final battle in the quest for the truth will be fought five years after Mr Justice Stegmann said that his decision was neither final nor binding. This time, Ferdi Barnard will square up to Anton Ackermann, determined to get his man and armed with a bag full of new evidence.

'You will be pissing in your pants when I'm finished with you.'

These were the words uttered to a bewildered Willie Smit minutes before he withdrew his evidence against Ferdi Barnard.

Facing the Springbok sprinter was Constable Eugene Riley, a black-belt karate expert and close friend and associate of Ferdi Barnard. Later, it would turn out, also a Military Intelligence operative, murderer, robber and smuggler.

When Riley got home that night, he jokingly told his live-in lover of seven years, Julie Wilken, what he had said to Smit to trigger his complete turn-around.[8]

At the time, Riley was still a policeman, but had not reported for duty for three-and-a-half years. In April 1989, he had suffered a knee injury and he had since then been too sick to report for duty at the Internal Stability Unit where he was based, although he still received his monthly salary. Instead, he set up a security company which offered security surveillance, access control, and civil and industrial investigations.

Eugene Riley was probably Barnard's closest friend. They were both Narcotics Bureau detectives in the early 1980s. When Barnard was released on parole, Riley said to Wilken: 'My buddy is out of prison.'

For the next five years, Riley and Barnard would be closer than brothers. They would form a gang that included diamond smuggler Corrie Goosen, former Narcotics Bureau detective and drug dealer Sam Malgas and a convicted bank robber. They were involved in several 'knocks', a term for robbery, often involving diamonds or utilising deceit. They also worked as Military Intelligence agents, ran a brothel, and sold illegal weapons. At least two men, Barnard and Riley, committed murder. The gang bribed policemen to steal dockets and paid them 'protection money'.

Before his death in May 1997, Goosen had proudly described himself as the country's 'best diamond smuggler' and had several previous convictions for illegal diamond dealing. When I met him in October 1995, Goosen and Ralph Haynes had appeared in the Johannesburg regional court on charges of diamond theft. According to evidence in their bail application, eight dossiers had been opened against them, but in every case witnesses had been afraid to testify against them.[9]

Goosen was eventually granted bail of R20 000. As he left the Johan Coetzee police station in Johannesburg and thanked policemen for their hospitality while he had been in detention, I picked him up and took him for a drink. He boasted openly about his diamond exploits and his ability to avoid prosecution. Washing down double rums and coke at an alarming rate, he would approach women in the pub, asking them: 'Don't you want to meet a man with a clean record?'

Ralph Haynes has an even more impressive criminal record that includes convictions for assault, illegal diamond dealing, theft, illegal possession of fire-arms and robbery with aggravating circumstances. He has been sentenced to altogether 16 years' imprisonment.

Haynes, Goosen and Barnard are a frightening trio – heavily built physically with bloodcurdling reputations to match. Not the kind of people to cross swords with, or to testify against.

Sam Malgas said that Barnard called him 'Boesman' (Bushman). 'We did everything together. We were so close, that I never thought anything can go wrong. We stole, smuggled, committed arson, robbed and "knocked". I won't tell about the other stuff,' said Malgas.[10]

I met Sam Malgas for the first time in 1995 at The Palace, where he worked as manager. I traced him again in December 1996 to the southern suburbs of Johannesburg where he said that Barnard had tried to kill him. He said he feared for his life and that he had had to hide in Hillbrow for six months.

Malgas, classified under apartheid law as 'coloured', was also a Narcotics Bureau detective and had served in the police for 12 years, but had left the force after he had been arrested for diamond smuggling.

He became, in his own words, one of Johannesburg's 'biggest drug smug-glers' and was involved in bringing mandrax tablets from India via Zambia to Johannesburg. He said he bought as much as a million rands of mandrax in India at a time and smuggled it into the country.

According to Malgas, Barnard's gang started 'knocking' in around 1988 and learned the skill from a drug lord in Johannesburg, for whom they acted as body-guards from time to time. 'We also did debt collecting for organised crime. We burnt down four houses and fired shots at these places to intimidate people.'

Julie Wilken confirmed that her lover had worked for a drug lord and had been involved in 'hitting houses'. She said that Riley was at the time still in the police force and had stolen Uzi machine guns from the Internal Stability Unit where he was based. The Uzis were used in some of the 'knocks'.

Wilken talks about several 'knocks' they performed in Swaziland. In August 1992, Riley, Barnard and Goosen went to Swaziland for a 'knock'. They took an Uzi, a shotgun and pistols with them. Before he left, Riley said: 'Baby, I'm going to make a million rand.' He came back with R100 000.

She remembers the day that Webster was shot: 'It was a public holiday and we went to Riley's parents in the morning. There was a report over the radio about the murder, and Riley became pale.'

He said to her: 'Baby, there's going to be shit.'

'Why?'

'There's years of shit coming. That dumb cunt didn't know what he was doing.' Wilken says when Ferdi Barnard was detained for more than three months at the end of 1989, Riley said to her there were 'things we have to move'. She said they had had to fetch a bundle of CCB documents that were stored in a metal box and had buried them somewhere on a farm.

Sam Malgas says it was common knowledge that Barnard had shot Webster. 'He told me he shot Webster. He only had to do observation on Webster, but he shot him to make a good impression on his superiors. I knew he got a R40 000 production bonus.'

Amor Badenhorst, a former 'escort girl' and strip tease artiste, who met Barnard in 1991 and started living with him soon afterwards, said in her statement that Barnard had also told her how he had murdered Webster and had even shown her the dam near Nylstroom in the northern Transvaal where he had discarded the shotgun. She said he confessed to her a day after Mr Justice Michael Stegmann had found that there was no proof beyond a reasonable doubt that Barnard had pulled the trigger.[11]

'Webster wasn't suppose to die, he was only supposed to be monitored. Ferdi said that Webster was involved in underground activities and that he wanted to blow up a bus full of children … One day when we drove past Nylstroom, he showed me the dam in which he threw the shotgun that was used to kill David Webster.'

When drug addict Mark Francis decided to co-operate with the state and swore an affidavit against Eugene Riley and Ferdi Barnard about their 'knocks', he signed his own death warrant. A few months later, he was found dead in a back street in Berea in Johannesburg, his face and head smashed with a baseball bat.[12]

Previously, one night in February 1991, the trio of Ferdi Barnard, Eugene Riley and Mark Francis, accompanied by Corrie Goosen, got into their fast cars and headed for Taung in Bophuthatswana to steal diamonds from a diamond dealer and businessman.

On the Wednesday night before they left, Julie Wilken pleaded with Riley: 'Please don't go tonight.' She said she felt that something was going to go wrong, but Riley told her: 'Don't worry, it is a hell of a deal. I will be back the next morning.'

Riley didn't come back. Barnard phoned Wilken and told her that she should not worry, but eventually knocked on her door and said he didn't know where her lover was.

Two days later, she discovered that Riley and Francis had been arrested on a charge of attempted murder and had been imprisoned in Pampierstad in the Northern Cape. The 'knock' had gone horribly wrong. Riley later told her that when they entered the house where the diamonds were, there were two men armed with AK-47s guarding the precious stones. Shooting broke out and Riley was lightly wounded in the face. Goosen and Barnard thought that Riley was dead and drove away, leaving him and Francis behind. They were arrested and thrown into jail.

When Julie Wilken got to the prison, Riley was chained hand and foot, his chin wound untreated and dirty. 'He was in a bad state and had a wild look in his eyes. He said he had to stand on his toes with his hands against the wall for hours. All he said to me, was: 'I love you.' She later discovered that he had been assaulted and sodomised in prison.

By the time that Riley was released on bail, Francis had already turned state witness and had sworn an affidavit implicating him in the attempted murder. 'Francis had to die, otherwise Riley would have gone to prison. He wouldn't go back, and in any case, Francis was a scum and a weasel,' says Wilken.

Wilken says that one Sunday night in August 1991, Riley went to Ferdi Barnard's home. Before he left, he took a baseball bat with him. She knew that Francis was going to die. 'He came back late that night. He took my cigarette lighter, a can of petrol and said he had to go and burn his clothes. When he returned, he took a bath and got into bed without saying a word.'

The next morning, Wilken heard that Francis was dead. That afternoon, several policemen came to her house and took her lover away. A security guard saw the killers beating Francis with the baseball bat, but couldn't identify Riley at a police parade. Riley was released and the attempted murder charge withdrawn because of lack of evidence.

Amor Badenhorst said in her statements to the Transvaal Attorney General that the baseball bat was sawn into smaller pieces and thrown away.

The murder of Mark Francis is part of the Attorney General's indictment of Ferdi Barnard.

When investigators of the Goldstone Commission raided a highly secret operations unit of the SADF in a plush Pretoria suburb and confiscated five files, they were astonished at what they found: less than a year after the CCB had ostensibly been disbanded, Ferdi Barnard had been rehired by Military Intelligence to create a dirty tricks unit. Its task: to find embarrassing information on ANC leaders by using prostitutes, homosexuals and drug dealers.[13]

Barnard's gang of desperadoes comprised criminals, prostitutes and a Mozambican refugee. Amongst them were Eugene Riley, Sam Malgas and a former Mozambican army deserter by the name of Joao Alberto Cuna, who had entered South Africa illegally in 1987.[14]

Despite his suspected involvement in the murders of David Webster and Anton Lubowski, Barnard was appointed a 'chief agent' in August 1991 on the recommendation of General Rudolph Badenhorst.

Barnard's unit was part of the Directorate of Covert Collection (DCC), a cloak-and-dagger unit within Military Intelligence. In December 1992, Mr Justice Richard Goldstone said in a commission report that the DCC had been involved in third-force activities and had attempted to derail the peace negotiations between the ANC and the National Party government. Nineteen Military Intelligence officers and operatives, including two generals, four brigadiers, colonels, handlers and agents, were then sacked by FW de Klerk in an attempted purge of his security forces.

According to Goldstone, Barnard's madcap plan to cripple the ANC included the recruitment of members of Umkhonto we Sizwe as Military Intelligence agents, but 'where such members could not be recruited they would be criminally compromised. For that purpose, use would be made, inter alia, of prostitutes, homosexuals, shebeen owners and drug dealers.'

Barnard's gang of whores and killers set up a brothel in Waverley in Johannesburg. Amor Badenhorst said she met Eugene de Kock at a hotel where he gave her R3 500 to set up the brothel. A prostitute and former mistress of Barnard, Carol Ann Burton, said he wanted her to recruit white prostitutes who would be prepared to sleep with black men.[15]

Badenhorst said that the brothel was not only used to 'entertain' and debrief ANC members who were recruited as Military Intelligence spies, but was also used by the gang as a meeting place to plan 'knocks'. Barnard stored an arsenal of weapons, which included Uzi machine guns, AK-47s, hand grenades and explosives, at the brothel.

Sam Malgas said he sold cocaine to Barnard in return for weapons, including AK-47s, shock grenades, hand grenades and and RPG rocket launchers. 'He once gave me seven AKs for five grams of coke, which I sold to Inkatha. On another occasion, he gave me 17 hand weapons.'

Barnard was, according to the Goldstone report, fired in December 1991, but Military Intelligence continued to employ him long afterwards. He operated under the pseudonym 'Tony' and concentrated on discrediting the ANC and gathered information about the Azanian People's Liberation Army (Apla) in the Transkei. He had a PAC source named 'Mr B' in Umtata. Barnard said in his intelligence reports that 'Mr B was an influential drug smuggler who had regular contact with the PAC President Clarence Makwetu.'

Barnard says he was part of a campaign to discredit Winnie Mandela when he leaked evidence of her affair with attorney Dali Mpofu to newspapers. In August 1992, an envelope was delivered to the offices of the *Sunday Star* in Sauer Street, Johannesburg. It contained a sensational love letter, addressed to lawyer Dali Mpofu, in which Mandela confessed how her passionate love for the young lawyer had helped to destroy her marriage. According to the newspaper, Mpofu has told friends he never received the letter.[16]

Barnard told me about plans, masterminded by former Rhodesian Geoffrey Price, one of Barnard's handlers, to blow up Zimbabwean Prime Minister Robert

Mugabe in the Sheraton Hotel in Harare with a bomb, and to blow up anti-apartheid activist Klaas de Jonge in Amsterdam in the Netherlands. A bomb would have been placed in a postbox used by De Jonge – but like so many other elaborate plans devised by apartheid's secret forces, nothing came of it.

On a Sunday night in January 1994, Julie Wilken and her lover, Eugene Riley, watched the violent gangster film *Bugsy* on television. The film ends with the mobster being shot dead by his cronies, who suspect him of cheating them.

Wilken didn't see the end of the film as she left Riley in the lounge of their Brixton home to go to bed. She was woken by a shot around midnight, and when she stormed into the room, she froze and started screaming. Riley sat slumped in a chair, his face covered in blood. His mouth slowly opened and he made a gurgling sound. Next to him was a revolver.

Half an hour later, he lay in hospital, his face covered in bandages. His eyes were half-open, but Wilken said his body was cold. The machine keeping him alive was switched off and he died without saying a word.

Just after she got home, Ferdi Barnard and Corrie Goosen arrived. Riley's father, Tom Riley, said Barnard wanted to know whether his son had handed 'certain documents' to him.

Wilken said more than a month before his death, Riley 'was sleeping with his hand on a shotgun'. She said he was providing Military Intelligence with information about Barnard's alleged weapon smuggling. The Tuesday before his death, he told Wilken: 'I will not protect him any more.'

Amor Badenhorst said that two days before Riley died, Barnard had discovered that his friend had turned against him. 'Ferdi was furious. Riley was the only person he really trusted.' She said the death of Riley had had a devastating effect on him as he increasingly used crack and cocaine.

According to Wilken, Riley did a 'knock' with Corrie Goosen just before he died. 'He took his shotgun and left. He came back later and said it wasn't as successful as they had hoped, but that he had made R50 000. He gave me R10 000 to give to his parents. Shortly afterwards, there was a falling-out between Riley and Goosen. On the Sunday morning before he died, he took his pistol and said: "Now I'm going to see Corrie." He later came back, but said nothing.'

Goosen was one of the coffin bearers at Riley's funeral, but Barnard was conspicuous by his absence.

Despite the mysterious circumstances in which Riley died and his connections with the underworld and covert security force units, police investigators treated his death as a common suicide. They later admitted that they should have launched a murder investigation. Wilken says a bundle of Military Intelligence documents she typed for Riley disappeared at the time of his death and she received a host of death threats. An inquest into his death has never been held and the dossier regarding his death is gathering dust at the Brixton Murder and Robbery Squad.

Julie Wilken, who maintains that Barnard had something to do with the death of her lover, said she won't rest until the killer is brought to justice. Of Barnard, she says: 'He reminds me of a fly, something that has to be crushed to death.'

When Amor Badenhorst had dared to turn her back on Ferdi Barnard and leave him, he traced her down to Nigel, east of Johannesburg, and arrived in town with eight of his men. He waited for her to arrive at the Nigel Hotel, where she was dancing, and threw a shock grenade through the window. Barnard meant it as a warning: 'You are mine and cannot get away from me. I will find you, wherever you are.'[17]

Badenhorst and their daughter, Shanika, went back to Barnard, where she said she lived a day-to-day existence as the personal property of one of Johannesburg's most infamous godfathers. She has a son from her previous marriage.

When Badenhorst decided to turn against Barnard in late 1996 and make a statement to the Attorney General, she and her children were whisked away on a witness protection programme to the Western Cape. It took Barnard a few months to trace her, and this time, he didn't threaten her again: he made her an offer she couldn't refuse.

Amor Badenhorst left home at the age of 15, and three years later, was a prostitute in Johannesburg. She married a policeman, but two years later he was sentenced to 15 years' imprisonment for murder. It was then that she met Ferdi Barnard and started living with him. It was a life, she says, of abuse, crack, cocaine and crime.

'I was his possession, but I loved him very much. I was probably the only one who thought there was something good in him. Life with him consisted of four walls. From time to time, I was allowed to take my son to the drive-in or visit my parents in Nigel. I was the dumb blonde on the side … From the very first day I met him, he was involved in illegal deeds.'

She says that about two years after they started living together, Barnard introduced her to cocaine and she became an addict. 'At the beginning, it was only once a month, then it became twice a month. I later started smoking crack … The past winter was hell. Ferdi refused to give me money for medicine and food for Shanika. There was no electricity in the house and only cold water. He would give me cocaine for two days, and then keep it away for two days. He likes to play games with people.'

When Ferdi Barnard went to prison in 1984, he said that it was his hate for drugs that caused him to kill the two addicts. However, a few years later he was an addict himself, supporting his cocaine and crack habit through crime and prostitution.

Sam Malgas said he sold up to R40 000 of cocaine at a time to Barnard. He said in the beginning he didn't know that Barnard was snorting it himself, but after a while he did it openly and in the presence of Malgas. 'I also started using cocaine and lost everything because of my abuse. There was a time when I lived on R2 000 (of cocaine) a day.'

Badenhorst says she was involved in several of the 'knocks' performed by Barnard and his gang. She remembers how Barnard and Riley once came back from Lesotho with a million rand. When she walked into the kitchen, the money was lying on the floor. She took R80 000 and stuffed it under her bath.

The 'knocks' didn't stop with the death of Eugene Riley. At the time of the writing of this book, Barnard was standing trial in the Klerksdorp Magistrate's Court for stealing diamonds from Western Transvaal prospectors. According to evidence in court, things went horribly wrong during the Klerksdorp 'knock'.

The prospectors were a typical Western Transvaal farming family who had ventured into diamond digging during one of the droughts of the late 1970s and early 1980s. They accumulated a fortune in diamonds and locked some 2 000 carats away in a bank vault as 'insurance' for the future when, they believed, the white man might be driven out of the country. The diamond mine was on *'oom'* (uncle) Fanie Nel's farm, while his sons Marius and Deon mined the barren land.

According to evidence given in court, both Goosen and Barnard claimed that they had had an 'Israeli buyer' who had been willing to buy diamonds at 20% more than the market value. The buyer had wanted to inspect the diamonds first and a meeting had been arranged in a hotel just outside of Klerksdorp.

Once the diamonds were produced for inspection, Goosen grabbed the metal box containing the diamonds, jumped into his BMW M5 and raced away. The prospectors were not prepared to give up their fortune that easily, and immediately gave chase through the Western Transvaal in their truck.They had a machine gun and fired at the BMW, narrowly missing Goosen.

The police then joined in the chase and Goosen was eventually arrested hiding in a mealie field. He was covered with dry leaves and branches. In one hand he held a cellphone and in the other a pistol. The diamonds have never been found and in all likelihood were thrown out of the car window by Goosen to be picked up again on his release from jail.

Although Goosen already had several previous convictions for diamond smuggling he had always manged to stay out of jail by threatening to kill state witnesses and by bribing policemen to steal dockets. He was always armed to the teeth and always carried a baseball bat with him in his luxury car.

Warrant Officer Flip Kruger, who investigted the Klerksdorp case, said that when Goosen was detained, he offered four policemen R100 000 each to release him and steal the case docket. There is evidence that at least one accepted the bribe. A policemen at the Criminal Bureau was paid to remove Goosen's fingerprints from all police records.[18]

I have often wondered how the prospectors could even have contemplated doing a deal with these gangsters whose trademarks were flashy cars, ostentatious jewellery and 'poodle-cut' hairdos.

Marius Nel said that it had been known that Barnard had worked for the CCB.

'It was an organisation that had a good image in the old South Africa. They said they had high contacts in the security forces and we believed them.'[19]

Deon Nel said that Barnard went as far as telling him how he had gunned down David Webster. 'He said that Webster was a political activist and that he had been ordered to remove him from society. He said to me that he had shot Webster from a short distance with a shotgun ... Maybe he told us because we were politically rightwing. Maybe he just wanted to impress us.'[20]

Johannesurg businessman and mining engineer Bill Douvan said that he had been 'knocked' and swindled out of R4 million by Barnard and Goosen. In one instance he had become involved in an uncut diamond venture in Swaziland that had promised to 'harvest' between R50 and R100 million. The gangsters asked him to provide security to the value of R2 million.[21]

He had given them R700 000, but a day or two later he was requested to get another R1,4 million in cash. 'They said the deal was as good as sealed. Barnard went with me to collect the cash. He carried two bags full of money ... And then he and the money just disappeared. They were terrific crooks. When the utmost conmen come up with fantastic schemes, even princesses fall ... I tried to chase them and get my money back, but I was helpless. Barnard had once shown me seven Uzi guns; another time he showed me two. They are very dangerous.'

Amor Badenhorst said in her statements to the Attorney General that Barnard is protected by a 'cabal' within the Brixton Murder and Robbery Unit, while Sam Malgas told me that he personally had to hand over 'protection money' of R10 000 a month to a senior police oficer.

I asked Barnard about his friendship with Lieutenant Rassie Erasmus of the police's Organised Crime Unit, and he assured me that his friend was one of the 'straightest cops around' and wouldn't hesitate to arrest him should he obtain sufficient evidence. How straight a cop, I wondered, could one be who drove around with counterfeit American dollars in his car and who allowed Barnard to abuse crack and cocaine in his presence?

Ferdi Barnard's feedom seems to have come to an end. After snorting another line and knocking back another rum and coke, he said: 'I want to lead a straight life now, I want to be left alone because I want to get on with my life. I'm turning 39 next year and want to settle down. All this talk about my arrest has a devastating impact on my domestic life. I cannot plan anything for the future. I can offer no woman a future. It destroys my life.'

South Africans are in the future probably going to look back at the life and times of Ferdi Barnard and ask themselves why he was not stopped earlier. Why did the authorities allow this man to act with so much impunity and in the process destroy more lives?

And then there are going to be those who will wash their hands in blamelessness and say: we never knew.

Chapter Nineteen

Oranje, Blanje, Blues[1]

It was early morning, May 4, 1978, in Cassinga, a former iron-mining town 250 kilometres north of the Namibian border. Three hundred South West African People's Organisation (Swapo) soldiers were lined up on the parade ground, while in the rest of the little town, family members and refugees from Namibia prepared for another day of exile in the Angolan bush.[2]

Three hundred kilometres south of Cassinga at a military air base inside Namibia, four South African Air Force Canberra bombers and four Buccaneer fighters, loaded with thousand-pound bombs, took off.

A few minutes later, six C-130 transport planes carrying 257 paratroopers took off and turned north towards the Angolan sky. One of the soldiers was Lieutenant Rich Verster, a young and decorated soldier of A Company of 3 Parachute Battalion.

The target was Cassinga, which was, according to intelligence, Swapo's major forward operational headquarters where 1 200 soldiers had been trained to undertake military operations in Namibia. Aerial photographs showed that the town was well-defended and that it had an extensive network of deep zigzag trenches and bunkers.

The attack on Cassinga was one of the SADF's most ambitious raids ever into Angola and one of the largest airborne assaults ever performed. It was called 'Operation Reindeer' and was approved by Prime Minister John Vorster and Minister of Defence PW Botha.[3]

At eight o'clock that morning in Cassinga, death came from the sky. Bombs rained from the silver bellies and wings of the Canberras and Buccaneers and turned the parade ground into a muddle of dust and flesh and blood.

Women and children screamed and cried as bombs exploded in and around Cassinga, blowing people to pieces and buildings apart.

Inside the transport planes, the elite of the army's airborne forces prepared themselves for one of the lowest action jumps in paratrooper history. They were led by the legendary Colonel Jan Breytenbach, the SADF's most accomplished fighting commander.

Sitting across from Verster was his friend Anton Steyn who handed him a note with the words: 'Forever and ever, goodbye my friend. Forever we meet again, we shall smile. If not, this party was well made.'

Like most men in the aircraft, Rich Verster was scared. Some prayed, others joked, most were just silent. The paratroopers were armed with R1 rifles, a few 60 millimetre mortars and captured RPG rocket launchers. They had to overrun Cassinga in one swift, violent assault, and withdraw again as quickly as possible. Twenty kilometres south of Cassinga was a force of mechanised tanks and armoured vehicles, manned by Angolan soldiers and Cubans.

As they approached Cassinga, the order came: 'Get ready!', and the men lined up, clutching their assault rifles.

The red light went on and the Staff Sergeant started counting: 'Ten, nine, eight … zero!', and then came the sound of the beep.

Rich Verster was the second paratrooper to jump from the C-130. While still in the air, he saw a Buccaneer diving down on Cassinga and dropping its load of death before screaming up into the sky again. Smoke and flames billowed from the burning town.

On that autumn day in May 1978, Rich Verster jumped into an abyss of horror.

The next few hours would transform his life and haunt him for ever.

Over the next two decades he changed from soldier to killer to Military Intelligence agent to diamond miner to drug smuggler.

Nineteen years after the raid on Cassinga, he told me his story in a prison in the south of England.

Amidst the green valleys, sweet fields and gentle downlands of south England and on the banks of the river Fromme lies Dorchester, a village shrouded in the mists of early history and immortalised in the novels of Thomas Hardy.

In the centre of town and built on the site of a Roman temple stands the medieval church of St Peter's. A hundred yards further down North Square is a three-storey red-brick building with 15 chimneys rising into the sky, not unlike the many castles and historical buildings sprinkled accross the Dorset country-side. The entrance to the castle-like building, built in 1790, is a fine Portland stone gateway overlooking the river and the green cornfields beyond.

A sign in front of the gateway states that this is the entrance to 'Her Majesty's Prison, Dorchester', and this was where I was heading in May 1997 to request a visit with prisoner number 3964: Rich Verster.

Minutes later, the burly man gripped my hand and shook it like an old friend. As we sat down at a small table, more inmates were led into the visitor's room and I then realised that the ancient and quaint surroundings of Dorchester obscured the grim realities of just another prison.

Next to me, a heavily tattooed gangster (in prison for bank robbery) with 'The Idols' and a swooping bird of prey immortalised on his forearm, comforted his crying wife, while across the room, an inmate grasped at the breasts of his girlfriend until a warder snarled at him that a 'contact visit' did not entail intimate and arousing physical fondling.

Verster was an awaiting-trial prisoner on charges of attempting to smuggle 170 kilograms of compressed marijuana into the United Kingdom. At the end of January 1997, Verster, a Port Elizabeth millionaire businessman and a British citizen were arrested at Hurn airport near Bournemouth in the south of England after arriving from Spain in a private jet. British customs officials searched the plane and found six suitcases containing the marijuana, with a street value of £500 000 (R3,7 million).[4]

While custom officials searched the plane, Verster took off, jumped over the airport fence and ran away. Late that night, he handed himself over to the British police and has been in custody ever since.

Verster admits that he is 'as guilty as hell' and that his fingerprints were found on the suitcases containing the drugs. He said he ran away because he was delirious with fever after he had contracted malaria in the West African country of Sierra Leone. Until shortly before his arrest he had mined a piece of land there for diamonds. The marijuana originated from Sierra Leone, a country frequently plagued by coup d'etats and civil war.

But I wasn't in Dorchester to speak to Verster about his drug exploits. I had made the journey to England to ask him to repeat a story he had told to me four years earlier, but because it was in confidence, I could then not publish it.

It was a story so poignant that it had brought tears to the battle-hardened soldier's eyes.

Rich Verster has been haunted and tormented for many years by the memories of Cassinga and the day he had had to perform mercy killings on behalf of the SADF. Within the confines of Her Majesty's Prison in Dorchester, he agreed to speak about Cassinga again. Twenty years on, he was still unable to forget the unforgettable.

The air in and around Cassinga was filled with the smell of smoke, gunpowder and death. Verster landed in a tree, but managed to free himself. He started looking for the rest of his platoon and found that his mate Skillie Human had plunged to his death after his parachute had failed to open.

The parachute drop did not go according to plan. Smoke billowing from the burning camp conspired with a stronger than expected wind and the result was that some of the paratroopers landed up on the wrong side of the Culonga River. However, at two minutes to nine, the ground attack unit had regrouped and started the assault on Cassinga.

Verster was decorated for bravery for neutralising an enemy anti-aircraft position. Paratrooper Norman Reeves was bleeding to death, but the Air Force helicopter couldn't get close enough to evacuate him. Verster took an RPG rocket launcher, crawled towards the enemy position and blew it up.

For the next few hours, fighting raged in and around the town as the last Swapo guerrillas fought from the trenches and bunkers. And then the guns fell silent, and

Verster and his men could enter Cassinga to wipe out the attempts at resistance.

As they approached the town, they could hear the lamenting and moaning of the wounded. The bombs from the Canberras and Buccaneers had spared no one. People were buried underneath rubble and shrapnel had ripped off limbs and torn bodies open.

Verster said that from the corner of his eye, he saw a silhouette of someone crouched in a corner, his rifle pointing in the air.

He turned around and fired his R1 at the figure. As he walked closer, the body convulsed and the person died.

'It was a nine-or-ten-year old boy, clutching a wooden rifle.'

When he saw his own child a few days later, he just cried.

SADF video footage shot after the raid shows young, white soldiers in brown uniforms walking through the smoking ruins of Cassinga. Young children cry with pain and shock and in bombed-out buildings ragged and torn posters of Swapo leader Sam Nujoma dangle from the walls.

In a mass grave lie dozens of bodies of women, children and soldiers, their legs and arms and broken bodies entangled in a mass of flesh.

'They never told us beforehand that this was what it was going to be like. They never told us about the women and children. Many thought it was going to be an adventure.'

In the meantime, Air Force helicopters arrived to evacuate the casualties and airlift the paratroopers back to safety in Namibia. In the choppers were a team of medical orderlies and three doctors to treat the wounded. There were only 11 wounded on the South African side, so the orderlies could attend to Swapo's injured, especially the women and children.

There were only three SADF doctors and too many wounded on the enemy side to treat, too many survivors who were so badly mutilated that they were doomed to die.

Verster and two of his men were given orders: comb the killing area and decide who we can save or take back to Namibia. If people are too badly wounded or hurt, shoot them.

On that day, Rich Verster had to choose: who to let live, and who to let die.

He walked into a bombed building, filled with scorched and charred bodies. They were all dead, except for one, whose eyes showed signs of life. The person was so badly burnt that Verster couldn't see whether it was a man or a woman. The person made no sound, but looked at the paratrooper, who lifted his rifle and pulled the trigger.

In some of the trenches, he said, people were piled three high. There were people in agony and pain everywhere. They shot the badly wounded as they went along.

In one of the trenches, he says, he heard a baby cry. He started searching for the child, and found a baby girl full of blood, but she appeared to be unhurt. The infant was lying on top of her mother, who was holding her with one hand.

Verster wanted to pick the baby up, but the mother grasped her child and held on to her with what was probably her last strength. They had to tear the child from her.

A piece of shrapnel had ripped the woman's abdomen open. Her intestines were showing and she was so badly wounded that she was breathing through a gash in her stomach. Verster said he could see that she was pregnant.

She looked at them holding her baby, and stretched her arm out in desperation for her child.

'Shoot her!' somebody said next to Verster.

He did.

On his way back to Namibia, Rich Verster cried. 'I didn't become a parabat to slaughter innocents. I just wanted to be the best. We killed many Swapo soldiers during our assault on Cassinga. That was war, but nobody told me that I would have to kill people who were dying and unarmed.

'I suppose there were just too many wounded and we couldn't leave them to die in pain. I don't know why I was chosen to kill. Some were conscious, some were not. Some were making sounds, others not.'

He often thinks about the women and her baby, and wonders what happened to the child and where and how she ended up. She must be the same age as his own son.

'This is the dark side of my being, the dark room inside me. I am a soldier, but that day in Cassinga I killed in cold blood. But there was no hope for her. I had to shoot her. She looked at me. I can never describe what it did to me.'

Most military observers agree today that Cassinga was both a military base and refugee camp. Swapo guerrillas were trained in a base in the town and armed infiltrations into Namibia were planned from Cassinga. But it was also a safe haven for thousands of Namibian refugees who had fled South African repression in Namibia.

Nobody seems to be sure how many Swapo soldiers and Namibian refugees died at Cassinga. The SADF said more than 850 'terrorists' died, while other military observers put the death toll as high as 1 600. Whatever the real figure, amongst the dead were hundreds of women and children. The body count on the South African side: three dead, one missing, and eleven wounded.[5]

Rich Verster is a man who is mentally scarred by the sheer horror of war. He also suffers from post-traumatic stress disorder, but unlike killers like Wouter Mentz, Rolf Gevers or Willie Nortje who led their blindfolded victims into woods to execute them, blew bodies to smithereens or assassinated deaf people in their beds, Verster contracted his illness at Cassinga, a battle hailed by apartheid's top brass as a glorious and decisive victory for South Africa in its battle to maintain control of Namibia and to stop Swapo from crossing the Angolan border. In Parliament, PW Botha spoke about a 'defeat for the dark and evil forces of Communism and terrorism'.

After the raid, Verster was decorated for bravery. But when the generals pinned the medal to his chest, they were unaware of the strife and conflict within the young soldier.

The trauma that Rich Verster suffered in Cassinga was only diagnosed three years later as post-traumatic stress disorder. By that time, he was in jail, facing multiple murder charges. He was accused of murdering 14 tribesmen during a faction fight in Msinga in KwaZulu in 1979. He also faced charges of conspiracy to murder, terrorism, and illegal possession of arms and ammunition.

According to evidence produced in court, Verster became embroiled in a faction fight between the pro-Inkatha Sithole and pro-ANC Zwane clans in the Msinga area of KwaZulu in June 1979.[6]

He denied in court that he had ever taken part physically in the faction fight, although he had agreed to help the Sitholes. He admitted that he had cleaned and oiled guns for them and had helped them with planning the attack. Evidence was that he had tried to recruit fellow paratroopers to come along and shoot 'houties' (a derogatory name for black people). During the trial, Verster acquired the nickname of the 'Soldier of Terror'.

It was whilst in jail that his psychological condition was diagnosed by a military psychologist. He relived the events at Cassinga and under hypnosis saw and described the eyes of the dying mother when her baby had been taken away. His psychologist wrote a letter to Magnus Malan in which he warned him: 'The machine that made him, is now manipulating him.'

Verster was found guilty of conspiracy to commit murder, participating in terrorist activities, illegal possession of firearms and contravening the Defence Act. He was sentenced to eight years' imprisonment.[7]

In Dorchester Prison, Verster told me he became involved in the faction fight when one day in 1979, he was approached by a Zulu man who had grown up with him as a child in the Msinga area. Ben Sithole's mother worked as the domestic worker in his family's house. Verster says that Ben was probably his best childhood friend, and that they did everything together, although, he does add: 'I *donnered* (smacked) him quite often.'

On entering adulthood, Ben went to work on the mines and Verster went to Potchefstroom University to study law. Verster comes from a prominent Afrikaner family which includes a former head of the South African Air Force, a head of the South African Prison Services and a general in Military Intelligence.

Verster was an academic failure, but great fun to be with. He had a pilot's licence and was doing part-time crop-spraying at this time. Male students would line up for a flip over the women's residence where female students were tanning on top of the building!

One of his fellow law students was Anton Ackermann, the state advocate in the Msinga trial and the prosecutor who would put Eugene de Kock behind bars for life. Shortly after my visit to Dorchester, Ackermann flew to the United Kingdom to consult with Verster about using him as a possible witness against Ferdi Barnard.

After Cassinga, Verster abandoned his studies. His name was published in the newspapers as one of the SADF soldiers to be decorated for bravery. Ben Sithole saw it, looked him up and the two were reunited.

Ben was looking for help. He said that the Zwane clan was killing the Sithole women and children and Verster had to assist them. Verster agreed, and for the next few weeks, trained and armed the Sithole clan and planned an attack.

On the night of the attack, he attended the rituals of the the sangomas, at which the men smoked marijuana and prayed to their forefathers. Ben made a small incision next to Verster's eye. His Zulu friend explained that since he had no forefathers he could pray to, the cut would help his spirit to escape his body if he should be killed. Verster joined the Sithole clan, armed with pistols and short stabbing spears, in their attack. The next morning, 14 mutilated bodies of the Zwane clan were discovered. Ben himself was killed and his liver removed.

Verster says he was already working for Military Intelligence at the time of the massacre and that the operation was approved by his superiors, but I didn't have enough time during my visit to him in prison to question him in more detail to substantiate his story.

What is true, however, is that he served less than half his sentence, and when he was released he walked out of prison into a full-time Military Intelligence position.

Rich Verster became a spy master within the Directorate of Covert Collection (DCC), a secret unit within Military Intelligence. He is vague when he talks about his role in DCC, but he gave instructions to Eugene Riley, Sam Malgas and, in later years, Ferdi Barnard, whom he had met in prison. After Barnard had left the CCB, Verster invited him to use his criminal talents in the DCC. Verster also worked closely with Eugene de Kock and his men at Vlakplaas.

Verster says he worked on organised crime and used Barnard and Malgas to introduce him to, and infiltrate, the underworld, but like so many of his cohorts, he himself became involved in crime, although he said he never made any money from his activities.

According to evidence led in the Eugene de Kock trial, De Kock received two rhino horns and 1 743 counterfeit R50 notes 'from a friend in Military Intelligence' and submitted claims for a bogus informant. Chappies Klopper testified that he received counterfeit American dollars from De Kock which he had to hand in at the syndicate fraud unit in Pretoria and write out false claims.

The counterfeit money and rhino horn came from Rich Verster, and although the Vlakplaas men made tens of thousands of rands out of false claims for bogus informers, he said he got nothing. He was also involved in supplying weapons to them, for which they submitted false claims.

Verster was never in the 'inner circle' of the DCC – simply because he wasn't trusted and he was often out of control. His financial statements seldom balanced, and if ever questioned about it, he would simply say: 'But we're busy with an operation!'

While still a DCC agent, he formed private business partnerships to export diamonds from Namibia and import food into Angola and was also investigated for smuggling gold from Zimbabwe. At one stage, he drove a black Porsche 911.

Verster said he was Ferdi Barnard's closest confidant, and that Barnard had confessed to him in great detail how he had shot David Webster and that Calla Botha had been in the car with him. Verster said he had reported Barnard's confession to Colonel Gerrie Bornman of Military Intelligence, but his superior officer told him not to get involved in the affairs of the CCB.

He said he knew that his agents were involved in drug smuggling and diamond 'knocks', but allowed these activities to continue as they provided him with invaluable information about organised crime which he reported to his superiors.

'There were times when I felt desperately sorry for Ferdi, but there were also times when I thought I should kill him because he was such a menace to society. I once found him at the Summit Club in Hillbrow, and when I saw him, blood was coming from his nose because of all the cocaine he had snorted. His head fell and he was ashamed that I had to see him in that state.'

I first met Rich Verster in January 1993, days after he and a group of Military Intelligence officers had been fired by State President FW de Klerk. The purge of the security forces was the result of a raid by the Goldstone Commission on the offices of the DCC. Mr Justice Richard Goldstone reported to the State President that the DCC could have been involved in third-force activities and even in murder.

Days later, I knocked on Verster's door and asked if he would speak to me. He invited me in. My most vivid memory of Rich Verster, a likeable and amiable man, was of him standing in his lounge practising his golf swing. (He is a scratch golfer.)

Verster was destitute, bitter and angry. He couldn't understand why he had been fired. He said FW de Klerk was like a commander who deserted his men in the field without food.

'Everything we did, every project we executed, had the full blessing and knowledge of our superiors. I don't want to go to jail again. I want to forget and start a new life.'

While he had been spending his nights in Soweto devising diabolical plots against the ANC and PAC, he said, some of the generals had already been negotiating their retrenchment and early pension packages.

I spent several days with Verster while he was contemplating telling me about the activities of the DCC. While we were negotiating the terms under which he would speak, Inkatha leader Chief Mangosuthu Buthelezi (today the Minister of Home Affairs) unexpectedly held a press conference in Durban, at which he accused me and a colleague at the *Sunday Star* of being National Intelligence Service agents.

Four months earlier, we had written an investigation about gunrunning by Inkatha, and Buthelezi said at the press conference that this was nothing but a smear campaign by the National Intelligence Service against him and his organisation. Buthelezi's allegations were made just as Verster was about to reveal the dirty secrets of the DCC – which included the supply of weapons to Inkatha.

Verster saw reports of the allegations against me on national television and when I knocked on his door a few days later, he refused to speak to me. He thought I had been 'planted' on him and that I reported our conversations back to my 'handler' in the National Intelligence Service.

Verster disappeared into obscurity, until I learnt of his arrest in the United Kingdom.

After his dismissal from Military Intelligence, Rich Verster was left to fend for himself. And so he finally turned to Sierra Leone, a country engulfed in a brutal civil war.

In May 1995, the South Africa mercenary organisation Executive Outcomes, one of the world's leading purveyors of private military muscle, arrived in the capital of Freetown with a contract and a promise to restore law and order in exchange for $15 million and a share of the country's diamond riches.

Much of Executive Outcomes' military might was focused in Kono, the rich diamond-mining province in the east of the country. Ten months after the South Africans had captured the region, tens of thousands of foreigners had flocked in behind them, hoping to get rich.

One of them was Rich Verster, who had come to Sierra Leone hot on the heels of the mercenaries. He wasn't part of Executive Outcomes, but he had contacts in the organisation as he had fought and worked with many of its men.

He would join the men of EO – as they became known – in their home-made bush saloon, replete with stools, carved bar, a refrigerator and beer. Every Friday night, they had a real braaivleis, with steak flown in from South Africa. Like the EO mercenaries he was a battle-hardened soldier who had been at war for more than 15 years.

American journalist Elizabeth Rubin, on a mission to Sierra Leone in 1996 to investigate the involvement of Executive Outcomes in that country, found Rich Verster in Kono. One afternoon, Rubin wrote in the American *Harper's Magazine,* she drove with Verster and his Sierra Leone workers along a muddy track he had cleared through the bush. He was transporting his workers to a mining site on the Bafi River, and they took the occasion to complain that he wasn't providing them with enough food.[8]

'Rich said nothing. Then, suddenly, he slammed on the brakes, jumped out, ran behind the Land Rover, and returned to the window holding a small poison-ous night adder. The Africans shrank back in terror as he dangled the snake over his face, bit off its head, spat it out, and dropped the body in his mouth. His jaws and cheeks shook as he chewed up the snake and swallowed it. The Africans murmured words to God.

'Rick spat out some adder mulch and, trying to ape the local tongue, said: "Why you always wait for me for food? You hungry, go to de bush and get food. De snake and de bush food build de body immunity against disease. That is what they teach us in the South African Defence Forces."

'Later,' Rubin said, 'the local chief gathered the people around Rich under a corron tree. He said that Rich was an African, a black man with a white skin who understood the black man's troubles and had come to end their suffering. The chief dubbed him Moses: like Moses saving the Israelites from Pharaoh, Rich had saved the people from their corrupt former overlords.

'Behind the myth, the facts were much more prosaic, and typical of the coarse brutality of the place: Rich, a 220-pound former paratrooper, had punched out the teeth of the corrupt mining boss who had preceded him and promised the same for anyone else who tried to mess with him.'

The Dorchester prison authorities allowed me two one-hour sessions with Verster, far too short to record a history of secret wars and covert operations spanning a period of 20 years. I doubt whether Her Majesty's warders in Dorchester knew who Johann Friedrich Verster really was, but when I requested the visit, one said: 'Nice bloke, that. Pity what he did.'

When I arrived for my second visit, Verster was dressed in a Northern Transvaal rugby sweater, and when he saw me, he said: 'Take me with you. I can't take it any more. I want to go home.'

Verster has pleaded guilty to the charges of smuggling and possession of marijuana, and has turned state witness against his millionaire accomplice. Verster admitted in court that he was a former employee of Military Intelligence and had been involved in smuggling drugs-for-arms from South Africa.

Verster realises that he will probably have to spend some years in prison in the United Kingdom, unless some deal can be made between the justice departments of the two countries so that he can serve his sentence in South Africa.

Like most of the apartheid killers and fighters I have described in this book, Rich Verster fought for a way of life he believed in deeply. As the political land-scape shifted, these former heroes and guardians of apartheid and white civilisa-tion became social and moral outcasts on the margins of society. In a bizarre way, we have inherited a new 'lost generation'. Rich Verster is one of them.

Chapter Twenty

Guns for September

'Who was behind her killing?' I asked him.[1]

He looked at me with his bleak green eyes, hurled another whisky down his throat and said: 'No, if I tell you, you will tell others. Then I will have to kill you.' He laughed hysterically in a high-pitched voice.

The man sitting in front of me was Dirk Francois Stoffberg. Alias Francis Borg, Herbert Tanzer, Derek Strauss. A former bank clerk and Sunday school teacher who became an international gunrunner. Also a murderer, fraudster, smuggler, money launderer, spy and self-confessed apartheid assassin.

But unlike so many others who made killing their business: flamboyant, eccentric, at times even funny and likeable. There was a time when he had driven two Italian sports cars, trained race horses and stayed in penthouses in the finest hotels in Europe and Asia. He had entertained His Excellency the Chilean ambassador to South Africa and the exiled King Leka of the Albanians in his living room, while underneath the floor was a cellar where hundreds of thousands of United States dollars were locked away – money he had accumulated from arms smuggling.

Dirk Stoffberg was above all a playboy. When I met him in June 1993, he was married to wife number seven. She was a German – whom he described as 'teutonic' – who had four years earlier left her husband and two children to join Stoffberg as he was fleeing justice in Europe. Before her, it seems, he had been married to two women at the same time, one Chinese, the other South African. There were also Israeli, French and British wives.

He kept a file on each of them, together with the respective marriage and divorce certificates, a photograph of each wife naked, and a brassiere and a pair of panties. At times, mostly when he was drunk, he would play German march music, put on his Nazi uniform, parade up and down his verandah, click his heels, do the goosestep, salute and enjoy himself. Like a little boy playing Hitler.

He was also cruel and ruthless. He abused and assaulted women. When his son's dog snapped at him, he hung the dog in a tree. He peddled arms, ranging from missiles to mustard gas, to some of the worlds's most notorious regimes: Libya, Iran and Iraq. In Hong Kong, he lured a man to the seventh floor of a building, from which he was thrown out of a window.

'People disappeared and they would have accidents. There are various ways and means of solving an accident. If blackmail or financial destruction doesn't work, then certain accidents come into play,' Stoffberg said to me.

He had extensive links with the South African security establishment. Every time he returned from an overseas mission, a senior National Intelligence Service agent would debrief him. He had close ties with the police and started working for Military Intelligence in 1987. In fact, Stoffberg was prepared to do whatever for whoever was prepared to pay. Money was his supreme master.

He loved to boast about his achievements in the international weapons trade, his money, his women and his James Bond-like lifestyle. He would justify assassinations by saying: 'Well, every soldier is a killer, isn't he? So what's the difference between the soldier on the frontline and me fighting behind enemy lines so that you can sleep peacefully at night? We both have to kill.'

Stoffberg would often – especially in bars – talk about the assassination in 1988 of Dulcie September, the ANC's chief representative in France. Shortly after September was gunned down, Stoffberg was linked to the murder by a French newspaper quoting French and Belgian intelligence sources. The influential *Le Monde* said in a leading front-page article that South Africa had a special death squad in Europe that was headed by a man by the name of Dirk Stoffberg.

'I still don't know how they got my name,' he would say, start talking about September, stop himself, get aggressive, threaten me and drink more. But he did admit that he had been involved in her assassination. He told me about the assassins that had been hired to shoot her, the money they were paid and a hit list Scotland Yard had found in his possession.

But he never told me who he was working for at the time, who masterminded the killing and who gave him his instructions.

Dirk Stoffberg took his secrets to his grave. Shortly before nine o'clock on Wednesday night, July 20, 1994, at least four shots were fired in his luxurious house overlooking Hartebeespoort Dam, west of Pretoria. Police found the bodies of Dirk and Susanne Stoffberg on the patio. At first, it looked as though Stoffberg had shot his wife and then himself. A few weeks later, police opened a murder docket.

It wasn't suicide. Dirk and Susanne Stoffberg were murdered.

He died as he had lived: by the sword.

Early morning, March 29, 1988. An assassin waited for Dulcie September to arrive at the ANC's office near the Gare du Nord in the Tenth District of Paris. No one heard the shots, no one saw the killer flee. The 45-year-old activist had her key in one hand, the mail in the other, as the gunman fired five, 22-calibre bullets into her head and body. The pistol was fitted with a silencer. It was a highly professional execution, planned with precision.[2]

The assassination of September followed days after Belgian police defused a bomb placed outside the ANC's office in Brussels. Seven weeks earlier, an unidentified gunman had fired two shots through a window of the same office, narrowly missing Godfrey Motsepe, the ANC's chief representative in Belgium.

Dulcie September, born into a 'coloured' family in the Cape, completed her teacher training at Battswood College, and had been teaching for some years when the expulsion of friends from whites-only residential areas stung her into active politics towards the end of the 1960s. She was arrested and detained several times before leaving the country to join the ANC, but friends say she was never actively involved in the military structures of the ANC.

The ANC blamed the killing on South African hitmen. Foreign Minister Pik Botha dismissed the allegations, suggesting instead that September was the victim of an internal struggle within the ANC.

September was the first prominent ANC leader to be gunned down in Europe. French President Francois Mitterand said the murder had revived the question of economic sanctions against Pretoria. He added: 'I have had suspicions about the South African regime for a long time, but with regard to the assassination of September, I can say nothing definite, even if my intuition tells me something else.'[3]

Two days after the murder, Dirk Stoffberg made a phone call from Frankfurt in Germany to Linda Stoffberg, his estranged wife (wife number six) back in South Africa. According to Linda, he said to her: 'A terrible thing has happened. I had to go to Paris, but I'm back again. They're accusing me of killing that black bitch.'

'What happened?' she asked him.

'I didn't actually do it. But you know me, I get people to do things.'

Stoffberg phoned Linda throughout the the week. He was frantic. He eventually said to her he had hired assassins to pull the trigger. At the time, he was a member of a criminal gang in Europe that specialised in assassinations, blackmail, arms smuggling and money laundering. They called themselves the Adler Group, and could have been involved in the murder of September – on a contract from South African Military Intelligence.

Le Monde said that a South African death squad had been operating in Europe a few months before the killing of September. The newspaper said that Stoffberg and another South African had been questioned by British security officers at London's Heathrow Airport after a list of ANC names had been found in their possession. The death squad – called the 'Z-Squad' by the newspaper, was supported by an extreme right-wing Frenchman working for the South African Embassy. He had been named by the media as Jean-Dominique Taousson, a former member of the clandestine OAS movement which had fought against President Charles de Gaulle when he had decided to quit Algeria. Taousson published a far-right newsletter which was reportedly funded from South African secret funds and distributed to European parliamentarians and businessmen with South African interests.[4]

Stoffberg told me about the agent who had been questioned with him at Heathrow Airport. 'There was this fellow Mitchell, who was stationed in Geneva. He had just come from South Africa and was linked to Military Intelligence. He gave me a list of names and addresses of all the ANC operatives that were based in London. I met Mitchell in the airport coffee room where we were approached by two customs officers who asked us to accompany them to a room. I told them the list was names of friends and acquaintances and their addresses to whom I wanted to send Christmas cards. They let us go.'

'What was the list?' I asked him.

'These were future targets, to put it that way, if you want to know the truth,' he said, and laughed hysterically. He wouldn't tell me to whom he had to give the list, but it could have been the same agent or agents that were behind the killing of September.

The Mitchell that Stoffberg referred to was David Campbell Mitchell. According to the magazine *Private Eye,* he shared an office in Geneva, Switzerland with the Honorary Consul for Malawi. 'He has even more interesting friends: he is very close to the South African government. He has a holiday property in Knysna, and was on a holiday visit there last year to attend to commercial work when he was approached by South African Military Intelligence. They were looking for someone who could move a lot of money around, set up front companies and assist in sanctions busting.'

A few months after the murder of September, Stoffberg befriended a German journalist by the name of Jurgen Roth in Frankfurt. 'First he talk about arms dealing, especially dealing with Iran. And after some drinks, he's talking about Dulcie September, and he told me he was involved in the murder of September. He never directly said that he was engaged, but said he was part of the network who organised the killing of September. I believe he's very aggressive. He told me several times if I talk about this, he will kill me. Always when I saw him, he was drunk. In the morning he drank whisky, till the evening.'[5]

When Jurgen Roth met Stoffberg, the arms smuggler was a member of the Adler Group and was trying to peddle chemicals and nuclear material to Middle Eastern countries. He was constantly drunk and on the run from the German and Swiss authorities. The South African playboy who had once driven a Ferrari, dressed his women in lace and had had a million dollars at his feet, was heading for his final fall. A dark life of deceit and secrecy was about to come to an end.

Linda Stoffberg thought she was going to be wife number three and that the flamboyant man who sent her roses and French champagne minutes after he set eyes on her was in the 'import-export' business and that the Arabs, Chileans and Chinese who visited him were just ordinary business associates.

Linda was, in fact, at least wife number five or six, his companies 'Fire-Arms International', 'Iran International Trading Company', 'Air Swaziland' and 'Teiger Handels AG' were nothing but front companies for moving arms around the world illegally, and many of the eccentric and fascinating people who visited him were surplus merchants who dealt in instruments of death. And then there was the spy from the National Intelligence Agency, the security policemen and the man from Military Intelligence consulting him behind closed doors.

Linda Stoffberg is an intelligent woman. She knows who Dirk Stoffberg was. She knows about the killings, the weapons smuggling, the money laundering. He betrayed her, lied to her, and abandoned her and their young child.

And yet, she adores him. Her loyalty to him is absolute. 'I had the best time of my life with him and nobody can ever take his place,' she said. To her, he was a good man who was never fully understood. In turn, Stoffberg said to me that Linda was the only woman he had ever really trusted.

They met at the beginning of 1980 when Linda, visiting a friend and just divorced, saw Stoffberg walking in and out of an office with the sign 'Teiger Handels AG'. He was dashingly handsome, flamboyant and interesting people were with him: a Frenchman, a Spaniard, an Arab.

Out of curiosity, Linda walked up to him and asked him: 'What work do you do?'

'Export-import,' he said, and ten minutes later, the champagne and roses arrived. Six weeks later, he asked her to marry him. He said he had prayed to God, who had told him she was the right person for him.

Linda knew little about him. He was a son of a bank manager who became a bank clerk himself. He was at one time also a Sunday school teacher. His father died when he was 12 years old and he had an unhappy childhood. When his mother died, he refused to attend her funeral. When his brother died, he said: 'Good, he was a mean shit anyway,' and didn't go to the funeral either.

Linda thought she was number three, not number five or six. When they got married, Stoffberg had three children, although he accepted only two as his own. His son Anton died when he was six by falling out of a window, while his daughter Cheryl has four children with four different men as fathers. Francois was born when Stoffberg was married to Monique, his second wife. Shortly after the birth, Stoffberg denied that Francois was his child and chased Monique away.

Stoffberg and Linda were married in November 1980. Linda wore a white lace dress. 'All his weirdo friends were there, but none of my family was allowed to attend. The reception went on for three days.'

It took Linda two months to realise that something strange was going on. 'I heard him talk about tanks and helicopters late at night, but when I asked him what was going on, he said he would confide in me once I had signed an oath of secrecy.'

Each and every person who has ever had any secret dealing with Stoffberg, including his wives, had to sign his personal 'oath of secrecy'. 'In case of violation of this statement on my part I shall be subject to punishment according to the related laws of the Kingdom of Saudi Arabia and/or Republic of South Africa.'

When I asked Stoffberg about his oath, he said: 'I used it as a psychological weapon.'

'Did you ever have to use it?'

'Only once. There was a certain German accountant in Frankfurt. I gave him a sample of chemicals the Libyans wanted. He wouldn't pay me. I took out my knife, grabbed him by the tie and cut his face – as a warning.'

After she had taken the oath, Stoffberg told Linda that he was busy selling 50 American-built M48A tanks and 7 500 rounds of ammunition to Taiwan – despite an arms embargo against that country. A contract between Stoffberg and three Taiwanese generals, acting on behalf of the Combined Services Forces of Taiwan, was signed on September 11, 1979. The tanks were ostensibly to have been sold to Spain, where they would have been refitted by Chrysler of Spain, before ostensibly being resold to the Royal Thai Army, although they were in fact intended for Taiwan. The contract was worth more than $36 million.[5]

A false end-user certificate stating that the final destination of the tanks was Thailand, was obtained through a local businessman who got a commission on the deal. The Nigerian military attache in London was allegedly paid R20 000 for providing a false end-user certificate stating that spare parts for the tanks were going to the Nigerian Army, when in fact they were to go to Taiwan. (End-user certificates are issued by countries wishing to buy arms, and state that the country issuing the certificate is the genuine and ultimate buyer of the weapons.)

Suddenly, Linda Stoffberg found herself embroiled in the murky world of arms smuggling. She was introduced to his handlers in the National Intelligence Service and the security policemen who frequently visited their house. One of his handlers in National Intelligence was Colonel At Nel, who more than a decade later was exposed as a commander of the Directorate of Covert Collection, a Military Intelligence dirty-tricks unit and death squad.

Linda brought hundreds of thousands of United States dollars into South Africa. Stoffberg was at the pinnacle of his career. Neil Hooper, a journalist friend at the *Sunday Times* whom he had endlessly wined and dined, named him Dirk 'Sanctions Buster' Stoffberg and an 'international businessman extraordinary'.[6]

Stoffberg had started working for the Security Branch at the age of 21 when he married Anne Steyn, the daughter of Brigadier Louis Steyn. He was still a bank clerk when he became involved in the transfer of secret police funds from France to South Africa. He eventually received special intelligence training.

Stoffberg's brother-in-law was appointed South Africa's ambassador to Iran, and before long, the gunrunner had set up 'Iran International Trading Company' to foster relations between the two countries.

He ventured into the arms market in the late 1970s when he marketed a Rhodesian-made sub-machine gun in South Africa and Europe. The nine-millimetre hand carbine was called the 'Kommando', and Neil Hooper called it 'Dirk's supergun'.

In the next year or two, Stoffberg would team up with some of Europe's most notorious gunrunners: the Britons Mike Aspin and Len Hammond, jailed in London in October 1982 for smuggling weapons to South Africa in contravention of the United Nations arms embargo; the Belgian Francois Laroche and the

American fugitive, gunrunner and 'bounty hunter' Reinier Jacobi. Stoffberg founded ten front companies throughout the world to conduct his arms deals.

In 1981, South African passport in hand, he obtained the advanced blessing of the Iraqi government and flew with a chartered jet into Baghdad to conduct arms deals. A week after his arrival, Israeli aircraft bombed Iraq's nuclear reactor at Tamuz, about 20 kilometes from the Baghdad hotel where he was staying. He was detained in his hotel room on suspicion that he was a spy, but was eventually released and introduced to Iraqi generals. He signed a contract of $7,7 million for the delivery of small arms and ammunition to Iraq.[7]

Shortly afterwards, Stoffberg, Aspin and Hammond were implicated in the sale of 1 000 British-manufactured machine guns to Iran, at the time holding three British citizens hostage. The guns were destined for the Revolutionary Guard, principal arm of the Ayatollah Khomeini's Islamic regime.

But Stoffberg was also a supreme conman. He offered the Iranians 50 Bell helicopter troop transporters at $1 million a piece. Contracts were drawn up and Volkskas Bank in Pretoria was notified of the deal. The arrangement rapidly fell apart when the Iranians wanted to inspect the helicopters – impossible because they were in bits and pieces all over South Africa.

One of his more odd relationships was with King Leka of the Albanians. The king, who has never even sat on the throne, left his fatherland in 1939 when his father, King Zog, was exiled during Mussolini's invasion of Albania. King Zog and Queen Geraldine were forced to flee to Greece with the one-day-old Leka.

The exiled king and his family came to live in South Africa in 1980. Stoffberg and Leka had several meetings to discuss the training and arming of a guerrilla force that would eventually invade Albania and overthrow the Communist regime. In a letter to Stoffberg, Leka wrote about 'the feasibility of training a unit of 300 men with a possibility of eventually accepting 1 500 men'. Nothing ever came of it.

Stoffberg said he became a Security Branch agent at the end of 1982 and was instructed to spy on the Afrikaner theologian Dr Beyers Naude and the South African Council of Churches (SACC). He said he recruited an SACC employee by the name of Andre, equipped him with a spy camera and listening devices, and told him to photograph financial statements and to bug budget meetings. Stoffberg said the investigation unearthed some corruption in the SACC and the information was leaked to Naude's funders and to the World Council of Churches.

Neil Hooper wrote afterwards in the *Sunday Times:* 'A West German intelligence agent is in South Africa to probe spending by the South African Council of Churches.'[8]

But Stoffberg's espionage wasn't always as fortuitous. He went to London to try and recruit a local journalist to spy on the ANC. 'Unbeknown to me, this man wasn't as right wing as I thought. In fact, he was communist.' Shortly afterwards, *Private Eye* described Stoffberg as a 'comical figure' and the 'world's worst spy'.[9]

Linda Stoffberg then became part of Dirk Stoffberg's twilight world. 'I was shit scared. I didn't know what was going on.'

In 1980, a Belgian by the name of Francois Laroche entered South Africa under the name of 'JF de Bernard' and became Stoffberg's business partner. Laroche was wanted in France for illegal arms sales to various African countries and an Interpol warrant had been issued for his arrest for the alleged murder of a policeman in Chile and for escaping from prison.[10]

Stoffberg and Laroche set up a front company by the name of 'Air Swaziland' which chartered aircraft all over the world to transport arms to South Africa and the Middle East. Stoffberg introduced Laroche to his handlers in the National Intelligence Service and the Security Branch.

Stoffberg said that while Laroche was in South Africa, French authorities found out about his whereabouts and sent a security agent by the name of Commandant Piaget to investigate his activities. 'Piaget was like a bloodhound. He visited our offices and got hold of telex tapes and documents which he stuffed into his briefcase.'

Stoffberg said they had to stop Piaget. When the Frenchman was returning from the Air Swaziland office at Lanseria, a hired marksman shot out the front tyre of his car. The car overturned and Piaget was rendered unconscious. Stoffberg said he and Laroche then took the tapes and destroyed them.

Not so, says Linda Stoffberg. She claims that Laroche and Stoffberg decided to get rid of Piaget because he knew too much. After the car accident, the Frenchman, seriously injured, was taken to the Edenvale Hospital. The two gunrunners, dressed as male nurses, went to the hospital to kidnap him.

'I was sitting in the car when they came out with Piaget, covered in bandages, in a wheelchair. In the car, Laroche held a pistol against his head and we drove to a private hangar at Jan Smuts Airport.'

Piaget was taken from the car, put into a light aircraft, and flown away. She did not see him again and Stoffberg never spoke about it. Laroche left the country and fled to Paraguay.

Shocked by what had happened, Linda decided to leave Stoffberg. She told him she was visiting an aunt in Durban, but planned to fly from there to a friend in the United States. Just after she arrived in Durban, Stoffberg phoned her and said he knew about her plans. He came to fetch her and said to her: 'There is no way you can get out of this marriage. You are mine for ever.'

She stayed, and started travelling around the world with him to do weapons deals. 'We only flew first class. We stayed for weeks in a penthouse in the Hyatt Hotel in Hong Kong where Dirk had to fetch US dollars stuffed into his safety deposit box at the hotel every day.' She was introduced to Reinier Jacobi, nicknamed 'Teddybear', and Ross Wood, known as 'Spiderman'. Jacobi, who used the names of Rex Johnson and Ralph Koenig, is widely described as a 'bounty hunter' and was arrested for drug trafficking in Hong Kong in 1991.

Jacobi was the leader of the Adler Group. I asked Stoffberg what the Adler Group was.

'This was a dirty tricks organisation, involved in assassinations.'

'Was Adler also involved in arms deals?'

'Yes, of course, all sorts of dirty business. We used the Union Bank of Switzerland and several front companies. Our group was based in Hong Kong. We were also involved in the moving of certain nuclear materials and operated a brothel out of Macau. This was a wonderful source of information. Blackmail was extensively used by the Adler Group. One highly placed American security official was into whipping and he visited the brothel often. He was also blackmailed.'

One night, Stoffberg said to Linda: 'Somebody has double-crossed us. I must leave.' When he came back later that night, he was 'killing' himself with laughter. He told her how he had lured the 'double-crosser' – a Belgian gunrunner – to the fifth floor of a building where 'Spiderman' had waited for him. The man had fallen from a window to his death.

When I asked Stoffberg about this, he simply said: 'That was a very unfortunate accident. Accidents did come into play. Spiderman and Jacobi were very effective killers. They were very sturdy men and had no morals.'

Stoffberg claimed that the Adler Group worked for the American Central Intelligence Agency (CIA). It is possible, but what is more clear is that the Adler Group was a gang of freelance criminals prepared to work for whoever was prepared to pay.

South African customs records show that Jacobi and Wood visited South Africa in 1982. According to Stoffberg, their purpose was to meet security policemen and Military Intelligence officials. The authorities were concerned about links between the Palestine Liberation Organisation (PLO) and the PAC and the ANC. There were also rumours that Carlos 'The Jackal' Ramirez was training South African guerrillas in Libya.

After a stay of several months in Hong Kong, Stoffberg and Linda moved to Taiwan where they stayed for three months in a penthouse in the Ritz Plaza Hotel in Taipei. One day, Stoffberg consulted a Chinese fortune teller, who took his hand and told him that he would die a violent death. The gunrunner was very upset.

Linda fell pregnant and wanted to come home. Stoffberg said she had to bring some money with her, and two leather bags were stuffed with $1 million in cash. 'This was my hand luggage. At Jan Smuts, I declared a few items I bought as gifts and walked through customs.'

Stoffberg came back shortly afterwards, and the couple moved to a smallholding in North Riding near Johannesburg. The money was put into a safe underneath the house. Stoffberg would say to her: 'I never asked God for this, because as a child I had nothing.'

He bought himself Ferrari and Maserati sports cars and gave Linda a Mercedes sports car for her birthday. 'He didn't know what to do with all the money. He bought a thousand bottles of good red wine and employed a wine steward.'

Linda said Stoffberg had a special way with women. He had his own bathroom and would groom himself for hours. 'He would make women feel beautiful. He always smelled divine. Women from all over the world wrote him love letters.' He said to Linda not to worry as he would never have extra-marital affairs: 'If I get tired of one woman, I move on to the next.'

He had an incredible temper. He threw things around and screamed at business associates. Black workers on the smallholding bore the brunt of his temper – for example, he tied a maid to a lamp post for the whole night. Linda said he would take his gun, walk into the veld, and start shooting. When her beef and Yorkshire pudding weren't perfect, he would take them and smash them against the wall.

Stoffberg had a goose he loved and admired. He would carry the goose around and bath with him. When his rottweiler Zorba snapped at the goose, Stoffberg took his pistol, held it against the dog's head and pulled the trigger. The pistol jammed. 'God meant for this dog to live,' he said and walked away. He hanged another dog in a tree. Yet, every time a pet died, he held a funeral on the smallholding for it.

Stoffberg's documentation shows several more deals during the middle 1980s: American-manufactured TOW missiles and gyroscopes for the Iranians, arms and ammunition for the Iraqis, minesweepers for the Taiwanese and in later years, chemicals for Libya.

Stoffberg was 'highly expert', believes British arms specialist and investigator Alex Manson after studying his documentation. 'These people are different. They are adventurers. They are wheeler dealers. Some of them are used by intelligence services, others are mercenaries who want to supplement their income. It is not a normal world, it is a fantasy world, and it was within this world that Stoffberg lived and survived for many years. He was highly expert in military hardware and his *modus operandi* made it evident that he had considerable security and intelligence experience.'[11]

But by 1987, Dirk Stoffberg was broke. The fortune which he had stored under his house was gone, spent on lavish overseas trips, Italian sports cars, race horses and entertaining. Arms deals didn't materialise. Stoffberg got desperate: he tried to sell cement to Nigeria and smuggled diamonds. But he faced an even greater threat: the South Africa arms manufacturer Armscor charged him for trying to sell their weapons without a licence. Annscor failed to obtain witnesses to testify against Stoffberg and the charges were withdrawn.

It was then that the gunrunner turned politician. He put his Nazi uniforms away and joined the liberal Progressive Federal Party (PFP). He had meetings with PFP leader Dr Van Zyl Slabbert and several MPs and told them that he could expose the dirty secrets of Armscor. The PFP wanted him to stand as their candidate against Minister of Defence Magnus Malan, but veteran politician Helen Suzman would not have a gunrunner in her party. Stoffberg backed down.

In October 1987, Stoffberg told Linda that he had to fly to Europe for a few days. 'He said he had to meet an Iranian in Frankfurt to clinch a deal. He had just concluded a diamond deal and took the money with him. He left me and his son with only R30 and a pile of debt,' said Linda.

The day before he left, Linda found him in his study crying over photographs of her and their son Ivan. 'I then knew that something was wrong and that I might not see him for some time.'

Stoffberg would return to the country only five years later. In the meantime he divorced Linda and married wife number seven, smuggled chemicals and went to prison. He continued his work for the security forces of South Africa and according to his own account, became involved in the murder of Dulcie September.

A few months after Stoffberg left the country, Linda and his estate were sequestrated. He owed the bank R600 000. As Linda went through his documents, she discovered files on all his wives. She wasn't number three, she was number five or six. While he was still married to her, he had tied the knot with a Chinese woman in Taiwan.

'The files would start with the marriage certificate and end with the divorce papers. Each file contained love letters, a naked photograph, bra, panties, hair and intimate details of each woman. There were magazine cuttings of his fantasies of hairstyles, clothes and underwear he would have liked us to wear. I discovered a letter from one of his former wives, which he intercepted and never gave to me, in which she warned me that Dirk used to beat her up and knocked her head against the wall.'

I once asked Stoffberg to describe his wives to me. 'Where shall we start? Let's see. Anne was South African, the first one. Black hair, very, very attractive. Now who was the second one? The second was Monique. French. She was blonde, very petite, small. Nanette, Israeli, very vivacious, dark-haired. Very good figure. Anne from the UK, also dark-haired, tall, statuesque, attractive. Where are we now? Niki, very petite, very attractive, Chinese. Susanne, very teutonic. German, blonde, blue eyes.'

'You missed one. Linda.'

'Of course yes, how could I? Also petite, black-haired, attractive. They never knew what I was doing, except Linda and later Susanne.'

The gunrunner met Susanne Tanzer, mother of two boys and wife of a dentist, in March 1988 in Frankfurt. She had an import-export business and wanted to do business with South Africa. Somebody had referred her to Stoffberg.

'There was something special in his eyes, and to me he looked very exotic. His face was nice and brown, his hair grey and shining. He was different to other men I had met and I immediately fell in love. I was married to a dentist for 15 years, but life was boring for me. I was excited about Dirk's international life. Maybe it was like an adventure for me. It was similar to James Bond.'[11]

Stoffberg continued to write letters to Linda and told her he still loved her and would be back home soon. He said the Iranian deal was about to be concluded. He never told her about Susanne. He lived in Frankfurt and continued to work for Jacobi and the Adler Group.

Stoffberg told me that towards the middle and end of the 1980s, South African Military Intelligence increasingly used the services of the Adler Group. They wanted a list of names and addresses of ANC operatives in Europe and asked Stoffberg to find out where the ANC's bank accounts were held and what the account numbers were. Stoffberg said he opened bank accounts at the Bank Societé Generale in Brussels and Credit Suisse in Zurich in order to pay informants. He said he also made use of bank accounts in London and Frankfurt.

Stoffberg maintained contact with his 'friends' in the National Intelligence Service and the Security Branch, but said they had nothing to do with the assassination of Dulcie September.

When September was gunned down in Paris on March 29, 1988, Stoffberg claimed he was in Frankfurt. He wrote to Linda that he was in Paris. He told me, however, that he was in London paying each of the assassins £20 000.

Over a period of months, Stoffberg gave me small pieces of information about the assassination. He said the assassins were two former French legionnaires who had been recruited by the Adler Group. The same men were involved in the attempt on the life of Godfrey Motsepe.

'Why was she killed?' I asked him.

'Because it was so simple. She was an easy target. We knew where she lived and worked and what her movements were. There was no particular reason. I did not even know who she was. I didn't decide to have her killed either. I just had to pay the killers.'

When Stoffberg spoke about Dulcie September, he was usually drunk. But never too drunk to know what he was saying or to stop himself mentioning the names of the other people involved in the killing.

Stoffberg said that after he left South Africa in 1987, he maintained all his old security force contacts, amongst them At Nel of the Directorate of Covert Collection. Another was Colonel Martin Smith, a Military Intelligence Service officer. In fact, Smith was one of his very best friends.

He also had friends and contacts in the police. One was Colonel Stef Grobler, today a senior officer in the new South African Police Service. In fact, when former Vlakplaas commander Captain Dirk Coetzee spoke out in November 1989, Grobler sent a series of faxes to Stoffberg asking him to help to discredit the former policeman. Stoffberg had to leak dirt about Coetzee to the media.

'I have no doubt that he (Coetzee) is a liar who is making wild allegations as a result of one or other mental derangement,' Grobler wrote.

The media in Germany and Switzerland exposed Stoffberg as a South African agent, gunrunner and possible assassin of Dulcie September. Questions were raised in the German Parliament about his presence in the country. Police surrounded the Frankfurt hotel in which he was staying, but Susanne managed to hide him in her car and that same night they crossed the border into Switzerland. He hadn't paid his hotel bill of 30 000 German Marks.

In August 1988, Stoffberg and Susanne Tanzer lived in Lucerne, Switzerland, in a penthouse in the Hotel National, one of Europe's most opulent establishments. Stoffberg operated a front company called 'Atlantic Bankers Corporation' from the hotel.

Back in South Africa, Linda Stoffberg and their son were in dire financial straits and they had to live with her parents. She divorced him, but Stoffberg continued to phone and write every week, saying he would be back soon. He never said a word about his new mistress.

'He said he'll look after me and that one day I will not have to work. I asked him if he was having an affair, which he denied. He said he was in a lot of danger, but things would eventually turn out okay.'

In 1990, the disgraced homeland leader Brigadier Oupa Gqozo, 'Chairman of the Military Council of State of the Republic of Ciskei', appointed Stoffberg to trace R47 million which had allegedly been paid in bribes to former Ciskei despot Lennox Sebe. According to Gqozo's documentation, the money was deposited into bank accounts in Switzerland, the United States, Panama and Israel.

Documentation shows that Stoffberg became increasingly involved in the smuggling of chemicals like mustard gas and nuclear materials.

His long-time friend and business associate, Durban-based Malcolm Roelofsz, asked him in July 1990 to find a buyer for 700 grams of 97% bomb-grade uranium. 'Packed in triple cylinders in units of 100 grams each. Sellers looking for offer of approximately US$100 000 per gram,' Roelofsz wrote to him.

In January 1991, he sent this fax, which referred to the enriched uranium, to 'Andres' in Spain: 'This highest grade – 97% pure – and you can make payment subject to inspection. Remember I have been there and seen goods and spoke to scientist.'

In March 1991, the company Brightstar International Trading in Tunis asked Stoffberg to find the ingredients they needed to manufacture mustard gas: 'We will be pleased if you arrange to send us your best offer for the following items', and the fax listed 200 tonnes of phosphoroustrichloride, 300 tonnes of thionychloride and several other substances. Stoffberg asked another South African arms dealer, Don Lange, if he could supply the ingredients: 'Chemicals – here is the full requirement: please give me best price for delivery to Tunis.'

A few days later, Stoffberg sent another fax to Lange: 'We need to hurry. Elghellali won't wait. Please send earliest date of delivery. We need certificate of validity. Can you get it here this week? If we can pull this one off – there are more buyers.'

I asked Stoffberg: 'Why deal with pariah states like Libya, Iran and Iraq?'

'The whole world supplies them and that is what the arms industry is all about: supply and demand.'

'Don't you feel guilty about it?'

'Not at all.'

The correspondence between Lange and Stoffberg continued for some time, but it is unclear if chemicals were supplied to Brightstar. However, three years later, Don Lange was dead. Stoffberg died 20 days after him.

The Rhine-Main border post between Switzerland and Germany. April 25, 1991. Dirk Stoffberg and Susanne Tanzer tried to enter Germany. In her handbag was a list of chemicals the Libyans wanted. They crossed the Swiss frontier without any problems, but as they entered Germany, a customs official asked them for their passports and disappeared for half an hour.

The next moment, the car was surrounded by armed guards and Stoffberg was arrested and manacled. The Germans said there was an Interpol warrant for his arrest for selling a thousand handguns to Chile – a country under a United Nations arms embargo at the time.

'They said I was dangerous man and I was put half-naked in a cell for the whole night. I thought the charges were ridiculous as I would never have become involved in such a small transaction.'

By the time Susanne was searched she had already flushed the Libyan chemical 'shopping list' down the toilet.

Stoffberg was incarcerated in Konstanz, awaiting his extradition to the United States. Six months later, he boarded a TWA flight from Frankfurt to New York. 'I was moved from prison to prison across the state of New York. They didn't know what to do with me. I often had to strip naked in front of other prisoners and they would lift my testicles to see if I wasn't hiding anything. I was always locked up with blacks, who called me a white shit.'

Stoffberg was formally charged under the US Arms Export Control Act for selling 1 000 9mm Smith and Wesson handguns to a US customs agent posing as a Chilean broker. In November 1991, he pleaded guilty and faced a possible sentence of eight to fourteen months in prison.

But Stoffberg had an ace up his sleeve. While in prison, he played his 'October surprise' card. According to the 'October surprise' theory, in 1980 Ronald Reagan's presidential campaign had persuaded Iran to delay the release of the 52 American hostages then being held by the Iranians until after the presidential election, thereby ensuring the defeat of President Jimmy Carter. In return, Reagan's campaign had allegedly promised arms to the Iranians.

Stoffberg testified in prison before a special US task force investigating the 'October surprise' theory that in the summer of 1980, he had met two Reagan presidential campaign officials in London to discuss the issue of the American hostages held captive in Iran. The two officials were William Casey, who became Reagan's CIA chief, and Richard Allen, who was to serve briefly as national security advisor. Because of his close ties with Iran, Stoffberg claimed, Casey and Allen asked him to broker an arms-for-hostages deal.[13]

'October surprise' investigator R Spencer Oliver wrote to trial judge Jack S Weinstein: 'Mr. Stoffberg has to date provided the House of Representatives Committee on Foreign Affairs with substantial assistance in an ongoing investigation. Although Mr Stoffberg's co-operation may not lead to any criminal action, the information which he has provided to us has already been helpful and, to some extent, has been corroborated by other evidence.'

In January 1992, Judge Weinstein ruled that based on 'the importance of the defendant's co-operation with Congress', Stoffberg should only serve two to eight months' imprisonment. Because he had already served eight months, the judge ordered his immediate release from New York's Rikers Island.

The media and Republicans in the Senate and the House of Representatives cried foul. Republican Congressmen introduced a resolution demanding an investigation. The magazine *Village Voice* called Stoffberg 'as bad as a mother-fucker'. The New York *Newsday* said the gunrunner had 'every incentive to stretch the truth'.[14] The 'October Surprise Task Force' said in its final report: 'There were inconsistencies in Stoffberg's evidence which proved difficult to reconcile.'

Stoffberg might have conned his way out of prison. Days after his release, Dirk Stoffberg and Susanne Tanzer arrived back in South Africa.

Upon his arrival, Stoffberg phoned Linda Stoffberg and arranged a meeting. 'There he was, five years later. He looked haggard and much older. He must have been through a lot in prison. He said that what he had done was for his country and his people. He never tried to explain what happened after he left me and his child, and simply said he wanted a plate of home-cooked food.'

Stoffberg said he was quitting the arms business, and for a while at least, it seems as though he meant it as he tried to get involved in property development near Pretoria. Susanne and Stoffberg were married in July 1993 and moved into a double-storey house overlooking the Hartebeespoort Dam.

Stoffberg's long-lost son, Francois, tried to reconcile with his father. Stoffberg said to him that if he was willing to join the army and become a soldier, he would accept Francois as his son. Francois refused, and was chased away. When Stoffberg died, neither Francois nor Cheryl attended his funeral.

I met Stoffberg in 1993 in a 'bush pub' near the Hartebeespoort Dam. He was already drunk, but immediately ordered another bottle of wine, and another, and another. Stoffberg had a desire to talk and wanted others to know about his supposedly incredible life. He saw himself as a hero, fighting an enemy behind the battle lines.

Anthony Sampson, author of *The Arms Bazaar,* said that this is often the case with arms dealers. 'They have no problems with their self-respect. I've always noticed that they feel a need to justify themselves and also to talk to other people, including journalists, about their remarkable achievements, because they feel themselves on the one hand to be loners, on the other hand they are doing something which is rather specially important and unique. There's no doubt in my experience that arms dealers are very prone to show off and need to display their wealth. A kind of arrogance or defiance.'[15]

Stoffberg was no different, and over bottles of wine in the 'bush pub', the story of Dirk Stoffberg started unfolding. Each time we met, he provided me with another piece of the puzzle. He gave me documents and started saying things about Dulcie September. But however drunk he became, there was always a point where he stopped and would threaten me if I ever talked about what he had said. He claimed he was too scared to tell the whole story.

At the time of the writing of this book, the TRC said it was investigating certain leads about the murder of September. I believe they have to look no further than Military Intelligence and Dirk Stoffberg.

Rich Verster, a former spymaster in the Directorate of Covert Collection of Military Intelligence, said from his Dorchester prison that region six of the CCB could have been involved in the assassination. Ferdi Barnard made the same allegations. The CCB had a European region, about which we know very little. If it was involved, it could have been a joint operation between the CCB and Military Intelligence.

I believed Stoffberg when he said he was involved in the murder and acted upon orders from his handlers in Military Intelligence. It was never something that he boasted about or wanted the world to know. He was simply too scared. He phoned Linda Stoffberg two days after the killing and confessed his complicity in it. He did the same to Jurgen Roth. Why would he have lied?

What does French Intelligence know? How did the French discover Stoffberg's name so soon after the killing and what special death squad were they talking about?

Stoffberg has always hinted at the complicity of the Adler Group in September's assassination and said that it could have been involved in recruiting assassins and in paying them. According to Stoffberg, there was a close relationship between the Adler Group and Military Intelligence, which used the Group's services in Europe.

Dirk and Susanne Stoffberg seemed to be happy. 'I know about all his marriages, but the time we spent together, we suffered a lot, and because of that we love each other very much, our love is so strong, it will be forever, there will be no other marriage for me and for Dirk.'

But a few months later, the bodies of Dirk and Susanne Stoffberg lay in a pool of blood on the balcony of their home, both with bullet wounds in their heads. It looked as if Stoffberg had shot Susanne, then himself.

On that Wednesday night in July 1994, Susanne had been speaking to one of her sons in Germany on the phone when he had heard a scream and a shot being fired. She had dropped the phone and thousands of kilometres away, her son had heard three more shots. He had broken the connection and telephoned the couple's neighbours, who contacted the police.

Days after the killings, Susanne's two teenage sons were granted an urgent application by the Pretoria Supreme Court to seal the house and to prevent any of the contents being removed by anyone except the police until an executor had been appointed to sift through the mountain of paper in search of a will.[16]

But by then, the safe in the house had disappeared. Four people swore affidavits that there had been a safe, and I saw the safe once myself when Stoffberg had opened it to give me a document. Some of South Africa's most closely guarded secrets might have disappeared with the safe.

It was a business associate of Stoffberg and friend of Susanne who provided the first clue as to what could have happened on the night of the killing. 'A week before her death, Susanne cried and said that Dirk's chemical operations got out of hand and that she was frightened.'

I met Margaret Turner in the basement of a parking garage at Johannesburg International Airport. 'What was the relationship between Susanne and Dirk?' I asked her.[17]

'Disastrous.'

'Why?'

'Perpetual beating and criticism. In fact, there was nothing that Susanne could do to please Dirk. He treated her like dirt and yet she did everything for him. I urged her to leave him after he had beaten her very badly one night. She looked horrible.'

'Nonsense,' said Colonel Martin Smith, Stoffberg's long-time friend and contact in Military Intelligence. 'Susanne was a trouble-maker. She had affairs with other men. She even tried to seduce me.'[18]

'Could he have killed her?'

'No, Dirk would have chased her away. He's had six wives. He was finished with her. He wanted her out of his life.'

Linda Stoffberg had another story. She said she spoke to Stoffberg a few hours before he died. 'He was fine. The normal Dirk. Happy. He spoke about coming to his son's karate grading and we set up a meeting the next day to discuss personal affairs.'

She said Stoffberg had already told her that he was divorcing Susanne. 'He did not have to kill any wife. If he wanted to get divorced, he got divorced. He had been married plenty of times. That really didn't worry him very much, and he already told me they were getting divorced.'

All three people spoke about one thing: chemicals.

According to Turner, Susanne had said it was getting out of hand. Turner said she didn't know what kind of chemicals had been involved, but that people were desperately looking for files that had disappeared.

'I have not only been offered money by three different people, I have also been told that unless I hand over certain documents, and what they are I don't know, I shall be killed.'

Col Smith said Stoffberg was doing deals with Iran and other countries in the Middle East. Ten days before he died, Stoffberg told him that he feared for his life.

'What was he busy with?'

'A few months ago, he mentioned a chemical by the name of red mercury. He said it had something to do with the enrichment of uranium.'

Linda Stoffberg also said that people had looked for documents. 'A lot of people appeared from nowhere that nobody knew. They claimed to be friends of Dirk and Susanne. I had phone calls from certain of Dirk's associates overseas who wanted to know what had happened to the documentation.'

'Did he ever mention the name red mercury to you?'

'Yes, he said he was working on some deal.'

It has been called the twentieth century's biggest hoax. A brilliant swindle. A conman's dream. A red herring.

Others say that it exists: that it is a top secret and unique substance. It makes nuclear bombs smaller and more efficient. In the dying days of the Soviet Union, they say, nuclear scientists perfected this wonder substance that could be used to trigger a small nuclear bomb of the fusion type.

Red mercury. It has become one of the most lucrative exports to the twilight world of nuclear arms trafficking. Red mercury has been touted by gunrunners and conmen throughout the world since the collapse of the Soviet Union. Vendors of this fantastic substance have been asking prices as high as $250 000 per kilogram.[18] But the Uranium Institute, the International Atomic Energy Agency, the US Department of Energy and its Russian counterpart say that it doesn't exist. Most 'red mercury' on sale has turned out to be ordinary quicksilver dyed red.[19]

But there are nuclear scientists who believe it's real. One is Dr Frank Barnaby, who once worked in Britain's nuclear programme. I spoke to him at his house in the south of England.[20]

'I have talked to Russian scientists who have been involved in the manufacture or testing of red mercury. And talking to them scientist to scientist you get a feeling whether these fellows are telling the truth or pulling a hoax. I talked to them over a long period. I am pretty convinced that they were telling the truth.'

Whatever the case, conclusive evidence of the existence of this substance has yet to be produced.

Dirk Stoffberg believed it was real, and he tried to buy and sell red mercury. A few months after his death, I was handed a file which contained documents on some of the deals he had worked on before his death.

Stoffberg tried to buy a 40-square-kilometre teak forest in the Yei and Yambio districts of southern Sudan, not far from the Ugandan border. The estimated value of the teak was several hundreds of millions of dollars. Stoffberg's partners in the deal were Margaret Turner and a South African company by the name of Septagon Export Services. This company is one the major weapons suppliers to the Sudan People's Liberation Army (SPLA), the Christian rebel movement occupying the southern region of Sudan. The SPLA has been involved in a three-decade armed conflict with the Muslim government of the Sudan in Khartoum.

Stoffberg and his business partners would have paid the SPLA with weapons: mines, mortars, missiles, rocket launchers, light armoured vehicles, combat rifles, ammuntion and Russian-manufactured Antonov aircraft.

And then there was the red mercury file. It started with a fax from his friend and business associate Malcolm Roelofsz: 'I am told 60 kilograms is available, 40 kilograms in Namibia, 20 kilograms was sent to RSA for analysis. I am told asking price is US$250 per gram (US$250 000 per kilogram).'

Stoffberg offered the red mercury and a quantity of highly enriched uranium 235 to one Zuhdi Alkatib in Jordan in the Middle East: 'No contact has yet been made by your friends. We have first option on this material, but another party also wants to purchase. Please advice me urgently today if we must secure this for you.'

The red mercury file ended on an eerie note: the inside back cover was covered with streaks of blood.

Col Smith said that about ten days before Stoffberg died, he had seen people from the Middle East. He said the gunrunner had feared for his life and had said he was busy with a dangerous operation. Smith urged him to carry a weapon.

Days after I discovered the documents, police opened a murder docket. The investigation was handed to controversial Brixton Murder and Robbery Squad commander Colonel Charles Landman, who was at the time investigating several other red mercury-related murders.

Twenty days before Stoffberg died, arms dealer Don Lange, with whom Stoffberg had tried to do a chemicals deal in 1991, was found dead in his Durban flat. There was a plastic bag over his head which was connected to a gas cylinder. It also looked like suicide, until police did a second autopsy and found that there was no gas in his blood. It was murder. Lange often spoke about red mercury and asked a business associate to find him the substance. A suitcase full of documents and two false passports disappeared after the murder.[21]

Another case was one of the most macabre killings police ever investigated: in the boot of a car was the dismembered body of a man. His torso, buttocks, arms and legs had been amputated. He was smeared with an oily, black substance. He was Alan Kidger, marketing manager of Thor Chemicals.

Three years after his death, police investigators said they believed he had been assassinated because he was supplying Middle Eastern countries with high-technology chemicals that could be used in the manufacture of nuclear weapons. The name red mercury was mentioned.

Police haven't solved any of these murders. Landman said he believed that the Israeli secret service Mossad could have been behind the killings. He is yet to provide any convincing evidence, and these murders will probably remain a mystery.

Dirk and Susanne Stoffberg were cremated at separate services. Her ashes were flown to Germany, while Stoffberg's were divided between his children Ivan and Cheryl Stoffberg, although Cheryl didn't attend his funeral. A stone was erected for Stoffberg alongside that of his father, mother and brother in the Primrose cemetery in Germiston.

Linda said that Stoffberg always knew he was going to die a violent death. But he didn't fear death. He believed God had a cloud waiting for him to float around on. He said he had fought a brave fight and had led a good life.

Chapter Twenty-One

A sour and sullen soul

The commissioner spreads the photos on the table. A slope of tamboekie grass, a wind-blue sky, some fresh soil.

He shows us the place ... we dig ... we find red topsoil mixed with black subsoil ... we know ... and then the spade hits something ...

'She was brave this one, hell she was brave,' says the grave indicator, the perpetrator, and whistles softly through his teeth. 'She simply would not talk.'

The skull has a bullet hole right on the top. 'She must have been kneeling ...' says the commissioner.

Ribs. Breastbone that once held heart. Around the pelvis is a blue plastic bag. 'Oh yes,' remembers the grave indicator. 'We kept her naked, and after 10 days she had made herself this panty.' He sniggers: 'God ... she was brave.'
– The Afrikaans poet Antjie Krog, writing in the *Mail and Guardian* about TRC investigators digging up the body of a murdered activist.[1]

July 1997, and at a Cape Town hearing of the TRC, a portly and florid-looking former security policeman took the stand to face his victims.

Captain Jeffrey Benzien was a master torturer. Breaking people down and subjecting his victims to the worst possible hell was his business. And he relished his reputation – that he needed only 30 minutes to break open the can of silence and get his victims to spill the beans.

Mere mention of Benzien's name struck fear into the hearts of Western Cape activists during the 1980s. Activist Robert Maliti was so severely beaten by Benzien and three other security policemen that he suffered brain damage and is now partially paralysed.

But the South Africa of 1997 was no more the apartheid state of a decade earlier and in an amazing turn of events, the tortured turned into inquisitors. Former ANC activist Ashley Forbes asked Jeffrey Benzien: 'When I was arrested, do you remember saying to me that you were able to treat me either like an animal or a human being?'

Benzien: I concede I may have said it.

Forbes: Do you remember when you used the wet bag I was undressed and my pants were pulled to my ankles, and thereafter the wet bag was put over my head and I was suffocated?

Benzien: I cannot remember that specifically, but I can concede, yes. (Benzien was notorious for the 'wet bag' treatment, which involved covering his victims' head with a wet cloth bag and squeezing until they were on the verge of suffocation and unconsciousness.)

Forbes: Do you remember while I was lying on the ground someone inserted a metal rod into my anus and shocked me?

Benzien: No sir, as heinous as it may sound I used an electric generator on only one person …

Forbes: On the second occasion I was tortured, do you remember I was wrapped in a carpet?

Benzien: I concede that I assaulted you, that was on the Monday evening … after that we went for the steak, am I correct? After that, I took you on investigation to the Eastern Cape, and you said it was the most Kentucky Fried Chicken you've ever eaten … Your trip to Colesberg, where you braaied with me that night and with the rest of the unit? Do you remember?

Forbes: Do you remember putting me on a chair and telling me you were going to burst my eardrum?

Benzien: No sir, I remember hitting you, but only after a few days.

Forbes: Do you remember saying you were going to break my nose, and then putting your thumbs in my nostrils and pushing up until my nose started to bleed?

Benzien: No sir.

Forbes: After I tried to commit suicide I went to hospital. Do you remember trying to use the wet-bag method again while I was in hospital?

Benzien: Your honour, it shocks me and causes me to be sad that I had presumed that this meeting was about truth and reconciliation, and that Mr Forbes now puts it to this forum that I tried to put a bag over his head in Groote Schuur Hospital.

Former ANC activist Peter Jacobs asked Benzien: 'At some point you gave electric shocks to me. Where did you give me those shocks? In which parts of my body?'

Benzien: Can you help me? If I said to Mr Jacobs I put the electrodes at his ears, I may be wrong. If I said I attached it to his genitals, I may be wrong. If I put a probe into his rectum, I may be wrong. I could have used any one of those three.

Truth Commissioner: Did you during your service use all three methods?

Benzien: In the case of Mr Jacobs, yes sir … That he was intensively abused and molested, I concede.

Security policemen don't come much more depraved than Jeffrey Benzien. He has admitted having a poster of Ashley Kriel, an ANC operative he allegedly shot in cold blood, in his office. The poster was defaced and inscribed with the words: 'One down … to go.'

In one of the most dramatic moments at the hearings of the TRC, Benzien demonstrated his 'wet bag' technique on a volunteer. The manacled detainee would be forced to the floor, face down, with Benzien seated on his back. Benzien would pull the damp sack over the detainee's face and twist it tightly around his neck. Questions would be fired at the detainee while he or she was fighting the clinging, suffocating cloth for air.

Many of the torturers and killers of our past have been forced into confession at the TRC. They still wear their tinted glasses, thin snorretjies (moustaches) and grey shoes, but old tragic stories have been retold in new ways.

Many of the men who once sent shivers of fear through those they interrogated and tortured are now frail and pathetic. Twenty years ago, Major Harold Snyman of the Eastern Cape Security Branch was the chief interrogator of Steve Biko, South Africa's foremost proponent of the Black Consciousness Movement. The security policemen were then defiant, claiming that they had acted in selfdefence when they slammed the activist's head into a wall during a scuffle in Room 619 of Port Elizabeth's Sanlam building, where the Security Branch had its headquarters.

Harold Snyman, now 71 years old, and four of his former colleagues took the witness stand at the TRC in September 1997 to give a new and 'true' version of Biko's death. Amongst the policemen were Gideon Nieuwoudt, who has applied for amnesty for ten murders.

According to their 'new evidence', the men pummelled Steve Biko with their fists, beat his naked body with hosepipes, manacled his hands and shackled his feet to an iron grille before loading him into the back of a Land Rover for the 1 200 km journey to Pretoria.

Among Biko's sins? 'He tried to sit down and Captain Daantjie Siebert ordered him to stand up. He did not react ... According to the state system of the time, that was the way it had to be done,' Snyman said.

After cross-examination by Advocate George Bizos, acting for the Biko family, Snyman crumpled into a helpless heap. 'I am tired, your honour. I am not healthy and I don't feel I can go on any longer. I am on medication, and my old age should also be taken into account.'

What has become known as the miracle of South Africa – the coming of democracy and the building of a single nation – has also brought its madness. The killers and torturers are not only walking free: Jeffrey Benzien is still a serving captain in the South African Police Service. A week before his testimony, three former Azanian People's Liberation Army cadres asked for amnesty for killing 11 people and injuring more than 50 in a hand-grenade and machine gun attack on the St James Church in Cape Town in July 1993. Two of them are now officers in the South African National Defence Force. Dirk Coetzee, Brood van Heerden and Willie Nortje are now spies in the National Intelligence Service.

None of the generals who gave the orders have been charged. They haven't even been forced to repay the booty they stole. On the desk of the Transvaal Attorney General lies an indictment against several generals, including Krappies Engelbrecht and Nick van Rensburg, and Inkatha leaders, amongst them Themba Khoza and Celani Mthethwa, for charges ranging from murder to gun smuggling. The indictment has been completed a long time ago, but the Attorney General says he has difficulty in prosecuting because of a lack of manpower.

PW Botha is not just too old to be charged for apartheid crimes, it seems, but also too fragile to be hauled in front of the nation at the TRC and asked to explain his role in dehumanising black people to the extent where it became easy for Eugene de Kock and Dirk Coetzee and Paul van Vuuren to kill.

When Eugene de Kock was sentenced in October 1996, South Africa had its first taste of justice as South Africa's most odious policeman was locked away for life. Notorious Eastern Cape security policeman Colonel Gideon Nieuwoudt was sentenced to 20 years' imprisonment when he was found guilty of blowing up four people with a car bomb in 1988. He has appealed against his sentence and has applied for amnesty for the killing.

The prosecution of other alleged apartheid criminals has been less successful. The difficulty of prosecuting apartheid-era crimes was made painfully obvious when Magnus Malan and 19 co-accused, amongst them two former Chiefs of the Defence Force, the Chief of Staff Intelligence, senior Military Intelligence officers, a security police colonel, the Deputy Secretary-General of Inkatha and six Inkatha recruits, were acquitted on charges of conspiring to massacre 13 people at KwaMakhuta in Natal in January 1987. Malan was alleged to have authorised a programme that trained Inkatha fighters in the Caprivi in northern Namibia in 1986, who eventually formed an anti-ANC death squad. According to the indictment, the massacre was ordered because the newly trained killers were bored; the victims, seven of whom were children, were not the intended targets.

It was strong stuff, but not strong enough to reach Malan. In the end, the judge said that the SADF trained the soldiers at a government base, but that the state had not succeeded in directly linking Malan and the other defendants to the crime.

Because South Africa has opted for a process of finding the truth and allowing the granting of amnesties for full and frank confessions, most of apartheid's assassins are going to walk free. Eugene de Kock – if he doesn't get amnesty – is essentially going to remain the symbol of evil perpetrated during the apartheid years, a Rudolf Hess-like character locked away behind the high walls of Pretoria Central Prison.

All this has left him not only a lonely man, but a sour and sullen soul.

Greeting me at the entrance to the Maximum Security section of Pretoria Central Prison is a black board with a Bible verse scribbled in white chalk: 'John 21: 17: A third time Jesus said: 'Simon son of John, do you love me?' Peter was sad because Jesus asked him the third time: 'Do you love me?' So he said to him:

'Lord, you know everything; you know that I love you!' Jesus said to him: 'Take care of my sheep.'

Beyond the blackboard, an endless row of steel and barricaded doors lead to the belly of the yellow-bricked building and what was once death row. This was apartheid's death factory, where condemned criminals were executed, many of them black ANC cadres who had been sentenced to death for committing acts of terror against whites. At the height of the ANC's 'people's war' against apartheid in the latter half of the 1980s, up to seven people were hanged in one session to make space for incoming souls who had been condemned to death. In 1989, 14 residents of the township of Paballelo near Upington in the Northern Cape were sentenced to death for the killing of a single policeman.

Looking at my own reflection in the polished floor to avoid the searching eyes of the inmates, I cannot help but think about prisoners who were reprieved and escaped the noose and lived another day to tell their tale, and of how those who were destined for execution got deboned chicken on the eve of their meeting with the hangman and had the circumference of their necks measured a day or two earlier. And then, at sunrise, the silence would be broken by the clangour of a door and footsteps that echoed towards the death chamber.

But the Constitutional Court, founded after the 1994 elections to guard our infant democracy, ruled that the clause which guarantees the right of life prohibits the state from killing, and the death penalty was abolished.

Today, Maximum Security is home to some of South Africa's most hardened criminals, none more hardened than Eugene de Kock. His cell, unlocked at eight in the morning and locked again at four in the afternoon, is not far from the old death chamber.

It is a winter's morning in June 1997 as he is ushered into the waiting room. It is the first time I've seen him since he was sentenced to life imprisonment and 212 years behind bars more than six months ago. The man who was then led down the stairs of court number GD in the Pretoria Supreme Court looked grey and tired after losing a court battle of more than two years. Since then, he has made one more brief appearance in the Supreme Court: to end his marriage of ten years to Audrey de Kock.

He is now dressed in a green prison uniform, but looks fit and rested, his face tanned, probably from spending several hours every day in the small outside square where maximum security inmates can relax and exercise. For the first time ever, I shake his hand, as our previous meeting was behind glass. His handshake is firm, even intimidating.

'It's hard inside,' he says, and tells of fellow inmates who spit in his food. He has complained that unless they are tested for AIDS, Hepatitis B and other diseases, he won't eat. Gone are the days of peri-peri chicken.

A month earlier, De Kock had submitted his amnesty application of 1 200 pages to the TRC. His submission details 20 international and 87 local incidents, ranging from murder to gunrunning to fraud, all of which he was either directly involved in or had knowledge of. The index to his application mentions several 'new' incidents which did not emerge at his court case, amongst them: 'An attempt to kill Sam Nujoma (Namibian president)', 'Instruction from General (Krappies) Engelbrecht to kill Joe Verster of the CCB', and 'Supply of weapons to Renamo'.

De Kock's application for amnesty is a last, desperate attempt by the former Vlakplaas commander to prevent him from growing grey and old, even dying, in Pretoria Central Prison. In evaluating his application, the Amnesty Committee of the TRC will have to decide if his crimes were committed with a political objective in mind, and whether the crimes befitted the objective.

De Kock is going to the TRC armed with arguments about the 'political realities of the time, the security police culture, the communist and total on-slaught, the secret war ...', and one can already see the words formulated on his lips: 'We were just doing our jobs, it was difficult to refuse, I carried out orders from the generals and implemented the policies of the government of the day.'

What to do about the banality of all his murdering, his determination to show that he was only the executor of his master's policies – this is one of the great moral issues which will confront the Amnesty Committee when they weigh up De Kock's application.

Can a nation afford to pardon a man for brutalities such as the murder of Japie Maponya – his skull cleaved open by a spade because he had a brother who was a member of the ANC, Moses Nthehelang – smothered with a tube in the madness of a Vlakplaas drinking orgy, the Nelspruit Four – led into an ambush, executed and set alight, and Tiso Leballo, blown to smithereens with explosives?

He will face not only the Commissioners, but also the families of his victims. Fortunately for him, the amnesty process does not require remorse, but it does give victims an opportunity to express an opinion as to whether or not amnesty should be granted. Catherine Mlangeni, mother of bombed lawyer Bheki Mlangeni, has already appeared before the TRC and begged that Eugene de Kock should never be granted amnesty.

Reconciliation is not a notion the victims entertain just now. During his amnesty hearing, Dirk Coetzee turned towards Charity Kondile, whose son he had burnt to ashes on the bank of the Komati River: 'I ask your forgiveness. I am sorry for what I did ...'[2]

The legal representative of Charity Kondile read her statement to Coetzee: 'You said that you would like to meet Mrs Kondile and look her in the eye. She asked me to tell you that she feels it is an honour ... you do not deserve. If you are really sorry, you would stand trial for the deeds you did ...'

A long uncomfortable silence filled the hall. The judges, the legal representatives, the audience ... everybody looked distraught – the only movement was that of Dirk Coetzee as he slowly turned away and clutched his hands.

In an interview afterwards, Kondile said: 'It is easy for (Nelson) Mandela and (Desmond) Tutu to forgive ... they lead vindicated lives. In my life nothing, not a single thing has changed since my son was burnt by barbarians ... nothing. Therefore, I cannot forgive.'

Gillian Slovo's search for her mother's killers led her to one of Johannesburg's industrial areas, where she confronted a man who 'must have been all of twenty stone: his head looked tiny, perched as it was on top of all that fat'. He was Craig Williamson, who has asked for amnesty for blowing up her mother, Ruth First, with a parcel bomb in 1982.[3]

'I was in the loop that killed your mother,' he said.

'Loop? What was he talking about? A baton race? A high tech circuit? Or a group of men sitting in Pretoria's Wachthuis working out ways to rid themselves of Ruth?

'... I was seized by anger. Perhaps stabbing would have been easier than sitting and listening to this bully's bloodless tale of murder ... those other qualities that I'd been searching for – regret, repentance, or conscience – had been conspicuously absent.'

Marius Schoon, whose wife and eight-year-old child were blown up by Williamson in 1984, feels the same: 'If I were in the same space as that man, I wouldn't be able to stop myself from stabbing him ... I would like to see him in the sight of an AK.'[4]

Eugene de Kock is entering his final battle: to obtain amnesty and to bring the generals down with him. He has lost all his other wars: against the liberation armies in Rhodesia and Namibia, against the ANC, against the quest for democracy and against the Transvaal Attorney General's special investigations team.

Eugene de Kock is soon going to be history, but the questions he raises are about South Africa's future: how are we going to deal with narrow culpability and broad responsibility, about where the essential guilt for the country's shameful past lies?

What about the majority of white South Africans who were the complicit and silent beneficiaries of apartheid? Not just whites, but the many Joe Mamaselas who collaborated, informed and served? What about the bureaucrats who did all the apartheid paperwork needed in order to classify, remove, disinherit and control? Judges and magistrates that ignored the pleas of tortured detainees and absolved the inquisitors and killers? The Afrikaans churches that were nothing but the National Party at prayer? Big business that grew fat and elephantine through cheap labour? Newspaper editors that helped to cover up and hide the truth?

And yet, there is no moral outcry by white South Africans about what Eugene de Kock did in their names. No condemnation of FW de Klerk and his predecessors who used their money to prop up and fund their death squads. Little understanding of the pain and suffering laid bare at the TRC.

'We didn't know … why must I feel guilty about something I knew nothing about? … FW de Klerk didn't know about it, how were we supposed to know?'

The TRC is uncovering a large chunk of our past, but has been less successful in achieving reconciliation, because there has been no collective apology from the white community for what was committed in its name.

Says Gillian Slovo: 'And yet, in the face of the displaced responsibility and the empty justifications that the likes of Craig Williamson produced, forgiveness felt like just another effort, in a long string of previous efforts, that the victims, and not the perpetrators, would have to make.'

When the TRC was set up in November 1995, the nation was looking for an essential gesture to take it beyond the scapegoating. To start with, they wanted what post-war Germany got when Willy Brandt went down on his knees at the Warsaw ghetto memorial and asked the world for forgiveness. They needed reconciliation and the quest for forgiveness to come from the heart.

But what they had hoped for will never be. FW de Klerk's 'big denial' has not only brought Desmond Tutu to the brink of tears, but has left the people of this country further apart than ever before.

Antjie Krog wrote: 'De Klerk and his hostile delegation leaves. The room and passages are filled with rage. People swamped with fury and desperation. Desmond Tutu's skin hangs dull and loose from his face, his shoulders covered in defeat. I want to go to him in one or other infantile gesture. To kiss his ring, to touch his dress. When De Klerk walked out, it was as if something forever slipped through my fingers. Speechless, I stand before Tutu. From whence will words now come? For us. Us hanging, quivering, ill, from this soundless space of the Afrikaner past? What does one say? What the hell does one do with this load of skeletons, shame and ash?'[5]

The philosopher and author Albert Camus, writing of Algeria at a time when the French authorities were seeking to justify torture and assassination, said: 'The fact that such things could take place amongst us is a humiliation we must henceforth face. Meanwhile, we must at least refuse to justify such methods, even on the score of efficacy. The moment they are justified, even indirectly, there are no more rules or values; all causes are equally good, and war without aims or laws sanctions the triumph of nihilism. Willy-nilly, we go back in that case to the jungle where the sole principle is violence.'[6]

I sit in Maximum Security with Eugene de Kock. In the room, four chairs and one table, chained to one another. One window, heavily barricaded. Bare white walls. An inmate brings coffee. Eugene de Kock speaks, bitterness and resentment rolling off his tongue and filling the empty and hollow space around us.

In a few hours from now, he'll be locked away for the night, perhaps after a meal of samp and rice into which somebody may spit. Dirk Coetzee will go home to his barricaded home in Soutpansberg Avenue in Rietondale, Paul van Vuuren will tend to his cattle on the farm Drooglaagte near Warmbaths and Ferdi

Barnard will prepare for another night of sleaze at 92 Oxford Road, Rosebank.

An inmate calls De Kock for lunch. I leave and shake his hand. He strolls down the dark artery that leads to the heart of the prison and his figure fades away.

Outside, the warm Pretoria winter sun bakes down on the cement pavement leading me out of the prison. The clamour of another steel door propels me back to Potgieter Street – and normality.

It's a sight Eugene de Kock may never see again. It's too late now. It may for ever be too late.

Notes

PREFACE

1. The information in this preface is based on interviews and conversations with Ferdi Barnard in Johannesburg in January 1993, November 1995, October and December 1996, and June 1997.

CHAPTER ONE

1. Minutes of the State Security Council, Number SVR 12/83, June 28, 1983.
2. FW de Klerk, National Party submission to the Truth and Reconciliation Commission, May 1997.
3. Magnus Malan, submission to the Truth and Reconciliation Commission, May 1997.
4. Paul van Vuuren, interviewed on his farm near Warmbaths, March 1997.
5. Evidence in the case of the State versus Eugene de Kock, Pretoria Supreme Court, 1995 and 1996.
6. Rich Verster, interviewed in Pretoria, January 1993.
7. Peter Casselton, interviewed in Beira, Mozambique, November 1996.
8. Evidence led in the case of the State versus Eugene de Kock.
9. *Ibid.*
10. Paul van Vuuren, interviewed, March 1997.
11. Evidence led in the case of the State versus Eugene de Kock.
12. Peter Casselton, interviewed in the Northern Transvaal, December 1995.
13. Guy Bawden, interviewed in Johannesburg, March 1995.
14. Kenneth W Grundy, *The Militarization of South African Politics,* Oxford University Press, 1988.
15. Jacques Pauw, *In the Heart of the Whore,* Southern Book Publishers, 1991.
16. M Dippenaar, *Die Geskiedenis van die Suid-Afrikaanse Polisie, 1913-1988,* Promedia, 1988.
17. Craig Williamson, interviewed in Johannesburg, November 1995.
18. Beyers Naude, interviewed in Johannesburg, March 1996.
19. *Ibid.*
20. Viktor E Frankl, *Man's Search for Meaning,* Washington Square Press, 1984.
21. *Business Day,* November 8, 1996.
22. FW de Klerk, National Party submission to the Truth and Reconciliation Commission, May 1997.
23. Joyce and Sipho Mtimkulu, interviewed in Port Elizabeth, May and June 1996.

24. Truth Commission Special Report, South African Broadcasting Corporation (SABC), January 29, 1997.

CHAPTER TWO
1. The information in this chapter, except where otherwise indicated, is based on personal conversations and visits to Eugene de Kock in Pretoria Central Prison in December 1995 and January and February 1996; Evidence led in the case of the State versus Eugene de Kock in the Pretoria Supreme Court, 1995 and 1996; and conversations and meetings with several former Vlakplaas operatives and security policemen.
2. Jacques Pauw, *In the Heart of the Whore,* Southern Book Publishers, 1991.
3. Marthinus Grobler, interviewed in Johannesburg, January 1990; *Vrye Weekblad,* 26 January 1990.
4. LTC Harms, *Report of the Harms Commission of Inquiry into Certain Alleged Murders,* 1990.
5. Vossie de Kock, interviewed in Springs, December 1995.
6. *Ibid.*
7. Paul Erasmus, interviewed in Pinetown, November 1995.
8. Dirk Coetzee, interviewed on several occasions from 1989 to 1997.
9. Riaan Stander, interviewed in Pretoria, November 1995.
10. Lukas Kalino, interviewed in Pretoria, January 1996.
11. Eugene de Kock, submission to the Truth and Reconciliation Commission, May 1997.
12. Shaun Callaghan, evidence to the Truth and Reconciliation Commission, June 1997.
13. John Deegan, interviewed for the Truth Commission Special Report, SABC, July 1997.
14. Craig Williamson, interviewed in Johannesburg, November 1995.
15. Vic McPherson, interviewed in Johannesburg, February 1996.
16. Jack Cronje, conversation in Pretoria, April 1997.
17. Joe Mamasela, interviewed in Johannesburg, January and February 1996.
18. *Mail and Guardian,* February 2, 1996.
19. *Ibid.*
20. Johan van der Merwe, submission to the Truth and Reconciliation Commission, October 1996.

CHAPTER THREE
1. The information in this chapter, except where otherwise indicated, is based on evidence led in the case of the State versus Eugene de Kock, Pretoria Supreme Court, 1995 and 1996.
2. Daniel Maponya and Maureen Zondi, interviewed in Krugersdorp, January 1996, and several meetings and conversations since then.

3. *Ibid.*
4. Riaan Stander, interviewed in Pretoria, November 1995.
5. Peter Casselton, interviewed in the Northern Transvaal, December 1995.
6. lvor Jenkins and Bea Roberts, interviewed in Pretoria and Johannesburg, January and April 1996.
7. Daniel Maponya and Maureen Zondi, interviewed in Krugersdorp.

CHAPTER FOUR
1. The information in this chapter, except where otherwise indicated, is based on evidence led in the case of the State versus Eugene de Kock in the Pretoria Supreme Court, 1995 and 1996, and conversations and meetings with several former Vlakplaas operatives and security policemen.
2. Ronald Bezuidenhout, interviewed in Brakpan, December 1995.
3. Leon Flores, interviewed in Johannesburg, February 1996.
4. Ferdi Barnard, interviewed in Johannesburg, November 1995.
5. Peter Casselton, interviewed in the Northern Transvaal, December 1995.
6. Joe Mamasela, interviewed, January and February 1996.
7. FW de Klerk, National Party submission to the Truth and Reconciliation Commission, May 1997.
8. Don Foster, Dennis Davies and Diane Sandler, *Detention and Torture in South Africa,* James Currey, 1987.
9. N Chabani Manganyi, André du Toit (Eds), *Political Violence and the Struggle in South Africa,* Southern Book Publishers, 1990.
10. *Ibid.*
11. Donald Woods, *Biko,* Penguin, 1987.
12. Joe Mamasela has refused to apply for amnesty, but has agreed to testify *in camera* before the Truth and Reconciliation Commission. These are excerpts from his evidence, handed in at the case of the State versus Dirk Coetzee and Others in the Durban Supreme Court, 1997.
13. Willie Nortje and Brood van Heerden, affidavits sworn in Denmark, April 1994.
14. Eugene de Kock, conversation in Pretoria Central Prison, June 1997.
15. Stephen Ellis and Tsepo Sechaba, *Comrades against Apartheid,* James Currey, 1992.
16. Jacques Pauw, *In the Heart of the Whore,* Southern Book Publishers, 1991.
17. *Ibid.*
18. *Ibid.*
19. *Network,* Television News Productions, SABC, December 18, 1986.
20. *Beeld,* January 21, 1966.
21. Brood van Heerden, affidavit sworn in Denmark, April 1994.
22. *The Citizen,* June 21, 1997.
23. Desmond Tutu, remark made during the submission of FW de Klerk and the National Party to the Truth and Reconciliation Commission, May 1997.

24. Brood van Heerden, affidavit.
25. *Die Volksblad,* January 11, 1989; *Die Burger,* January 11, 1989.
26. *South,* August 30, 1990.

CHAPTER FIVE
1. *Vrye Weekblad,* November 17, 1989.
2. The information in this chapter, except where otherwise indicated, is based on evidence led in the case of the State versus Eugene de Kock, Pretoria Supreme Court, 1995 and 1996.
3. Ronald Bezuidenhout, interviewed in Brakpan, December 1995.
4. Joe Mamasela, interviewed in Johannesburg, January and February 1996.
5. Krappies Engelbrecht, affidavit concerning his investigation into the disappearance of Japie Maponya, handed in at the Harms Commission of Inquiry into Certain Alleged Murders, Pretoria, 1990.
6. Evidence presented to the Harms Commission.
7. Riaan Stander, interviewed in Pretoria, November 1995.
8. FW de Klerk, Addressing policeman at the Police College, November 28, 1989.
9. Jacques Pauw, *In the Heart of the Whore,* Southern Book Publishers, 1991.
10. *Ibid.*
11. Craig Williamson, interviewed in Johannesburg, November 1995.
12. Evidence presented to the Harms Commission.
13. Joe Mamasela, interviewed in Johannesburg.
14. Peter Casselton, interviewed in the Northern Transvaal.
15. Eugene de Kock, evidence to the Harms Commission.
16. Willie Nortje, affidavit sworn in Denmark, 1994.
17. Wouter Mentz, evidence to the Truth and Reconciliation Commission, February 1990.
18. Joe Mamasela, interviewed, January and February 1996.
19. Wouter Mentz, evidence to the Truth and Reconciliation Commission.
20. LTC Harms, *Report of the Harms Commission of Inquiry into Certain Alleged Murders,* 1990.
21. Jacques Pauw, *In the Heart of the Whore.*
22. Report of the Independent Board of Inquiry into Informal Repression, 1990.
23. Seipati Mlangeni, interviewed in Soweto, February 1991.

CHAPTER SIX
1. The information for this chapter was obtained through interviews with Ronald Bezuidenhout in the Weskoppies Psychiatric Hospital in Pretoria, May 1991; an interview with Ronald Bezuidenhout in Brakpan, December 1995; an interview with Marilyn Bezuidenhout in Brakpan, December 1996; and evidence led in the case of the State versus Eugene de Kock, Pretoria Supreme Court, 1995 and 1996.

CHAPTER SEVEN

1. The information in this chapter, except where otherwise indicated, is based on evidence led in the case of the State versus Eugene de Kock, Pretoria Supreme Court, 1995 and 1996, and conversations with several former security policemen, including Chappies Klapper.
2. Report of the Independent Board of Inquiry into Informal Repression for the Month of March 1991.
3. Craig Williamson, interviewed in Johannesburg, November 1995.
4. Ferdi Barnard, interviewed in Johannesburg, November 1995.
5. Corrie Goosen, interviewed in Johannesburg in October 1995.
6. *Rapport,* December 1, 1996.
7. Riaan Stander, interviewed in Pretoria, November 1995.
8. Bill Douven, interviewed in Johannesburg, August 1997.
9. Evidence about the assassination attempt by Leon Flores on the life of Dirk Coetzee was led at the judicial inquest into the death of Bheki Mlangeni, Johannesburg Supreme Court, 1992.

CHAPTER EIGHT

1. The information in this chapter, except where otherwise indicated, is based on evidence led in the case of the State versus Eugene de Kock, Pretoria Supreme Court, 1995 and 1996, and conversations with several former security policemen who participated in the event.
2. Ferdi Barnard, interviewed in Johannesburg, November 1995.
3. Nicky Swart, interviewed in Krugersdorp, May 1993.

CHAPTER NINE

1. *The Star,* January 13 and 14, 1991.
2. *The Star,* May 17, 1994.
3. Adriaan Vlok interviewed for SABC, Roving Report 9044, 1991.
4. The evidence of the involvement of Eugene de Kock and Vlakplaas in the supply of weapons to Inkatha and the training of Zulu impis in Natal was obtained from evidence led in the case of the State versus Eugene de Kock, Pretoria Supreme Court, 1995 and 1996; affidavits sworn by Willie Nortje and Brood van Heerden in Denmark, April 1994; and the evidence of Nortje before the Goldstone Commission, March 1994.
5. *The Star,* March 11, 1982.
6. FW de Klerk, second submission of the National Party to the Truth and Reconciliation Commission, May 1997.
7. Special Hearing of the Truth and Reconciliation Commission on the Caprivi Trainees held in Durban, August 1997.
8. The information on the Boipatong massacre was obtained from a series of newspaper articles that appeared in *The Star, Sunday Times* and *The Citizen.*

9. Riaan Stander, interviewed in Pretoria, November 1995.
10. Corrie Goosen, interviewed in Johannesburg, October 1995.
11. Thys du Plessis, interviewed in Krugersdorp, June 1993.
12. Nicky Swart, interviewed in Krugersdorp, June 1993.
13. Daluxolo Luthuli, affidavit sworn in Denmark, March 1995.
14. *The Star,* January 29, 1993.
15. *Saturday Star,* January 23, 1993.

CHAPTER TEN
1. The information in this chapter, except where otherwise indicated, is based on evidence led in the case of the State versus Eugene de Kock, Pretoria Supreme Court, 1995 and 1996.
2. *Sunday Times,* April 2, 1990.
3. Joe Mamasela, interviewed in Johannesburg, January and February 1996.
4. Joe Mamasela, *in camera* evidence to the Truth and Reconciliation Commission.
5. George Nene, interviewed, December 1995.
6. *Mail and Guardian,* March 7, 1997.
7. Brood van Heerden, evidence to the Goldstone Commission, April 1994.
8. Riaan van Rensburg, interviewed in Pretoria, March 1996.
9. Craig Williamson, interviewed in Johannesburg, November 1995.
10. Peter Casselton, interviewed in the Northern Transvaal, December 1995.
11. Riaan Stander, interviewed in Pretoria, November 1995.
12. Ferdi Barnard, interviewed in Johannesburg, November 1995.
13. Eugene de Kock, evidence led at his bail application in the Pretoria Supreme Court, August 1994.
14. Wim Cornelius, interviewed in Pretoria, February 1997.
15. Ivor Jenkins, interviewed in Pretoria, January 1996.
16. Chappies Klapper, evidence to the Goldstone Commission, March 1994.
17. Willie Nortje, evidence to the Goldstone Commission, March 1994.
18. Mr Justice Richard Goldstone, 'Third Force' report of the Commission of Inquiry Regarding the Prevention of Public Violence and Intimidation, March 1994.
19. Brood van Heerden, affidavit sworn in Denmark, March 1994.
20. Eugene de Kock, evidence led at an application by the Transvaal Attorney General, Pretoria Supreme Court, December 1994.

CHAPTER ELEVEN
1. The information in this chapter is, except where otherwise indicated, based on personal interviews and conversations with Dirk Coetzee over a period of several years, 1985-1997; testimony to the Harms Commission of Inquiry into Certain Alleged Murders, 1990; the civil case of Neethling versus *Vrye Week-*

blad, Du Preez, Pauw and Others, Johannesburg Supreme Court, 1990; the trial of the State versus Eugene de Kock, Pretoria Supreme Court, 1995 and 1996; and his own murder trial in the Durban Supreme Court, 1997. My book *In the Heart of the Whore* was also partly based on his life story.

2. Eugene de Kock, testimony in his murder trial in the Pretoria Supreme Court, 1995 and 1996.
3. Joe Mamasela, interviewed in Johannesburg, January and February 1996.
4. Yorkshire Television, 'Confronting the Hitman', 1995.
5. *Mail and Guardian,* February 7, 1997.
6. *The Citizen,* August 5, 1997.

CHAPTER TWELVE

1. The information in this chapter is based on interviews conducted with Joe Mamasela in Johannesburg, January and February 1996, and interviews with Dirk Coetzee about Mamasela. I met Mamasela for the first time in 1994 and have had several conversations with him since then.
2. Joe Mamasela was the main state witness in the case of the State versus Dirk Coetzee, David Tshikalanga and Almond Nofemela in the Durban Supreme Court, 1997. They were the first security policemen to admit their complicity in the murder of Mxenge in 1981. They have since been convicted of murder, but were granted amnesty by the Truth and Reconciliation Commission in August 1997.
3. Joe Mamasela, evidence in the case of the State versus Eugene de Kock, Pretoria Supreme Court, 1995 and 1996.
4. Jacques Pauw, *In the Heart of the Whore,* Southern Book Publishers, 1991.
5. *Rand Daily Mail,* November 30, 1981.
6. Paul van Vuuren, interviewed on his farm near Warmbaths, March 1996.
7. Evidence in the case of the State versus Eugene de Kock, Pretoria Supreme Court, 1995 and 1996.

CHAPTER THIRTEEN

1. The information in this chapter, except where otherwise indicated, is based on an interview with Paul van Vuuren on his farm near Warmbaths, March 1997; and evidence led in the amnesty applications of Paul van Vuuren, Jacques Hechter and Jack Cronje at several sittings of the Truth and Reconciliation Commission, October 1996, and February and March 1997.
2. Joe Mamasela refused to apply for amnesty, but has made a series of affidavits to the Transvaal Attorney General and has testified *in camera* before the Truth and Reconciliation Commission.
3. Elizabeth Maake, interviewed in Pretoria, February 1997.
4. Mabel Makupe, interviewed in Pretoria, February 1997.

5. Kenneth W. Grundy, *The Militarization of South African Politics,* Oxford University Press, 1988.
6. Donald Woods, *Biko,* Penguin, 1987.
7. FW de Klerk, first submission of the National Party to the Truth and Reconciliation Commission, August 1996.
8. Gloria Hlabangane, interviewed in Pretoria, March 1997.
9. The meeting between Van Vuuren and Tshidiso Motasi was set up and filmed by the Truth Commission Special Report, SABC.

CHAPTER FOURTEEN
1. The information in this chapter, except where otherwise indicated, is based on interviews with Peter Casselton in the Northern Transvaal, December 1995; Beira in Mozambique, November 1996; and conversations with friends.
2. *Mail and Guardian,* February 14, 1997.
3. Peter Dunnwoodie, interviewed in Halfway House, February 1997.
4. Al J Venter, *Challenge: Southern Africa within the African Revolutionary Context*, Ashanti Publishing, 1989.
5. Peter Casselton, Application for amnesty submitted to the Truth and Reconciliation Commission, December 13, 1996.
6. Eugene de Kock confirmed Williamson's attempt to have Casselton killed in his testimony at his own trial, Pretoria Supreme Court, 1995 and 1996.

CHAPTER FIFTEEN
1. The information in this chapter, except where otherwise indicated, is based on a series of interviews and conversations with Pieter Botes in April and May 1990 and evidence led before the Harms Commission of Inquiry into Certain Alleged Murders, 1990.
2. Albie Sachs, *The Soft Vengeance of a Freedom Fighter,* David Philip, 1990.
3. The information on the origins and structure of the CCB was obtained from evidence led at the Harms Commission, conversations with CCB operatives and from *In the Heart of the Whore.*
4. *Sunday Independent,* April 28, 1996.
5. Jacques Pauw, *In the Heart of the Whore,* Southern Book Publishers, 1991.
6. *Vrye Weekblad,* September 15, 1989.
7. *Sunday Independent,* April 28, 1996.
8. *Sunday Star,* May 13, 1990; *Saturday Star,* May 12, 1990.
9. *Cape Times,* February 27, 1990.
10. *The Star,* February 27, 1990.
11. Judicial inquest into the death of David Webster, Johannesburg Supreme Court, 1992.
12. *The Star,* June 24, 1994.
13. Willie van Deventer, interviewed in London, April 1990.

CHAPTER SIXTEEN

1. The information in this chapter, except where otherwise indicated, is based on interviews with Leslie Lesia in October 1990 and testimony in the civil case of Neethling versus *Vrye Weekblad,* Du Preez, Pauw and Others, Johannesbugr Supreme Court, 1990.
2. *Eastern Province Herald,* May 16, 1987.
3. Guy Bawden, interviewed in Johannesburg, March 1995.
4. Miriam Lesia, interviewed in Bloemfontein, October 1990.
5. Miriam Lesia, interviewed in Bloemfontein, March 1995.

CHAPTER SEVENTEEN

1. Minutes of the State Security Council, Number SVR 12/83, June 28, 1993.
2. FW de Klerk, National Party submission to the Truth and Reconciliation Commission, May 1997.
3. Magnus Malan, submission to the Truth and Reconciliation Commission, May 1997.
4. Des and Irene Bawden, interviewed on their farm in Matabeleland, Zimbabwe, March 1995.
5. Joseph Hanlon, *Beggar Your Neighbours,* Catholic Institute for International Relations, 1987.
6. *Ibid.*
7. *The Herald of Zimbabwe,* December 19, 1981.
8. *Parade Magazine,* Zimbabwe, June 1990.
9. Joseph Hanlon, *Beggar Your Neighbours; Parade Magazine,* Zimbabwe, June 1990.
10. Al J Venter, *Challenge, Southern Africa within the African Revolutionary Context*, Ashanti Publishing, 1989.
11. Diana Gammack, 'South Africa's War of Destabilisation', in Glenn Moss and Ingrid Obery (Eds), *South African Review,* 1990.
12. *Parade Magazine,* Zimbabwe, June 1990.
13. Joseph Hanlon, *Beggar Your Neighbours.*
14. Jeremy Brickhill, interviewed in Harare, March 1995.
15. Guy Bawden, interviewed in Johannesburg, March 1995.
16. *Parade Magazine,* Zimbabwe, June 1990.
17. *Sunday Star,* September 2, 1990; *Vrye Weekblad,* April 30, 1990.
18. Kitt Bawden, interviewed in Cape Town, March 1995.
19. Eileen Smith, interviewed in Johannesburg, March 1995.
20. Channel Four Television, 'The Hidden Hand', 1992.
21. Michael Lapsley, interviewed in March 1995.
22. Dumiso Dabengwa, interviewed in Harare, March 1995.
23. Sapa, May 27, 1997.

CHAPTER EIGHTEEN

1. The information in this chapter is based on interviews and conversations with Ferdi Barnard in Johannesburg in January 1993, November 1995, October and December 1996, and June 1997; and several friends and associates.
2. *Eastern Province Herald,* November 1, 1995.
3. *Sunday Star,* May 17, 1992.
4. Jacques Pauw, *In the Heart of the Whore,* Southern Book Publishers, 1991.
5. *Sunday Star,* May 13, 1990.
6. Jacques Pauw, *In the Heart of the Whore.*
7. Information about evidence led at the judicial inquest into the death of David Webster, Johannesburg Supreme Court, 1992, was obtained from court records and newspaper clippings.
8. Julie Wilken, interviewed in Johannesburg, December 1996 and January 1997.
9. Corrie Goosen, interviewed in Johannesburg, October 1995.
10. Sam Malgas, interviewed in Johannesburg, December 1996.
11. *Rapport,* December 1, 1996.
12. *Beeld,* November 18, 1992.
13. *The Star,* November 17, 1992; *Beeld,* November 18, 1992.
14. *Sunday Times,* November 22, 1992.
15. *Rapport,* December 1, 1996.
16. *Sunday Star,* September 6, 1992.
17. *Rapport,* December 1, 1996.
18. Flip Kruger, interviewed in Klerksdorp, July 1997.
19. Marius Nel, interviewed at Hartebeesfontein, September 1997.
20. Deon Nel, interviewed at Bloemhof, August 1997.
21. Bill Douven, interviewed in Johannesburg, August 1997.

CHAPTER NINETEEN

1. Under white rule, South Africa's national flag sported the colours of orange, white and blue, and was referred to as the Oranje, Blanje, Blou.
2. The information in this chapter, except where otherwise indicated, is based on conversations and interviews with Rich Verster in Pretoria, January 1993, and Dorchester, England, May 1997.
3. Willem Steenkamp, *South Africa's Border War, 1966-1989,* Ashanti Publishing, 1989.
4. *Sunday Times,* February 2, 1997.
5. Willem Steenkamp, *South Africa's Border War, 1966-1989.*
6. *The Star,* August 28, 1981.
7. *The Star,* February 16, 1982.
8. *Harper's Magazine,* February 1997.

CHAPTER TWENTY
1. The information in this chapter is, except where otherwise indicated, based on a series of meetings and interviews with Dirk Stoffberg at the Hartebeespoort Dam near Pretoria between June 1993 and March 1994; and interviews with Linda Stoffberg in October 1993, December 1996 and January 1997. Dirk Stoffberg also provided me with files of documentation about his weapons transactions in the later 1970s and 1980s.
2. *The Star,* March 30, 1988.
3. *Cape Times,* April 5, 1988.
4. *The Star,* April 10, 1988.
5. Jurgen Roth, interviewed in Frankfurt, Germany, October 1993.
6. *Sunday Times,* June 2, 1981.
7. *Sunday Times,* January 3, 1981.
8. *Sunday Times,* July 11, 1982.
9. *Private Eye,* September 17, 1982.
10. *Sunday Times,* May 24, 1981.
11. Alex Manson, interviewed in London, October 1993.
12. Interview with Susanne Tanzer at the Hartebeespoort Dam near Pretoria, October 1993.
13. *New York Newsday,* January 18, 1992; *The Wall Street Journal,* February 6, 1992.
14. *Village Voice,* February 3, 1992.
15. Anthony Sampson, interviewed in London, October 1993.
16. *Sunday Times,* July 24, 1994.
17. Margaret Turner, interviewed in Johannesburg, October 1994.
18. Martin Smith, Interviewed at the Hartebeespoort Dam in October 1994.
19. *Daily Telegraph,* March 19, 1994; *Sunday Times,* August 21, 1994.
20. Frank Barnaby, interviewed in England, October 1994.
21. *Saturday Star,* June 25, 1994

CHAPTER TWENTY-ONE
1. *Mail and Guardian,* June 13, 1997.
2. *Mail and Guardian,* February 7, 1997.
3. Gillian Slovo, *Every Secret Thing,* Little, Brown and Company, 1997.
4. Marius Schoon, interviewed in Johannesburg, November 1996.
5. *Mail and Guardian,* June 13, 1997.
6. Jacques Pauw, *In the Heart of the Whore,* Southern Book Publishers, 1991.

Index